Additional Praise for *Asymmetric Returns*

"The book is comprehensive and provides a very good overview on issues that many institutional investors are currently facing. The examples used throughout the book are as helpful as they are entertaining."

—Kurt Silberstein, Portfolio Manager, Absolute Return Strategies, California Public Employees' Retirement System

"In Asymmetric Returns, Ineichen advances the practice of active management by distilling the essential elements of the craft from the pedestrian pursuit of index-tracking strategies. Broadly expanding on his seminal work, In Search of Alpha, this treatise is resplendent with assessable facts and reasoning that will recalibrate the focus and attention of thoughtful investors."

—Bryan White, Chief Investment Officer, Quellos Group, LLC

"Once again, Alexander Ineichen is at the forefront of observations about the industry. . . . a must read for investors and asset managers alike!"

—Tanya Styblo Beder, CEO, Tribeca Global Management LLC

Founded in 1807, John Wiley & Sons is the oldest independent publishing company in the United States. With offices in North America, Europe, Australia and Asia, Wiley is globally committed to developing and marketing print and electronic products and services for our customers' professional and personal knowledge and understanding.

The Wiley Finance series contains books written specifically for finance and investment professionals as well as sophisticated individual investors and their financial advisors. Book topics range from portfolio management to e-commerce, risk management, financial engineering, valuation and financial instrument analysis, as well as much more.

For a list of available titles, please visit our Web site at www.Wiley Finance.com.

Asymmetric Returns

The Future of Active Asset Management

ALEXANDER M. INEICHEN

BICENTENNIAL
1807
WILEY
2007
BICENTENNIAL

John Wiley & Sons, Inc.

Published by John Wiley & Sons, Inc., Hoboken, New Jersey.
Published simultaneously in Canada.

For general information on our other products and services or for technical support, please contact our Customer Care Department within the United States at (800) 762-2974, outside the United States at (317) 572-3993 or fax (317) 572-4002.

Wiley also publishes its books in a variety of electronic formats. Some content that appears in print may not be available in electronic formats. For more information about Wiley products, visit our Web site at www.wiley.com.

Library of Congress Cataloging-in-Publication Data:

Ineichen, Alexander M.
    Asymmetric returns : the future of active asset management /
Alexander Ineichen.
        p. cm.—(Wiley finance series)
    Includes bibliographical references and index.
    ISBN-13: 978-0-470-04266-3 (cloth)
    ISBN-10: 0-470-04266-4 (cloth)
    1. Investment analysis. 2. Investments. 3. Hedge funds.
I. Title.
HG4529.I54 2007
332.6–dc22

2006020137

Printed in the United States of America.

10 9 8 7 6 5 4 3 2 1

*To my late parents Mircea Juan Ineichen
and Diana Ethel Ineichen-Garthwaite*

Contents

"I wish Karl would acquire some capital, instead of just writing about it."

—Mother of Karl Marx

For his statue of David in 1501, Michelangelo used a single block of marble. In fact, it was a block that had been started upon but abandoned by another, lesser talent, years earlier. At the time, everyone thought that this block of marble was ruined, that its potential had been exhausted, and that nothing further could be extracted from it. But Michelangelo took on this discarded block, and from it he created one of the masterpieces of all times.

For Michelangelo, to sculpt meant to take away, not to add, because the "work of art" already existed inside the stone. The block of marble was just the covering of a work of art; the sculptor only had to take away the part in excess. The sculptor's hand, guided by skill and experience, could only "liberate" what was already there inside the block of marble. His task was to free the "idea" inside from the superfluous matter surrounding it.

One could argue that, similarly, the alpha in capital markets is already there. But special talent is required to hedge ("take away") all the various unwanted risks in order to carve out the gains—the "alpha."

As markets become more and more efficient, carving out the alpha will be increasingly difficult without using all of the risk management tools available. Constraining managers in their field of expertise and the use of the tools to execute their craft, therefore, cannot be optimal. It's like giving Michelangelo only a hammer. In this book, we argue that the key tools required to extract alpha are risk management tools. In our view, investors cannot manage returns, but they can manage risk. Achieving sustainable positive absolute returns is the result, we believe, of taking and managing risk wisely. The result, when successful, is an asymmetric-return profile.

An asymmetric-risk/return profile is the result of an *active* risk management process. By *asymmetric returns,* we mean a return profile that is not available through long-only buy-and-hold strategies. Achieving an asymmetric-return profile requires a dynamic and flexible risk management process that truly corresponds to the end investors' risk preferences, tolerances, and aims. We claim that the delivery of these asymmetric-return profiles is the goal, and the future, of active asset management. This claim is based on some assumptions about what investors really want. An important one of these is that all investors are loss averse, that is, they do not perceive volatility on the downside in the same fashion as volatility on the upside. Hence our focus on asymmetry and our use of the term *asymmetric returns*.

The term *hedge fund* is a misnomer because there are no hedge funds that hedge all risks. If all risks were neutralized, so would be the returns. As Mario Andretti put it: "If everything is under control, you're driving too slow." Returns are a function of taking risk. Absolute-return investing implies that the risk-neutral position is cash (i.e., no risky positions at all). Generating alpha by definition means to take some risk. However, there are risks that are more likely to carry a reward, and risks that are less likely. This is where the asymmetry comes in. In financial markets there is both—randomness as well as predictability. The process of differentiating the two, the "sculpting," is then a function of intelligence, knowledge, insight, savvy, effort, experience, and skill. Luck helps, certainly, but in the long run, that cannot be the determinant of success.

The ultimate goal of an active investment management process is "alpha." In traditional investment management, success is typically referred to as outperforming a benchmark. This means that losing 28 percent when the benchmark fell 30 percent is actually quite an astounding achievement because the outperformance was two percentage points. However, in the absolute-return world, there are no benchmarks. The active risk manager, unlike the relative-return manager, has additional objectives that go beyond beating an arbitrary benchmark. We believe this new terminology of *asymmetric returns* goes beyond "the search for alpha." In fact, the term *alpha* originally stems from a linear model. We believe alpha is an option.

An asymmetric-return profile is achieved either through absolute-return managers driven by profit and loss or, more passively, through financial engineering using hedging techniques. What we call a *hedge fund* today is really part of the risk management business. Given that many investors expect the 2000 to 2020 period to be less investor friendly than the 1980 to 2000 period, we could currently be witnessing the convergence between what we referred to as the *asset management industry* and what we have come to understand to be the *risk management business*. Taking this line of thought further, we could say there is a convergence between the long term (as in "equities outperform bonds in the long term") and the short term (as in "interim volatility matters"). The synthesis of the two would be, in its active form, managers seeking investment opportunities while managing total risk.

An institutional or private investor allocating money to an active risk manager is essentially outsourcing to that manager the task of managing *total risk*. This is one of the main differences to the relative-return approach, wherein the manager does not have a mandate to manage capital at risk, but has a mandate to manage *tracking risk* relative to a market or liability benchmark. We believe that managing tracking risk is a passive risk management process, not an active one. Confusion arises because risk is sometimes defined in relative terms and sometimes in absolute terms. During the 20-year equity bull market, the traditional asset management industry used a more relative metric, whereas the risk management industry (essentially trading departments of investment banks and hedge funds) focused on an absolute metric to define and manage risk. Among the pivotal objectives of *active* risk management—unlike with relative-return investing—are avoiding absolute financial losses (especially large ones) as well as *actively* managing downside volatility.

The active approach to risk management has many advantages, but it also has some disadvantages. A major advantage for a hedge fund allocator is the substantial diversification benefits that can be achieved by combining many *independently* managed portfolios. (Diversification is the only scalable and repeatable free lunch in financial economics that is available to all investors.) One disadvantage is that the absence of a market benchmark can result in lower transparency.

With respect to transparency, it is important to distinguish between risk *measurement* and risk *management*. Risk measurement is fairly objective. Risk management, however, is subjective. The heterogeneity of the hedge funds industry with respect to the way risk is managed is an indication that this is true. Our main point is that the pure reliance on a process or a few metrics is very dangerous. We therefore believe that an open-minded, dynamic, and flexible approach to risk management is superior to a static (purely rule-based) and dogmatic process. With respect to transparency, this means that investors' demand for transparency should not interfere with the nimbleness and flexible maneuverability of the manager. Successful risk management in an ever-changing environment is like shooting a moving target: It is difficult but improves with practice. We don't think that successful risk management will trade at a discount anytime soon. As Oscar Wilde put it: "Experience is one thing you can't get for nothing."

We believe that in active risk management it is important to apply a skill that carries a reward in the marketplace within an opportunity set where the risk/reward trade-off is skewed in favor of the risk taker. What we herein refer to as *structural change* in the asset management industry is about finding skill (which is difficult enough), as well as the optimal setup for that skill to be operational in a value-added fashion. In terms of applying skill, we believe there is a trade-off between transparency and standardization on the one hand, and entrepreneurial maneuverability on the other. Interestingly, traditional asset managers are becoming somewhat more entrepreneurial by venturing into the absolute-return space, while hedge funds by and large are moving in the opposite direction, that is, they are becoming more transparent (as in self-constrained, disciplined, and process driven) to cater more to high-quality (quite often institutional) investors.

We believe these trends to be consistent with our claim in our first book, *Absolute Returns*—namely, that the hedge fund industry is slowly converging with the traditional asset management industry. In other words, from now on we should be talking about product differentiation in asset management—that is, distinguishing between *active* and *passive* risk management, and not between hedge funds and non-hedge funds. An active risk management process seeks asymmetric returns. We believe this to be the future of *active* asset management.

Some investors argue that the market is currently wrong in the way it prices active risk management services—in other words, that the fees in the hedge fund industry are too high. We believe that absolute-return strategies incorporating active risk management techniques and passive long-only buy-and-hold strategies offer entirely different value propositions and therefore merit entirely different dimensions in pricing, that is, costs to the end investor. In other words, we believe the market is right in the way it distinguishes between the two value propositions through different levels of fees. Searching for bargains when selecting an active risk manager is somewhat akin to searching for the cheapest parachute: By the time you notice the deficiency, it is too late. (Of course, this analogy has its limitations, as the parachutist's remorse period is short lived.)

We have designed this book to be readable by all financial professionals, whatever their particular area of expertise. However, at times, we somehow felt the urge to part from the main style. In some instances we have introduced break-out sessions called "Out-of-the-Box." Throughout the book these sections are add-ons that are related to the topic in discussion but are somewhat a digression from the main story line. In Chapter 1, for example, we digress to discuss a conference call with seven luminaries of the financial world. In another vein, we have sometimes added an appendix to a chapter. This is generally where the subject demanded more technical treatment than we gave it in the main body of the text or where we took the liberty to bring across a point more colloquially.

Alexander M. Ineichen, CFA, CAIA
Oberägeri, Switzerland
May 1, 2006

Acknowledgments

In my close to 20-year tenure in financial markets, I have had the good fortune to meet many interesting and dull, honest and dishonest, wise and unwise, ambitious and lazy, and insightful and ignorant characters. I am blessed to have learned something from all of them.

Many financial professionals have contributed to this book by examining the whole book, parts of the manuscript, or earlier versions thereof. In particular, I would like to thank Larry Chen and Sanjay Tikku, whose reviews and comments of the entire book were invaluable. I also benefited from discussions, debates, comments, and insights from Martin Boldt-Christmas, Bill Brown, Charlotte Burkeman, Meyrick Chapman, Alex Ehrlich, Arun Gowda, Jens Johansen, Kevin Maloney, Alan Scowcroft, James Sefton, and David Smith. I would also like to thank Bill Falloon, Laura Walsh, and Emilie Herman of John Wiley & Sons for their help and flexibility.

Opinions expressed in this book represent solely my own viewpoint and may or may not reflect the opinions or activities of any organization with which I am associated. Anyone interested in investing in an active risk manager should first seek *independent* advice. It goes without saying that all errors, omissions, and ambiguities, as well as any lack of humor, are entirely my own responsibility.

CHAPTER 1

Survival of the Richest—Volatility Matters

"It is not the strongest of the species that survive, nor the most intelligent, but the one most responsive to change."
—Charles Darwin

I magine you're a frog. You live the good life. You and your comrades, that is, the frog population, live happy and unchallenged lives. Your community prospers and grows. But then, one day, out of the blue and without warning, a frog-eating snake suddenly enters your habitat. What do you do? There are three options: (1) you run; (2) you and your comrades somehow adapt to the change in circumstances; or (3) you end up as snake food. Suddenly, life seems unfair. But you have to act; otherwise, you know it's going to be option 3 and you'll be history.

In our recent work (to be referenced later), we highlighted the aggressiveness, and the appetite, of the snake entering the frog's habitat and also commented on the fear, but also ignorance of large parts of the frog population. Today, things have moved along a bit. The frogs now realize that their environment—and therefore their life—has changed forever. Slowly but surely, the frogs have realized that in order to survive, they must adapt. The snakes, on the other hand, have lost some of their initial edge. They no longer have the advantage of "surprise" that they had when they first entered the habitat of the frogs. With this, they have lost some of their momentum. They, too, have to get smarter. This book is essentially about the coexistence of frogs and snakes.

THE FUTURE OF THE ASSET MANAGEMENT INDUSTRY

The asset management industry (essentially the habitat of both relative and absolute-return managers, beta providers and alpha providers, fish and sharks, frogs and snakes—however you want to think about it) started to change around the year 2000. The year 2000 is the turning point at which hedge funds started to seriously compete with the traditional asset management industry for institutional assets. Since then, institutional investors distinguish more carefully between alpha and beta, absolute returns and relative returns, and skill-based and market-based strategies. Quite early on, we referred to this change as a paradigm shift in the asset management industry. Our most serious advice in the early part of the decade was from John Maynard Keynes:

> *"When circumstances change, I change my view. What do you do?"*

Today—roughly half a decade after our initial hypothesis—we continue to believe that the asset management industry is going through structural change. The difference to five years ago is the evidence for this idea's taking shape in the marketplace, as well as an increasing population of investment professionals who agree that this is indeed a structural change in the asset management industry. We first presented these ideas in Ineichen, "In Search of Alpha" [2000] and continued to refine our thoughts in Ineichen [2001; 2003a, b, c; 2005]. We also believe ourselves to be in good company as we find credible confirmation for at least some of our elaborations in Cliff Asness's "An Alternative Future"[1] as well as Peter Bernstein's five inflection points for the asset management industry.[2]

Change in Risk Perception

Change in the asset management industry is driven by changes in their investors' change in risk perception. Investor needs are in the process of changing fundamentally, driven on the retail investor front by the looming retirement uncertainty with respect to a huge demographic shift and increased longevity, and on the institutional investor side by a combination of worsening pension deficits and a significant different approach to evaluating and eventually paying for performance. All of this is taking place amid an uncertain market environment that is breeding enormous levels of anxiety among investors of all stripes.

The catalyst that triggered this recent change was the equity bear market starting in 2000. We call this—for want of a better term—the "oops-effect." Following the sharp decline in equity prices, many investors realized that, "oops," ignoring short-term portfolio volatility is not in line with their investment objectives after all. (In cartoons, this is shown by a light bulb popping up above the head of the character with the effect. We are unaware of a formal term in the behavioral sciences that describes an observer's sudden switch from ignorance to enlightenment of an obvious fact. Nevertheless, an Internet search revealed that this could be called the *light bulb effect*.) More formally, this means that investors migrated to the belief that volatility matters and time does not reduce risk.

Figure 1.1 illustrates the negative effects of a volatile portfolio and its implications for short-term as well as long-term financial health or solvency. The bear market triggered a change in risk perception among a wide array of investors. Note that nothing at all has changed with respect to the underlying concept of "risk." A volatile portfolio is still and always has been a volatile portfolio, irrespective of equity markets going up or going down. Nor were there any significant theoretical breakthroughs in finance that brought about the change in perspective. It was the live experience of capital depreciation that was the catalyst for this change in perspective. We believe that what has changed is not risk itself but how investors *perceive* risk.

Figure 1.1 shows the impact of large drawdowns on compounding capital over time. We have added the potential time it could take for some

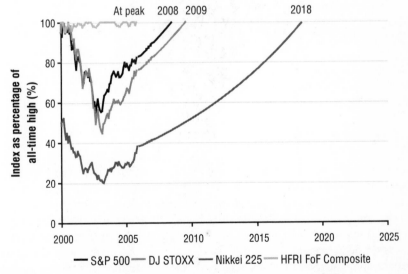

FIGURE 1.1 Underwater Perspective and Potential Time to Recovery
Note: December 2005 inclusive. Based on local currencies, HFRI in U.S. dollars (USD). Loss recovery line was based on assumption that indices compound at 8 percent per year.
Source: Author's own calculations; data from Thomson Financial and Bloomberg.

of these indices to recover to their previous peak. The Nikkei 225, for example, reached 38,915.87 in December 1989, fell to 7,607.88 in April 2003, and then recovered to 16,111.43 by year-end 2005. In other words, the index fell by 80.5 percent. In Figure 1.1 this is shown as a line falling to 19.5 percent (of peak value). Assuming the Nikkei 225 recovers from 16,111 at an annual rate of 8 percent, the index will not have recovered from its losses until 2018. It is probably true that equities outperform bonds in the long term. However, what the graph shows is that you might not live long enough to experience the long term. We discuss long-term returns in more detail in Chapter 9.

We call this the "underwater perspective" as it shows an index as a percentage of its previous all-time high; that is, it shows by how much an investment is "under water." This book advocates an investment approach that is designed to minimize these "underwater" periods, that is, to preserve capital even when market conditions are difficult. The problem with large drawdowns is that they kill the rate at which capital compounds. Any approach that takes an asset or liability benchmark as a risk-neutral base does not give the avoidance of large drawdowns the high priority we believe it deserves. We could argue that investing is like swimming: In both cases the survival-appreciating economic agent—after diving under water—has an incentive to reach the surface level at some stage in the future. As Warren Buffett—arguably an absolute-return investor—puts it:

> *"When we can't find anything exciting in which to invest, our 'default' position is U.S. Treasuries... Charlie and I detest taking even small risks unless we feel we are being adequately compensated for doing so. About as far as we will go down that path is to occasionally eat cottage cheese a day after the expiration date on the carton."*[3]

The idea of what we believe is an absolute-return investment philosophy is to try and stick close to the surface level in Figure 1.1, as digging oneself out of a deep hole can be rather time consuming. In other words, we prefer an asymmetric-return profile, that is, many and large gains versus few and small losses, to a symmetrical profile. More formally, we argue that the post-dot-com bubble period is characterized by a transition from the second into the third stage of asset management. In the preface of *Absolute Returns*[4] we defined the three stages as follows:

1. Absolute-return approach with low degree of manager specialization.
2. Relative-return approach with high degree of manager specialization.
3. Absolute-return approach with high degree of manager specialization.

We believe it is fair to argue that there was an asset management industry before there were benchmarks. This first stage was characterized by an absolute-return focus and a low degree of specialization on the part of the manager. Managers had "balanced" mandates in which top priority was given to an asset allocation decision rather than security selection. This approach suffered from poor performance in the mid-1970s. More fundamentally, it suffered from what is known in economics as an "agency problem": The objectives of the manager were not aligned with those of the principal. Managers were incentivized to beat the peer group rather than to invest in an economically sensible fashion based on their individual edge and overall opportunity set.

This first stage was replaced by the second stage: the relative-return game. In this second stage, managers shifted to a relative-return approach. The asset allocation mandate was essentially taken away from the manager and this led, quite naturally, to higher specialization on the part of the manager. Next to poor performance and principal/agent issues, the introduction of the Employee Retirement Income Security Act (ERISA) in the United States in 1974 was yet another catalyst for the industry to move from the first to the second stage. ERISA changed the fiduciary responsibility of the end investor.

The introduction of an index was an improvement of the status quo as it somewhat resolved the agency problem through using a rigid benchmark. Around the same time, the efficient market hypothesis (EMH)* was rising to academic prominence through the work of Samuelson [1965] and Fama [1965, 1970], and the investment community was intellectually gradually moving away from the merits of active asset management in general and the feasibility of stock selection in particular. The main product to emerge from the 1964 to 2000 consensus thinking in the investment community was the index fund. Hedge funds are (or, more precisely, until recently were) somewhat antithetical to the EMH and the consensus view.

We classified active managers exploiting absolute-return strategies as the third stage in asset management. The third stage combines the absolute-return investment philosophy from the first stage with a high degree of manager specialization of the second stage.† The absolute-return approach

---

*As a matter of priority, investment professionals who read small-printed footnotes of finance books (such as this one), should certainly also read "The Adaptive Markets Hypothesis" (AMH) by MIT professor Andrew Lo [2004]. The AMH can be viewed as a new version of the EMH and is based on an evolutionary approach to economic interactions, taking into account some recent research in the cognitive neurosciences that has been transforming and revitalizing the intersection of psychology and economics.

†One could argue that there is a fourth stage. Hedge funds now have also launched long-only funds alongside their absolute-return products and there are increasingly

seeks to solve some of the issues of the relative-return approach. Investors introduce an absolute yardstick against which managers get measured. This avoids some of the pitfalls of the relative-return approach, namely peer-group hugging, search for mediocrity, and misalignment of interests between manager and investor. However, the absolute-return approach introduces new issues to be resolved. First, the loose mandate of absolute-return managers (i.e., the lack of tracking error constraints) results in a wide dispersion between managers. This means that the costs and risks of manager selection as well as potential benefits are higher with the absolute-return approach than with the relative-return approach. Second, a paradigm shift (i.e., the introduction of something new) reduces transparency and increases costs. This is an advantage for first movers and early adapters, but potentially a disadvantage for latecomers.

Recent consultant survey material adds some credibility to the preceding discussion. Figure 1.2 shows answers to a survey question. The survey was published in fourth quarter (Q4) 2005 and represented $3.5 trillion of global pension assets. The question was phrased as follows: "Which factors have fueled the worldwide growth in hedge funds in the recent past, and which, if any, are likely to do so over the next three years?"

Figure 1.2 confirms that a bear market was the catalyst for pension funds getting interested in hedge funds. The long-only culture came under

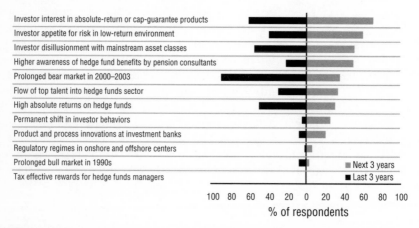

FIGURE 1.2   Reasons by Pension Fund for Investing in Hedge Funds
Source: Create/KPMG [2005].

fewer specialist-focused funds. Many funds, at least within mainstream strategies, now have diversified focus, that is, they keep opportunity set as widely as possible, as some strategies are overcrowded and inefficiencies arbitraged away.

severe scrutiny, as pension funds watched their assets going from surplus to deficit. (Later in this chapter we will argue that "volatility matters," a notion that was subdued during the 1990s bull market.) However, this is not the main reason mentioned for investing in hedge funds going forward. The main two factors mentioned by the pension funds surveyed were interest in absolute returns and investor appetite for hedge fund risk in a low-return environment. These two factors are driving flows.

LIVING LEGENDS ON THE FUTURE OF INVESTMENT MANAGEMENT

300 YEARS OF COLLECTIVE WISDOM

The Chartered Financial Analyst (CFA) Institute (formerly Association of Investment Management and Research [AIMR]) issued its inaugural issue of CFA Magazine *in January/February in 2003. The cover story was "Words from the Wise"—a conference call from November 2002 that was chaired by Charles D. Ellis (author of* Winning the Loser's Game *[1993]). The "wise" were John Neff, Gary Brinson, Peter Bernstein, Jack Bogle, Warren Buffett, Dean LeBaron, and Sir John Templeton. Together, these legends share more than 300 years of collective experience.*

One of the questions was the following:

Looking back over the last 30 years, what are the most important changes in the fundamental nature of our profession? And then looking out over the next 30 years, what do you think will be remembered from today that's really significant?[5]

Here are some quotes from some of the participants. The quotes are in chronological order but are taken slightly out of context, as we did not reprint the whole debate. Our first quote is from Jack Bogle, founder and ex-chairman of the Vanguard Group:

"This business has really changed. It used to be about stewardship, and now it's about salesmanship. There used to be about 300 broad-based equity funds, and now there are 5,000, many of them narrowly based and speculative specialty funds, often created and sold just when they shouldn't be bought. ...."

Bogle then pitches for investing in index funds and finishes response to the question:

"... In all, the mutual fund industry has turned from a profession into a business. The challenge for the next 30 years is just as obvious as the smiles on our faces: This industry should return to its roots."

Bernstein (author of Against the Gods [1996]) on the same question listed above:

"One of the problems with this market has been, particularly for professional managers, 'benchmarkitis' on the part of the clients. I think there are forces at work that are going to break that down. One is the hedge fund, which you can approve or disapprove of as an animal, but it's focused peoples' attention away from the conventional benchmarks. This is a very, very important development."

Another question posed at the conference call of legends was about corporate governance. Corporate governance could, we believe, be improved through implementation of the absolute-return approach. The main decision for buying a stock under the relative-return approach is balancing outperformance potential with its marginal contribution to tracking error. Most of the relative-return manager's portfolio is dead weight, that is, long positions held to manage tracking risk. The main reason to buy a stock under the absolute-return approach is balancing potential capital appreciation versus potential capital depreciation. One could argue that corporate executives will pay closer attention to investors who not only can buy or not buy the stock but also sell short the stock.

Here are some soundbites on corporate governance from the legends. Ellis phrases the question as if the U.S. president were calling the panelists on the subject of corporate governance. Some of the responses were:

LeBaron: "Sunshine, sunshine, sunshine, disclosure and more of it. And the president should start with it himself. "

Buffett: "The only real way to get improvement in corporate governance is to have big investors demand it."

Bogle: *"But most important is for institutions to wake up and behave like owners."*

Bernstein: *"The president should understand that we run the risk of ending up with corporations run by bean counters instead of risk takers if we push this thing too far. Sunshine is essential. And the tax thing is an interesting idea, but otherwise try to keep the sticky fingers a little off."*

BOTTOM LINE

We believe that at least some of these quotes point toward an absolute-return approach. Diverging interests between principal and agent have come a long way. Some of the current problems in the economy in general, and in the financial industry in particular, could be solved (or the status quo improved) by realigning interests between principal and agent. What safer way than principals requesting that agents become at least a little bit principals? For this not to work, capitalism and free enterprise needs to be a flawed idea.

DEFINING ASYMMETRIC RETURNS

Introduction

What do we mean by "absolute returns"? This question was addressed in your author's first book: *Absolute Returns: The Risk and Opportunities of Hedge Fund Investing* [Ineichen, 2003a]. The distinguishing feature of an "absolute-return" approach is that it gives priority to capital preservation. This can be contrasted with a "relative-return" approach, which links risk and return to some benchmark; capital preservation is not a major objective in a "relative-return" approach. The argument of this book is that the absolute-return approach is the preferred investment philosophy and that asymmetric returns are the implementation thereof.

What do we mean by "asymmetric returns"? In the first place, we mean a return profile that is not symmetrical, that is, a profile that departs from the so-called normal distribution. The specific "asymmetry" we are concerned with here is between positive outcomes (of which we cannot get enough) and negative outcomes (which we do not like). In an asymmetric-return profile risk and return depart from linearity. The simplest way to illustrate what we mean is with options.

Think of a strategy whereby $95 is invested in a money market instrument yielding the risk-free rate and $5 is invested in call options. We therefore begin with a portfolio worth $100. Assume for a moment that over a period the value of the options increases threefold, so the $5 investment is now worth $15. During the same period, the $95 investment in money market instruments grows to $100. At the end of the period, the value of the portfolio is therefore $100 + $15 = $115. The return on the portfolio is 15 percent.

Now consider instead of buying options that increase threefold we bought options that expired worthless. In this case the value of the portfolio at the end of the period would be $100 + $0 = $100. So we would still not have made any loss on our portfolio. Our initial capital of $100 was preserved.

In this simple example the relationship between potential gain and potential pain is very *asymmetric*. Our potential gain was unlimited, whereas the capital base was safe.

The central claim of this book is threefold:

1. *Asymmetric returns* are about finding investment opportunities where the risk/reward relationship is asymmetric, that is, situations in which the potential profit is higher than the potential loss or where the probability of a profit is higher than the probability of a loss of the same magnitude, or a combination thereof.
2. Finding and exploiting these asymmetries requires an active risk management process.
3. The future of active asset management is about finding and exploiting these asymmetries.

We believe this new terminology of "asymmetric returns" goes beyond our previous model of "the search for alpha" [Ineichen, 2000a]. In fact, the term *alpha** originally stems from the capital asset pricing model (CAPM), which is a linear model.

---

*The Economist, in a survey of human evolution, on alpha: "Students of animal behavior refer to the top male in a group as the 'alpha.' Such dominant animals keep the others under control and father a large proportion, if not all, of the group's offspring. One of the curiosities of modern life is that voters tend to elect alpha males to high office, and then affect surprise when they behave like alphas outside politics too." ("The Proper Study of Mankind: A Survey of Human Evolution," *The Economist*, December 24, 2005.)

Background

Traditional asset management has a bias toward long-only investment strategies. Both index funds and long-only managers define risk relative to a market benchmark. Hence, their operation is structured in a fashion wherein replication and access are key elements.

In Ineichen [2001, 2003a, 2004a] and elsewhere, we made the point that what today is referred to as *active* management is in fact *passive*, because it uses the same risk management techniques as indexing (which is considered passive money management) and the same definition of risk (tracking risk) as do index funds. The distinction between passive and active long-only investment management is merely the magnitude of the tracking error constraint, that is, the predefined and accepted deviation from a market benchmark. If risk management is passive, the return distribution of the managed portfolio will be similar to that of the underlying market. Putting it crudely: If volatility is at 10 percent, the passive (or the so-called active) portfolio will have a volatility of around 10 percent, with higher moment risk characteristics similar to the benchmark. If volatility is at 50 percent, the portfolio volatility will also be around that level, as risk is defined and managed relative to the market benchmark.

We discuss tracking risk versus total risk and active versus passive risk management in more detail in Chapters 2 and 6, respectively. Table 1.1 gives a foretaste what this discussion entails: controlling downside risk and avoiding losses, especially large ones.

Table 1.1 shows the quarterly performance of the average hedge fund as well as the average U.S. mutual fund in quarters in which the Standard and Poor's (S&P) 500 index was negative. The sum of all negative quarterly returns for the S&P 500 index was −111.4 percent. This compares to −115.6 percent for the average mutual fund. This slight underperformance of active long-only asset management is fairly consistent with most of the empirical research suggesting that active long-only underperforms. (Note that index funds underperform, too.) The average hedge fund lost only 8.5 percent in these negative quarters. We believe this a big difference to −115.6 percent of the average mutual fund, assuming compounding capital positively and survival is a major objective. (Note that the sum of all negative quarterly returns of the Van U.S. Hedge Fund Index was 26.8 percent, which compares to 111.4 percent in case of the S&P 500.)

One key claim for which we will argue throughout this book is that all investors should prefer asymmetric returns to symmetric returns. This conclusion is based on the following three factors that, we believe, apply to all investors. The first two notions are from Markowitz [1952, 1959] and the third from Kahneman and Tversky [1979]:

TABLE 1.1   Hedge Funds versus Mutual Funds in Down Quarters

	S&P 500	Van U.S. Hedge Fund Index	Morningstar Average Equity Mutual Fund
1Q 1990	-3.0%	2.2%	-2.8%
3Q 1990	-13.7%	-3.7%	-15.4%
2Q 1991	-0.2%	2.3%	-0.9%
1Q 1992	-2.5%	5.0%	-0.7%
1Q 1994	-3.8%	-0.8%	-3.2%
4Q 1994	-0.02%	-1.2%	-2.6%
3Q 1998	-10.0%	-6.1%	-14.9%
3Q 1999	-6.2%	2.1%	-3.4%
2Q 2000	-2.7%	0.3%	-3.2%
3Q 2000	-1.0%	3.0%	0.6%
4Q 2000	-7.8%	-2.4%	-8.1%
1Q 2001	-11.9%	-1.1%	-12.7%
3Q 2001	-14.7%	-3.8%	-17.2%
2Q 2002	-13.4%	-1.4%	-10.7%
3Q 2002	-17.3%	-3.6%	-16.7%
1Q 2003	-3.2%	0.7%	-3.7%
Sum of returns*	-111.4%	-8.5%	-115.6%
Cumulative return	-69.4%	-8.8%	-70.9%

*Author's own calculations, not in original.
Source: VAN Hedge Fund Advisors, LLC.

1. More return is preferred over less.
2. Certainty is preferred over uncertainty.
3. Losses weigh stronger than profits; that is, disutility from capital depreciation is larger than utility from capital appreciation.

The first factor (more return) is obvious. More is always preferred to less as you can always give away what you do not want, so less is never preferred to more. All investors, everything else being equal, prefer more over less, not only with respect to returns.* An absolute-return manager, unlike a relative-return manager, also actively addresses the second and third of the three factors mentioned above: First, most absolute-return

*For the sake of argument, we ignore here the very special case wherein an increase in wealth can result in negative externalities, tipping marginal utility into negative

managers have some sort of target risk (e.g., volatility or VaR) and control portfolio risk accordingly. Second, capital preservation is crucial; that is, avoiding large drawdowns is a major part of the objectives as well as the investment process. In other words, the difference in market behavior and investment process between relative and absolute-return managers does not manifest itself by examining returns but by examining risk. What we mean by risk will be elaborated in more detail in following chapters. It has many aspects: risk definition, risk control, risk perception, risk management philosophy, corporate risk management culture, and so on. Put simply, if a manager defines risk relative to a benchmark, the portfolio will mimic the return distribution of the underlying market benchmark. However, absolute-return managers are not driven by market benchmark but by profit and loss (P&L). This means risk is defined in absolute terms. We use the term *total risk*. If risk is defined as total risk and the investment process is driven by P&L, the manager will be taking into account these three factors.

VOLATILITY MATTERS

The Thing about Compounding Capital

As previously mentioned, one of our claims is that volatility matters. Volatility can kill the rate at which capital compounds. Visualize:

- A 10-year investment of $100 that is flat in the first year and then compounds at 8 percent will end at $200.
- A 10-year investment of $100 that falls by 50% in the first year and then compounds at 8 percent will end at $100.

This, to us, seems to be a big difference. What we find puzzling is that not everyone agrees with our notion that long-term investors cannot be indifferent to short-term volatility. Note that a 10-year investment of $100 that compounds at 8 percent in the first nine years and then falls by 50 percent will end at $100, too. Figure 1.3 shows these three investments graphically. We assume that the three portfolios are diversified portfolios; that is, idiosyncratic risk is diversified. Note that we have added some casual remarks on compounding, survival, and dull financial products to the appendix of this chapter.

---

territory (e.g., kidnapping, media attention). These negative externalities do not apply to institutional investors, as it can be safely argued that the probability of a trustee of a pension fund being kidnapped or hunted down by a hoard of groupies is minuscule.

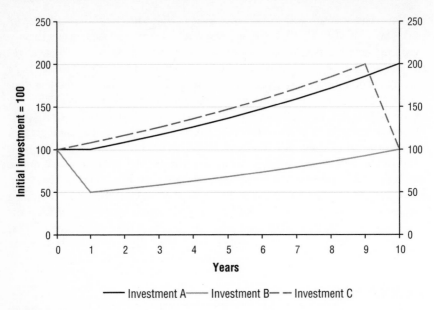

FIGURE 1.3   Effect of compounding
Source: Author's own calculations.

Note that investment C has outperformed investment A for a long time. We believe the proper response to a presentation of outperformance akin to the one shown in Figure 1.3 is: Who cares? Any form of return examination without a discussion of the risk involved is useless. If we do not know the risk, the next period could be materially different from the past. Examining realized volatility and historical return distribution properties is a start but purely backward looking. We do not see a shortcut for investors that allows intelligent investment decisions without knowing what they are doing, that is, without having as clear as possible an understanding of risk going forward.

While we believe investors' change in risk perception is largely structural, loss aversion and perception of risk could be cyclical. We possibly have found a simple way to measure investors' loss aversion. (We discuss loss aversion and prospect theory more formally in Chapter 5.)

Figure 1.4 is a 200-day moving average of the U.S. and Japanese indices. We have normalized the peak to 100 and then synchronized the peaks. We are actually serious in claiming that risk aversion varies a lot. We also feel very strongly about the notion that it was the 2000 to 2002 bear market that put hedge funds, and therefore absolute-return strategies, on the agenda of many institutional investors. Although we equally strongly believe that the asset management industry is fundamentally changing, and that the end

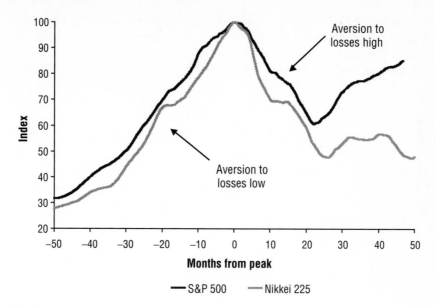

FIGURE 1.4 Change in Loss Aversion
Lines in graph show 200-day moving average based on daily returns. All-time highs were indexed to 100 and synchronized. Highs of 200-day moving average were September 2000 (S&P 500) and February 1990, respectively.
Source: Author's own calculations; data from Thomson Financial.

of this decade will have little resemblance to the previous one, we need to acknowledge that there is a cyclical element in all this. We also believe that, as low interest rates have caused liquidity to swell, by early 2006 equity strategists were falling over themselves with bullish commentary for the year. Flows into hedge funds somewhat slowed in 2005. It is not entirely unthinkable that the flow of institutional funds into absolute-return strategies has slowed because investors are having positive returns in the rest of their portfolio as well. We actually have a mini-theory on this.

In technical analysis there is an oscillator called the *Coppock curve*. According to investopedia.com, the Coppock curve is "A long-term price momentum indicator used primarily to recognize major bottoms in the stock market. It is calculated as a 10-month weighted moving average of the sum of the 14-month rate of change and the 11-month rate of change for the index."[6] The interesting thing about this curve is that the 14-month and 11-month periods were chosen based on research suggesting that it takes normal, grown-up human beings around 11 to 14 months to recover from the loss of a loved one. This might sound somewhat awkward, but judging from the author's own experience, this could actually be more or less correct. If this is true, our theory is that it takes around 11 to 14 months until the pain from a large loss is filed in a different part of the brain, that is, does not influence day-to-day decision making anymore. So we do not think it is pure coincidence that flows into hedge funds started to slow roughly one year after the lows in equity markets, that is, one year into the recovery. Aversion to losses was largest when markets were in freefall. It is not entirely unthinkable that flows into absolute-return space will pick up again as soon as markets start falling again and real losses are experienced.

Back to Basics　　The adoption of the absolute-return approach is to some extent the industry "returning to its roots," at least for the active part of the asset management industry. The negative effect of large drawdowns on compounding capital was not lost on Benjamin Graham (1894–1976):

> *"An investment operation is one which, upon thorough analysis, promises safety of principal and an adequate return. Operations not meeting these requirements are speculative."*[7]

Nor was it lost on Albert Einstein:

> *"Compound interest is the eighth natural wonder of the world and the most powerful thing I have ever encountered."*

What we refer to as the third stage of the asset management industry is a combination of the absolute-return approach from the first stage, and the high degree of specialization of the second stage. Combining an absolute-return approach with a high degree of manager specialization* results in the manager's having a mandate to balance investment opportunity with capital at risk. This is a more flexible approach than adding value with respect to a benchmark. It takes into account the fact that market inefficiencies have a tendency to go away when identified by too many investors, as well as the fact that the reward from a certain skill falls over time. Today, we call this

---

*We believe this to be the case for the asset management industry as a whole. One could argue that within the subspace today called the hedge fund industry, there is a trend toward broader mandates, that is, less specialization as many single-strategy managers seem to be migrating toward multistrategy approaches. We believe this to be related to the scalability (or nonscalability) of an absolute-return venture, as well as the adaptability and flexibility of skill in the marketplace, two issues addressed in more detail later in this book. Another reason is that successful managers migrate to less risk as the downside is perceived as larger (less time to recover from loss, potential kink to reputation and ego, etc.).

a *hedge fund*. However, the term, essentially a misnomer characterizing a legal construct, might disappear.

A different view from our own is the belief that the absolute-return investment philosophy will somehow be integrated into the status quo— what we call the second stage of asset management, the relative-returns game. After all, the end investors (pension funds, insurers, etc.) have a multiple set of objectives, some of which are defined in relative terms. We do not share that point of view. As a matter of fact, we are inclined to treat the benchmarked long-only and absolute-return approaches as opposites, or, more formally, as passive and active risk management. Why?

Our angle (or bias) comes from looking at the world from what we believe is a risk perspective. The bottom-up stock selection process of a long-only manager and a long/short manager might be identical or very similar. However, there is a big difference in the way risk is defined. If the definition of risk is different, it is obvious that the whole risk management process differs as a result. In a benchmark-driven investment process, risk is defined as some form of *tracking risk*, while, in an absolute investment process, risk is defined as *total risk*. Managing tracking risk means participating in any boom/bust cycle unhedged, whereas managing total risk means reducing risk when the risk/return opportunity set changes to the investor's disadvantage. The investment philosophy and culture resulting from this differentiation could not be farther apart. Indeed, we believe they could be considered opposites.

We believe, however, that some sort of convergence between "traditional" and "alternative" management has become more apparent over the past two to three years. For instance, it is true that many hedge funds are becoming somewhat more like traditional investment managers, that is, more transparent, regulated, investor friendly. Some hedge fund firms are even launching long-only products. At the same time, the traditional asset management industry is launching what look like absolute-return products or are buying into the absolute-return boom through mergers and acquisitions. But does this trend also reveal any convergence in investment philosophy and risk management culture? We're not yet convinced.

Evolution Is Jumpy, Not Smooth

Generally, progress is not smooth and gradual, but erratic and jumpy due to new discoveries and new ideas. A new development or idea is typically ridiculed first, then it is contested because it does not fit nicely with the current doctrine, then the opposing camp adapts to the changed environment, and then—finally—goes on to argue that "we knew this all along." With respect to absolute-return investing, we have safely passed the first phase. There is only a minority of die-hard contemporaries from the popular press and a minority of institutional investors left arguing that the search for alpha, the preference for an asymmetric-return profile over exposure to randomness, the quest for independent return streams (portfolio diversification), and thinking about the extreme impact of large losses to investor survival probability is ridiculous. We believe we are somewhere in the second phase where there is still opposition, as the "new" idea does not fit nicely with "old" beliefs.

Here, the term *incommensurability* used by Thomas Kuhn (American philosopher and historian of science) in the context of paradigm shifts and scientific change comes to mind.* Kuhn [1962] held that at certain moments in the development of science the abandoned paradigm and the newly embraced one are "incommensurable." By this he means that the fundamental concepts of one paradigm cannot be rendered by the terms of the other. In other words, according to Kuhn, the old and new paradigms are conceptually so different that a debate is not possible. We find this image extremely apt for the asset management industry, in the sense that the concepts and perceptions of risk between the relative-return paradigm and absolute-return paradigm are so wide as to be incommensurable. A quote from the late Professor Robert Heilbroner, author of *The Worldly Philosophers: The Lives, Times, and Ideas of the Great Economic Thinkers,*[8] potentially also applies to the current regime switch in the asset management industry:

> *"The high theorizing of the present period [in economics] attains a degree of unreality that can be matched only by medieval scholasticism."*

The theorizing of scholars over abstracted ideas is a common feature of the end of paradigms. The incredibly complex math employed to explain anomalies in Newtonian physics before Einstein posited his comparably simple relativity is a case in point. Comparing the current regime switch in asset management with the move from Newtonian physics to Einstein's relativity or from the Ptolemaic system to Copernicanism is arguably somewhat over the top. However, risk-uncontrolled exposure to market forces could one day—looking back—be compared to the unsheltered exposure of our ancestors to the whims of natural forces. Most people probably agree

---

*The term *incommensurable* derives from a mathematical use, according to which the side and diagonal of a square are incommensurable by virtue of there being no unit that can be used to measure both exactly. Kuhn stressed that incommensurability did not mean noncomparability (just as the side and diagonal of a square are comparable in many respects).

that finding ways to control and shelter life and belongings from the natural elements is considered progress. We believe the same is true for controlling capital at risk. (Nudists might disagree, though.)

CHAPTER SUMMARY AND CONCLUSIONS

The asset management industry is often considered a zero-sum game (or even a negative-sum game after fees). A zero-sum game implies the presence of both winners and losers. The gains of the winners are matched by the losses of the losers. If a paradigm shift results in all investors managing risk more aligned to their individual preferences, then all investors win. (Except those who miss the shift, of course.)

We believe that the purpose of risk management and risk management products is to achieve asymmetric returns. By asymmetric returns we mean a risk/return profile that is not available in "nature," but is artificially controlled to match the end investors' risk preferences more accurately and more efficiently. Our belief is based on some assumptions, an important one of which is that investors are loss averse; that is, volatility on the downside is not the same as volatility on the upside, hence the key importance of asymmetry.

The asymmetric-return profile is achieved either through absolute-return managers driven by P&L or through financial engineering using hedging techniques. We believe that what we call a hedge fund today is really part of the risk management business. Given that many investors expect the 2000 to 2020 period to be less investor friendly than the 1980 to 2000 period, we could currently be witnessing the merger between what we referred to as the asset management industry and what we have come to understand to be the risk management business. One could view this as a merger between the long term (as in "equities outperform bonds in the long term") and the short term (as in "interim volatility matters"). The synthesis of the two would be, in its active form, managers seeking investment opportunities while managing total risk. In its more passive form, it would be structured investment products (e.g., capital guarantees or overlays).

We believe that one of the main sources of confusion, myth, and misrepresentation with respect to risk comes from the observation that risk is sometimes defined in relative terms and sometimes in absolute terms. During the 20-year bull market, the asset management industry used a more relative metric, whereas the risk management industry (essentially trading departments of investment banks and hedge funds) focused on absolute metrics to define and manage risk. The pivotal objectives of absolute-return investing are in sharp contrast with those of relative-return investing. The absolute-return approach aims to avoid absolute financial losses, preserve principal, and *actively* manage portfolio volatility. One of the major disadvantages of all this is that the absolute-return approach does not fit as nicely into the traditional asset allocation process of the institutional end investor. One could conclude that the absolute-return approach is not fit for survival because there is limited transparency and one cannot budget for risk as well as one can with the relative-return approach. We believe that this view is similar to the assessment of individual transport 100 years ago and the migration to the automobile. Because of the lack of proper roads, there was the belief that "the horse is here to stay."

APPENDIX: ON COMPOUNDING, SURVIVAL, AND DULL SWISS

> *"It takes 20 years to build a reputation and five minutes to ruin it. If you think about that, you'll do things differently."*
> —Warren Buffett

Your author is Swiss. One of the many stereotypes of the Swiss is that they are perceived—by the global non-Swiss community—as dull. One of the reasons the Swiss are so dull—according to an article we came across some years ago—is that the Swiss never had victories on battlefields to speak of, never had colonies, never had social upheavals, never had social disasters. The Swiss, unlike their neighbors, don't even strike. The article went on to argue that periods of stress, such as war, bring out the best in terms of human inventiveness and creativity. The article went on to say that the works of Michelangelo, da Vinci, and the like fell into such stress periods. As a result of the Swiss being so peaceful and dull, the article went on, they are extremely uncreative.* One famous psychiatrist and one partly famous reformist theologian aside, the Swiss have no poets, no composers, no philosophers, hardly any writers, or painters of international acclaim to speak of. So the only creative legacy from the Swiss to the world—according to this article—is the cuckoo clock.

However, Switzerland—by any standard—is also among the world's richest nations. Has the reader ever thought that there might be a relationship between dullness and riches? Potentially, there is.

---

*Which is, of course, entirely untrue. According to the United Nations Human Development Report 2001, Switzerland is top-notch when inventiveness is measured by patents per capita. In addition, it does actually require a beautiful mind to come up with the idea of stirring pieces of bread on an oversized fork in a pot of melted cheese for dinner.

We started examining the hedge fund space in 2000. One of the fund of funds marketing one-liners we came across at the time was something along the lines of "We offer dull products." In finance, there is a measure for the degree of dullness: the standard deviation of returns or—in its annualized form—the volatility. So a fund of funds could argue that if survival and sustainable compounding of capital (two elements that are arguably related) are major objectives, then large erratic swings, especially on the downside, are to be avoided. The bottom line of this analogy is the following: The Swiss—supposedly—are dull but somehow got compensated for their collective loss of sense of humor by creating an environment that allowed a long-term and sustainable creation of prosperity that has been handed over from one generation to the next. Fund of hedge funds—with volatilities in some cases of less than two percentage points these days—are dull, too. But chances are that fund of funds also—when risk is managed diligently—will survive and compound capital sustainably for the foreseeable future.

One way to make the case for the dull is the following: Table 1.2 shows five different investment alternatives whereby we calculated returns over the past ten years. The first row is a simple average of the ten annual returns from 1996 to 2005. The second row shows the compound annual rate of return (CARR). This is the return that shows if one had invested on day one, in this case January 1996, and held on to the investment until the end of the investment period, in this case 2005. However, this is not really a practical assumption for most investors, institutional as well as private. Most investors continuously add new money to old.

The third method in Table 1.2 is more realistic for most investors. It assumes the investor adds an equal amount of capital in regular intervals, in this case ten equal contributions at the beginning of every year. The rate shown is the fixed rate that matches all cash flows. There are some observations we can draw from the table. First, the higher the volatility of the investment, the more the internal rate of return (IRR) differs to the average annual return. In the case of the NASDAQ, the average return was

TABLE 1.2   Returns from 1996 to 2005

	S&P 500 Total Return Index	NASDAQ Composite Index	MSCI World Total Return Index	JPM Global Gov. Bond Index	HFRI Fund of Funds Comp. Index
Average	10.7	13.8	9.0	5.5	8.8
CARR	9.1	7.7	7.5	5.2	8.4
IRR	5.7	4.1	6.3	5.4	7.4

CARR: compound annual rate of return; IRR: internal rate of return.
Source: Author's own calculations; data from Thomson Financial and Bloomberg.

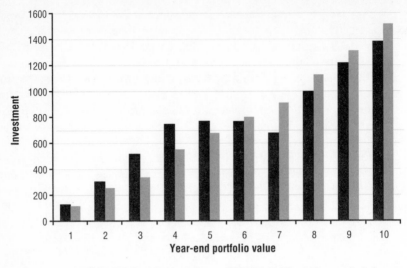

FIGURE 1.5 Example of an Exciting versus a Dull Investment (1996 to 2005)
Source: Author's calculations; data from Thomson Financial and Bloomberg.

13.8 percent. An investor buying the NASDAQ in January 1996 and selling in December 2005 compounded at 7.7 percent. However, had the investor added an equal amount every year, his investments would have compounded at a rate of 4.1 percent. This is probably much closer to many investors' experience with tech stocks. Second, fund of funds have by far the highest IRR. What is interesting here is that fund of funds have underperformed the S&P 500 Total Return Index. Or have they? We don't think so. We do not believe that many investors have put money in the S&P 500 in 1996, left the investment untouched throughout all the turbulence, and looked at the performance at the end of 2005. Adding to an existing investment over time is far more realistic. Figure 1.5 shows the two investments whereby $100 was invested at the beginning of every year. The bars measure year-end values.

Going forward, many investors will come to realize that the light-grey bars in Figure 1.5 represent the more attractive investment, that is, portfolios with high risk-adjusted returns are superior to portfolios with lower risk-adjusted returns. That's why dull is good and volatility matters. Oscar Wilde might have been thinking of the Swiss when he said: "It is better to have a permanent income than to be fascinating."

CHAPTER 2

Risk and Transparency

"Investors will want to make sure that they don't start out with the money and the hedge funds start out with the experience, and then when all is said and done, the hedge funds have the money, and the investors have the experience."
— John Webster, Greenwich Associates[1]

R isk and transparency considerations are key to any investment process. Today, post-Enron and during what someone once described as the current "regulatory and compliance bubble," considerations with regard to risk and transparency are probably more important than ever before in investment management. In this chapter we discuss issues surrounding transparency and risk. We make the argument that risk is far too complex to be captured by a single aggregate risk figure or daily risk report.

We introduce a somewhat esoteric definition of risk, where we define *risk* as "exposure to change." We believe that, with respect to transparency, there is some confusion between risk *measurement* and risk *management* and that the latter is scarce and difficult, whereas the former is not. We believe Winston Churchill was on to something when he said that "most economists use statistics like drunks use lampposts: for support more than for light."

RISK IS "EXPOSURE TO CHANGE"

The Boiling Frog Syndrome

Transparency is an evergreen issue in absolute-return investing. The consensus among new institutional absolute-return investors seems to have moved away from real-time and position-level transparency, which was commonly demanded a couple of years ago. The focus is now increasingly on process, rather than position, transparency. In addition, institutional investors are now more likely to emphasize aggregated risk measures and periodic reporting. The focus on aggregate risk measures, however, creates its own set of problems.

Investors attempt to quantify risks because doing so makes risk management more precise as well as more transparent. Expressing risk in quantitative rather than qualitative terms provides some sort of "common language" for financial professionals to compare, contrast, and debate.[2] The history of risk management and its instruments, such as derivatives, is all about breaking down products and contracts into their component risks. Once risk is divided into components, these risk components can be aggregated and the risk managed separately.

We believe that risk measurement can be narrowly defined and is probably to a large extent objective, whereas risk management is a much broader task and is subjective by definition. Although the two are not entirely unrelated, the underlying skill sets required for the two are totally different. In addition, different investors have different definitions of risk.

A suitable analogy is the difference between accounting and entrepreneurism. Accounting is objective (at least in the axiomatic, fraud-free laboratory environment of the actuary). However, sound accounting does not automatically result in entrepreneurial success. (It is somewhat like being short a put option: Good accounting does not guarantee success, but bad accounting almost certainly eventually results in disaster. Accounting is therefore important, just as risk measurement is.) Entrepreneurial success is much more complex and difficult. It requires experience, creativity, intelligence, passion, drive, and so on. Most importantly, founding and running a business successfully is subjective. There is a consensus as well as objective guidelines to do accounting. However, there is more than one approach that leads to entrepreneurial success (most of which, potentially, are not taught at business school). To complete this analogy: Risk measurement is similar to accounting where a somewhat inflexible approach (rules and guidelines) has merit, as the task requires objectivity and transparency. Risk management, on the other hand, requires a more flexible approach, is entrepreneurial in nature, and is subjective by definition.

Risk management is at least as much a craft as it is a science. A craftsman needs a combination of skills, that is, a balance between outright knowledge and street-smartness (practical tricks of the trade) to execute his job successfully.* One could argue that this combination of skills goes far beyond, for example, econometric modeling of (historical) risk factors, or the abstract theorizing under laboratory conditions. As we will elaborate throughout this book, risk is about what you don't know, not about what you know. Outright knowledge alone has its limitations. Perhaps there is, beyond craftsmanship, even an element of art. As Albert Einstein put it:

"I am enough of an artist to draw freely upon my imagination. Imagination is more important than knowledge. Knowledge is limited."

In the practitioners' literature, risk management is often described as both art and science. Parker [2005], for example, defines the art bit as follows:

"The art of risk management is the experience and skill, creating an edge, which the practitioner develops over time."[3]

This definition summarizes more or less two thirds of this book as it touches on three elements that we will be trying to bring home in various different ways: experience, skill, and an alertness (as opposed to ignorance) for change. It is especially in this latter bit, that is, alertness to change in market circumstances, that some of our writing peers—from our point of view—display ignorance, or putting it more mildly, underweight the hindsight bias of all empirical undertakings. In our view, far too much research in the field of finance is based on historical data. We appreciate the importance of testing hypotheses. However, in the social sciences, the aim for absolute precision can turn the undertaking into pseudoscience. Historical returns show only what did happen, not what could have happened or could happen going forward. Applying complex mathematical tools and techniques to the (often very imprecise) financial data can be misleading at best, fatally inappropriate, and damaging at worst.[†] We would go so far as to argue that an investor who stops learning, adapting, and improving in a dynamic marketplace is as good as toast: Only luck is keeping him solvent.[‡]

---

*A risk manager with deep theoretical knowledge but lacking street-smartness is essentially akin to someone who knows the Kama Sutra by heart but cannot find a mate.

†Quoting Albert Einstein again: "Since the mathematicians have invaded the theory of relativity, I do not understand it myself anymore."

‡Alternative definition of an *equity bull market*: "A random market movement causing the average investor to mistake himself for a financial genius."

It's the boiling frog syndrome: the gradual warming of the comfortable water that finishes off the unsuspecting creature.

Some investment professionals who select and monitor hedge funds for a living go as far as arguing that giving money to a theoretical economist (presumably this is an economist or strategist who never managed money) is futile, as he lacks the tricks of the trade; that is, he is "street-unwise." The theoretical understanding might be there, but the practical "market savvy" is missing. In selecting a macro or currency manager, one looks for both an excellent understanding of the big picture, that is, how the economy works as well as trading experience (i.e., an understanding of flow of funds), and the humble acknowledgment that market forces can sometimes be stronger than one's ideas and convictions. (Here the obligatory Keynes quote: "Financial markets can remain irrational far longer than you can remain solvent.")

Risk versus Knightian Uncertainty

According to Knight [1921], there is a difference between "risk" and "uncertainty." Risk describes situations in which an explicit probability distribution of outcomes can be calculated, perhaps on the basis of actuarial data. In contrast, uncertainty describes situations in which probabilities are unknown, and more importantly, where they are impossible to calculate with any confidence due to the uniqueness or specificity of the situation. Ellsberg [1961], for example, demonstrated that most people prefer betting on a lottery wherein the probabilities are known to betting on lotteries with unknown probabilities, that is, displaying an aversion against "Knightian uncertainty." Knight argued that profits should be defined as the reward for bearing uncertainty. Note that Knightian uncertainty is incompatible with the traditional expected utility framework of Von Neumann and Morgenstern [1947] and Savage [1954]. The expected utility theory is based on the notion that outcomes are unknown but their probabilities are known. Knight (as well as John Maynard Keynes [1921]) argues that not only are the outcomes uncertain, the probabilities are unknown, too.

We believe that a lot that has been written in the field of risk management in general, and absolute-return investing in particular is focused on risk measurement. The typical method used is factor or style analysis. This approach aims to construct a model based on historical returns and come up with some risk factors that explain some of the observed variation in this time-series data. More often than not, assumptions have to be made as to how returns are distributed, that is, how the world *should* look, not how it does. While such an analysis sometimes yields interesting results, it only covers a small part of the complexities of risk management. Why?

As put in Ineichen [2003c], one of the (many) definitions of risk is*:

$$\text{Risk} = \text{exposure to change}$$

This definition is very simple and somewhat unscientific, but nonetheless we believe it is a very powerful one. In a recent article called "Defining Risk" in the *Financial Analysts Journal*, Holton [2004] comes up with a very similar definition:

> *"It seems that risk entails two essential components: exposure and uncertainty. Risk, then, is exposure to a proposition of which one is uncertain."*

Risk measurement deals with the objective part. The risk measurer either calculates risk factors, simulates scenarios, or stress tests portfolios based on knowledge available today according to an objective (and, preferably, statistically robust) set of rules. However, any assessment of risk is based on knowledge that is available today.

Risk, however, has to do with what we do not know today. More precisely, risk is exposure to unexpected change that could result in failure to achieve one's desired outcome (e.g., meeting future liabilities). By definition, we cannot measure what we do not know. We are free to assume any probability distribution, but that does not imply an objective assessment of risk. In other words, risk management is complex, primarily qualitative and interpretative in nature. Risk measurement, however, is more quantitative and rule based, and has a rear mirror view by definition. As Peter Bernstein [1996] put it in the last chapter of *Against the Gods: The Remarkable Story of Risk*:

> *"Nothing is more soothing or more persuasive than the computer screen, with its imposing arrays of numbers, glowing colors, and elegantly structured graphs. As we stare at the passing show, we become so absorbed that we tend to forget that the computer only answers questions; it does not ask them. Whenever we ignore that truth, the computer supports us in our conceptual errors. Those*

---

*There is more than one definition of risk. Rahl [2003], for example, defines risk as "the chance of an unwanted outcome." This definition also implies that the two sides of a return distribution (or, more importantly, the investors' asymmetric utility thereof) are different and that the risk management process should be structured accordingly. Warren Buffett on risk: "Risk comes from not knowing what you're doing." Your author sympathizes with these two definitions, for both private and institutional investors (and their agents!).

who live only by the numbers may find that the computer has simply replaced the oracles to whom people resorted in ancient times for guidance in risk management and decision-making."[4]

Prevention versus Cure

Jaeger [2005] makes a very valid distinction when discussing issues related to risk and risk management: the distinction between prevention and cure. The former is cheaper than the latter. In other words, in the field of risk management, *"staying out of trouble* is much more desirable than *getting out of trouble."*[5] As Jaeger puts it:

> *"The keys to avoiding a crisis are diversification, prudent levels of leverage and liquidity, and a continuing respect for one's own fallibility. The keys to managing a crisis are more limited and less satisfactory: either do nothing, or reduce positions sharply."*

The two tasks are entirely different. Preventing disaster is forward-looking and creative, while responding to a disaster is reactive and analytical. We believe both are important tasks in the tool kit of the active risk manager. While preventing disaster is laudable, accidents—or worse, disasters—happen. When the accident or disaster is exogenous, the active risk manager will naturally find himself in the position of "getting out of trouble" mode. Exogenous shocks happen also to prudent and foresighted managers (while endogenous accidents and disasters do not—or to a lesser extent.) Given that exogenous shocks happen, we believe there are two remarks to be made in this respect: (1) experience matters and (2) a shock can be a great opportunity for the well-funded manager.

Experience Matters   We argue that experience matters for fairly obvious reasons. Arbitrageurs who lived through and survived autumn 1998 have more experience than those who have not. As poet Heinrich Heine put it: "Experience is a good school. But the fees are high." We address the costs of "experience" in the next chapter.

We believe in the concept of "learning by doing." Someone who has dug himself out of a hole once in the past might have an edge next time around, certainly relative to someone who has thought this could never happen to him, that is, never imagined finding himself in a hole. We subscribe to Louis Pasteur's view: "Chance favors only the prepared mind." However, there is the argument to the contrary. As David Dreman, chairman of Dreman Value Advisors, puts it:

"There is an impressive and growing body of evidence demonstrating that investors and speculators don't necessarily learn from experience. Emotion overrides logic time after time."[6]

We believe there is certainly a lot of truth in this statement. Nevertheless, we rate experience highly. Of course, there are investors who learn and those who do not. This would just indicate that those who learn have an edge over those who make the same mistakes over and over again. If this is true, we then could argue that experience is not nonexistent in the financial world, just scarce. This could serve as an explanation why some investors can charge 2 + 20 (2 percent management fee plus 20 percent performance fees) and why others cannot (although a cynic might turn the notion around and argue that some investors can charge 2 + 20 because those who pay 2 + 20 have no experience).

What we believe is scarce is risk management experience where risk is defined in absolute-return terms, and not relative to a benchmark. The complexities of derivatives (of which the pricing is both science and art, the trading a craft, and the accounting a mystery), short selling, and leverage (both a craft) require a skill set that is materially different from managing money relative to a benchmark. Experience in disaster management is even scarcer than risk management skill (mainly—and fortunately—because there have not been that many disasters). The supply of "disaster experience" is limited because both survivors and nonsurvivors often exit the market (albeit for different reasons). We would not be too cynical to believe there is a cyclical element in the demand curve for managing risk under market stress. It's just interesting to note that some investors demand it predisaster and others postdisaster.* In other words, experience matters. Note that experience is not taught at business school. As Mark Twain put it: "Don't let schooling interfere with your education."

Ashley [2003] has an intuitive way of classifying different kinds of information that we can use as proxy for skill and experience and also for its pricing:

- **Data:** Facts that can be used for reasoning, discussion, or calculation.

---

*As mentioned in Chapter 1, it was the 2000–2002 equity bear market that put absolute-return investing on the agenda of institutional investors. Less known is that the 1987 crash actually resulted in a similar conversion of perception, albeit on a smaller scale. Many (or some) investment professionals clearly steered away from a long-only investment style after the crash. Their argument was that a strategy that can wipe out 20 percent of one's money in one day is simply not an intelligent way of managing money.

- **Information:** Data with context, obtained from investigation, study, or instruction.
- **Knowledge:** Information with meaning and understanding.
- **Wisdom:** This term can be ridiculed, but let's say it is knowledge with insight.[7]

We would argue that the price is related to the preceding list: The further down we go on the list, the more value is *potentially* added and the higher the price—insight we normally get through experience. Note that we said *potentially*. In investment management, we do not know with certainty whether we are getting wisdom by paying a high price. A good track record could be a result of either knowledge and wisdom or luck. In Chapter 5 we therefore argue that alpha is an option from the perspective of the investor.

Experience in absolute-return space potentially is best visible in managing liquidity risk. Liquidity risk comes in two related forms: one associated with the excess cash available to meet margin calls, and the other with unwinding positions. The former is somewhat related to anticipation, that is, looking forward, while the latter is more reactionary, that is, backward looking. For example, in convertible arbitrage, the second quarter of 2005 was a period with investor redemptions and forced selling.* Managing liquidity risk is probably not a science, but a craft. Often, a "scientific" way to measure risk assumes frictionless markets, that is, a marketplace with free and abundant liquidity. However, in dislocating market conditions, the assumptions do not hold. A suitable analogy would be driving a car on an icy road during thick fog. While forecasting weather conditions might help avoid the risk, once unexpectedly on an icy patch of road, an experienced Ferrari test driver will probably manage risk more skillfully than a meteorologist.

Funding   The capital invested in a hedge fund should be stable. There are two distinct components of this capital: the "equity" the fund receives from its investors and the "debt" it receives from its prime broker. Measures that indicate the stability of capital are the redemption periods or the portion of the fund that belongs to the managers. Hedge funds are long-term investments. Hence, hedge funds have long redemption periods and, nowadays, in some cases, long lock-ups. There is good reason for this: If a fund's capital base is not secure, there is a chance that capital might be

---

*Note that there is little or no empirical evidence in the financial literature for our claim that experience matters. In convertible arbitrage in Q2 2005, one could argue, it was actually size (not the lack of experience) that caused losses due to redemptions and forced selling. Some of the larger (and more experienced) funds lost the most.

withdrawn at exactly that moment when it is most needed. Note that many of Long-Term Capital Management's (LTCM's) trades would have been profitable if it had been able to hold on to its assets for some months longer (and some broker/dealers—not to be mentioned here—had not traded against them).

Assuming sound funding, an exogenous shock can be a great investment opportunity instead of a disaster—as it turned out for LTCM. Typically, markets overreact (to good and) especially to bad news; that is, market prices overshoot on the downside. Citadel founder and CEO Ken Griffin makes the point well:

> *"If you're Avis, and the lights suddenly go off at Hertz, you had better be in a position to make a lot of money."*[8]

In other words, in exogenous shocks the wheat is separated from the chaff. While the majority panics and runs for the exit, some investors—the ones who have no need to worry about their funding—will be facing a great investment opportunity.

RISK MEASUREMENT VERSUS RISK MANAGEMENT

The fate of LTCM is often quoted as an example of the dangers of the reliance of any risk model output in dealing with uncertainty. Note, however, that LTCM probably employed both—the best scientists (academics) in the field of risk measurement, as well as the best craftsmen (traders) on Wall Street. The late Leon Levy [2002], cofounder the Oppenheimer Funds and Odyssey Partners, puts the limitation of pure science more boldly while discussing the failure of LTCM:

> *"What can be made of this chain of events [failure of LTCM]?*
>
> *First and foremost, never have more than one Nobel laureate economist as a partner in a hedge fund. LTCM had two. Having had one Nobel Prize winner as a limited partner over the years, I can say that had our firm followed his advice, we too might have lost a lot of money."*

Note that this quote is taken slightly out of context. There is more praise for LTCM in Levy's *The Mind of Wall Street* than there is criticism. For example, Levy argues that the "willingness to take personal risk stands in refreshing contrast to all too many Wall Street players." As did many before him, Levy isolates hubris as the main catalyst for LTCM's failure (and not the failure to measure "risk"). In other words, our interpretation of the lesson for investors is this: A successful risk measurer comes up with an "objective" correlation matrix or any other metric for "risk." A successful risk manager, however, knows that this metric is, at best, a biased view on future relationships and, at worst, a tool upon which slavish reliance can result in disaster.

The Musical Chairs Effect

In the years after the dot-com bubble burst, many investors experienced risk according to the aforementioned definition (risk = exposure to change), as market environment and return expectations had changed. As the decade progresses, it is becoming increasingly apparent that some of the beliefs and assumptions that were formed during the 20-year bull market are, potentially, false.

Risk management (as opposed to risk measurement) deals with changing one's portfolio according to an ever-changing environment or changing rules that happened to have worked fine in the past. The future is uncertain. The only thing we really know for sure is that the status quo is going to change. As economist Hyman Minsky put it: "Stability is unstable." Risk management, we believe, is the thought process that balances the investment opportunities with the probability of capital depreciation, or the risk of not meeting the objectives one has established. This means that it is, as mentioned, subjective by definition. It also means that someone with investment experience will most likely have a competitive advantage over someone who has none. To some extent, investing and managing risk is like musical chairs—if you're slow, chances are you are not going to win.

In risk measurement as well as in risk management, codependence of returns and risk is of crucial importance. Arguably, one of the greatest achievements of modern portfolio theory is that the combination of risky assets with positive expected returns and different volatility levels can reduce portfolio risk if the correlation between them is less than one. As a result, analysts and risk measurers calculate correlation factors. The correct (and objective) way to do this is by calculating the covariance between log returns of time series. The returns are either daily, weekly, or monthly, and the period of observation varies depending on data availability and personal preference (which goes to show that there is even subjectivity in risk measurement). However, measuring correlation matrixes is a different task than managing risk, irrespective of the degree of sophistication of the model or model input. Risk measurement is just one tool for the risk manager (albeit an important one).

In this example, the result of the analysis is a correlation matrix. The correlation matrix calculated using historical data is assumed to hold true for the future. However, given that we defined risk as exposure to change, true risk is manifested only when the real world deviates from the assumed (or modeled) world, or precisely when the correlation matrix proves worthless. This observation is neither new nor undocumented.[9]

Correlation can be misleading. For example, in a portfolio of insurance risk transfer products, one would assume that there is no correlation from insurance premiums underlying airline disasters and natural disasters. When a plane crashes due to malfunction, human error, or terrorist activity, it is normally not because of a natural disaster, so correlation can be assumed as low. However, the tails can be correlated. An earthquake in Japan could cause damage to planes on the ground, triggering an insurance liability depending on how the contracts are defined. When unpleasantness hits the proverbial fan, instruments and strategies can become correlated even though they might appear uncorrelated 99.9 percent of the time. As Lord Bauer, economic adviser to Margaret Thatcher, put it: "A safe investment is an investment whose dangers are not at that moment apparent."

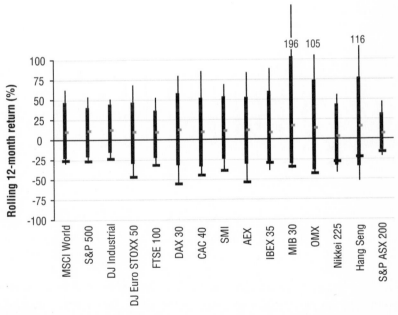

FIGURE 2.1 Rolling 12-Month Returns in Developed Equity Markets, 1983 to 2003

Vertical line measures 20-year trading range of 12-month returns. All returns are simple returns in local currencies. Observation period is 20 years to March 2003 except DJ Euro STOXX 50 (since 1987), CAC 40 (1988), SMI (1989), AEX (1984), IBEX 35 (1988), OMX (1987), and S&P ASX 200 (1993).

Example Recent stock market history is a good example for high and increasing correlation. Econometric models have not come close to picking up the 2000 to 2003 level of high correlation in equity markets. Gustave Le Bon [1982] popularized the term *contagion* in 1896. Le Bon observed that in a group, individuals who may by very different from one another in every respect are transformed into a unified body with a collective mind that causes its members to behave very differently than they would if each person were acting in isolation. The sentiment of the crowd as well as its acts, Le Bon argued, is highly contagious. History shows that correlation increases in market downturns: The greater the fall, the higher the correlation. The following graphs should illustrate this point.

Figure 2.1 shows rolling 12-month returns for some equity markets among a sample of so-called developed economies as of March 31, 2003,

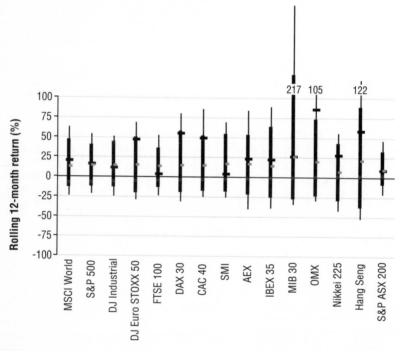

FIGURE 2.2 Rolling 12-Month Returns in Developed Equity Markets, 1980 to 2000
Vertical line measures 20-year trading range of 12-month returns. All returns are simple returns in local currencies. Observation period is 20 years to March 2003 except DJ Euro STOXX 50 (since 1987), CAC 40 (1988), SMI (1989), AEX (1984), IBEX 35 (1988), OMX (1987), and S&P ASX 200 (1993).
Source: Author's calculations, data from Thomson Financial.

in local currencies. The thin vertical line measures the trading range of 12-month returns over a 20-year period, whereas the bold vertical line shows the 90 percent range, that is, cutting off the most extreme 5 percent on each side of the distribution. The long horizontal tick measures the 12-month simple return (i.e., excluding reinvested dividends) as of March 31, 2003. The small tick measures the mean.

The graph shows that major markets were all under water by a significant amount as of March 2003. From the 15 indices shown, seven were at their 20-year low at the end of March 2003 based on this measure. The 12-month return of six additional indices was in the 5 percent tail on the left-hand side of the return distribution. Only two were above the five percent left tail (Nikkei 225 and Hang Seng). So global equity markets were extremely correlated.

Figure 2.2 shows how Figure 2.1 looked in March 2000 (showing rolling 12-month returns for the period from April 1980 to March 2000). The horizontal ticks in Figure 2.2 are scattered all over the place. Any econometric estimation of correlation most likely would have underestimated correlation, that is, overestimated diversification benefits.

TRACKING RISK VERSUS TOTAL RISK

Different investors can have different investment objectives that can result in different ways they define, perceive, and subsequently manage and control risk. In a relative-return context, risk is defined, perceived, and managed as tracking risk. In the absolute-return space, risk is defined, perceived, and managed as total risk.* Risk management of the former is driven by a benchmark (asset or liability benchmark), while risk management of the latter is by a profit and loss (P&L). Defining risk against an absolute yardstick (i.e., capital depreciation) is different from the relative-return approach, in the sense that the capital preservation function under the relative-return approach is not part of the mandate. In institutional investment management, the mandate to manage total risk was taken away from the manager in the 1970s (explicitly in the United States and United Kingdom), on the basis that it yielded unsatisfactory results and amplified the agency problem as briefly mentioned in Chapter 1.

Table 2.1 contrasts the two relative-return models, indexing and benchmarking, with the absolute-return model in investment management. For indexing we mean index funds, and for benchmarking we mean a long-only investment process tied to a benchmark.

---

*Note that relative-return managers also have a business motive to manage total risk, as a halving of assets under management roughly halves revenues (assuming profit margins stay constant).

TABLE 2.1   Tracking Risk versus Total Risk

	Relative-Return Models		Absolute-Return Model
	(Indexing)	(Benchmarking)	
Return objective	**Relative returns**		**Absolute returns**
General idea is to	*Replicate benchmark*	*Beat benchmark*	*Exploit investment opportunity*
Risk management	**Tracking risk**		**Total risk**
General idea is to	*Replicate benchmark*	*Beat benchmark*	*Preserve capital*

Source: Ineichen [2001].

Defining risk as tracking risk means that the risk-neutral position of the manager is the benchmark and risk is perceived as deviations from the benchmark. A benchmarked or indexed equity long-only manager moving, for example, into cash (yielding the risk-free rate) is increasing (tracking) risk as the probability of underperforming the benchmark increases. In other words, the probability of meeting the (return) objective declines—hence the perception of increased risk. In the absolute-return space, the risk-neutral position is cash. A move from a long equities position into cash means reducing total risk as the probability of capital depreciation decreases. Note that some call active long-only asset management (that we believe is passive risk management) *constrained active management.**

Put simply, under the absolute-return approach, there is an investment process for the upside (return-seeking by taking risk) and for the downside (some sort of contingency plan if something unexpectedly goes wrong or circumstances change). This could be a sudden exogenous market impact, excess valuations, heavily overbought market conditions, a concentration of capital at risk, a change in liquidity, marginal dollar being funny money, the sudden death of a marginal buyer, and so on. Absolute-return investing therefore means thinking not only about the entry into a risky position, but also about the exit.

This is an elementary contributing factor to seeking an asymmetric-return profile. If this is not the case, we are essentially dealing with a buy-and-hold strategy that is more or less the opposite of seeking asymmetric returns. With an absolute-return strategy seeking an asymmetric-return profile, we put our faith and money in the—ideally capable—hands of an

---

*This is a somewhat newer term that appeared on the firmament of—sometimes ridiculous—financial jargon. *Constrained active* sounds like being old enough to date but having to be home at dusk.

experienced active risk manager. With a buy-and-hold strategy we essentially put our faith and money in the hands of God. Note that the former of the two is much harder but potentially more profitable, or as Thomas Jefferson put it: "I find that the harder I work, the more luck I seem to have."

Under the relative-return model, the end investor is exposed to mood swings in the asset class in an uncontrolled fashion. Defining the return objective and risk management relative to an asset benchmark essentially means that the manager provides access (beta) to the asset class—that is, risk and return are nearly entirely explained by the underlying asset class. This means the investor is exposed (has access) to the asset class on the way up as well as on the way down. Investing in a long-only fashion is like driving uphill in a car with no brakes: As long as it's going up, you're fine. However, when it goes down you need some additional tools to control your risk. Transparency under the relative-return model is high, because a change in market circumstances does not materially affect the investment process and the asset allocation. Access to the benchmark is always close to 100 percent (hence the transparency).

Controlled versus Uncontrolled Risk

Myopic investors have difficulty differentiating between exposure to uncontrolled and controlled risk. It seems to us that a bear market or large financial losses have a sobering effect on investors, clearing their vision somewhat. Figure 2.3 compares what we believe is uncontrolled exposure to risk with controlled exposure to risk. We believe managing total risk means having a higher compounding rate of return with lower downside risk. It is therefore not a big surprise that hedge funds have been on some investors' agendas since the equity market fell in 2000 to 2002 (as discussed in Chapter 1). Under normal market conditions of positively trending returns, the difference between controlled and uncontrolled total risk is somewhat difficult to spot (for myopic investors just examining returns but not risk, that is).

We believe that a fund of hedge fund index can serve as a proxy for controlled total risk, as it measures the average portfolio of what we believe are actively managed portfolios. Active risk management takes place on two levels, capital market risks are managed on single-manager level while other idiosyncratic risk such as for example selection risk is managed on a fund of funds level.

Controlled Total Risk   Note here that we are not selling past returns. (In the financial world these days every PowerPoint presentation that includes a graph such as the one shown in Figure 2.3 requires a disclaimer somewhere on the page stating something along the lines that "past performance is no

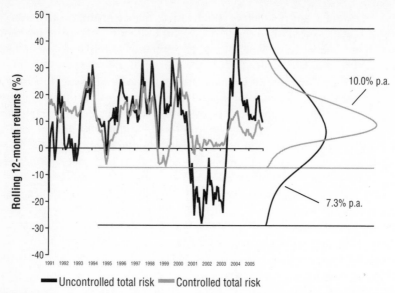

FIGURE 2.3 Controlled versus Uncontrolled Exposure to Risk
Controlled total risk: HFRI Fund of Funds Composite Index in U.S. dollars (USD) (in effect, a total return index); Uncontrolled total risk: MSCI World Total Return Index in USD; December 2005 inclusive. Distributions are conceptional.
Source: Author's own calculations; hedge fund data from Bloomberg, and stock index data Thomson Financial.

guarantee for future performance," essentially implying that private as well as institutional investors are about as fiducial and astute as baboons.) We are selling the concept of controlling downside risk in the real world.

Figure 2.3 shows that downside swings are smaller (and hence lower overall volatility as well as downside volatility) and the compound rate of return (as well as internal rate of return [IRR] and mean) is higher. The compound annual rate of return, volatility, and maximum 12-month drawdown for the HFRI Fund of Funds Composite Index from 1990 to 2005 were 10.0 percent, 5.5 percent and −6.6 percent. In Ineichen [2001]—formalized in this book—we called this risk/return profile to be the future of active investment management, as we believed (and still do) that all investors have positive utility from compounding capital and negative utility from absolute financial losses, especially large ones.

Uncontrolled Total Risk   To contrast controlled risk with uncontrolled risk we have chosen an equity index, which we use as a proxy for a long-only strategy. We view the terms *long-only, buy-and-hold,* and *benchmarking* as the opposite of what we believe is active risk management. Note here that we are not comparing like-for-like. The HFRI Fund of Funds Composite Index is net of fees (in fact, net of two layers of fees) while the MSCI World is gross of fees.

By *uncontrolled risk* we mean erratic swings on both sides (positive as well as negative) and a lower compound rate of return. (Note that with "both sides" we implicitly assume zero or the risk-free rate as point of reference, not the mean of the return distribution.) The compound annual rate of return, volatility, and maximum 12-month drawdown for the MSCI World Total Return Index (assuming reinvestment of dividends) were 7.3 percent, 14.4 percent, and −27.9 percent.

The Asymmetry   The highest returns from equities are higher than those from diversified hedge fund exposure, while the lowest returns are lower. However, the lowest returns are much lower, while the highest returns are only somewhat higher (hence lower compounding).

Figure 2.4 shows the distribution of quarterly returns from the two indices in Figure 2.3 (MSCI World Total Return Index and HFRI Fund of Funds Composite Index). There were a total of 64 quarterly returns spanning the 16-year observation period. The ratio between positive and negative in the case of what we believe is uncontrolled total risk was 45:19. The relationship with controlled risk was 55:9. In other words, controlled risk has not just smaller negative returns, but also fewer of them. In Chapters 6 and 7 we examine these two forms of asymmetries (smaller *and* fewer negative returns) in more detail.

After viewing Figure 2.4 and not knowing the underlying indices, which bars would most investors prefer? We would argue—judging by intuition alone—that most investors would opt for the dark bars. However, large parts of academia went to great length arguing that it is actually the dark bars that suffer from fat tails. We will spend some time on this fat-tail notion throughout this book (because it is important). As for now, the intuitive response to the dark bars suffering from fat tails (implicitly assuming that the gray bars do not) is: "You must be kidding." (That is actually the response by many absolute-return practitioners when confronted with some of the conclusions coming from the hedge fund–bashing fraternity of academia.)

Note here that we present the data somewhat differently than the "standard" way in finance. The standard way of looking at the abnormality of a return distribution is by looking at the third and four statistical moments of a distribution. The first two moments are the mean, that is, average return, and the standard deviation of returns, which, in its annualized form, is referred to as *volatility*. These two variables are enough

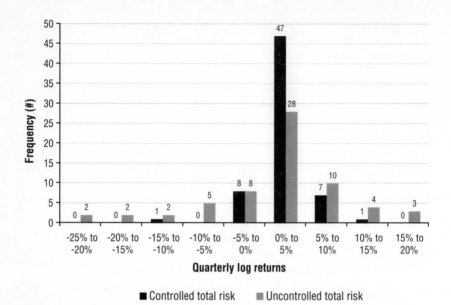

FIGURE 2.4 Distribution of Quarterly Returns (1990 to 2005)
Source: Author's own calculations; hedge fund data from Bloomberg, and stock index data Thomson Financial.

to explain a normal distribution. However, since the normal distribution in finance is an extremely unrealistic approximation of reality (since October 1987 it is difficult to argue otherwise) variables that show a departure from normality are also added. The third moment of a return distribution is the skew or skewness. A positive number will tell us whether it is somewhat more likely to have a return above the mean relative to a return below the mean. The simple options example in Chapter 1 would have a positive skew because more than 50 percent of returns would be widely scattered on the right-hand side of the mean.

The fourth statistical moment is the kurtosis or excess kurtosis. A normal distribution has a kurtosis of three. (We prefer the term *excess kurtosis* because it is clearer. Often, authors use the word *kurtosis* and mean excess kurtosis. So when we see a figure of 2 called *kurtosis,* it is not always clear whether the author means kurtosis of 2, which is an excess kurtosis of -1, or the author means excess kurtosis of 2, which is a kurtosis of 5). This fourth moment of the return distribution is also designed to show a departure from a normal distribution. A positive excess kurtosis means that there are more returns closer to the mean than suggested by a normal distribution and more returns in the wings of the distribution.

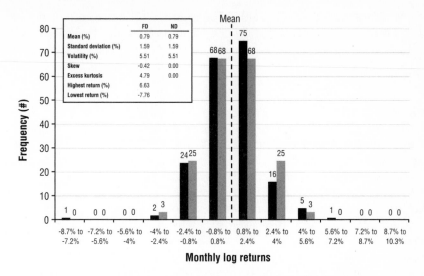

	FD	ND
Mean (%)	0.79	0.79
Standard deviation (%)	1.59	1.59
Volatility (%)	5.51	5.51
Skew	-0.42	0.00
Excess kurtosis	4.79	0.00
Highest return (%)	6.63	
Lowest return (%)	-7.76	

■ Frequency distribution (FD)　■ Normal distribution (ND)

FIGURE 2.5　Distribution of HFRI Fund of Funds Composite Index (1990 to 2005)

The x-axis has been designed for the mean of 0.8 percent to visualize the symmetry of the normal distribution, that is, labels of the x-axis have been rounded for display purposes. Size of return buckets of x-axis are 1.6 percent, that is, one standard deviation. Figures above bars of ND have been rounded. Frequency distribution is based on log returns, as log returns are supposed to be normally distributed, while simple returns are log-normally distributed.

Source: Author's own calculations; data from Bloomberg.

Figure 2.5 shows a real-world example of the difference between a frequency distribution and a normal distribution. The return buckets of the x-axis have been designed for the normal distribution to display its main characteristic: symmetry. A normal distribution is, to some extent, a proxy for a model world, whereas a frequency distribution is essentially what happened in the past in the real world. The exhibit visualizes what we refer to as an *asymmetric-return profile* (the achievement of which we argue in this book is difficult and active and is potentially the future of active asset management).

The frequency distribution (dark bars in Figure 2.5) is based on 192 monthly USD total log returns from January 1990 to December 2005. The compound annual rate of return (CARR) of the HFRI Fund of Funds Composite Index (not shown in graph) was 10.0 percent over the 16-year period. The normal distribution serves as a comparison and was calculated using the mean monthly return from the index of 0.8 percent and the standard deviation of monthly log returns of 1.6 percent. (A normal distribution is fully explained by the mean and standard deviation. The normal distribution is both simple and elegant.* This is probably the main reason why financial scholars are hooked on it. It's too bad that it really does not explain much of what is going on in the real world.)

The skew statistic of the frequency distribution is slightly negative, which is actually quite funny[†] for two reasons. First, it is funny (or at least strange) that skew is negative because there are 75 observations in the 0.8 to 2.4 percent bucket, that is, the first bucket immediately to the right of the mean, while a normal distribution suggests only 68. Second, it is funny because your author has a regular laugh every time he reads an empirical study where the negative skew feature (and positive excess kurtosis) is overemphasized and compared to picking up nickels in front of a steamroller. In other words, statistics tells us that—when compared to the model world of the normal distribution—the frequency distribution is negatively skewed. However, when compared to a long-only strategy, that is, comparing real world with real world (as in Figure 2.4), the situation is different. In addition, there is anecdotal evidence: Investors with *diversified* equity long-only portfolios lost between 50 percent and 90 percent during the last bear market. Investors with *diversified* hedge fund portfolios actually had positive returns (albeit tiny ones) in that period. And *hedge fund investors* are exposed to fat tails? Hilarious.

In the laboratory environment of the financial scientist, however, things can look quite scary. We pick this up by looking at the extremes, that is, those returns not within the four middle buckets in Figure 2.5, that is, outside of the two-standard-deviations range. In the frequency distribution there are nine observations outside the middle four buckets. This is only two more than a normal distribution suggests, which suggests around seven observations (frequency numbers on top of bars in Figure 2.5 have been rounded). The normal distribution places these outliers symmetrically to the right and left of the middle (otherwise, it would not be a normal distribution)—in this case, 3.4 returns on each side of the middle four buckets, each 0.2 in the next bucket, and so on. The frequency distribution shows extreme asymmetry: Of the nine outliers, only three are on the left-hand side, that is, the negative side, while the other six are on the right-hand side.

The worst monthly (log) return of the HFRI Fund of Funds Composite Index was −7.8 percent in August 1998 (followed by −2.6 in September

---

*Someone once even mentioned that the normal distribution has something erotic to it. Some people really should go out more often.

[†]People who find humor in return distributions probably should go out more often, too.

and −2.0 in October, implying autocorrelation). What happens to the fourth moment of the distribution if we replace the −7.8 percent return in 1998 with 0.0? The mean changes from 0.79 to 0.84 percent, and volatility decreases from 5.51 percent to 5.08 percent. What happens to skew? Skew changes from −0.42 to +0.43. In other words, one single observation in 16 years causes skew to be negative. Generalizing that hedge fund strategies have negative skewness or that hedge funds are systematically selling disaster insurance based on one data point is highly misleading. Only a fundamental understanding of the strategies and risk exposures, including their optionalities, gives us a hint whether a strategy or portfolio is risky, that is, whether our decision making today is intelligent or not. Accidents happen. We do not know the timing or magnitude by examining historical time series.

What happens to excess kurtosis? Excess kurtosis of the HFRI Fund of Funds Composite Index was 4.79, which is a fairly large departure from the normal distribution. The excess kurtosis does not necessarily come from more returns in the middle (although this depends somewhat on how the buckets are chosen) but from more observations in the wings, that is, so-called fat tails. If we take out the August 1998 return, the excess kurtosis shrinks to 1.49. In the appendix to Chapter 4, we discuss some of these more technical issues in greater detail.

One paper by Brulhart and Klein [2005] on higher moments actually stands in refreshing contrast to most articles on the subject. As a collaboration between a practitioner and an academic, the paper won the 2005 AIMA Canada Research Award. In this paper, the authors argue that—strictly statistically speaking—skew and excess kurtosis are actually not synonymous with third and fourth moments of the return distribution, despite everyone's treating them as such. Referencing statistical papers, the authors argue that the skew and kurtosis measures are "normalized" by the standard deviation. So their findings show that skew and kurtosis are more inflated with absolute-return strategies because volatility is lower, whereas third and fourth moments that are not normalized by the volatility are much lower when compared to long-only strategies. We made this point in Ineichen [2004b] and stress this (somewhat) excessively in this book: When comparing systematic risk with systematic risk, it is a long-only strategy that exposes the investor to tail-heavy-event-type risk, not an absolute-return strategy in which managing total risk is a major objective. This is why the analysis of drawdowns shows a different picture than the examination of excess kurtosis and skew. The drawdown measure is not normalized by the volatility but shows the absolute (historical) loss either relative to time (e.g., 12 months) or previous level of wealth (e.g., peak to trough).

The next graph, Figure 2.6, shows why we first had to write a book called *Absolute Returns* before we could elaborate on the implementation,

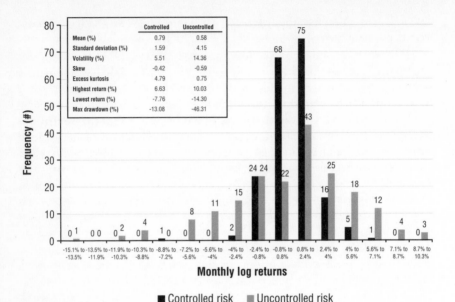

	Controlled	Uncontrolled
Mean (%)	0.79	0.58
Standard deviation (%)	1.59	4.15
Volatility (%)	5.51	14.36
Skew	-0.42	-0.59
Excess kurtosis	4.79	0.75
Highest return (%)	6.63	10.03
Lowest return (%)	-7.76	-14.30
Max drawdown (%)	-13.08	-46.31

FIGURE 2.6 Frequency Distribution of Controlled and Uncontrolled Risk
The x-axis has been designed for the mean of 0.8 percent to be analogous to
Figure 2.5. All based on log returns. Controlled risk: HFRI Fund of Funds Composite
Index. Uncontrolled risk: MSCI World Total Return Index.
Source: Author's own calculations; hedge fund data from Bloomberg, and stock
index data Thomson Financial.

that is, asymmetric returns. The graph shows the same data as Figure 2.3
(controlled versus uncontrolled risk) but based on monthly returns and
with the mean of the controlled risk portfolio being the center of the
distribution. So Figure 2.6 compares the frequency distribution of the HFRI
Fund of Funds Composite Index (which we labeled as *controlled risk*) and
the frequency distribution of the MSCI World Total Return Index in USD
from 1990 to 2005 as a proxy for a long-only strategy, that is, uncontrolled
risk. We have chosen the same mean and return bucket size as in Figure 2.5
for comparability purposes.

We have discussed the first two moments before, that is, fund of funds
outperformed equities with a fraction of the volatility. Let's focus on the
higher moments and search for asymmetries. First, compare the best and
worst one-month returns of the two portfolios. The best monthly total return
in equities is 340 basis points higher than the best return of a diversified
hedge fund portfolio (remember that we are comparing two time series, one
of which is net of fees, while the other, the MSCI World, is gross of fees).

However, the worst monthly return in equities is lower by 653 basis points. That is the first asymmetry.

The most obvious observation from the Figure 2.6 is the difference in magnitude of the negative returns—the second asymmetry. To include equities we needed to expand the axis from the previous graph by four buckets on the left-hand side. The worst monthly total return (i.e., including dividends) of the MSCI World was 14.3 percent. (Note that this return was also in August 1998 implying occasional high correlation of hedge fund portfolios to capital markets in global stress scenarios.) Here again, there is a difference between eye and statistics. The calculated excess kurtosis of the long-only strategy is smaller than with the fund of funds index, that is, only 0.75 versus 4.79. By looking at these two numbers, it seems it is fund of funds that are selling disaster put options, that is, the likelihood of losing one's shirt seems large. Eye and statistics differ in the case of comparing a risk-controlled with a risk-uncontrolled portfolio because we are comparing a portfolio with a volatility of less than six with a portfolio with volatility nearly three times higher. In the case of the HFRI Fund of Funds Composite Index, the worst return of −7.8 percent is a staggering 5.4 standard deviations away from the mean of 0.8 percent. A −7.8 percent return does not register if risk is uncontrolled, that is, volatility is high. A −7.8 percent return in the case of the MSCI World would only equate to a 2.0 standard deviation move from the mean of 0.6 percent, as one standard deviation is 4.1 percent. And since a two-standard-deviations move is fairly "normal" (around 95 percent of occurrences are within plus or minus two standard deviations, assuming returns are normally distributed), it does not register as excess kurtosis, that is, fat tails. That's why we argue that not being scared of the potential losses of a long-only strategy because it has no fat tails (as measured by the excess kurtosis statistic) is about as intelligent as a frog not fearing a frog-eating snake because it has no horns. A two-standard-deviation negative return of the HFRI Fund of Funds Composite Index is only a −2.4 percent loss. One important message of this book and previous work is that losses hurt investors more than does excess kurtosis. The worst loss of the risk-uncontrolled sample of −14.3 percent translates into "only" 3.6 standard deviations from the mean of 0.6 percent. (If we were able to analyze weekly or daily returns, we would find that the numbers would change but the logic would not.) So our line of argument is that a −14.3 percent loss hurts more than a −7.8 percent loss irrespective of the former being only 3.6 and the latter 5.4 standard deviations from the mean. It hurts even more if you have many large losses. So let's look at frequency (as opposed to magnitude) of losses.

As mentioned earlier, the HFRI Fund of Funds Composite Index (controlled risk) has nine observations beyond the four buckets in the middle, three negative outliers, and six positive outliers. How does this compare to what we call uncontrolled risk? The MSCI World had 78 of its returns outside these four buckets, 41 on the downside and 37 on the upside, and therefore also displayed a slight asymmetry but of the wrong kind to the loss-averse investor. This, we believe, is a big difference. The message here is that it is not only *magnitude* that kills the rate at which capital compounds—*frequency* matters, too. We are more specific on these asymmetries in Chapter 6.

One could argue that the previous analysis is unfair because we compared a portfolio with a volatility of 5.5 percent with one with volatility nearly three times higher. In Figure 2.7, we have delivered the long-only portfolio in the previous example to have the same volatility as the HFRI Fund of Funds Composite Index. In other words, we combined the MSCI World with cash to get a portfolio with 5.5 percent volatility. Figure 2.7 shows the distribution.

In Figure 2.7, we have left the label *uncontrolled risk* unchanged, as we believe reducing volatility symmetrically—which is what the introduction of cash does—is not an active task. We believe this new comparison is the

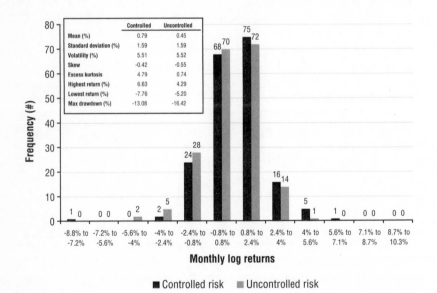

FIGURE 2.7 Frequency Distribution of Two Portfolios with the Same Volatility
The x-axis has been designed for the mean to be 0.8 percent. Return buckets are 1.6 percent. All based on log returns. Uncontrolled risk: 38 percent MSCI World and 62 percent USD one-month London Interbank Offered Rate (LIBOR), monthly rebalanced.
Source: Author's own calculations; data from Bloomberg and Thomson Financial.

most fair. It allows us to see the alpha. The alpha is essentially having higher black bars on the right side of the distribution and lower and fewer black bars on the left-hand side. It is this asymmetry that is the value added from active risk management and that allows the investor to compound capital with fewer accidents. In Chapter 5, we argue that alpha is an option on this asymmetric payout (and the sustainability thereof), as the investor, looking forward, does not know with certainty whether he is going to get it or not.

The portfolio labeled *uncontrolled risk* in Figure 2.7 (38 percent MSCI World and 62 percent one-month cash) had a CARR of 5.6 percent. This compares to 10.0 percent of the sample labeled *controlled risk,* despite a 5.4 standard deviation outlier on the left-hand side of the distribution. The cumulative of all returns below zero was 52.6 percentage points in the case of controlled risk and 84.5 percentage points in the case of uncontrolled risk. Note that compounding at a (nominal) rate of 5.6 percent over 16 years takes the investor from 100 to 239. Compounding at 10.0 percent instead results in an end value of 459. This is a big difference. So these subtle differences in the way the returns are distributed have a big impact to long-term wealth creation and preservation. The myopic investor can easily underestimate these differences.

Note that there are still some investment professionals and scholars who claim the idea behind absolute returns in professional asset management is a fluke. In a recent article titled "The Myth of the Absolute-Return Investor," Waring and Siegel [2006] reiterate the case for relative returns. Their argument is more or less the mirror image of Ineichen [2003a] and this book, and it is inconsistent with the findings of a broad survey displayed in Figure 1.2. One of their claims we challenge is the notion that hedge funds are also relative-return investors (and therefore there is no such thing as "absolute returns"). The claim is based on what the authors call the "normal portfolio" or "home," a risky portfolio on which the hedge fund adviser supposedly falls back to when the managers do not know what to do with their capital. Waring and Siegel wrote:

> *"For a purported absolute-return manager, the normal portfolio may not have been purposefully or thoughtfully designed—and may be more implicit than explicit—but somewhere in the manager's investment style lies a "home," a set of factor exposures or betas that the manager goes to when he or she has no reason to go somewhere else."*[10]

The authors even claim that Warren Buffett is a relative-return investor and has a benchmark. This clearly is inconsistent with Mr. Buffett's own words quoted in Chapter 1 ("Charlie and I detest taking even small risks unless we feel we are being adequately compensated for doing so"). The default position of the absolute-return investor is cash or Treasuries. If this is not the case, the term *absolute returns* does not apply, as the investment decision-making and risk management process will be geared to managing tracking risk, that is, deviations from the "normal portfolio" or "home" or benchmark. If you do not know what to do as an absolute-return investor, you do not fall back to some arbitrary set of risks. Why would you want to do that? If the view of the opportunity set goes to zero, the risk of the portfolio goes to the position where the probability of losing money is closest to zero. (Temporarily hedging all market-type risk would have the same effect.) In some instances, the capital is even returned to investors due to the manager's assessment of the opportunity set (or the manager's wish to improve his golf handicap or a combination of the two).

One recent example of this behavior is distressed securities—a strategy that is cyclical. This means the opportunity set changes in a business-cycle, semipredictable* and mean-reverting fashion. Default rates in the United States fell from 12.8 percent in 2002 to 1.2 percent in 2004. What did managers do in 2004 when the game was over? What they certainly did not do is what Waring and Siegel [2006] claim, that is, fall back to a "normal portfolio."† Some distressed funds closed and gave money back to their investors, thanked them for lending them their trust during the ride, and said that they will be calling them when the next cycle begins.

---

*If default rates are at 1.2 percent, the probability that the default rate will be higher or lower in five years' time is not equivalent to flipping the proverbial fair coin. The probability that default rates will be higher than 1.2 percent is higher than the probability of their being lower. (Equivalently, distressed debt trading at 16 cents to the dollar is not the same as distressed trading at 86 cents to the dollar.) An increase is more likely than a decrease. Come to think of it, this is actually—unlike some others—quite an important footnote: If everything were random, there would be no such thing as "asymmetric returns." The asymmetry would be a function of randomness. However, for generating asymmetric returns, there needs to be some form of predictability where insight, skill, and experience of the manager allows variation of the capital at risk (as opposed to moving back to an arbitrary "home," i.e., benchmarking). This arguably judgmental active risk management activity is the cause whereby the asymmetric risk/return profile is—when successful—the effect.

†To be fair to the authors, they do mention (p. 18) that "sometimes, hedge funds are characterized as having a benchmark of cash." However, they view it as the exception. (A technology sector long/short fund probably will always have a net exposure to the underlying sector.) We believe it is the rule, not the exception. Whatever the debate, we do not think that the terminology and doctrines of benchmarking and relative returns lends itself very well to what is going on in hedge fund space. In Chapter 1, we used a Thomas Kuhn term that describes the two worlds (relative and absolute returns) as *incommensurable*.

Others, more the multistrategy type of investors, reduced capital at risk in the strategy where the opportunity set was limited and increased it in a strategy where they thought the opportunity set was plentiful or, if nothing attractive was found, into cash. (The peak of the distressed cycle is somewhat the reverse of merger mania, that is, the opportunity sets of the two strategies are somewhat reciprocal. At the most distant level, this reverse synchronicity is a function of greed and fear of investors and corporates alike.)

Waring and Siegel end their paper:

"Beating a benchmark is all that matters; it is the only thing that is worth paying high fees to achieve."[11]

We believe this view was the consensus from the mid-1970s to the peak of the bull market in early 2000. Today, there are more and more investors who believe that it is *not* worth paying high fees for a 28 percent loss when the benchmark is down by 30 percent, especially not if the 200-basis-points difference is perceived as random. For compounding capital negatively, no external help is required. Most investors can do it on their own. We believe risk perception has changed for good. Survival probability; loss aversion; limited practicability of time diversification; and option-like, that is, asymmetric risk/return trade-offs in absolute-return space, have entered the equation of investment management.

The discussion of tracking risk versus total risk leads to a discussion of what a risk management process should protect, that is, preserve from adverse impact. Should a risk management process protect the investor or his money?

INVESTOR PROTECTION VERSUS CAPITAL PROTECTION

Based on investor protection (regulation, transparency of investment portfolio, and market benchmark) as well as wealth protection (through risk management techniques utilizing the use of derivatives, leverage, and/or short selling), the absolute-return approach could be viewed as the pure opposite of the relative-return approach. Today, we, the financial community, know that investor protection is not the same as protecting principal. Investors exposed to Germany's NASDAQ look-alike, the "Neuer Markt," lost between 80 percent and 100 percent despite being diversified and despite the market's being regulated. Regulation, transparency, and a market benchmark protects the investor, but not necessarily his money. As a manager from a large North American pension fund put it:

TABLE 2.2   Investor versus Wealth Protection

		Relative return mandate	Absolute return mandate
Investor protection	Regulation	High	Low
	Transparency	High	Low
	Benchmark	Yes	No
Wealth protection	Derivatives	No	Yes
	Leverage	No	Yes
	Short selling	No	Yes

Arrows not in original.
Source: Updated from Ineichen [2003c].

"Regulation in North America is not a big deal: unwittingly, it is promoting a false sense of security. On either side of the Atlantic, the biggest blow ups have occurred under the very nose of regulators."[12]

In the relative-return approach, the investor's principal is not entrusted to a fiduciary who tries to preserve it in difficult times but whose mandate implicitly or explicitly dictates that the principal is exposed to the full extent of market volatility—the volatility of the market benchmark. This exposure has been considered acceptable up until recently because the wealth protection function was held by the end investor and because of some strong-held beliefs with respect to return expectations, time diversification, and investment processes during the long bull market.

Table 2.2 shows a matrix comparing an investor protection function as well as a wealth or capital protection function for the relative-return as well as the absolute-return approach.

Table 2.2 is a static description of the status quo a couple of years ago when we first published this table. Since then, there has been change. We believe that the relative-return and absolute-return worlds are merging, essentially our hypothesis in Ineichen [2001, 2003a]. (Note that the hedge fund universe is also increasingly overlapping with private equity.) As shown through the arrows, we believe that hedge funds are somewhat becoming like traditional managers, while traditional managers are somewhat becoming like hedge funds. We see the trends as follows.

Investor Protection

Regulation   Hedge funds are certainly on the agenda of most regulatory bodies around the world. We believe it is fair to claim that the gap between traditional asset management and hedge funds with respect to regulation is in the process of closing and will continue to do so in the coming years. (One interesting remark made on the record from one of the five Securities and Exchange Commission [SEC] members after the SEC's 2002–2003 probe into hedge funds was that, potentially, one need is to deregulate mutual funds, rather than regulate hedge funds.)

SEC commissioner Cynthia A. Glassman on SEC registration in the United States starting February 1, 2006:

> *"Another initiative I want to discuss briefly is the hedge fund adviser registration rule that went into effect earlier this month. As I said last year, in my view, the Commission adopted this rule to combat perceived evils, i.e. retailization and growing fraud, which I do not believe had been demonstrated even after an extensive staff review was completed in 2003. In my view, the registration requirement for hedge fund advisers we adopted (and that I voted against) was not well thought out. Had we approached the hedge fund issue more analytically at the outset—deciding what information we really needed and how best to get it—I believe we would be in a much better position today to provide effective monitoring and to see red flags. Further, we should have considered alternatives, such as raising the financial qualification criteria for eligible investors, especially if we were really concerned about retailization."*[13]

Note that (retail) investor protection was only one of the drivers behind the SEC's probe. Another was the concern that, while the SEC knew that hedge funds were growing in terms of both number and assets under management, there were no reliable data indicating just how many hedge funds there were and just how much money they had under management. As hedge funds are frequent traders of securities, this raises concerns of their market impact's being disproportionately large relative to their (growing) size. This was potentially a stronger driver (and somewhat more justified) than trying to protect retail investors.

The new hedge fund registration rule has created extra burdens for the SEC without protecting investors. The new rule has proven "costly and ineffective," commissioner Paul S. Atkins said at a gathering sponsored by Boston University's Morin Center for Banking and Financial Law. In the period before the rule went into effect, roughly 1,000 hedge fund advisers had filed paperwork to be reviewed by the agency, which will not do much to deter fraud, he said. Also, the new rule forces the SEC to police the holdings of perhaps 100,000 hedge fund investors, who tend to be wealthier, at the expense of its work overseeing the mutual funds held by 90 million people of more modest means on average, Atkins said. And it creates too many burdens on the funds themselves. While the new policies might seem appropriate, he said, "a closer look reveals them to be rooted rather tenuously in reality."[14]

Transparency   Generally speaking, hedge funds and hedge fund investments are becoming more transparent over time. A hedge fund might have an incentive to meet the higher transparency requirements of an institutional investor, as the capital could be considered "smart money," which is more stable, as opposed to "dumb money," which is more responsive to fads and return chasing (and ultimately to untimely withdrawals)—that is, less stable and hence of lower quality to the manager. (The increased use of lock-ups could be seen partly as a way to manage the occasional and proverbial "weak hand.")

Benchmark   Generally speaking, we believe the obsession with benchmarks among sponsoring bodies has cooled off somewhat. Many investors have noticed that their liabilities do not follow the Standard & Poor's (S&P) 500 or MSCI World index. (Someone once said—upon retirement—you cannot eat a relative sandwich.) Remarkably, however, in the more recent past, some hedge funds have been launching long-only funds with a benchmark. This, we believe, is an interesting development, supporting our central hypothesis that we should be thinking about product differentiation in asset management rather than hedge funds and non-hedge funds.

Wealth or Capital Protection

Derivatives, Leverage, and Short Selling   Regulation might "protect" the investor but not necessarily his money. We believe it is risk management that preserves capital from depreciation. Regulation did not protect investors' money from Enron, WorldCom, NASDAQ fallout, Germany's "Neuer Markt" literally evaporating, and so on.* It is risk management that protects investors' money, not regulation. To do risk management, one requires risk management tools and techniques. These happen to be the use of derivatives, flexibility to lever and delever exposure to market risk exposures, and the

---

Financial News (April 20, 2006) reported that the head of information technology at German financial services regulator, Bundesanstalt für Finanzdienstleistungsaufsicht, has reportedly confessed to taking roughly EUR2.6 million (USD3.2 million) in bribes. He faces being jailed for up to 10 years. These headlines are rare. Interesting but perhaps not overly surprising is that they appeared in hedge fund–averse and overregulated Germany, where a left-wing politician branded active shareholders (who in double-digit-jobless-rate Germany have a record of creating jobs) as *locusts*.

ability to sell short. We believe the use of risk management tools in active investment management is somewhat akin to the use of telescopes in the field of astronomy or the introduction of jet engines in the field of aviation. That is to say, the development is structural: There is no way back. In other words, the future of active asset management is about managers trying to achieve an asymmetric-return profile, which is possible only by being able to use the full spectrum of risk management instruments and products. Long-only investing is like playing golf with only a 7-iron.

Note that not every strategy requires the same level of sophisticated risk management tools. The more complex a strategy, the more developed the risk management tools need to be. A cash-based, long/short strategy requires less sophisticated tools than, for example, a relative-value mortgage-backed security strategy with significant prepayment risk, that is, complex optionality.

Change is never applauded by all at the same time. Rather, a minority introduces or innovates, and then it takes a while for contagion to kick in and a majority consensus to build. First, however, there is disagreement, or as Thomas Edison put it: "Discontent is the first necessity of progress." Even long-only investments in equities were considered as inappropriate for conservative investors a couple of decades ago. At a hedge fund conference in Cape Town, South Africa, in November 2005, a speaker opened his speech by explaining how his grandfather one day came home and explained to his grandmother that he bought stocks, that is, was now a shareholder. Grandmother apparently kicked him out of the house. She didn't want any association with a speculator. By replacing the word *stocks* with *hedge funds* or *derivatives* and the word *grandmother* with *actuaries,* we have a situation not unlike today.

One amazing observation we regularly make is the long and continuous aversion to derivatives among a large majority of investors and market observers. This is amazing because we believe that derivatives are just an instrument to complete a task efficiently. Being generally opposed to the use of derivatives in finance because its misuse has caused casualties is like opposing the use of morphine in medicine because of its misuse. Potentially, the ongoing criticism of derivatives by politicians and press (who might not know better) and famous investors (who should know better) is as helpful to progress in the field of finance as Cheech and Chong are helpful to progress in the field of medicine.

Derivatives are often considered complicated financial instruments. Often, derivatives experts are referred to as "rocket scientists," implying that if you have not been part of NASA's Apollo program, it is unlikely that you are going to understand derivatives anytime soon. However, the use of derivatives is fairly straightforward. In this respect, derivatives are similar to cars: An automobile is a highly complex piece of engineering. It is unlikely that you are able to dismantle a car, understand the mechanics and electronics, and then reassemble the machine. However, one needs only a couple of driving lessons in combination with common sense to unlock the benefits of the machine and control risk. Most drivers do not really understand what happens when they press the accelerator. The same is true for derivatives. Some derivatives can be highly complicated such that most financial professionals will not be able to dismantle and replicate the instrument. In addition to common sense, one needs some elementary understanding of the basic strategies (essentially long and short calls and puts) and how it changes portfolio risk parameters. An investor does not necessarily have to understand the *Archimedes exposure path* or *exponential generalized autoregressive conditional heteroskedasticity (EGARCH)* for derivatives to add value.

Asset Allocation and Manager Constraints   Typically, the end investor manages absolute levels of risk through asset allocation. If the end investor decides to have an allocation to long-only equities through a benchmarked manager, then obviously the manager needs be fully invested at all times. In the past, this was supported by the beliefs that market timing does not work consistently, that long-term investors (e.g., pension funds) need to be fully exposed to market volatility at all times to capture the equity risk premium, and that equities outperform bonds in the long term. One of the market benchmark's purposes, therefore, was to reduce uncertainty from a manager's deviating too strongly from the market benchmark that was part of the asset allocation process.

We believe that some of these long-held beliefs are currently being challenged. In our opinion, the most obvious erroneous belief is the paradox in constraining a skilled manager. If Grinold [1989] and Grinold and Kahn [2000] are right in arguing that the value added of an active manager is a function of his skill and the number of independent decisions the manager can make (breadth), that is, implying some sort of flexibility with respect to investment opportunities, then finding managers with investment skill and then constraining them cannot be efficient. It is unlikely that Warren Buffett or George Soros would have compounded at 25 to 30 percent for so long had they used the S&P 500 Index as their benchmark and a tracking error constraint of 200 basis points. Constraining a talented manager is like tying a golfer's legs together: He will still be able to play golf, but it won't necessarily improve his swing. (Hopping from one hole to the next with tied legs would not be efficient, either, and would also look somewhat foolish.)

The search for investment talent and the subsequent manager constraint for investor protection purposes is suboptimal at best and highly inefficient at worst. The adoption of an absolute-return approach by the active asset management industry is essentially the synthesis of the investor protection and wealth protection functions in Table 2.2. This means a skilled manager has the mandate to manage investment opportunity and balance the change in the opportunity set based on his individual assessment of total risk. The flexible and benchmark-free mandate is, we believe, superior to a constrained mandate if we assume that it is a manager with an edge close to the investment opportunity who is best suited to judge when the risk/reward trade-off changes its characteristics. A further argument for the risk management mandate moving from the end investor to an active risk manager is the observation that committee-based decision making is both slow and return-chasing in nature.

This paradigm shift is, obviously, going to happen only if the fee-paying end investor buys into it (that said, we actually believe the shift is already well under way.) The increase in flexibility comes with a price. Idiosyncratic risk is higher. In the following section we contrast systematic and nonsystematic risk. In Chapter 6 we examine systematic risk and in Chapter 7 nonsystematic risk in greater detail.

SYSTEMATIC VERSUS NONSYSTEMATIC RISK

Another way to contrast the relative-return approach with the absolute-return approach, with respect to transparency and risk, is to distinguish between systematic and nonsystematic risk. Table 2.3 classifies financial risks as systematic risk, that is, risk the investor can expect to get compensation from taking; and operational risk, which is purely idiosyncratic risk, that is, should be eliminated through diversification, as it carries no premium.

TABLE 2.3 Systematic versus Nonsystematic Risk

	Relative return industry	Absolute return industry
Systematic risk		
Marketrisk	Unmanaged	Managed
Nonsystematic risk		
Alpha	Variable	Variable
Default risk	Low	High
Key person risk	Low	High
Model risk	Low	High
Etc.	Low	High

Source: Ineichen [2003c].

The only common denominator between the traditional asset management industry and the hedge funds industry from Table 2.3 is with respect to alpha: Both industries promise alpha and, according to some fee-paying and cynical investors, both fail to deliver on a net basis. As we mentioned in the preface and will elaborate in Chapter 5, alpha is an option. The investor cannot be sure that he will be receiving net alpha. He can only surmise, that is, elaborate whether investment process and investment staff are fit to potentially deliver what they claim they are able to. We also could have inserted arrows showing trends in Table 2.3 as we did in Table 2.2—the two industries are converging.

Systematic Risk

Market risk is systematic risk as single-stock or single-constituent risk is diversified. A benchmarked relative-return manager will have a mandate that dictates that the market risk is fairly constant. If it is an active mandate—or *constrained active*, to use the modern term—the portfolio can have a small degree of variation in beta, for example, by tilting the portfolio to high-beta stocks relative to the equity market benchmark. However, the overall beta is constant when compared to absolute-return managers, as it is part of the mandate. The benefit to the end investor is that it allows for proper asset allocation as well as risk budgeting. Without this consistency in beta exposure, the transparency to the end investor is largely compromised or nonexistent.

A flexible mandate results in lower transparency. Given that the absolute-return manager focuses on total risk as opposed to tracking risk, other systematic risk factors are managed actively and therefore change dynamically. Managing risk is not the same as hedging the risk. Hedging risk is the opposite of taking risk, while managing risk is the opposite of ignoring it. This means it is the manager's call to be exposed to any sort of risk in an underlying asset class, any spread, or illiquid instrument. Transparency, therefore, is much lower to the end investor. The cry for transparency on the part of the institutional end investor is understandable. A fiduciary requires transparency. Transparency is required to fit these new instruments into a traditional framework of the existing investment process. However, potentially, the "traditional framework of the existing investment process" is in need of an overhaul. In addition, there are different levels of transparency. Transparency with respect to the investment process is a requirement for understanding risk. However, position-level transparency is costly and of little value to the end investor.

Many investment professionals who have been in the hedge fund business all or most of their professional career view a long-only buy-and-hold strategy as much more risky than, for example, a relative-value or event-driven strategy, that is, what today is referred to as an *alternative investment strategy*. For at least some of them, a typical pension fund is following a strategy that is of higher financial risk than the strategy they pursue. An amusing anecdote from our perspective is that both pension funds and alternative investment staff believe their strategy to be conservative.* A pension fund with a 75:25 mix between equities and bonds, for example, is fully exposed to the volatilities and correlations of these two markets. The total risk is unmanaged (in practice, although not in theory). It is no wonder, then, that a majority of fee-paying institutional investors preferred to hand mandates to managers who have an approach that does not have managing total risk as a primary objective. Financial conservatism is indeed in the eyes of the beholder.

In Warren Buffett's opinion, the term *institutional investor* is an oxymoron: Referring to money managers as investors is, he says, like calling a person who engages in one-night stands romantic. Buffett is not at par with modern portfolio theory. He does not run mean-variance-efficient portfolios. Critics argue that, because of the standard practices of diversification, money managers behave more conservatively than Buffett. According to Hagstrom [1994], Buffett does not subscribe to this point of view. He does admit that money managers invest their money in a more conventional manner. However, he argues that conventionality is not synonymous with conservatism; rather, conservative actions derive from facts and reasoning. We find it difficult to challenge this last point.

Nonsystematic Risk

While financial risk is often lower in the case of the absolute-return industry (because market risks are actively controlled), the opposite can be

---

*Another amusing anecdote is that Warren Buffett is perceived as the ultimate long-only investor. This is amusing because Berkshire Hathaway is much closer to a multistrategy absolute-return vehicle than a benchmarked long-only vehicle: Warren Buffett is not indifferent to overall valuation of a stock market (ending his predecessor partnership in 1969 due to a lack of value), exploits short-volatility strategies (current insurance business; risk arbitrage in the 1980s), is actively involved in distressed securities (bailing out Salomon Brothers in 1991, offering to bail out LTCM in 1998), has huge macro bets (short the dollar), is active in commodities (through investment in Petro China and bets on silver), is active in fixed-income arbitrage (through investment in a fixed-income arbitrage fund), and so on. The fact that Mr. Buffett publicly condemns derivatives and, recently, also hedge funds certainly increases the entertainment value of investment management as well as giving this anecdote a somewhat ironic overlay.

said for operational risks. The investor's risk to the operation is higher with hedge funds than it is with traditional asset managers (this is, of course, a generalization). Operational risk, however, is nonsystematic or idiosyncratic risk. This means exposure to nonsystematic risk does not carry an economic risk premium (unlike exposure to systematic risk). However, nonsystematic risk can largely be eliminated through diversification alone.

One could view a hedge fund as having operational risk similar to an early-stage venture capital firm in the private equity market or a micro cap (tiny small cap) in the stock market. Many hedge funds start as a small operation in which their own money is managed next to some funds from friends, family, and, often, former colleagues. This start-up phase, obviously, is of much higher operational risk than, for example, a multibillion-dollar traditional or alternative asset management firm. As the absolute-return management operation moves through its own life cycle, this idiosyncratic risk—assuming going concern—decreases (often in line with returns). Figure 2.8 references a report wherein the breakdown of fund failures attributed to operational risk in the absolute-return world was examined, thus adding some color to idiosyncratic risk.

To some extent this is a contradiction: On one hand, we argue that there is no compensation for bearing idiosyncratic risk; on the other, we

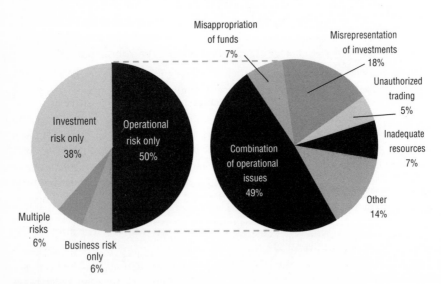

FIGURE 2.8 Operational Risk
Source: Capco [2003].

observe that returns are often higher when managers are smaller (and leaner), but idiosyncratic risk is higher. We therefore suspect that there is some sort of inflection point where size, available capacity, and maturity of the operation are just about right (i.e., reasonable idiosyncratic risk), but the nimbleness and flexible maneuverability and entrepreneurial incentives and drive are still intact (i.e., reasonable returns). A pragmatic response from an investor's perspective to this is to diversify the maturity life cycle, that is, include early-, medium-, and later-stage hedge funds in an absolute-return portfolio.

The optimal number of hedge funds in a hedge funds portfolio is still an ongoing debate. Mean-variance fetishists argue that between 12 and 15 hedge funds are optimal because adding another hedge fund does not improve portfolio efficiency. This might be true in mean-variance space. However, we challenge that argument as follows. If we have a portfolio of hedge funds that contains 50 managers, say, in the United States and Europe and add a further manager operating in Asia with a positive alpha that is higher than the average alpha of the 50 existing managers, then the inclusion of manager number 51 adds value by definition. The reason is threefold: First, nonsystematic risk of the portfolio is further diversified. A default, by definition idiosyncratic risk, will have a smaller impact on the portfolio. Second, portfolio efficiency is increased because the return stream is independent, that is, weakly correlated to the return streams of the existing 50 managers. Chances are that there is crowding in at least some of the 50 managers, for example, in European stock exchange stocks. The diversification benefits therefore could be significantly lower than perceived, as correlations can jump when markets dislocate. Third, the portfolio alpha relative to assets under management and capital at risk is improved because we found a manager with higher alpha than our existing managers. So the marginal contribution of adding manager number 51 is positive in terms of reducing nonsystematic risk further, improving portfolio efficiency, and potentially increasing portfolio alpha. There is actually a further reason: One of the issues in hedge fund investing is access, that is, finding and securing capacity. This means a hedge fund allocator (fund of funds or any other investor) has an incentive to build a relationship with the hedge fund managers that is built on mutual trust and professional respect. There is an incentive to build and maintain business relationships. In the preceding example, firing manager number 50 to make room for manager number 51, who has higher alpha, might not be optimal from a business perspective. Burning bridges in the absolute-return industry is far from optimal. There are actually allocators who have a bad reputation in the marketplace for carelessly firing managers. These allocators are burning goodwill. Guess which hedge fund managers they will end up with.

The distinction between systematic and nonsystematic risk is cause for some debate on the regulatory front. Many regulators have already viewed, or are in the process of viewing, the financial risk of a diversified portfolio of hedge funds as lower than, for example, a diversified portfolio of stocks or a balanced portfolio containing only stocks and bonds. Part of the debate, however, is based on the question of whether a single hedge fund should be compared to an investment in a single stock or a single mutual fund. If a single hedge fund is compared to a mutual fund, then the idiosyncratic risk is most often higher or much higher with the hedge fund than it is with a benchmarked long-only fund (e.g., a mutual fund) of a large and established asset management firm. The comparison between a hedge fund and a mutual fund is much more frequent than a comparison between a hedge fund and a single-stock investment. However, from an idiosyncratic risk and portfolio construction point of view, one could argue that single hedge funds are more comparable to single-stock investments, while fund of hedge funds could be compared with mutual funds. Both fund of funds as well as mutual funds construct portfolios in which idiosyncratic risk is diversified.

In the stock market, even retail investors know (either by training or by experience) the concept of diversification, that is, that risk is reduced by holding not just one stock but many. The same logic applies to hedge funds. The common denominator with stocks and hedge funds is that occasionally a company as well as a hedge fund goes bankrupt, due to either fraud or some other failure. However, while any kind of bankruptcy is unfortunate, single-entity bankruptcy risk is fully diversifiable risk. The difference between single-stock investments and single–hedge fund investments, though, is the correlation among the single portfolio constituents.

With stocks, as we know today, correlation is high and is even higher in a bear market or during an economic shock situation. The correlation among different single hedge funds is of a completely different nature than the correlation characteristics in the stock market. In addition to lower correlation coefficients, the variance of the correlation statistics is lower with hedge funds, too. In other words, not only is correlation among constituents lower than with stocks, the correlation is also more stable than it is with stock portfolios. (This is a delicate subject open to some debate. While low correlation is the rule, there are exceptions to the rule. Short-volatility strategies, for example, have high correlation in dislocating or extreme market conditions. This event-type risk can be partly offset by holding long-volatility strategies, as well as short-volatility strategies. Nevertheless, a perfect storm scenario remains a possibility for all portfolios.) This low correlation and the stability of its constituents' correlations enables the construction of conservative, that is, low-volatility, portfolios. We believe it was the lack of appreciation about the importance of correlation in portfolio construction in understanding financial conservatism in the 1982 to 2000 bull market.* However, the situation has now changed.

From a regulatory point of view this distinction between systematic and nonsystematic (in addition to systemic[†]) risk is important. The function of any regulator is to protect the investor (see Table 2.2). If a naïve investor confuses a hedge fund for a mutual fund (as the two terms phonetically sound similar), then there is the risk that the investor is misled, irrespective of whether the financial risks of the hedge fund are lower than the financial risks of the long-only manager. The typical naïve investor will assess the bankruptcy risk of a typical mutual fund to be very low. In theory, if the idiosyncratic risks of single hedge funds are compared with the idiosyncratic risks of stocks, it is not entirely clear why the naïve investor can risk his financial wealth with single stocks but not with hedge funds. In practice, this line of argument depends on the amount of capital the naïve investor has at his disposal, because access to single hedge funds is different from access to single stocks.

We do not know how things will play out for the retail investor from a regulatory standpoint. What we do know is that if a frog-eating snake enters the habitat of the frog, the frog is on his own.

CHAPTER SUMMARY AND CONCLUSIONS

Risk Metrics Group, arguably a pioneer in its field, publishes and advertises what it believes to be "9 Rules of Risk Management."[15] We believe there is hardly a better way to summarize this chapter on risk and transparency:

1. **There is no return without risk**
   Rewards go to those who take risks.
2. **Be transparent**
   Risk should be fully understood.
3. **Seek experience**
   Risk is measured and managed by people, not mathematical models.
4. **Know what you don't know**
   Question the assumptions you make.

---

*Reason never causes a paradigm shift—an event is needed too. It wasn't the idea of "liberty, equality, fraternity" alone that widowed Marie Antoinette.
†For a good discussion of systemic risk in connection with hedge funds, please refer to Chan, Getmansky, Haas, and Lo [2005].

5. **Communicate**
   Risk should be discussed openly.
6. **Diversify**
   Multiple risks will produce more consistent rewards.
7. **Show discipline**
   A consistent and rigorous approach will beat a constantly changing strategy.
8. **Use common sense**
   It is better to be approximately right, than to be precisely wrong.
9. **Return is only half the equation**
   Decisions should be made only by considering the risk and return of possibilities.

An investor (institutional or private) allocating money to an absolute-return manager essentially hands over the mandate to manage total risk to the manager. This is one of the main differences from the relative-return approach, in which the manager does not have a mandate to manage capital at risk, but has a mandate to manage tracking risk relative to a market benchmark. The absence of a market benchmark has one major disadvantage: It will result in lower transparency.

The relative-return approach has some great advantages as it allows the end investor to undertake a fairly accurate asset allocation and budget for market risk factors. The desire to turn the absolute-return approach into a relative-return approach to capture the advantages of the latter is understandable but unwise. Investors demanding transparency for asset allocation and risk-budgeting purposes, in our opinion, should be focusing on the manager's ability to manage (as opposed to measure) risk. This task is labor intensive, subjective by definition and qualitative in nature. We are not at all implying that this is an easy job, nor are we implying that all investors are equally equipped to do the job. However, it seems that the main focus today, with respect to transparency and risk, is the search for an all-inclusive risk measure. While this search is commendable, it could also be a move in the wrong direction.

If our hypothesis turns out to be wrong (which is a possibility), then it is because the institutional end investor continues to perceive the utility of being able to control asset allocation and budget for risk accurately as higher than the utility of asymmetric returns. Although we feel quite strongly about the absolute-return approach taking over, there is one major reason why one could oppose our view: change. It is pretty safe to assume that the absolute-return industry cannot continue to deliver these superior risk/return profiles if everyone on the planet gives them their money. The hedge fund industry was more attractive as long as everyone believed it was not. Until recently, the hedge fund industry, we believe, was populated with the best risk managers. This was possible because an extreme selection process took place (as barriers to entry were high), as only about 1 percent of the investment community thought of hedge fund investing as a good idea. However, this situation has changed. An industry or investment process that 99 percent of the investing public believes is a bad idea is not the same as an industry that 99 percent of the investing public perceives as a good idea. We compare this with musical chairs: If you have fast research and decision-making capability, you are quicker to adapt to change and are, eventually, better off. Chances that you win are higher. There are potentially no gifts (and certainly no free lunches) for the slow investor. As Mario Andretti put it: "If everything is under control, you're driving too slow."

Over the past five years, investing in hedge funds has gained popularity. However, this is part of a problem. Throughout the last two decades of the twentieth century, investing through a buy-and-hold long-only strategy in the equity market was a good idea (unless you were a Japanese investor investing locally). However, in the past, it seemed to have been a better idea when everyone thought it was a bad idea (as price change happens at the margin). Coming out of the inflation-prone 1970s, equity investments were not popular. Interest rates were high, and equity valuations low. We would not consider the mood change that followed in the 1980s a paradigm shift but rather a turning point in a cycle. Our hypothesis is potentially wrong and the increase in demand of hedge fund products is not a paradigm shift (what we believe) but just part of a cycle; hedge funds were popular in the late 1960s, but then encountered some difficulties in 1969 and the early 1970s. So we could argue that it is the abundance of liquidity that is lifting all boats.

History, we believe, shows that there are both cycles and paradigm shifts. Distinguishing the two, potentially, is difficult.

We believe that the difference between risk measurement and risk management with respect to transparency and risk is an important one. Risk measurement is fairly objective. Risk management, however, is subjective by definition as well as by comparison. The heterogeneity of the hedge funds industry with respect to the way risk is managed, in combination with the observation that the hedge fund industry was able to steer through the difficult three-year period from 2000 to 2002 more or less (financially speaking) unharmed, is an indication that this might be true. Our main point is that the pure reliance on a process or a few metrics is very dangerous. We believe, therefore, that a dynamic and flexible approach to risk management is superior to a static (purely rule-based) and dogmatic process. With respect to transparency, this means that investors' demand for transparency should not interfere with the nimbleness and flexible maneuverability of the manager.

The confusion between risk measurement and risk management also has some beneficiaries. As Leon Levy [2002] put it:

> *"Most people believe that markets are driven primarily by economic factors, and that psychology plays a minor role.* I take the position that markets are driven by both psychological and economic factors. I owe great debt to economists for their inability to acknowledge the degree to which psychology moves markets. (In this sense, it's unfortunate that economics now seems to be embracing psychology.)"*

If a hedge fund manager can say that his daily value at risk is $4.33 million and explain the assumptions behind the figure, and, if need be, pop into the fund's own library and get copies of all relevant papers on the subject, then this surely is a blessing. However, it does not tell the investor a lot about risk management skill and experience. Risk management is the judgment call that (apart from questioning the $4.33 million figure) relates the total capital at risk with the investment opportunities the fund is exposed to. In addition, managing risk is a much broader task than just measuring it. Most importantly, it is the observation skill of the manager in noticing early when the risk/reward relationship is changing to the portfolio's disadvantage. Successful investing, we believe, has to do with often getting not only the entry strategy right, but also the exit strategy.

Since active risk management skill is scarce and managing risk is difficult, it carries a fairly high price tag. In the financial services industry, anything that is easy carries a low price tag. This leads us to the next issue: fees.

---

*Note that Robert Shiller [1981, 1989] showed that around two thirds of the volatility in equities cannot be explained by changes in fundamental variables. Fisher Black [1986] used the term *noise*.

CHAPTER 3

The Price of Asymmetric Returns

"I do it on behalf of my brothers Schubert and Mozart, who died in poverty."

—Igor Stravinsky in response to the notion that his fees were outrageous

Imagine you are a frog. You are enjoying the good life. Things are going well for you. But, unlike many of your more complacent comrades, you are a thoughtful frog and are concerned about the future. You have not ignored the lessons of history. You know that while things are going well now, they might change in the future. You know that there is a non-negligible probability that a frog-eating snake might enter your habitat. You ask yourself what you would do if this happened. There is no easy answer. You envy the owl, who can just fly away at the first sight of danger. How much would you pay for this optionality? As a literate frog you recall the exclamation from Shakespeare's *Richard III*, where the king cries out, "A horse! A horse! My kingdom for a horse!" after his horse was killed in battle, leaving him at the mercy of his enemies.

The dispersion of fees paid for active asset management is huge. Why? If markets were even close to being efficient and investors even halfway rational, the range between high and low fees charged by managers could not possibly be as wide as it is—hundreds of basis points per year. But it is. The reason, we believe, is simple: Not all investors are equally fit to assess an ever-changing market environment and make rational, diligent, and intelligent investment decisions. It is, therefore, very unlikely that all investment products are of equal value in terms of their proposition. There is variation.

FEES — AN EVERGREEN ISSUE REVISITED

Introduction

Economic theory distinguishes between two types of actors in the market: principals and agents. Principals are typically owners, for example, capitalists who put money at risk and expect income, proceeds, or capital appreciation as a reward for their risk-taking activity. Agents, on the other hand, are essentially wage earners; they are hired by the principals to act on their behalf. Agents work with the capital and might even control it on a day-to-day basis, but they do not "own" it. The relationship between principal and agent is typically referred to as the *agency relationship* and refers to the separation between ownership and control. Economists have long been fascinated by the motivational problems or conflicts that can arise between principals and agents. The *principal-agent problem*, as it commonly called in economics, treats the difficulties that arise when a principal hires an agent under conditions of incomplete and asymmetric information. A problem or conflict exists because the economic incentives faced by the agents and the principals, as well as the information available to them, are often quite different. Examples of agency relationships are between shareholders and management, investor and asset manager, pensioners and pension fund, and so on.

Fees (essentially the agent's income) are an evergreen issue in the investment management industry, in long-only asset management in general, and in absolute-return investing in particular. Generally speaking, investors view fees as being too high, while the providers of active asset management services—not too surprisingly—do not. (Providers of passive asset management services view the fees charged by active managers—also not too surprisingly—as high too.) The larger the manager's slice in percentage terms, the larger the issue. As returns from absolute-return strategies have been somewhat dampened over the past couple of years, fees are becoming an even greater issue as fees today are a larger portion of the return in percentage terms than they were in the 1990s. Consider a manager who achieves a 20 percent gross return. A fee of $2 + 20$ on this return results in an effective fee of 43 percent of net returns (6 percent of 14 percent). The same fee structure with 10 percent gross return results in a fee of 67 percent of net returns (4 percent of 6 percent).* It is not surprising that fees are a bigger issue when absolute returns are low. In addition, the appearance of the institutional investor, who has fiduciary responsibilities, in the absolute-return space has amplified the debate. Our experience in absolute-return

---

*Some define a hedge fund as "a compensation scheme masquerading as an asset class."

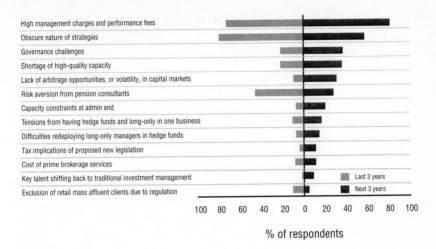

FIGURE 3.1 Perception of High Fees as Growth Dampener
Source: Create/KPMG [2005].

management is—unlike what some of the hedge fund investor surveys suggest—that investors are not indifferent to the level of fees. Someone even entrusted us with their idea to write a book called "Absolute Fees" in response to recent hedge fund performance, and in lieu of our first Wiley book entitled *Absolute Returns*.

Figure 3.1 supports the notion that fees matter.* In the survey referenced in the graph, pension fund managers were asked: "Which factors have hindered growth in hedge funds worldwide in the recent past, and which, if any, are likely to do so over the next three years?" The pension funds participating in the survey represented \$3.5 trillion of investments located across the globe.

One of the arguments against hedge funds is that their fees are higher than the fees charged by mutual funds. (Table 1.1 in Chapter 1, which compares performance in negative quarters between mutual funds and hedge funds, was a first hint why hedge funds might be getting away with charging higher fees.) In other words, it is not only the absolute level that is disturbing to investors, the comparison to an alternative investment vehicle matters, too. Following is a paragraph from an article discussing Sir John Templeton's views in reference to hedge fund fees in the *Financial Times*:

---

*Fees do not matter to all investors: One manager from a large European pension fund was quoted as saying, related to fees: "Fees are not an issue: If you pay peanuts, you get monkeys."

Sir John suggests that anyone with $10 m or more should do most of their investing through mutual funds. He doesn't like hedge funds. "The difference in a good mutual fund is only 2 per cent," he says, "whereas hedge funds charge fees that are much higher than that."[1]

We are not yet fully convinced whether the dispersion of mutual fund returns being as high as hedge fund fees is that relevant to the end investor. If someone had sold his company for $10 million and invested in mutual funds in January 2000, he would be holding around $9.3 million in mutual funds by the end of 2005 (assuming the mutual fund matched the performance of the Standard and Poor's [S&P] 500 Total Return Index). This investor would have seen his holdings melt to $5.8 million by September 2002 and recover to $9.3 million by December 2005. Potentially, this investor experienced some stress during the bear market. It is not entirely unthinkable that the investor would have sold in 2002 and not benefited from the recovery.

Had the investor instead invested the $10 million in a fund of hedge funds in 2000, his wealth would have increased to around $13.8 million by the end of 2005 (assuming the fund of funds matched the performance of the HFRI Fund of Funds Composite Index which is calculated net of fees). Interestingly, the investor would probably still have a full arsenal of stress hormones as the lowest value of his wealth was on day one, that is, $10 million in January 2000.

This makes one wonder whether fees matter, and if they do, how much? Potentially, it is net performance that matters, not gross performance or fees. Figure 3.2 compares these two methods of "wealth creation."

How long will it take for the S&P 500 index to catch up with the low-volatility fund of funds index? We do not know. Potentially, it never will. This is another demonstration that volatility matters. Investing in the gray line in Figure 3.2 might be dull, but at least it's prosperous. We believe the fact that mutual funds charge lower fees than hedge funds is somewhat missing the point.

The "point" is best described with the concept of asymmetric returns. Figure 3.3 compares cumulative performance of the HFRI Fund of Funds Composite Index with the MSCI World Total Return Index as a proxy for a diversified portfolio of stocks, the JPM Global Government Bond Total Return Index as a proxy for a diversified portfolio of government bonds, and cash as a proxy for the risk-free investment for the 16-year period from 1990 to December 2005. The annual compounding rates are shown in the graph. Note that the graph is based on total return indices, that is, shows performance assuming distributions are reinvested. The hedge fund index is net of fees, while the long-only indices are gross of fees. When the facts are

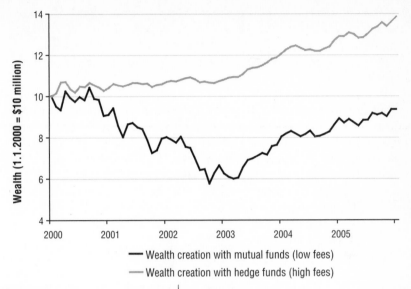

FIGURE 3.2   Difference between High and Low Fees
Wealth creation with mutual funds is based on S&P 500 Total Return Index; wealth creation with fund of hedge funds is based on HFRI Fund of Funds Composite Index.
Source: Author's own calculations; data from Bloomberg and Thomson Financial.

presented like this, it is pretty easy to argue that fees do not matter, only net results do. (In the appendix to Chapter 1, we have shown that the difference is even more extreme when we move from point-to-point analysis, as in Figure 3.3, to assuming the investor/saver adds new funds to his investment in regular or irregular intervals.)

Diversified hedge fund portfolios compounded at 10 percent per year over the past 16-year period. Both global equities and government bond portfolios compounded at around 7.2 percent per year over the same time period. According to most financial textbooks, the world should not work like this. First, equities should outperform bonds. That's what the scholars and equity sales staff of broker/dealers keep telling us. So what's wrong? There is nothing wrong—it just takes equities longer than 16 years to unfold their magic, that is, outperform bonds. We know this from studying the history of financial markets. (We discuss long-term financial market history in Chapter 9 in more detail.) Long-only equities are still a good investment, for example, for extraterrestrials who visit Earth in say 30- to 50-year intervals and therefore have no disutility from interim volatilities (assuming, of course, that these "foreign investors" do not have a Bloomberg terminal and a layman investment committee breathing down their neck).

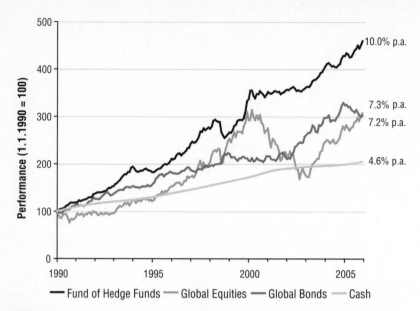

FIGURE 3.3   Hedge Funds versus Equities, Bonds, and Cash, 1990 to 2005
Indices: HFRI Fund of Funds Composite Index, MSCI World Total Return Index,
JPM Global Government Bond Total Return Index, U.S. dollar (USD) one-month
London Interbank Offered Rate (LIBOR).
Source: Author's own calculations; data from Bloomberg and Thomson Financial.

Second, how can a group of investors so consistently outperform
equities and bonds with lower (not higher) volatility?* Most textbooks
suggest that markets are fairly efficient and that investors are rational. How
can it be, then, that not all investors want to invest in the bold line in
Figure 3.3? Again, we must assume that 16 years is too short a time period
to draw any significant conclusions in this regard. Alternatively, we might
conclude that markets are not as efficient as we are taught at business
school. Many investment decisions are made by committees. There is a vast
amount of literature suggesting how inefficient committees can be in terms
of decision making under uncertainty. The cardinal quality of committees is
homogeneity and conformity. Nietzsche was probably onto something when
he said madness was the exception in individuals but the rule in crowds.

One of the key reasons we advocate the active absolute-return approach
in investment management is that it makes a lot of sense to us that managers

---

*Low volatility of diversified portfolios was not always as low as today. The hedge
fund universe was very directional until about 10 years ago.

control exposure to upside volatility differently than to downside volatility. An investment opportunity is then attractive when there is an asymmetry between the probability of making a profit and the probability of losing capital. If the outcome is like flipping a fair coin, no active manager is required. The absolute-return approach simply implies that the end investor (private investor, insurance company, pension fund, etc.) is not indifferent to swings on the downside, that is, essentially large and erratic negative returns. It is understandable that the organizations that pass on these (superior) asymmetric-return profiles to the end investor find themselves in the favorable position to charge higher fees. However, as the history of economics somewhat hints, high fees—under competition—have a tendency to turn into low fees over time.

Paying for the Balancing Act

The absolute-return approach is a balancing act between exploiting opportunities and managing total risk. The difference between achieving an asymmetric versus a symmetric return profile has everything to do with the mandate specification of the manager, as discussed in Chapter 2 and previous writings. The relative-return manager does not have the mandate to "manage the curve"*; that is, it is the market that determines how returns are distributed.

One-year implied volatility for S&P 500 and Financial Times Stock Exchange (FTSE) 100 options was 13.8 percent and 14.2 percent in December 1995, and 23.3 percent and 23.1 percent in December 1999, with interim peaks in the 30s and low 40s. (See Figure 3.4.) The absolute-return manager has a mandate to manage the elasticity of these returns. On the upside, the higher the volatility the better; and on the downside, the lower the volatility the better. The way the absolute-return manager achieves this asymmetry is by balancing investment opportunity with capital at risk: If opportunities are plentiful, the manager will put a higher amount of capital at risk or, in some cases, lever up. If opportunities are scarce, the manager will delever and/or move into the money market, that is, reduce capital at risk. In addition, the absolute-return manager prefers a situation in which predictability is high (e.g., arbitrage between a mispriced derivative and its synthetic) over a situation in which the outcome is highly random in the short term and very disperse in the medium term (e.g., buy-and-hold strategy in equities).

---

*In Ineichen [2002b] we reiterated the case for active managers using derivatives, as it is options that can help investors to introduce asymmetries according to one's investment views, that is, allow the investor to manage the curve (as in return distribution).

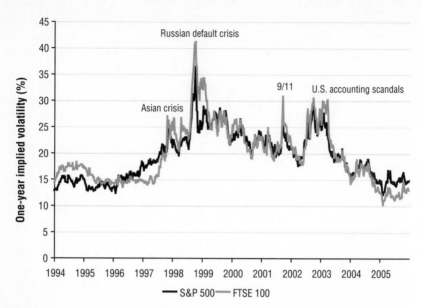

FIGURE 3.4 S&P 500 and FTSE 100 One-Year Implied Volatility, 1994 to 2005
Source: UBS Investment Research.

Change Is the Only Certainty in the Game of Risk   This brings us back to
our definition of risk from the previous chapter, namely, risk understood
as "exposure to change." We believe change is extremely relevant for
the absolute-return approach that aims to generate an asymmetric-return
profile, as there is a (moving) inflection point or zone between "plentiful
opportunities" and "scarce opportunities." The manager is paid to notice
early on when the investment opportunity (more precisely the risk/reward
relationship) changes. This is very important because it is commonly held
that the manager is paid for exploiting "proven market inefficiencies," or
picking up long established risk premiums, and/or should be fully invested at
all times. We challenge these common views for one major reason: change.

Market inefficiencies and investment opportunities do not hang around
forever—they come and go. Financial markets, investment opportunities,
and economies are not stable. The absolute-return manager, therefore, is
paid not only to find these opportunities but, in our view, is also paid to
notice early when the opportunity is gone or the risk/reward relationship is
in the process of changing. We believe exit strategies are at least as important
as entry strategies (indeed, one could even argue that the former are more
important than the latter). Most market opportunities change over time. The
most obvious determinant of change is the amount of capital deployed to

exploit an opportunity: If the opportunity is flooded with capital, the profits that can be derived from it diminishes. In other words, the opportunity goes away. This is true on a macro as well as a single-trade level. On a macro level it was economist Hyman Minsky* (1919–1996) who said famously that "stability is unstable." Minsky argued that long periods of stability cause all types of leverage and other risk taking to increase until they use up all the risk units freed up by the greater stability. This is also true on a micro level. An inefficiency disappears (or changes, i.e., become more risky) once everyone tries to put on the trade. Buchanan [2000] uses the analogy of earthquakes where over years or decades or centuries energy is built up by tectonic plates moving around. At one stage, the tipping point, all the built-up energy is released within seconds. For example, George Soros's notion of "reflexivity" in markets is inspired by the Heisenberg Uncertainty Principle (HUP): If something is closely observed, the odds are it is going to be altered in the process. The more a price pattern is observed by speculators, the more prone one's signals are to being false; the more the market is a product of nonspeculative activity, the greater the significance of technical breakout. This is another way of looking at optionalities/asymmetries in the financial marketplace.

We believe this to be also relevant for transparency: In a game of poker, showing your hand to the other players is not necessarily the most promising strategy for winning the game. As Peter Bernstein put it:

> *"Because of the danger that free-riders will hop aboard a successful strategy, it is quite possible that there are investors out there who beat the market consistently beyond the probability of luck, but who stubbornly guard their obscurity. Nobel Laureate Paul Samuelson, an eloquent defender of the hypothesis that markets act as though they were rational, has admitted that possibility: 'People differ in their heights, pulchritude, and acidity, why not in their P.Q., or performance quotient?' But he goes on to point out that the few people who have high P.Q.s are unlikely to rent their talents 'to the Ford Foundation or the local bank trust department. They have too high an I.Q. for that.' You will not find them on* Wall Street Week,

---

*Minsky argued that financial markets could move frequently to excess (the Financial Instability Hypothesis). He also underscored the importance of the Federal Reserve as a lender of last resort. Minsky stated: "A fundamental characteristic of our economy is that the financial system swings between robustness and fragility and these swings are an integral part of the process that generates business cycles." Historically low-risk premiums in the beginning of 2006 have resulted in Minsky's being quoted more often.

on the cover of Time, *or contributing papers to scholarly journals on portfolio theory.*"[2]

Samuelson's point of view, we believe, also supports our claim that the manager selection process (hiring and firing) is difficult and expensive in practice (as opposed to easy and cheap in theory).

Example   Figure 3.5 shows one example of a group of absolute-return managers who are renowned for responding to change (as well as being late, i.e., somewhat missing the inflection point by a tick or two). The graph shows the underwater perspective (index level as a percentage of previous all-time high) for a diversified portfolio of macro managers and a diversified portfolio of stocks. Both indices are based on monthly U.S. dollar total returns from January 1990 to December 2005. The compound annual rate of return (CARR) over the full 16-year period is also shown.

In the second quarter of 2000, macro managers were cause for negative headlines due to larger-than-average drawdowns (the fact that some of these managers had been compounding at 20 percent to 30 percent per year over multiple years did not seem to be viewed as relevant at the time). Some of the

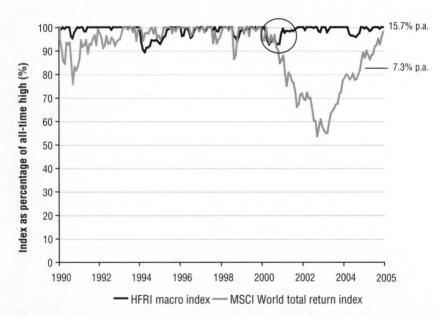

FIGURE 3.5   HFRI Macro Index versus MSCI World Total Return Index, 1990 to 2005
Source: Author's own calculations; data from Bloomberg and Thomson Financial.

more well-known managers experienced drawdowns and, as a result, mass redemptions. (Or the other way around—losses can lead to redemptions as well as redemptions to losses.) At the time macro managers, as a group, did not anticipate the bear market (especially not its magnitude).* (Often, these managers are long a trend and are referred to as *trend-followers or momentum investors.*†) So market timing is not the issue. The main point is that in the first half of 2000 the game changed. The risk/reward relationship changed. Most people knew that the late 1990s were extraordinary in terms of annual equity long-only returns (some well-known bears were bearish as early as the early 1990s). However, no one really knew when the music was going to stop. Only a very small minority noticed at the market peak that the game was going to change. All others noticed the change too early or too late. As a result of spotting change, the portfolio of an absolute-return manager changes. Whether a benchmarked long-only manager spotted change or not is not relevant, since he does not have the mandate to do anything about it anyway. Risk management in absolute-return space, that is, controlling downside risk in the case of benchmarked portfolios, is left to the end investor. With the absolute-return approach, however, it is the manager who decides on the relationship between portfolio and capital at risk. This is the origin of the asymmetry. It is judgmental and difficult. It would be unreasonable to assume that it carries the same price tag as benchmarking.

PAYING THE MILKMAN THRICE

What should the investor pay for? Figure 3.6 is an attempt to isolate the cost subfactors an investor pays to the manager. We have assumed that performance is attributable to three elements, namely, manager investment skill, a premium for liquidity and/or complexity, and an economic risk premium. We have also assumed that these three elements carry different price tags and that many investment strategies are a combination of these three elements.

We have placed long-only exposure to large caps in a developed economy in the left corner as it is passively attainable, that is, the return can be captured without the presence of investment skill (index funds, exchange-traded funds, swaps, etc.) and does not carry a premium for complexity or the lack of liquidity. No investment skill is required to capture the beta

---

*Most investors and managers who anticipated the bear market did most of the anticipating too early.
†Brunnermeier and Nagel [2003] find support that hedge funds in general were long the bubble and got out at the peak or shortly thereafter.

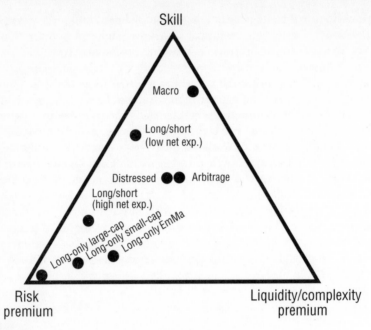

FIGURE 3.6   Skill versus Economic and Liquidity Premiums
Source: Ineichen [2003c].

of the asset class. Moving to the right, we have placed small-cap long-only and emerging markets (EmMa) long-only. Those disciplines carry an element of investment skill because the information-gathering process has a (empirically justified) positive expected return and liquidity is lower, as these markets are less efficient.

There is disagreement with respect to whether there is such a thing as "complexity premium." We recently came across a research report that stated that there were only two factors driving returns: an economic risk premium and investment skill. Skill was defined as outsmarting other market participants, and capturing an economic risk premium was defined as something that could be done entirely passively, that is, at low cost without the presence of skill. The report went on to make fun of relative-value managers because the captured premiums were just free money lying on the street and anyone could pick it up. This goes to show that, as the industry becomes institutionalized and mainstream, the amount of printed nonsense increases disproportionately.

Your author has spent 16 years of his 19-year professional career in derivative-related activity, and still does not understand, for example, convertible bonds (a derivative instrument). This could mean two things, of which we would rather only discuss one: It means that the convertible bond (CB) market and the arbitrage strategies employed in it are not that simple. The investment professionals who execute these strategies are not necessarily just researchers, but also craftsmen. Knowing and understanding option pricing theory in combination with knowing how to use a computer is surely a blessing. However, knowing how to use (risk management) tools in theory is not the same as using them in practice. The interpretation of short-term information and capital flows is also important. While your author would be capable of explaining CBs to his eight-year-old daughter or a pension fund trustee (both of whom know little about derivatives, although the former is eager to learn), it does not automatically result in applicable skill to succeed and survive in the CB marketplace.* Unlike some other market observers,† we have great respect for the managers unlocking these kinds of risk premiums and managing portfolio total risk and surviving difficult market conditions and unprecedented events. We strongly recommend that the ignorant do not start trading convertibles. As former president of Harvard University Derek Bok put it: "If you think education is expensive, try ignorance."

Arbitrage strategies such as CB arbitrage, risk arbitrage, and fixed-income arbitrage were placed in the middle of Figure 3.6, as the return is a function of all three elements, that is, investment skill, an economic premium (for example for being short volatility), and the degree of complexity being of a higher dimension than for a long-only investment style (assuming nonlinear return payoffs are more complex than linear ones, and assuming operating in illiquid markets is more difficult than in liquid markets). Any return from distressed securities is also a function of an economic risk premium (long distressed securities), skill (as there is no passive alternative and gathering information carries a reward), and a premium for the lack of liquidity. Long-short equity is primarily a function of stock-picking skill and the net exposure of the manager. A lower net exposure is generally considered of higher quality as the proportion of return attributable to skill is larger than if net exposures are high. (There are, obviously, exceptions to this.)

To Pay or Not to Pay—That Is the Question

How does all this relate to fees? Table 3.1 is an attempt to relate fees to the three performance elements discussed above. This analysis is very

---

*Barton Biggs [2006] on trustees: "... just because trustees are illustrious men doesn't mean they know anything about investing."

†Quote from Create/KPMG [2005] report: "Hedge fund managers are not geniuses with sixth sense; they are merely good at spotting mispricings. Even a monkey could make money in convertible arbs: they were priced too low."

TABLE 3.1 Fees in Relation to Skill, Liquidity, Complexity, and Risk Premiums

	Skill	Liquidity/ Complexity Premium	Risk Premium	Total	Rank
Value contribution factor	10	5	1		
Macro	5	1	0	55	1
Long-short, Beta = 0.2	4	1	1	46	2
Market neutral	2	2	2	32	3
CB arbitrage	2	2	2	32	3
FI arbitrage	2	2	2	32	3
Risk arbitrage	2	2	2	32	3
Distressed securities	2	2	2	32	3
Long-short, Beta = 0.8	2	1	3	28	8
Long-only small-cap	1	1	4	19	9
Long-only EmMa	1	1	4	19	9
Long-only large-cap	0	0	6	6	11

Methodology: A total of six points has been allocated to skill, liquidity/complexity premium, and risk premium for every strategy. Points are then multiplied with the value contribution factor and then summed and the product ranked.
Source: Ineichen [2003c].

rudimentary. The goal of this comparison is to gain some idea of what an investor should be paying a manager for. Note these issues are more complex than can be displayed by a table and a graph showing a triangle; that is, we simplify.

Performance attribution from a long-only strategy in large caps should have the lowest fees. There is no skill involved (because empirically the expected excess return from gathering information is zero or, after fees, negative) and liquidity is high and complexity low.* Performance attribution from other long-only strategies (e.g., small caps and emerging markets)

---

*One could argue that long-only managers charge fees similar to hedge funds. If 90 percent of the portfolio is held as dead weight (positions held to control tracking risk and where the manager has no insight) and fees are 30 basis points of assets under management, then the 30 basis points are actually 300 basis points on the 10 percent of the portfolio that is actively managed. Some investment professionals believe that for this reason, the 30 basis points is going to zero. Some use the phrase "Equities go FX," which means that equity exposure is as cheaply attainable as exposure in the foreign exchange markets. If this notion has merit (apart from being extreme), our earlier stated belief, that the whole investment management industry is at a crossroad, is strengthened. Whatever the argument, we advocate asymmetric fees (i.e., performance fees). It will be interesting to observe how the one or two dozen hedge fund managers will do

carry some premium for skill (as empirical evidence suggests that gathering information makes sense) and there is a premium for the lack of liquidity in small caps and emerging markets.

Performance attribution of relative-value strategies (market neutral and arbitrage) is balanced among skill, economic premiums, and a premium for liquidity and/or complexity. The same is probably true for distressed securities. The complexity premium is probably higher with relative-value strategies, and the liquidity premium higher for distressed securities. The economic premiums are difficult to replicate passively, that is, without any form of investment skill; despite Kat and Palaro [2005] suggesting otherwise. Information is scarce and difficult to obtain and assess. In other words, gathering information and managing risk can add value. We have associated nonlinear return payoffs of (for example) short-volatility strategies as more complex because, among other considerations, most off-the-shelf portfolio management software still cannot—very loosely phrased—deal with portfolios including derivatives properly.

Long-short equity is, in our view, a very heterogeneous subindustry. One could argue that if performance attribution is primarily a function of beta, then fees should be low. Low-net-exposure long-short equity has a performance attribution more skewed to skill, as performance is a function of stock picking (which can be fairly sustainable) as opposed to market timing (which we believe is less sustainable).

Macro is pretty high up on the investment skill scale (see next heading for debate). However, macro managers do not capture directional risk premiums. If they are long an asset class outright, it is because they expect the underlying asset class to appreciate in price in the short or medium term (and not because a buy-and-hold strategy yields a profit for the long-term and patient investor). Their value proposition is based on their belief that they can find catalysts that result in price moves earlier than the rest of the marketplace. The performance is therefore attributed to timing (and managing total risk) and investment themes, as opposed to capturing the premium of the asset class that is obtainable through a buy-and-hold strategy. There is a small premium for the lack of liquidity, as investors cannot cash an investment in a fund as easily as an investment in a traditional asset class in which there are derivatives available that allow fast liquidation.

---

with their long-only products where the performance fees is based on outperformance; that is, if there is outperformance, the manager gets a slice, and if there is underperformance, he needs to regain the underperformance (high-water mark applied to cumulative relative performance). To us, this actually makes a lot of sense.

Based on the assumptions made that underpin Table 3.1, macro should be able to charge the highest fees. How does this compare to the real world?

Some large and well-known macro managers have migrated to a multi-strategy approach. In such cases, fees as high as $3 + 30$ (3 percent management fee and 30 percent performance fee) is not unheard of. These larger macro organizations are as (or nearly as) diversified as fund of hedge funds. These higher fees, therefore, could be justified. The macro investor pays a similar amount of fees as the fund of funds investor. A fund of funds investor pays a 1 percent to 2 percent management fee and 20 percent to 25 percent performance fee for the single managers, plus $1 + 10$ percent on top of that for the fund of funds. This results in fees of 2 percent to 3 percent management fees plus 25 percent to 35 percent performance fees. However, while financial risk (as measured for example through volatility) between a multi-strategy macro manager and a fund of funds manager could be similar, nonsystematic (i.e., idiosyncratic) risk is distinctly lower with the fund of funds than it is with the macro manager.* An investor investing in a multi-strategy fund is exposed to one firm as all the different profits and losses are within the firm. In the case of investing in fund of funds, this risk is spread to multiple firms; that is, operational risk is distinctly lower. In the case of fund of funds, genuine diversification is achieved, as the main risk of absolute return investing is operational risk. (Losses from exposure to operational risk are discussed in the appendix to Chapter 4 as well as in Chapter 7.)

Tables 3.2 and 3.3 show the impact of fees on net returns to the investor with and without a hurdle rate. For example: a 20 percent gross return with a total fee burden of $3 + 30\%$, with a 5 percent hurdle rate to the end investor, would result in a net return of approximately 12.5 percent. Fees sum up to 7.5 percent (3 percent management fee plus 4.5 percent performance fee; 30 percent of 15 percent performance above hurdle rate of 5 percent).

Table 3.2 and Table 3.3 confirm what most investors already suspected: Charging high fees is attractive for the fee recipient. This is one of the reasons why the traditional asset management industry is not just sitting there and watching a small subindustry capture an oversize portion of the fees the fee-paying investment community is willing to spend. The expansion of the traditional asset management industry into the absolute-return world is

---

*This last notion is probably subject to debate as phrased too generally. Some multi-strategy macro managers carry less idiosyncratic risk than some fund of funds. This has been accentuated in the past two to three years, as some multistrategy (formerly) macro houses have become established and institutionalized and serious, while at the same time the barriers to start a fund of hedge funds seem to have fallen (as everyone and his dog has been starting one).

TABLE 3.2 Net Returns with 5 Percent Hurdle Rate

Fee Structure	Gross Return (%)					
	0	5	10	15	20	30
1 + 20 (%)	-1.0	4.0	8.0	12.0	16.0	24.0
2 + 20	-2.0	3.0	7.0	11.0	15.0	23.0
3 + 20	-3.0	2.0	6.0	10.0	14.0	22.0
1 + 30	-1.0	4.0	7.5	11.0	14.5	21.5
2 + 30	-2.0	3.0	6.5	10.0	13.5	20.5
3 + 30	-3.0	2.0	5.5	9.0	12.5	19.5

Source: Author's own calculations.

TABLE 3.3 Net Returns with No Hurdle Rate

Fee Structure	Gross Return (%)					
	0	5	10	15	20	30
1 + 20 (%)	-1.0	3.0	7.0	11.0	15.0	23.0
2 + 20	-2.0	2.0	6.0	10.0	14.0	22.0
3 + 20	-3.0	1.0	5.0	9.0	13.0	21.0
1 + 30	-1.0	2.5	6.0	9.5	13.0	20.0
2 + 30	-2.0	1.5	5.0	8.5	12.0	19.0
3 + 30	-3.0	0.5	4.0	7.5	11.0	18.0

Source: Author's own calculations.

already well under way. To many, this was unthinkable only a couple of years ago—a paradigm shift indeed.

Macro was placed in the skill corner of Figure 3.6 (which probably will please macro managers). There is no premium for complexity (which probably will displease macro managers)* or economic risk (as the directional exposure is biased toward market timing, momentum, or an investment theme, as opposed to capturing an asset class premium). There is some premium for the lack of liquidity. However, there is an ongoing debate whether macro is value added, that is, whether we can talk about alpha when discussing directional strategies. For example, if a manager was long the stock market from 1995 to 1999, exited the market around the market top (March 2000), and then started building up positions in commodities, that is, playing the China growth story through commodities (as opposed

---

*Note that many macro managers have added (complex) relative value strategies to their directional bets as these strategies are good complements from a portfolio efficiency point of view.

to buying stocks), are the manager's returns from being long equity market in the late 1990s and long commodities in the first half of the 2000s alpha or beta? Is it market timing, tactical asset allocation, or what? How should the manager be compensated for making money by riding secular trends skillfully? Some professionals argue that riding these trends is beta so it should not carry a high price tag. They argue that it was probably coincidence that the manager was long stocks then and long commodities now. And for every macro manager—so the line of argument—who was long, there is a manager who got these trends the other way around applying the zero-sum-game logic to the subset of financial markets instead of the whole marketplace. We even came across different versions of the history of macro when researching the topic. In the following, we therefore have added a section on *discretionary trading* (macro) as well as its brethren, that is, *systematic trading,* also known as managed futures. We wanted to add more color to these strategies than we did in *Absolute Returns*. Relevant to this chapter on fees, we hypothesize whether macro is the purest form of active asset management and therefore deserves the highest fees. It seems to us the marketplace already has made up its mind.

Is Macro the Purest Form of Skill?

Managed Futures   *Managed futures* refers to the active trading of futures and forward contracts on commodities, bonds, equities, and currencies. Managed futures is generally considered an alternative investment strategy. Generally speaking, investment in managed futures remains only a small part of a typical institutional investor's portfolio. Regardless of whether one likes them or not, managed futures as a strategy has a track record covering more than two decades, of which one characteristic is negative correlation during many of the past difficult market situations. (It also has a history of high manager attrition.)

Managed futures pools have been around for several decades, as have hedge funds. However, over the past couple of years, managed futures have appeared in classification systems of alternative investment strategies (as opposed to alternative investment assets such as private equity, real estate, timber, etc.) as a subgroup next to hedge funds, as both hedge funds and managed futures are so-called skill-based investment strategies. The term *skill-based* is often used as the opposite of buy-and-hold or market-based strategies.

Professionally managed futures (or systematic trading, whatever term you prefer) started in the commodity markets of the 1970s. The period was characterized as a period of large, upward price movements in agricultural and metals markets. Inflation, periods of crop disruption, and large movements of gold and silver provided attractive profit opportunities in the commodity futures markets. Often, the managers traded their own proprietary assets and pooled client assets in limited partnerships or traded them separately in managed futures accounts. Yang and Faux [1999] wrote:

> *"In the early 1970s, some of the basic forms of managed futures trading began to take place and were divided, as they remain today, between discretionary and systems trading. While discretionary traders used market judgement (generally based on fundamental information or interpretation of technical, price-driven market data) to trade in the commodities markets, other market professionals developed systematised trading methods, either on early computers or laboriously by hand, to be able to participate in directional price trends in the futures markets. Then, as today, success was frequently determined more by the risk-control characteristics of the trader's methods, and by the trader's consistency and discipline, than by the ability to find the directional price movement in the market."*

In the 1980s, opportunities in commodity futures diminished. New opportunities were spotted in the rising financial futures markets, namely, in fixed income and currency futures. As inflationary pressures that had helped commodity markets in the 1970s subsided, the performance of futures funds and commodity trading advisers (CTAs) was driven more by financial futures. In the mid-1980s, when Merrill Lynch was putting together the first large multi-adviser futures fund, MIT Nobel Laureate Professor Paul Samuelson, then a director of Commodities Corporation, the fund's trading manager, was asked for his thoughts on managed futures. His response included the comment:

> *"Diversification is the golden rule for prudent investment. If you add some judicious futures to the bonds, stocks, insurance, and real estate assets that are already in your portfolio, you can hope to sleep better at night."*[3]

The ever-rising power of computers allowed systematic as well as discretionary managed futures to grow. Increasing computer power added a new element to the game: speed. Some managers developed very quick, discretionary trading techniques, rapidly evaluating and anticipating the futures market movements from a fundamental and technical standpoint. Rapid trading techniques also mattered in computerized systems. Some systematic managers' very rapid trading required not just the computerized skill of seeking out and capturing the large number of frequently small-profit opportunities in the futures markets, it also required the development of advanced computerized order entry, execution, and trade reconciliation to transact the orders efficiently. Some of the models developed over decades remain fairly robust to this day.

The reason for the aforementioned ambivalence toward managed futures programs on the part of institutional investors is probably differing underlying beliefs about how capital markets work. Strong believers in the efficient market hypothesis (EMH) will have their reservations. The non-CTA camp believes that markets move due to economic fundamentals (and changes thereof) and that the rest is random noise. The pro-CTA camp is more of the view that markets are as much fundamentally driven as they are driven by nonrandom technicalities and the sentiment of the human pleasure machine (to use an Amos Tversky term), that is, the market participants and their rational—and from a utility-maximizing perspective, often irrational—flows. In addition, there is the belief that the sentiment part is not random noise but that there are repeatable patterns (e.g., trends) as there are repeatable patterns in human psychology.

We suspect that the consensus in institutional money management leans toward the belief that commodities or commodity-related strategies have no place in the relative-return world. Gold, for example, does not have an expected return (as stocks and bonds do). Yield is negative due to storage. The return on commodities (but not managed futures) is pure price change. However, the consensus could potentially change (as it did for hedge funds), depending probably on the performance of the asset classes that currently fit the consensus (as it did for hedge funds).

There is a difference between long-only exposure to commodities and managed commodity futures. One of the reasons why managed commodity futures exist is the theory of storage. The theory defines the relationship between the futures price and the spot price. It splits the difference between the futures price and the spot price into the forgone interest from purchasing and storing the commodity, storage costs, and the convenience yield on the inventory. The convenience yield reflects an embedded consumption timing option in holding a storable commodity. The theory suggests an inverse relationship between the level of inventories and convenience yield: At low inventory levels convenience yields are high and vice versa. A related implication is that the term structure of forward price volatility generally declines with time to expiration of the futures contract. This is caused by the expectation that, while at shorter horizons mismatched supply-and-demand forces for the underlying commodity increase the volatility of cash prices, these factors will fall into equilibrium at longer horizons.[4]

In oil, for example, Litzenberger and Rabinowitz [1995] found that oil futures often trade below spot, that is, futures markets are backwardated. Strong backwardation occurs when futures prices are below current spot prices. In weak backwardation, discounted futures prices are below spot prices. Litzenberger and Rabinowitz explained the phenomenon with the existence of "real options" under uncertainty. They show that production occurs only if discounted futures are below spot prices and strong backwardation emerges if the riskiness of futures prices is sufficiently high. A major consequence of a declining term structure of forward prices for investment in commodity futures is the opportunity to capture a positive roll return as investment in expiring contracts is moved to cheaper new outstanding contracts.

In many cases, returns from backwardation have diminished in the recent past and, in some cases, turned negative (contango). The effect has been most pronounced in markets where arbitrage is difficult due to difficult delivery (e.g., lean hogs) or storage (e.g., natural gas). Many researchers attribute this trend to an increase in assets to commodity indices.[5]

The "benefits" of financial literature for managed futures is mixed to slightly negative for the strategy. Performance persistence on the part of the manager is generally doubted. Attrition rates as well as survivorship bias in the available data are perceived to be high.

Irwin and Brorsen [1985] found that public commodity funds provide an expanded efficient investment frontier. Conversely, Elton, Gruber, and Rentzler [1987, 1990]; Schneeweis, Savanayana, and McCarthy [1991]; Irwin, Krukemyer, and Zulauf [1993]; and Edwards and Park [1996] concluded that publicly offered commodity funds are not attractive either as a stand-alone investment or as an addition to an equity/bond portfolio. For private commodity pools, Edwards and Park found that commodity pools are attractive either as stand-alone investment or as part of a diversified portfolio. Conversely, Schneeweis et al. concluded that private commodity pools do not have value as stand-alone investments but are worthwhile additions to a stock and bond portfolio. For separate accounts managed by CTAs*, Edwards and Park found benefits as a stand-alone investment as well as an addition to a diversified portfolio. McCarthy, Schneeweis, and Spurgin [1996] found valuable diversification benefits.

---

*A CTA is an independent commodity broker who meets additional requirements set by the Commodity Futures Trading Commission (CFTC). A commodity pool operator (CPO) is a centrally managed account. Commodity brokers gained a somewhat negative image as some brokers aggressively cold-called private investors, suggesting to trade, for example, heating oil "as it is about to go through the roof this winter."

More recently, Liang [2003] compares CTAs to hedge funds and fund of hedge funds. He finds higher attrition rates and survivorship bias in CTAs than in the other two classes. He also finds zero to negative correlation of CTAs to hedge funds, fund of hedge funds, and equities. On a stand-alone basis, Liang argues, CTAs trail hedge funds and fund of funds. The under-performance is attributable to high management fees, high attrition and survivorship bias, under-diversified portfolio positions in futures markets, and high leverage in futures contracts. However, the bottom line of the study is that while CTAs might not be an ideal stand-alone investment, adding CTAs can significantly improve the risk/return trade-off of a portfolio consisting of hedge funds, fund of hedge funds, and equities. Figure 3.7 shows why. (Chapter 7 will show negative correlation with other absolute return strategies in periods of stress on a single-manager level.)

Figure 3.7 compares a managed futures index with the MSCI World Total Return Index. The graph shows a selection of events in which MSCI World lost more than 5 percent of its value within one, two, three, or four months from 1980 to 2005 on a month-end basis. We then compare the negative MSCI World return with the performance of the Center for International Securities and Derivatives Markets (CISDM) CTA Asset Weighted Index during the same period. The graph speaks for itself. (That said, there is still a mini-debate as to whether this low correlation is a

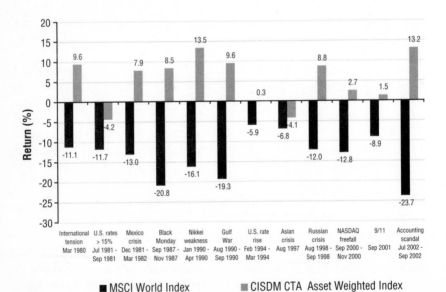

FIGURE 3.7 Managed Futures in Difficult Market Environments, 1980 to 2005
Source: Author's own calculations; data from Thomson Financial and CISDM.

coincidence. In theory, we are examining only one regime, the Greenspan regime of disinflation and falling interest rates. We do not really know whether the relationship of returns will be similar in a different market regime.)

Some hedge fund allocators consider exposure to managed futures a form of "long-volatility" strategy. The idea behind an allocation of managed futures is to balance some of the risk of the strategies that do poorly in difficult market conditions ("short-volatility" strategies).

We think long- and short-volatility strategies can be distinguished either by cause or by effect. A long-volatility strategy by *cause* is a strategy whereby the manager buys options and a short-volatility strategy is a strategy whereby the manager sells options. Convertible arbitrage, for example, is considered a long-volatility strategy because the manager is normally long optionality through the convertible bond. A long-volatility strategy by *effect* is a strategy where the risk/return profile resembles the payout of a long option position and a short-volatility strategy by effect is the opposite. Convertible arbitrage, one could argue, is a short-volatility strategy by effect, as the strategy does poorly in a stress scenario when spreads widen sharply and liquidity dries up (assuming the widening of the spreads outweighs the increase in implied stock volatility). Strategies that provide liquidity to the marketplace could be considered short-volatility strategies by effect as the return payoff resembles the payoff of a short put option position when liquidity dries up. In any case, hedge fund investors need to understand these different optionalities, ideally before investing.

Figure 3.7 shows graphically what some allocators describe as "long-volatility" characteristics (by effect but not necessarily by cause). Although the economic logic of such an allocation is somewhat ambiguous, Figure 3.7 shows that at least in the past such an allocation has worked very well as a diversifier of nearly any combination of stocks and bonds.

The correlation coefficient between the MSCI World Index and the CISDM CTA Asset Weighted Index for the period from 1980 to 2005 based on monthly log returns was −0.05.

Macro   The origins of macro are very much interlinked with the history of managed futures as well as with the original Alfred Jones (long/short equity) model. One could argue that managed futures and macro have the same origin in the commodity pits of the 1970s. In the early years, both strategies had a technical element. Managed futures then moved more in the direction of *systematic* trading, while macro moved toward *discretionary* trading. However, one could also argue that global macro grew out of the Alfred Jones model as some of the early players had their origins in equities, not in commodities.

We believe *Institutional Investor* originated the term *global macro* in 1986.[6] The article states that Julian Robertson made his first "global macro play" in 1985, anticipating that the U.S. dollar would decline against Swiss francs, deutsche marks, sterling, and the yen. Apparently, Robertson spent some $7 million on foreign currency options, limiting downside risk to less than 2 percent of capital. This essentially created the attractive asymmetric return profile of long option strategies. Over several months, profits from the bet exceeded several hundred percent of the capital at risk. Citing this example, the author of the article demonstrated how a good manager, operating from a base of equities, developed strong convictions from the best available information and, calculating risk, acted affirmatively on those convictions to generate exceptional profits. The article established Julian Robertson as an investor, not a trader. It showed how "newly developed financial instruments" (i.e., derivatives in this case) when used prudently, can improve on Jones's original (long/short equity) model.[7]

Macro is not only difficult to define, but is probably also the least classifiable absolute-return strategy. The flexibility of managers is high in all absolute-return strategies when compared with the constrained mandates of relative-return managers. The flexibility of the macro manager is greater than for any other absolute-return style. When compared with other absolute-return strategies, however, one could argue that the self-constraint (there is no benchmark-type constraint in absolute-return space) in macro is much lower than with, say, relative-value or event-driven strategies. In relative-value and event-driven strategies, the types of risks and tradable markets are more predefined than in macro. An equity market–neutral manager in the United States, for example, is unlikely to get involved in Danish debt, irrespective of the investment opportunity characteristics in the Danish bond market. In addition, portfolio concentration in macro can vary heavily from being extremely diversified to concentrated on a couple of positions in one or two themes.

Macro is probably the purest form of active management because the manager can, more or less, invest in any asset or strategy (full spectrum from directional to nondirectional, from purely discretionary to purely systematic, etc.) that he believes offers an attractive risk/return payoff. If there were a market for property options on land on Mars (perhaps soon a possibility, according to some "visionaries" in D.C.), the macro manager would be able to get active in the market. In any other type of fund, this would be considered "style drift." Many of today's so-called macro funds are involved in a broad array of absolute-return strategies.

Soros [1994] commented on his investment style in 1994:

"Our type of hedge fund invests in a wide range of securities and diversifies its risk by hedging, leveraging, and operating in many different markets. It acts more like a sophisticated private investor than an institutional investor handling other people's money. Since it is rewarded on absolute performance, it provides a healthy antidote to the trend-following behavior of institutional investors."

We could use this quote as an early definition for the macro category (although it probably also applies to many other absolute-return strategies). The quote covers at least some common aspects of macro: flexibility with respect to instruments and markets, unconstrained and absolute-return driven (as are private investors), and contrarian orientation (as in "healthy antidote" to benchmarking). However, the quote is more than 10 years old. We believe macro has transformed materially over the past 10 years, that is, the preceding definition does not capture all of the idiosyncrasies of the strategy today. There are, for example, multi-strategy (ex pure-macro) managers who derive large parts of their profit and loss not only from directional bets, but also from balanced exposures to various relative-value type, highly analytical/quantitative strategies. The borders to other strategies have become blurred, to say the least.

The macro strategy also has a history of betting against central bankers. As Jim Rogers [2000], cofounder of George Soros's Quantum Fund and potentially today's greatest commodities bull on the planet, described his investment philosophy:

"In all my years in investing, there's one rule I've prized beyond every other: Always bet against central banks and with the real world. In the seventies, the central banks were defending the United States' artificially low price of gold. Central banks and governments always try to maintain artificial levels, high or low, whether of a currency, a metal, wool, whatever. When a central bank is defending something—whether it's gold at thirty-five dollars or the lira at eight hundred to the dollar—the smart investor always goes the other way. It may take a while, but I promise you you'll come out ahead. It's a golden rule of investing."

Risk management, we believe, has changed what is generally referred to as *macro*. A decade ago, a macro manager would have considered his personal liquid net wealth as being enough to convince investors that "feeling the pain" with investors was incentive enough to manage risk.

In other words, the "trust me" factor was very high. We believe this has changed. Risk management has improved. Often, an independent (i.e., nonmanager) oversees (with the authority to control) overall group risk. (Just measuring or overseeing risk does not make a lot of sense without the authority to control risk.) This is especially the case with investment managers who are adopting a multi-strategy approach.

Generalizing further, the old school approach was where one lone "gunslinger" drove all the risk. Today, more emphasis is often given to a "multiple-alpha-silo" approach, whereby risk is managed similarly to the proprietary trading desk approach of a large investment bank. This newer approach results in the different trading books having low correlation, resulting in low fund of funds–like portfolio volatilities on a group level.

One reason underlying this low intergroup correlation might be that the multiple-alpha-silo approach allows several players to focus on the same idea (e.g., the flattening of the yield curve), via different time frames and different instruments within the same hedge fund. For example, one trading book might have a more plain vanilla directional approach with a medium-term (e.g., one to three months) outlook. Another book might be earning option premium in the short term by selling the opposite trade, while another has entered into a short-term contingent rate flattener that costs little but provides option-like insurance if the event occurs sooner than the managers of the other trading books expect. Single (silo) managers might have very different core expertise in different areas of the currencies, rates, equities, commodities, and options markets. Therefore, from both a portfolio construction perspective (i.e., fund of funds–like diversification benefit) and an elegance perspective, the individual multisilo risk takers can interact to the extent that their global macro (i.e., directional) trade ideas are expressed and executed in the best, cheapest, and most favorably asymmetrical way.

Some macro hedge funds are more focused on a hybrid of macro and fixed-income relative value. This is evidenced in the number of positions on the books. Typically, the old-school global macro manager had a dozen or less large core positions, while many of the macro/relative-value hybrid managers have hundreds or thousands of small trades, for example, relative-value butterflies, barbells, and basis trades, as well as a few larger directional trades. It goes without saying that risk management is more complex in such a hybrid structure than the old-school position-by-position stop-loss.

Ahl [2001] distinguishes three broad nondistinct approaches of macro managers: feedback-, model-, and information-based approaches. We believe the feedback- and information-based approaches are not just limited to macro.

The Feedback Approach The feedback approach is a behavioral approach. The idea is that markets are economically rational/efficient most of the time, but not always. Occasionally, markets are a couple of standard deviations from the mean due to investors' overreaction based on fear, greed, hysteria, or mania. The investment process focuses on market psychology and sentiment, and has its origins in the futures pits of the 1970s. Risk is normally managed by placing stop-losses on a position-by-position basis.[8]

What sounds like a contradiction in itself is that the feedback approach has an element of mean reversion as well as trend following. The idea is to sell into a bursting bubble (following the trend of a deflating bubble) and buy into, once in motion, the postbubble recovery (mean reversion). In the recent past, a short position in the U.S. dollar against, say, the euro, is an example of trend following, while a long position in exchange-traded funds (ETFs) on Brazilian stock market is an example of postbubble recovery. Trying to guess inflection points is not the major objective.

The Model Approach The model approach is based on the idea that central bankers and governments cause disequilibria in financial markets that can be exploited. Ahl quotes work by Jan Tinbergen,* coholder of the Nobel Prize in economics in 1969, as the origin for searching for market disequilibria. Tinbergen thought that policy makers can target only one economic variable with one instrument. For example, in a free-float currency regime, the central bank can control only short rates, but the exchange rate will often over/undershoot equilibrium. Ahl wrote:

> *"This was a fundamental insight that was effectively capitalized on by these macroeconomic practitioners from the late 1970s onwards. As these traders capitalized on the mistakes made by (predominantly European) politicians and central bankers, the electorate of the countries concerned paid the price."*

Ahl points out the short half-life of the model approach. After a while, commercially successful models, strategies, ideas, concepts, and frameworks are copied by the market: They become public knowledge. A cynical observer would probably argue that even central bankers moved up the learning curve and adapted a more market-oriented approach. (A more balanced observer would note that political Europe solved the problem of erroneous central bankers by getting rid of them altogether, except for one).

---

*Tinbergen [1962] argues that the relative lack of success of economic forecasts may be due to the fact that—other than in physics—economic behavior is not independent of forecasts published. This notion is central to Soros's [1987] reflexivity, which is discussed in more detail in Chapter 5.

The Information Approach The information-based approach is designed to gain an information edge in the marketplace. Information is collected and aggregated on a micro level to form a view of the macro picture. The main reason for focusing on the micro level (company revenues, earnings, balance sheet information, etc.) is that information on the macro level is often lagged as well as being erroneous (and corrected at a later date). The difficulty of collecting information on the micro level is that it is cumbersome (expensive), and the information often eclectic (as opposed to robust) and anecdotal (as opposed to statistically significant). It is for this reason, we believe, that macro is occasionally referred to being more art than science—a kind of alchemy of some sort.

Conclusion Does this section answer whether systematic and discretionary trading deserves a high fee? It is likely that the debate will continue. We believe these disciplines do actually deserve a high fee, as they involve an element of *active risk management.* If an empiricist plays around with some historical time series and then cries "Eureka" and declares that systematic and discretionary trading is all beta and easily replicable, he might convince the myopic. We just do not think the world is that simple. Data, data manipulation skill, and computer power are cheap. Risk management skill with market insight is not. The marketplace seems to have already made up its mind by pricing these two sets of skills accordingly.

ASYMMETRIC RETURNS THROUGH DERIVATIVES

Introduction

One of our claims in this book is that seeking asymmetric-return profiles is the future of active asset management. Note that the adjective *active* is quite important. We also believe ETFs, index funds, total return swaps, and so on have a great future. Investors are unlikely to remain altruistic forever (meaning that investors will continue to evaluate whether a manager adds value or not and they will pay the manager accordingly). So, do we really need an expensive manager to give us an asymmetric-return profile? The answer is no. An asymmetric-return profile is quite easily obtainable through, for example, the use of bonds and options. If an investor wants capital protection, there are also passive alternatives to an active risk manager. Generally, these investment products are summarized under the banner of "structured products." (Belgian dentists, apparently, love them.*)

---

*As do the financial engineers of investment banks around bonus time.

Asymmetric-return profiles can be obtained through a zero-coupon bond–like investment in combination with an option. If these asymmetric-risk/return profiles advocated in this book can be obtained passively, why pay an active fee? There is no need to pay an active fee if the same gross result can be achieved at a lower cost through a passive approach. If the same gross-return profile can be obtained at a lower cost, this means that the net return is higher. In other words, if we pay an active manager large fees we want either a higher return than with a passive alternative with the same risk or we want a lower risk with the same return.

In this section, therefore, we compare fund of hedge fund portfolios, a proxy for active risk management on two levels, the hedge fund level and the fund of fund level, with capital-guaranteed structures. Our conclusion is that active risk managers need not worry anytime soon.

Capital-Guaranteed Structures

Asymmetric returns can be achieved quite easily through the combination of a fixed-income element and options. The simplest example of such a structure is a zero-coupon bond combined with a call option on an equity index. One of the main attractions of such a structure is that the maximal "worst-case" loss at expiry is known in advance. If the zero-coupon bond is structured in such a way that it grows to 100 percent of the initial investment, then the maximal loss is zero; that is, capital is preserved (or guaranteed) at expiry (note that "maximal loss" refers to directional market risk but not credit risk of the issuer or inflation risk). Over time, such structures will have an asymmetric-return profile: In some years or periods the call option will end in-the-money and the investor will have his money back plus some capital gains from the long call option position. In other years or periods, the call option will end out-of-the-money; that is, the investor will get only his initial principal back but no proceeds from the call option (as the option expired worthless).

Before we compare these passive alternatives with what we believe is active risk management, we describe four simulated capital-guaranteed structures with one-year maturity. (Note that these capital-guaranteed structures can have substantially longer maturities than one year. We have chosen a one-year structure for presentation purposes, that is, to show the short-term capital preservation characteristics as opposed to just longer-term capital preservation.)

Two structures were based on the S&P 500 index (SPX), while the other two structures are on the TOPIX (TPX), the broad Tokyo stock exchange index. We have simulated two different types of structured products. One guarantees 100 percent of capital at maturity, while the other guarantees only 90 percent. The main variables of these structures are price and volatility of the underlying index and level of interest rates. The price of the index is obvious; the higher the appreciation, the more valuable the call option will become toward maturity, that is, the higher the return of the structure. The volatility determines how many options can be bought; that is, if volatility is low, more options can be bought. The more options purchased, the higher the participation on the appreciation of the index. Interest rates determine the discount of the zero-coupon bond. If interest rates are high, the discount is larger, which means there is more money left for the purchase of call options.

So the best case is high interest rates and low implied volatility at the time of purchase and then a booming stock market. In this case, the zero-coupon bond will be far below par and rise to 100 percent of principal over the maturity. The options, of which there are many because the discount is large and volatility is low, will explode as we have assumed a booming stock market resulting in a high payout from the call option.

Figure 3.8 shows the two underlying indices, SPX and TPX, for the 16-year period from 1990 to 2005 as well as the two 100 percent and 90 percent capital-guaranteed structures. We priced the capital-guaranteed structures at the beginning of every year and calculated month-end values. We then combined the 16 one-year structures to get a time series showing an investor's performance of entering such a structure at the beginning of every calendar year. The CARR of all six investments is shown in the graph. The average risk-free rate for the whole period was 4.5 percent and 1.8 percent for the one-year USD and one-year Japanese yen (JPY) rate, respectively. We have applied a log scale to the y-axis for presentation purposes.

There are several observations from Figure 3.8. The first and most obvious is that U.S. investors investing locally did better in terms of absolute returns than Japanese investors investing in their local stock market over the past 16 years irrespective of whether through long-only instruments or asymmetric structures using options. Depending on one's worldview, one could argue the former were somewhat lucky whereas the latter were—well—not. European investors were somewhere in between these two extremes. The lesson from this graph (and many others to follow in Chapter 9) is fairly simple: Markets can go up as well as down, not only in the short term, but also in the long term.

The second observation is about relative returns. In the U.S. example the long-only strategy (no risk management and therefore lower fees) outperformed the two asymmetric structures, while in the Japanese example the two capital-guaranteed structures outperformed the long-only investment. Note that this is intuitively what one would expect. A capital-guaranteed structure could be viewed as getting exposure to the stock market with an insurance policy. An insurance policy costs money. If the market performs,

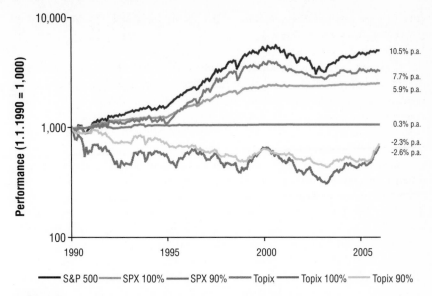

FIGURE 3.8 Comparison of Capital-Guaranteed Structures
Notes: Equity indices are total return indices. All returns are in local currency. The
zero-coupon bond (ZCB) is based on the one-year rates minus 15 basis points. Call
option was priced at-the-money based on historical volatility plus 20 basis points.
Historical volatility was based on a GARCH model that was calibrated to match
one-year SPX implied volatility from 1994 to 2005 (based on data availability.)
Source: Author's own calculations, data from Thomson Financial.

the performance is narrowed through the insurance expense. If the market
tanks, the insurance kicks in and the structured product outperforms the
long-only alternative. What is actually quite funny is that some investors
who opt for a guaranteed product are disappointed when it underperforms
(in a bull market, relative performance matters) and often go for a structure
without a guarantee in the next investment period, that is, essentially after a
market rally. The logic of these investors is similar to blaming the insurance
company, from whom they bought life insurance, for not dying prematurely.

One of the claims in this book is that it is possible for skilled investors to
reduce the cost of the aforementioned insurance premium. In other words,
get exposure to the upside but use active risk management to cap or control
the downside. Value is added if this can be obtained cheaper than through
a zero and call structure or a long-only vehicle with a put option. The
investment field for finding opportunities where capital can be put at risk
where risk is in an attractive relation to expected return is broad. It is

certainly not limited to the stock market. Bookstaber [2003] commented on the size of the opportunity set:

> *"The universe of alternative investments is just that—the universe. It encompasses all possible investment vehicles and all possible investment strategies minus the 'traditional' investment funds and vehicles."*

In the following example we contrast a long-only strategy (i.e., symmetrical return distribution) with both a passive and some active strategies, where asymmetric returns are the main objective. The results are summarized in Table 3.4. For the long-only strategies, we have chosen the S&P 500 index and the TOPIX index representing the U.S. and Japanese stock markets. Note that these two stock markets were the top two markets in 1990 in terms of market capitalization and had widely differing performances over the past 16 years. The observation period was from January 1990 to December 2005, determined by availability of data.

For the passive asymmetric-return strategy, we have simulated a zero-coupon bond plus call structure as outlined before. For the active asymmetric-return strategy we have chosen four hedge fund indices from Hedge Fund Research Inc. (HFRI), that is, fund of funds, macro, equity hedge (long/short managers with average low net exposure), and equity market neutral.

Many investors get excited by examining tables such as Table 3.4 showing long-term returns of hedge fund indices. Their excitement is based on the relatively high historical figures for CARR. There are many reasons for getting excited. Historical returns of hedge fund indices are not among them. Note that there is one row showing returns and several rows giving some information on risk. We believe this is a healthy relationship. (We even would not rule out the possibility that investors would be better served if historical returns were not shown at all. This would tilt the decision-making process away from [historical] returns to examining risk in a forward-looking fashion, that is, reason.) It is information on risk, not information about past returns, that might tell us something about the future. The 17.2 percent return of the Equity Hedge index is, apart from being upwardly biased by a couple of hundred basis points and not being investable for most investors, arguably high but potentially (or actually most likely) not sustainable. However, a volatility of 8.7 percent for a diversified portfolio of long/short managers is a reasonable assumption of the past, was experienced by most investors who were diversified, that is, was and is investable, and—most importantly—is a reasonable assumption and guide for the future. (However, there is variation in hedge fund portfolio volatility.

TABLE 3.4 Symmetric- versus Asymmetric-Return Profile (1990 to 2005)

	Symmetrical		Asymmetrical							
	SPX	TPX	SPX 100%	SPX 90%	TPX 100%	TPX 90%	FoHF	Macro	Equity Hedge	Market Neutral
CARR (%)	10.5	-2.6	5.9	7.7	0.3	-2.3	10.0	15.7	17.2	9.2
Average risk-free rate	4.5	1.8	4.5	4.5	1.8	1.8	4.5	4.5	4.5	4.5
Volatility (%)	14.4	20.4	4.8	13.3	2.1	10.8	5.5	8.1	8.7	3.1
Sharpe ratio	0.42	<0	0.30	0.24	<0	<0	1.00	1.38	1.46	1.51
Upside volatility (%)	8.1	12.2	3.8	8.9	1.6	7.6	3.9	6.4	6.2	2.5
Downside volatility (%)	10.3	13.4	3.2	8.5	2.3	7.3	4.2	4.5	4.9	1.7
Sortino ratio	0.59	<0	0.45	0.38	<0	<0	1.29	2.50	2.58	2.78
Max 1M drawdown (%)	-14.5	-20.2	-5.2	-14.9	-3.7	-13.9	-7.5	-6.4	-7.6	-1.7
Max 12M drawdown (%)	-26.6	-39.4	-3.0	-18.8	-5.4	-22.7	-6.6	-7.1	-8.3	-0.2
Max drawdown (%)	-44.7	-69.4	-5.4	-30.7	-5.4	-56.5	-13.1	-10.7	-10.3	-2.7
Recovery (months)	n.a.*	n.a.*	4	n.a.*	14	n.a.*	13	16	11	4
Rank Sharpe ratio	5	8	6	7	10	9	4	3	2	1
Rank Sortino ratio	5	8	6	7	10	9	4	3	2	1
Rank Max drawdown	8	10	3	7	2	9	6	5	4	1
Skew	-0.6	-0.2	0.2	-0.1	-0.6	0.0	-0.4	0.3	0.1	0.1
Excess kurtosis	1.1	1.0	2.5	1.7	13.2	3.2	4.8	0.6	1.4	0.4

CARR = compound annual rate of return. All returns in USD, except TPX. The zero-coupon bond (ZCB) is based on the one-year risk-free rate minus 15 basis points. Call option was priced at-the-money based on historical volatility plus 20 basis points and based on historical dividend yield. The HFRI indices are net of fees. All risk statistics are based on log returns, except the three drawdown statistics.
*As of December 2005, not yet recovered from lows.
Source: Author's own calculations; data from Bloomberg and Thomson Financial.

Twenty years ago, a typical fund of funds would have had a volatility of around 15 percent or higher, as the hedge fund industry at the time was by far not as heterogeneous as it is today.) In addition, the 8.7 percent figure is explainable through fairly low correlation for differing strategies in equity space and could be sustainable through many investment cycles to come. Let's have a look at some of the risk variables in more detail.

The capital-guaranteed structure did well: equity-like returns with bond-like volatility. Although it is interesting to see which strategy did well over the chosen observation period, it is not that relevant for the discussion of fees and risk management. Chances are that going forward, the return figures are going to be either different or materially different from the ones above anyway.

The lowest-volatility strategies were those in which 100 percent of capital was guaranteed. Interim drawdowns were all single digit. Recovery from interim losses was swift. Overall, the two 100 percent structures have similar risk statistics to a market-neutral strategy. We believe the difference between a 100 percent capital-guaranteed structure and a market-neutral strategy is that the former is passive and the latter active. While the risk statistics of the two might be similar, the Sharpe ratio or any other measure for risk-adjusted returns is much higher with the market-neutral strategy. The advantage of active risk management, therefore, is that the investor does not pay the insurance or option premium. The option premium is, one could argue, the alpha, that is, the value added by the manager net of fees. The advantage of the capital-guaranteed strategy is that it has an expiry date; that is, there is a date on which we can be confident that any potential losses will have recovered. In active risk management we do not have an expiry date. The degree of confidence in loss recovery can be very high but not as high as with capital-guaranteed structures.

Another interesting take-away from Table 3.4 is the three rows that show the ranking of three different measures, the Sharpe ratio, the Sortino ratio, and the maximal drawdown. (The Sharpe ratio divides the excess portfolio return over T-bills by the standard deviation of *all* returns, while the Sortino ratio has the standard deviation of *negative* returns or returns below a certain threshold in the denominator.) The ranking between the Sharpe ratio and the Sortino ratio is identical. The reason we find this interesting is that sometimes there is much debate as to which ratio or risk measure is better than others. However, if we then rank results, we often find that the difference is nil or indeed very small. So perhaps the Sortino ratio is a better ratio for our purposes of asymmetric returns than the Sharpe ratio, but (from a practitioner's point of view) who cares? They both rank the 10 strategies identically. The maximal drawdown statistic differs in the ranking, as it does not have a return statistic in the numerator. The maximal drawdown statistic ranks the market-neutral strategy first, and the 100 percent capital-guaranteed structures second (both having a maximum drawdown of −5.4 percent). However, the maximal drawdown is not a measure for risk-adjusted returns, just a measure for risk.

The two capital-guaranteed structures wherein 90 percent of capital is guaranteed are much more volatile. Volatilities were double digit and therefore much higher than with actively managed asymmetries. Drawdowns can be as large as with long-only portfolios. The reason is that we assumed one-year structures. If the underlying index falls a couple of years in a row, the maximal drawdown will be close to the number of years times the −10 percent loss tolerance, as shown in Table 3.5. The table shows calendar-year returns for the two underlying indices, the four simulations, and the four hedge fund indices. We have applied a color code for annual losses larger than −5 percent, −10 percent, and −15 percent.

Table 3.5 highlights some of the issues with capital-guaranteed structures in the past couple of years. Interest rates have been low. This means the zero-coupon bond is priced with only a small discount to par. This means

TABLE 3.5 Calendar-Year Returns (1990 to 2005)

(%)	Symmetrical		Asymmetrical							
	SPX	TPX	SPX 100%	SPX 90%	TPX 100%	TPX 90%	FoHF	Macro	Equity Hedge	Market Neutral
1990	-3.1	-39.4	0.0	-10.0	0.0	-10.0	17.5	12.6	14.4	15.5
1991	30.5	-0.4	15.4	28.5	0.0	-10.0	14.5	46.7	40.1	15.6
1992	7.6	-23.0	2.4	-1.7	0.0	-10.0	12.3	27.2	21.3	8.7
1993	10.1	11.0	4.3	6.7	2.6	0.1	26.3	53.3	27.9	11.1
1994	1.3	9.1	0.0	-10.0	1.4	-0.6	-3.5	-4.3	2.6	2.7
1995	37.6	2.1	23.4	46.5	0.4	-8.0	11.1	29.3	31.0	16.3
1996	23.0	-6.1	14.1	32.2	0.0	-10.0	14.4	9.3	21.8	14.2
1997	33.4	-19.4	15.6	34.7	0.0	-10.0	18.0	18.8	23.4	13.6
1998	28.6	-6.6	11.9	24.1	0.0	-10.0	-5.1	6.2	16.0	8.3
1999	21.0	59.7	6.6	11.5	0.6	29.3	26.5	17.6	44.2	7.1
2000	-9.1	-25.0	0.0	-10.0	0.0	-10.0	4.1	2.0	9.1	14.6
2001	-11.9	-18.9	0.0	-10.0	0.0	-10.0	2.8	6.9	0.4	6.7
2002	-22.1	-17.5	0.0	-10.0	0.0	-10.0	1.0	7.4	-4.7	1.0
2003	28.7	25.2	2.6	14.9	0.0	10.4	11.6	21.4	20.5	2.5
2004	10.9	11.3	1.4	3.9	0.0	0.6	6.9	4.6	7.7	4.2
2005	4.9	45.2	1.2	-4.0	0.0	36.4	7.3	6.9	10.7	6.6
CARR	10.5	-2.6	5.9	7.7	0.3	-2.3	10.0	15.7	17.2	9.2
Average	12.0	0.5	6.2	9.2	0.3	-1.4	10.4	16.6	17.9	9.3
Wealth start	100	100	100	100	100	100	100	100	100	100
Wealth end	498	66	252	329	105	69	459	1,028	1,261	407

Source: Author's own calculations; data from Bloomberg and Thomson Financial.

that fewer options could be purchased. Participation of such a structure from 2003 to 2005 in the SPX, for example, shows paltry returns when compared to the index. An even more extreme example is a capital-guaranteed structure on the TPX in 2005. With rates hovering around nil, there is no participation. Note that financial engineers have come up with ways to add other types of risk to the structure that, potentially, could increase returns.

Figure 3.9 shows the risk/return profiles of the 10 strategies, from January 1990 to December 2005. We have added capital market lines starting at the risk-free rate for both currencies. The idea of the capital market line is to show portfolio combinations with the same Sharpe ratio. Typically, in the long term, the capital market line should be upwardly sloped as investors expect more return for taking more risk. (Note here again that long term really means long term. We need to go far back for

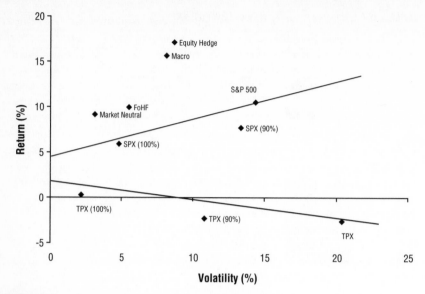

FIGURE 3.9   Risk/Return Comparison (1990 to 2005)
Source: Author's calculations, data from Bloomberg and Thomson Financial.

Japan to have an upwardly sloped capital market line.) In other words, by combining the risky asset class (in this case equities), the investor can move up and down the capital market line by either including cash (reducing expected return and volatility) or levering up (increasing expected return and volatility). We believe creating portfolios on this line cannot be considered active risk management. Reducing risk and return symmetrically is passive.

Note that all four capital-guaranteed structures are below their capital market line. These portfolios are less efficient than simple combinations of equity exposure and cash to reduce portfolio volatility. This is what we intuitively would expect as we buy insurance and know from intuition as well as experience that the investment banks offering these structures are not driven by altruism alone. What the graph does not show, though, is the utility of the investor. An investor might not just want to reduce volatility and stay on the capital market line. This investor could have great utility from knowing that 100 percent or 90 percent of principal is guaranteed at a certain time in the future. The value of the capital-guarantee feature to such an investor is outside crude analysis of return and risk, of which volatility is only a proxy. So whether these structures are overpriced or not is beside the point. They can still very much be value for money to the end investor, depending on his individual risk tolerances and preferences.

So the difference between capital-guaranteed structures and hedge fund portfolios is the difference between passive and active risk management. In active risk management the idea is to create this asymmetry, that is, move above the capital market line through active risk management. This means either more return with given risk, or lower risk with given expected return. This creates a new "capital market line" (which is not really a capital market line because it is not offered by the market but by something active, i.e., alpha). This new line also allows the investor to slide upward (more return, more risk) by levering up and downward by combining strategy with cash.

Equity hedge had equity-like (cumulative) returns during the bull market and was more or less flat in the aftermath of the bull market. Critics of the strategy argue that the strategy is unattractive because the correlation of long-short managers with the stock market is high. Figure 3.10 underlines the argument that this is literally only half the story. Often, long/short managers have equity-like returns when equities go up, and flattish or moderately positive or negative returns when equity markets fall. This is unlikely to be just a coincidence. We believe it is rather about actively assessing the opportunity set and putting capital at risk accordingly. When the broad market is falling, there are still sectors or styles that are increasing relative to

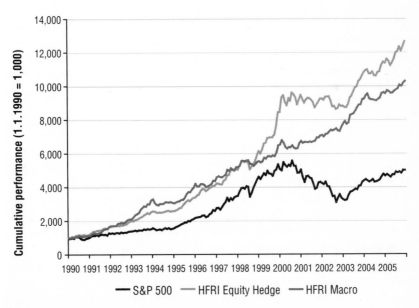

FIGURE 3.10 Cumulative Performance Long-Only versus Long-Short and Macro
Source: Bloomberg, Thomson Financial.

other sectors and styles or the broad market. These allocation decisions are active decisions. Trying to explain away the value added by arguing that the returns are correlated with the S&P 500 index is terribly naïve. The result of successfully trying to find the various asymmetries is obvious: higher compounding of capital in the longer term with lower downside volatility in the short term. Brunnermeier and Nagel [2003] add some credibility to this notion. They examined hedge fund behavior during the technology bubble. Their findings are that (1) many hedge funds were riding the bubble, not attacking it; (2) hedge funds reduced exposure before prices collapsed; and (3) their holdings outperformed characteristics-matched benchmarks. The authors highlight that their findings are inconsistent with the efficient market's view of rational speculation, but are consistent with models in which rational investors can find it optimal to ride bubbles because of predictable investor sentiment and limits to arbitrage. (In addition, they note that friction, such as short-sales constraints, do not appear to be sufficient to explain why the presence of sophisticated investors failed to contain the bubble.) We believe being predictable in secondary markets causes one to be on the wrong side of the alpha-generation process. It's potentially like bleeding in a shark pond: pretty hazardous and detrimental for long-term financial health.

We previously noted that macro is becoming more diversified by adopting a multi-strategy approach and, potentially, becoming a competitive force to fund of funds. The volatility of a diversified portfolio of macro managers has become less volatile over the past couple of years. While we would expect the dispersion of macro managers to be much wider than the dispersion of fund of funds managers, one could argue that the extremely low correlation among macro managers results in diversified portfolios of macro managers being not much more volatile than diversified portfolios of fund of funds. Low correlation among macro managers results in low volatility on a portfolio level. The reasons for low correlation among managers is, we believe, due to the high manager flexibility, that is, the absence of a market benchmark or any other idea the overall group could hug.

Those investors who do not invest in macro do so in the belief that the expected return of the speculator is negative. If the investor's expected return is negative, then other factors such as correlation to the rest of the portfolio are irrelevant. Investing and speculation are often compared to gambling. Those investors who shun directional strategies such as macro and CTA will (apart from having a bias to short-volatility strategies and therefore being stronger exposed to autumn 1998–type risk) compare the speculator with the slot machine user and relative-value managers with the slot machine owner.* Those investors who are open to some (essentially anti-EMH) directional strategies will probably agree more with Larry Summers, who in 1985 compared financial economists with "ketchup economists" obsessed with the relative prices of different-sized bottles of ketchup:

> "... *financial economists, like ketchupal economists ... are concerned with the interrelationships between the prices of different financial assets. They ignore what seems to many to be the more important question of what determines the overall level of asset prices.*"[9]

Combining those who seek relative value and those who seek mispriced value can result in reducing portfolio volatility. In the face of uncertainty, we recommend favoring an open and flexible approach to matters unknown or untestable, as opposed to a dogmatic and inflexible approach. This recommendation is built on our claim that risk management is as much a thought process (craft) as it is pure adherence to proven beliefs (science).

The main difference among symmetric- and asymmetric-return profiles is visible in the 12-month drawdowns (see Table 3.4 on page 97). The magnitude of drawdowns of all asymmetric-return profiles is a fraction of outright exposure to equities. If investors experience exponentially increasing disutility from the magnitude of drawdowns (and the state of the pension fund industry in some countries and the European insurance sector around 2002 suggests that this might be the case), the solution is to aim for asymmetric returns. (By "solution" we mean long-term solution as opposed to short-term solution.) The absolute-return approach results in asymmetric returns. The ultimate irony of all this is that in the halls of some regulators and pension funds, derivatives as well as hedge funds are still perceived as high-risk investments. (In 2002 some insurance companies were forced sellers of stocks for actuarial reasons, causing prices to free fall. Interestingly, they went on the record blaming hedge funds for falling stock prices.)

Figure 3.11 shows the annual returns of the S&P 500 (symmetrical returns), the 100 percent capital-guaranteed example on the S&P 500, and the HFRI Fund of Funds Composite Index (FoHF). The graph shows that over the past six years the return from a capital-guaranteed structure was paltry, either because the underlying index was negative for the year or because low interest rates resulted in a very low participation rate.

---

*Donald Trump on slot machines: "People think I'm a gambler. I've never gambled in my life. To me, a gambler is someone who plays slot machines. I prefer to own slot machines."

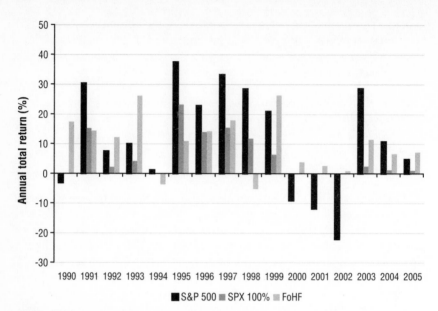

FIGURE 3.11 Annual Returns (1990 to 2005)
Source: Author's own calculations; data from Bloomberg and Thomson Financial.

Figure 3.12 shows the relationship between interest rates and equity participation of the capital-guaranteed structure. The chart shows that the equity participation rate is primarily a function of interest rates at the beginning of every calendar year in the observation period (and, though to a lesser extent, implied volatility). If interest rates are high, there is more capital available to buy upside volatility, that is, equity participation through long option positions. Participation was highest in 1994 to 1996 when interest rates were high and implied volatility low.

Figure 3.11 illustrates how the symmetric strategy and the passive (guarantee) and active (FoHF) strategies have performed in the past. Due to an unfortunate lack of market directional foresight, we do not know what these bars will look like over the next 10 years. What we do strongly suspect, though, is that asymmetric returns are superior to symmetric returns if disutility to losses is large. This could change the financial industry materially, because it means that financial products cannot be sold (or it will be more difficult) on the premise (and promise) that everything will be fine in the long term. The idea of asymmetric returns is based on the idea that interim volatility matters, too. As John Maynard Keynes put it, "In the long run we are all dead."

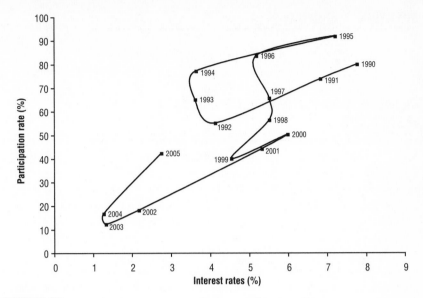

FIGURE 3.12   Equity Participation as a Function of Interest Rates
Based on one-year structure on S&P 500 with 100 percent of principal guaranteed.
Source: Author's own calculations; data from Bloomberg and Thomson Financial.

CHAPTER SUMMARY AND CONCLUSIONS

Delivering absolute returns to investors on a sustainable basis is difficult. It requires active risk management. Active risk management is an entirely different value proposition than that offered by traditional benchmark-linked long-only investment products. Structured products offer asymmetric-return profiles that suit the loss-aversion properties of investors. However, the cost of these products narrows returns significantly. There is no alpha in those products. They typically lie below the capital market line, not above. The idea of creating asymmetric-return profiles through active risk management should result in an efficiency improvement *and* a preferable risk/return payout. We believe these improvements to be alpha, as they are not available through passive strategies.

It seems that successful risk management in an ever-changing environment is like shooting at a moving target: It is difficult and improves with practice. This means experience matters. Running an enterprise successfully over a long period of time requires a huge—and even more importantly, a highly adaptive—set of skills. Luck is likely to be only one of the factors driving entrepreneurial success. It is, in our view, unlikely that successful risk management will trade at a discount anytime soon.

APPENDIX: AGGREGATE FEES

"There ain't no nice guys in big business."
                                                                    —Carl Icahn

A COMPARISON: MUTUAL FUNDS VERSUS
HEDGE FUNDS

The following estimates of aggregate fee income for the traditional asset management industry and the hedge fund industry were published in the appendix of Ineichen [2005]. While all our firepower was in the main section, that is, absolute-return investment philosophy, asymmetric-return profiles, manager adaptability under uncertainty, and so on, the one section that was heavily quoted in the financial press was the part in the appendix on fees. Motivation for this back-of-the-envelope calculation was a notion in the press that hedge funds now have surpassed the traditional asset management industry in terms of aggregate fees they charge their investors. This is obviously very interesting, as the hedge fund industry is a fraction of the U.S. mutual fund industry (then around $7 trillion)* or the global long-only industry (around $16 trillion).

Table 3.6 shows a wild estimate of aggregate fees generated by the hedge fund industry. The last line is essentially the gross margin for the whole industry (i.e., single hedge funds as well as fund of funds).

- Based on our rather crude assumptions, the hedge funds industry generated fees of around $46.3 billion in 2004 and $55.2 billion in 2005.
- Profitability (last row in the table) over the past 15 years was high, ranging from 2.1 percent of assets under management to 11.0 percent.
- According to Hedge Fund Intelligence, the hedge fund industry was not $1 trillion in terms of assets under management but $1.5 trillion in Q1 2006, of which $1 trillion was managed out of the United States ($375 billion in Europe and $125 in Asia). If we apply the 5.7 percent margin from Table 3.6 to the $1 trillion of hedge fund assets managed in the United States, the revenues could be around $57 billion in the United States alone.

---

*According to ICI (Investment Company Institute, www.ici.org) the U.S. mutual fund industry surpassed USD9 trillion in January 2006: USD5.2 trillion in stock funds, USD0.58 trillion in hybrid funds, USD1.03 trillion in taxable bond funds, USD0.34 trillion in municipal bond funds, USD1.7 trillion in taxable money market funds, and USD0.34 trillion in tax-free money market funds.

TABLE 3.6 Estimate of Aggregate Fees in the Hedge Funds Industry

USDbn	1991	1992	1993	1994	1995	1996	1997	1998	1999	2000	2001	2002	2003	2004	2005
Single hedge funds:															
HF AuM at beginning of year[1]	38.9	58.4	95.7	167.8	167.4	185.8	256.7	367.6	374.8	456.4	490.6	539.1	625.6	820.0	972.6
Net HF returns[2]	32.2	21.2	30.9	4.1	21.5	21.1	16.8	2.6	31.3	5.0	4.6	-1.4	19.6	9.0	9.2
Gross HF return[3]	41.5	27.8	39.8	6.4	28.1	27.6	22.2	4.5	40.4	7.5	7.0	0.1	28.1	14.1	14.3
Management fee[3]	0.4	0.6	1.0	1.7	1.7	1.9	2.6	3.7	3.7	4.6	4.9	8.1	9.4	12.3	14.6
Performance fee (no hurdle)[3]	3.2	3.2	7.6	2.1	9.4	10.3	11.4	3.3	30.3	6.8	6.9	0.1	43.9	28.8	34.8
Total HF fees[4]	3.6	3.8	8.6	3.8	11.1	12.1	14.0	7.0	34.0	11.4	11.8	8.2	53.3	41.1	49.4
Fund of hedge funds:															
FoHF AuM at beginning of year[1]	19.9	36.8	75.4	74.6	56.3	52.5	74.0	75.8	76.1	83.5	102.5	206.9	293.3	358.6	394.6
Net FoHF returns[5]	14.5	12.3	26.3	-3.5	11.1	14.4	18.0	-5.1	26.5	4.1	2.8	1.0	11.6	6.9	7.5
Gross FoHF returns[6]	17.2	14.8	30.4	-2.8	13.4	17.1	21.1	-4.6	30.5	5.6	4.2	2.2	14.0	8.7	9.5
Management fee of 1.0%	0.2	0.4	0.8	0.7	0.6	0.5	0.7	0.8	0.8	0.8	1.0	2.1	2.9	3.6	3.9
Performance fee of 5% (no hurdle)	0.2	0.3	1.1	0.0	0.4	0.4	0.8	0.0	1.2	0.2	0.2	0.2	2.1	1.6	1.9
Total FoHF fees[4]	0.4	0.6	1.9	0.7	0.9	1.0	1.5	0.8	1.9	1.1	1.2	2.3	5.0	5.2	5.8
Whole hedge funds industry:															
Total Fees[7]	4.0	4.5	10.5	4.6	12.0	13.1	15.5	7.8	35.9	12.5	13.0	10.5	58.3	46.3	55.2
Percentage of HF AuM	10.2%	7.7%	11.0%	2.7%	7.2%	7.0%	6.0%	2.1%	9.6%	2.7%	2.7%	2.0%	9.3%	5.6%	5.7%

[1] Based on year-end estimates from Hedge Fund Research for preceding year.
[2] Based on HFRI Fund Weighted Composite Index.
[3] Assuming 1 + 20 until 2001 and 1.5 + 25 from 2002 onward.
[4] Ignoring high-water mark, that is, 1995 and 1999 probably overstated.
[5] Based on HFRI Fund of Funds Composite Index.
[6] Assuming 1 + 10.
[7] Sum of fees generated by HF and FoHF.
Source: Updated from Ineichen [2005].

Profitability is not a function of randomness but, at least to some extent, the stock market. Figure 3.13 puts our crude estimate for the hedge fund industry's profitability (last line in Table 3.6) in relation to stock market performance. Profitability, not too surprisingly, is below average when equity markets free fall (2000 to 2002) or hedge funds free fall (1994 and 1998).

How does the $55.2 billion figure for hedge funds revenues in 2005 compare with that for the traditional asset management industry? *The Economist* (February 19, 2005) quotes research suggesting that the hedge funds industry is a sixth of the mutual fund industry (probably comparing global hedge funds with U.S. mutual funds), while generating more revenues.

We find aggregate global data on the asset management industry notoriously difficult to come by. In Table 3.7 we try to estimate aggregate fees in the traditional asset management industry (active and passive) as a function of assets under management and average profit margin.

- If we assume the U.S. mutual fund industry to be around $9 trillion and the average management fee to be 40 basis points, the aggregate gross

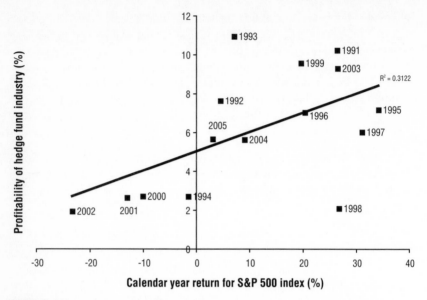

FIGURE 3.13 Hedge Fund Industry Profitability in Relation to Equity Market
Source: Updated from Ineichen [2005].

TABLE 3.7 Estimated Revenues from Traditional Asset Management

($bn)	Assets under Management in Mutual Funds (USDtr)						
Margin	7	8	9	10	12	14	16
0.20%	14	16	18	20	24	28	32
0.40%	28	32	36	40	48	56	64
0.60%	42	48	54	60	72	84	96
0.80%	56	64	72	80	96	112	128
1.00%	70	80	90	100	120	140	160
1.20%	84	96	108	120	144	168	192

Source: Updated from Ineichen [2005].

fee income would be (simplifying to the extreme) around $36 billion. In
other words, it is not entirely unthinkable that the global hedge funds
industry is generating more fees than the much larger U.S. mutual fund
industry. Depending on which base and which margin assumption we
use, it is conceivable that the U.S. absolute-return industry is generating
more fees than the U.S. mutual fund industry, which is at least nine
times larger.

- Based on our estimate of aggregate assets under management in global long-only active and passive asset management of $16 trillion, and an assumed average gross margin of 60 basis points, the revenues of the traditional asset management industry amount to around $96 billion, which is higher than the $55.2 billion of the $1.3 trillion global hedge funds industry. The matrix in Table 3.7 allows assessment of fee level in U.S. or global mutual fund industry with different assumptions for assets under management and gross margin.

Judging by these figures, it seems to us that the marketplace has already priced active risk management and asymmetric returns at a much higher rate. It looks as if we should have spent more time at the beach instead of writing a book.

CHAPTER 4

Fireflies before the Storm

"Man had always assumed that he was more intelligent than dolphins because he had achieved so much ... the wheel, New York, wars, and so on, whilst all the dolphins had ever done was muck about in the water having a good time. But conversely the dolphins believed themselves to be more intelligent than man for precisely the same reasons."

—Douglas Adams*

Why, we ask, is the financial industry in such a mess? By "mess" we refer to the fact that so many chief information officers (CIOs) of insurance companies in Europe went into early retirement following the bursting of the bubble. By "mess" we refer to the fact that many pension funds had their surpluses wiped out within a brief period of time—surpluses that, we might add, it had taken them many years to build. By "mess" we also refer to the extreme dispersion of ideas and beliefs in the financial industry today. We believe the bursting of the dot-com bubble caused a change in risk perception with a large array of investors (as mentioned in Chapter 1). The change in risk perception was the catalyst for new ideas and business models surfacing and replacing old ideas and business models. However, in the current period of transition from old to new, there is friction, that is,

---

*Rephrased: "Institutional investors, consultants, and analysts had always assumed that they were more intelligent than absolute-return investors because they achieved so much ... benchmarks, tracking errors, performance attribution analysis, and so on, whilst all the absolute-return investors had ever done was muck about making money. But, conversely, the absolute-return investors believed themselves to be more intelligent than institutional investors, consultants, and analysts for precisely the same reasons."

it is intellectually somewhat a "mess." A transition of large magnitude and implication takes years. Or as John Maynard Keynes put it:

> *"The difficulty lies, not in the new ideas, but in escaping the old ones, which ramify, for those brought up as most of us have been, into every corner of our minds."*

RISK, RETURNS, AND MARKET EFFICIENCY

Active versus Passive Asset Management

Here is an attempt to clarify or even explain the situation. The key factor, we believe, is the great influence that modern portfolio theory (MPT) has had on how most present market participants think about risk. One of the pillars of MPT is the efficient market hypothesis (EMH)* or its twin brother, the idea that security prices follow a "random walk"—a pattern of random movement similar to molecules colliding with one another as they move in space.

Given the sheer complexity of the market, the dynamic interplay of numerous price drivers, and the reflexive relationship between cause and effect (i.e., the feedback loops), we have no doubt that it is very difficult (and perhaps even impossible) to forecast the market in a persistent fashion. And we might note that, during the bear market, the number of investment professionals who point-forecast markets 12 months hence without giving a hint to the probability distribution certainly decreased dramatically. The same concept of randomness is occasionally used to explain the success of certain "star" managers. If markets are not predictable, the logic goes, then the success of these managers must be a function of randomness. In other words, those successful investors just got lucky. So Warren Buffett, for instance, is just one of the lucky outliers on the right-hand side of a distribution of investors who started out in the 1950s. It is an extreme form of survivorship bias where only the random winners are visible and the losers exit the game. We believe this point of view simply denies that there is such a thing as a good investor.

The different outcomes—success or failure—are just different points on the probability distribution of possible outcomes where any particular

---

*Note that we do not believe that anyone seriously believes in the strong form of EMH. Perfectly efficient markets are an impossibility, as demonstrated by Grossman [1976] and Grossman and Stiglitz [1980] more than 20 years ago. If markets were fully efficient, no one would bother to gather information, which in turn means market prices would not reflect all information. The debate is only whether the inefficiencies are large enough to reward those who try to exploit them. We will address EMH in the next chapter in more detail.

individual falls in this distribution is random, that is, just a matter of luck. In this view, investing is something like flipping coins.* And we agree that if there were a national coin-flipping contest, there would be a couple of winners in the end due to pure randomness. Who exactly wins would indeed be a matter of luck. But to this we reply: True but who cares? It is the wrong analogy. A better analogy is a national chess tournament. The outcome of a chess tournament is not a function of randomness but mainly skill, here loosely defined as practice, experience, intelligence, talent, and so on. We potentially could narrow down the high-probability winners of a national chess tournament with 270 million contenders down to two or three dozen individuals. With coin flippers this is impossible.

The leap from the "random walk" theory to the conclusion that successful investing is simply a matter of luck is, we believe, totally wrong. (Vendors of index funds, occasionally camouflaged as academics, will most certainly disagree.) To the contrary, we believe that the common denominator of successful investing is not luck (though, of course, it helps) but an entrepreneurial mind-set, in general, and risk management skill, in particular (as adapting to *change* seems important for short-term as well as long-term financial health). If change is part of the game, then adaptability and the flexibility to allow for it becomes obvious. The consequence of ignoring change is probably most evident in competitive sports, where blindly following convention can result in embarrassing results. The invention of the curveball changed the face of baseball; the topspin changed the face of tennis; and the forward pass changed American football, not to mention what it did to those refusing to adopt it. The world of investments is not immune to this concept. In fact, we would argue that active investment management is dependent on the willingness to embrace change and, more importantly, to capitalize on it. In this business, adaptability is the key to longevity. As H.G. Wells put it: "Adapt or perish, now as ever, is nature's inexorable imperative."[1]

Figure 4.1 is an intuitively appealing way to illustrate active versus passive asset management. Generally, we talk about alpha and beta or the bifurcation between the two. However, there is obviously a huge gray zone between the two extremes. The most passive form of asset management is indexing where the tracking error is managed to be zero, that is, no variation from the market benchmark. The return is entirely explained by the market. Then moving to the left is enhanced indexing, which is indexing with an active overlay. Moving further to the left comes benchmarking, that is, what is largely the traditional active asset management industry. However, there

---

*The proverbial national coin-flipping contest is often used as an example to demonstrate that due to pure randomness it is possible to get some highly superior coin flippers (managers).

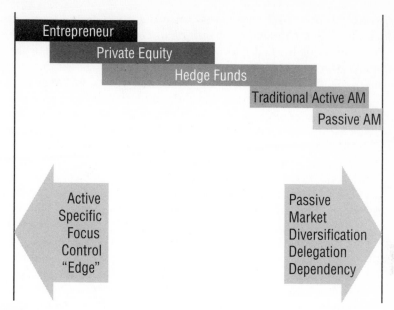

FIGURE 4.1 Active versus Passive Asset Management (AM)
Source: Rolf Banz, Pictet Asset Management.

is a huge overlap between these disciplines. There are long-only managers with very tight tracking error risk budgets and those with very concentrated portfolios and the flexibility to move large parts of the portfolio into cash, if need be. Then further to the left come hedge funds, then private equity. The other extreme is the entrepreneur setting up a shop from scratch. This is still the best way to leverage (and then later monetize) one's edge. It is purely active, specific, and focused. Note that there is overlap between, for example, private equity and hedge funds, as the two disciplines share some common features. In addition, hedge funds have become active in private-equity space and vice versa. Hedge funds overlap with entrepreneur as well as traditional active asset management. A hedge fund start-up is quite often an entrepreneur/investor with (hopefully) an edge setting up shop, that is, some form of hybrid between entrepreneur and asset manager. As the hedge fund survives the early years and succeeds, it moves to the right. From a business perspective, it becomes similar to a traditional shop with an operating officer, compliance officer, relationship staff, and so on. However, if the hedge fund moves into a private market, for example, private equity, it moves to the left in Figure 4.1. The graph therefore also shows that most generalizations regarding hedge funds are misleading because their spectrum of operandi is so large.

Nearly all successful absolute-return managers (Bernard Baruch, J.P. Morgan, Benjamin Graham, Warren Buffett, George Soros, Julian Robertson, Michael Steinhardt, Ed Thorpe, Jack Nash, Leon Levy—just to name a few) might or might not have outperformed a broad index benchmark had they given a tracking error constraint of 200 basis points. But what all these investors have in common is that they did not have such a constraint. They adopted a flexible (and absolute-return) approach to investment management, which involves constantly assessing and reassessing risk and constantly adapting to *change*. In this approach, risk management is an essential and integral part of the investment process. Arguing that these gentlemen "just got lucky" is like arguing that the success of Henry Ford, Sam Walton, John D. Rockefeller, Akio Morita, Thomas Edison, Andrew Carnegie, Walt Disney, Bill Gates, Michael Dell, Larry Ellison, and so on, was all due to luck. No doubt there was some luck involved. And no doubt it is true that for every successful entrepreneur there are many who failed to achieve success in their enterprise. But we cannot conclude from this asymmetry that the aforementioned individuals are not better than those who failed but were just luckier. Entrepreneurial success is most likely a function of many variables, for instance—and in no particular order: talent, intelligence, integrity, humility, hard work, diligence, drive (Lee Iacocca's "fire in the belly"), energy, passion, creativity, social network, adaptability (as in exposure to change), and, yes, some luck. (Capital also helps.) What is even more important is that all these variables can to some extent be assessed in advance—except luck.

On Bubbles and Market Efficiency   Given that the debate about whether markets are efficient is a very old one, is it relevant for the asset management industry today? Is it possible that there is no satisfactory answer as to whether, for example, equity markets are efficient and whether an active or a passive approach is called for? Indeed, most market observers would argue that the U.S. stock market is one of the most efficient. However, one could also argue that the U.S. stock market is among the least efficient. Why?

The NASDAQ (National Association of Securities Dealers Automated Quotation system) is part of the U.S. stock market.* The performance of the NASDAQ Composite Index probably looks pretty similar to a composite index of tulip bulbs during the tulip bulb mania some 300 years ago. Hardly anyone would argue for market efficiency in the case of tulips in seventeenth-century Holland.[†] However, the market dynamics were comparable. The

---

*It was not too long ago that the returns from the NASDAQ were referred to as "the new risk-free rate of return."

[†]The "greater fool theory" suggests that bubbles can exist even if all market participants are rational; that is, buyers buy on the premise that there is a greater fool around pushing prices even higher.

United States has the largest participation of retail investors in the stock market. This is pleasant for the brokerage community, but from a market dynamics point of view, it favors herding behavior. (One underlying assumption of this notion is that retail investors are less critical and therefore more receptive to what talking heads are selling on financial TV programs than are professional investment managers.) In addition, in the United States, the percentage of indexed money (index funds and other passive forms of investing) is highest globally. This is amplified by the fact that financial consultants are more influential in the United States (and in the United Kingdom) than elsewhere. Herding retail investors, indexed or quasi-indexed asset managers and consultants hugging the consensus results in market homogeneity. It is this market homogeneity that, one could argue, makes a market inefficient because it means that a large part of the market does the same thing at the same time (as opposed to idiosyncratically balancing fundamental economic variables with risk).[‡] Capital does not flow in projects or investments with the most favorable net present value because investors have objectives other than balancing potential return with an absolute measure for risk (e.g., buying Microsoft, Yahoo, and Google et al. with fresh cash for tracking risk considerations). If there is no absolute yardstick to assess risk, the probability is higher that all market participants either buy or sell (as was the case in the dot-com bubble for which the NASDAQ is a proxy). A trend becomes self-reinforcing. Expectations rise even further, amplified also through increased bullishness of various market participants (typical example of a feedback loop or Ponzi scheme). An asset bubble builds and, eventually, pops (an asset price bubble is then naturally succeeded by a regulatory and lawsuit bubble)—hardly the result of an efficient market. Conclusion: Small market inefficiencies can be arbitraged quickly, as the arbitrage requires small amounts of capital. Extremely large market inefficiencies can exist and persist longer because large amounts of capital are required to put on the arbitrage. Potentially, the arbitrageur runs out of capital long before proven right (as the 1995 to 2000 experience demonstrates to some extent).

Introducing a Flexible Approach to Managing Money

The bottom line, we believe, is that the asset management industry should stop worrying about whether markets are efficient. Potentially, this question has no answer. We believe a much more fruitful subject of debate is the degree of flexibility that investment managers should be given. This brings

---

[‡] As argued elsewhere, market homogeneity also increases systemic risk as it reduces liquidity, where liquidity is not defined by trading volume but by finding a buyer when one wants to sell.

us back to the hypothesized transition from the relative-return approach to an absolute-return approach. The absolute-return approach is essentially, as highlighted above, a flexible, more entrepreneurial approach to investment management. The absolute-return approach, that is, the search and desire for an asymmetric risk/return trade-off, is the merger of traditional asset management with risk management, where risk is defined in absolute terms. The task of a long/short equity manager, for example, on the investment analysis side is pretty similar to that of a long-only equity manager, that is, bottom-up company research. However, the big difference between the two is on the risk management side. If risk is defined as exposure to change, the long/short manager has a mandate to change the exposure of his portfolio (i.e., his capital at risk) according to his assessment of the market environment in which he is operating (note that a reassessment of risk and rebalancing are not the same as market timing). The assessment of the market environment is obviously subjective (as opposed to purely objective or rule based). A change could be triggered by a change in market conditions or a change in the beliefs held by the manager, or some other factor entirely—it doesn't really matter what exactly causes it. What matters is that the manager manages money in a flexible fashion where an ever-changing environment and a reassessment of the situation are an essential part of the equation. The incentive to act in a flexible and entrepreneurial fashion is further enhanced by the manager having his own net worth exposed to the same risks as his investors—an enhancement that we believe is very important.

IBM Chairman Louis V. Gerstner, Jr. was quoted in the late 1990s as referring to the new Internet companies as "fireflies before the storm." He called the storm that was arriving the real disturbance to the system, when companies transform themselves and seize the power of global computing and communications infrastructure (read: Change). The dot-com companies he referred to as just the fireflies before the storm "they shine now, but will eventually dim out." Are hedge funds the fireflies before the storm?

We could adopt this analogy for the asset management industry today. Hedge funds, potentially, are just the fireflies before the storm. They certainly are shining now but, potentially, they will dim out. However, the real storm could be the $16+ trillion asset management industry's adopting the absolute-return approach, that is, adopting the investment philosophy of the current $1.1 trillion hedge fund industry. Economic logic suggests that successful approaches are copied.

Compare the following:

1. Some pension funds conduct an asset liability study by their consulting actuaries every three years following the triennial valuation of the scheme.

2. An absolute-return manager seeking an asymmetric-return profile will observe geopolitics, social trends, and financial markets and assess risk on a tick-to-tick basis.

Assuming risk is defined as "exposure to change," which of the two do you believe is best suited to manage risk? How does this relate to fees? One could argue that every fee-based business is somewhat like the massage business: You can always do it yourself, but the result might not be the same.

TIME DIVERSIFICATION, RISK, AND UNCERTAINTY

Does Time Increase or Reduce Risk?

It is interesting that the capital-guaranteed structures discussed in Chapter 3 are generally considered suitable for private investors. Institutions, it is said, have a long-term perspective, and since equities outperform bonds in the long term, there is no need for hedging. This, we believe, is a fallacy because it is known that equities are more risky than bonds. If so, then why is it that having a large equity allocation is considered conservative in the long term? The empirically proven equity risk premium could be a historical accident caused possibly by a gigantic feedback loop of investors continuously convincing themselves that equities actually outperform bonds in the long term and bidding up equities as a result. Extrapolating this into the future is tricky. The error, we believe, has to do with the idea of time diversification, the definition of *long term*, and the understanding of risk.

There are essentially two schools of thought on the issue of time diversification. One believes that time reduces risk, while the other argues that time increases risk. How is this possible? Conventional wisdom suggests that over the long term, periods of above-average returns are offset by periods of below-average returns. In addition, the longer the time horizon being considered, the lower the volatility and the lower the probability of (end-of period) loss. However, if risk is understood in terms of the magnitude of potential loss, then risk in fact increases with time. The bottom line is, as Kritzman [2000] put it:

> "*The truth is that risk has no universal definition; rather, like beauty, it is in the eyes of the beholder.*"*

If time reduces risk, then it is true that investors just need to invest in equities and everything will turn out to be okay, as long as the investment

---

*We recommend Kritzman [2000] for a good summary of the issues with respect to time diversification.

horizon is long term (for example, infinite). However, if this were true, then equities could not be more risky than bonds. If it were true that equities outperform bonds in the long term, why bother investing in bonds in the first place? If equities outperform bonds in the long term, interim volatility and drawdowns do not matter in the short and medium term. Reliance on this notion to some extent implies indifference to volatility during the investment period. In addition, if it were true that equities outperform bonds in the long term, the pension fund industry would not be experiencing its current malaise. All participants (corporate sponsors, trustees, board members, advisers, government, pensioners, laborers, etc.) could just hang in there and wait until the "long term" materializes and asset growth catches up with liabilities. (Or wait until interest rates rise, and see the discounted value of the liabilities falling back into line with assets.)

Tyranny of the Status Quo

The consensus view in the industry is that time reduces risk. However, we believe the opposite, namely that time does not reduce risk but amplifies risk. Figures 8.9 and 8.10 in the appendix to Chapter 8 will show exactly what we mean, that is, that the range of outcomes 10 years hence is much larger than the outcome 12 months in the future. (A softer version of this argument would be to claim that time does not diversify risk as well as many investors thought it would during the 1990s.) Our line of argument is that true risk is perceived as large amounts of capital/wealth being wiped out. This is how risk has been perceived over thousands of years. This is in addition to the fact that disutility from losses is not linear; that is, a 40 percent loss is more than twice as bad as a 20 percent loss.* The logic behind this point of view is that the disutility (negative utility) from large losses is bad for all investors, that is, private as well as institutional investors. There are two important points to make:

"Everything is flux."—Heraclitus According to Greek philosopher Heraclitus (535 to 475 B.C.), there was no permanent reality except the reality of change; permanence was an illusion of the senses. Heraclitus was arguably one of the first (Western) philosophers. One of the last, Karl Popper (1902

---

*The idea that underlines the notion of asymmetric disutility from losses as well as a reference point can be traced a couple of hundred years back (Switzerland's Bernoullis come to mind) but was formalized by Kahneman and Tversky [1979], who defined their utility function in terms of gains and losses (as opposed to asset position or wealth), loss aversion (as opposed to risk aversion), and their utility function as S-shaped (as opposed to quadratic), that is, concave above the reference point and convex below it.

to 1994), popularized the notion that so-called scientific laws were not incorrigible truths about the world. (Most philosophers in between the two were in search of certainty.) Scientific laws were theories, and as such they were products of the human mind. For Popper, physical reality exists independently of the human mind, and so we can never apprehend it. We create theories to explain it, and use them for as long as they work. However, eventually each theory will prove inadequate, and we replace it with a better one. Popper stated: "All we can do is to search for the falsity content of our best theory."

There is no immediate solution to the debate on whether time reduces risk, as it depends on how we define risk. In other words, taking either side is speculative (the term *speculative* is here used as the opposite of conservative). If an investor believes in one argument, he takes risk, that is, he is exposed to his assumption being outright wrong or proven untrue over time (for example due to change in circumstances and market conditions). The notion that (high-duration) equities, for example, are a perfect match for (high-duration) liabilities was, at one stage, a good idea that was based on some strong beliefs and sound research. However, circumstances change. As Lord Keynes asked: "When circumstances change, I change my view. What do you do?"*

This means that taking a bet on something not known today or something unsolvable or untestable is an extreme leap of faith. The risk is that the assumption proves untrue or changes without the investor's spotting the change. This is, in our view, why many investors are in financial difficulty today. The dogmatic reliance on beliefs or assumptions is, we believe, the opposite of managing risk. Hugging the status quo might not be that good an idea when circumstances change. Milton Friedman called the lack of maneuverability or unwillingness to adapt to change the "tyranny of the status quo."

A successful risk manager, we believe (and assuming we are in the position to judge), has a probabilistic (as opposed to dogmatic) view on issues not known. In addition, the risk manager even questions "known" facts because knowledge in itself is uncertain by definition. This is true for the natural as well as social sciences.† If this were not true, civilization

---

*We apologize for falling back to this one-liner, but we strongly believe that if it weren't for change, investing would be easy. However, it isn't.

†We do not deny the existence of objective truth (because it would put us in argumentative difficulties); neither do we want to discuss Kant's subjectivism in this book (because we have no edge in doing so). We would just like to make the point that the degree of confidence is seldom absolute and is subject to change. To prove,

would not be evolving, and knowledge, therefore, not expanding with time. Knowledge is only "true" until someone comes along with a new theory that replaces the old.* Knowledge, therefore, has to be treated as temporal from the start. That is why we believe physicists, theologians, and economists have one thing in common: They all fall back on their belief.†‡ Risk management is, in our opinion, the discipline that deals with the beliefs changing or being proven wrong to the disadvantage of the investors' financial health.

"Volatility matters" The notion that equities outperform bonds in the long term is probably true, but this is potentially irrelevant for most investors. The reliance on equities outperforming bonds in the long term is rational only in the very special case where capital is infinite. The problem is, though, that there is no such thing as infinite capital in the real world. If there is uncertainty with respect to capital requirements before the end of history, the investor cannot be indifferent to volatility. In other words, interim volatility matters. In addition, the hypothesis of equities outperforming bonds in the long term is relevant only for the scientist trying to test the hypothesis in a controlled laboratory experiment. The scientist is constrained to the scientific approach of the natural sciences as someone in the past thought it was a good idea to lean the methodologies

---

for example, that "all polar bears are white" (this analogy also works with swans), one literally needs to check out all polar bears. If one examines only a small sample, the "fact" that all polar bears are white is not a fact but a belief where a certain degree of confidence can statistically be measured. If someone then spots a green "polar bear" with orange stripes walking down a glacier (sharing a similar genetic code as his white brethren), we then expand our knowledge by calling this "new" creature, for example, "glacier bear." The "fact" that all polar bears are supposed to be white proves to be false as new discoveries and definitions replace the old. (Of course, we will need to determine whether it is a hoax first, though.)

*Ptolemy also had a well-thought-out and "proven" theory underlying his point of view (until Copernicus and Kepler came along, that is).

†This belief about beliefs we got from John Adams [2002], a professor of geography at University College London, who has conducted research (among other things) on risk and road safety in the United Kingdom. His book *Risk* gives a fresh perspective on issues surrounding risk and uncertainty.

‡The idea of beliefs being important in decision making under uncertainty is probably as old as Western philosophy. In economics, for example, Kurz's [1994, 1997] theory of rational beliefs and rational belief equilibrium challenges the theory of rational expectations and game theory, which are based on the premise that economic agents know and understand a great deal about the structure of their environment. The theory of rational belief is based on the observation that intelligent economic agents hold diverse beliefs even when there is no difference in the information at their disposal.

of financial economics to the methodologies of the natural sciences (such as physics, astronomy, etc.) as opposed to the social sciences (history, sociology, psychology, etc.). The consequence of this (rather loosely phrased) remark is that relying on equities outperforming bonds in the long term is risky—especially when long term is not specified and the investor faces uncertainty with respect to needing the money before the long term is reached.

Experience Matters, Too   Because of our observation that experience matters in assessing risk, more experienced managers should do better. (Someone with an edge should do better than someone without.) However, experience in spotting change and assessing probabilities might be not enough. One could argue that the organizational set-up matters, too. The more nimble and flexible, the better. There is enough anecdotal evidence of pension fund managers risking (or terminating) their career prospects by trying to introduce a contrarian strategy. Several administrative overlays are unlikely to be optimal when managing risk. If our hypothesis has merit, that is, the end investor outsources parts of the wealth preservation function, then the most skilled risk managers will be managing an increasing pool of capital in chunks of $100 million to $10 billion blocks. This range seems to have proven as manageable before diminishing economics of scale kicks in. The most successful of this group can then go on and try to jump over the $50 billion and $100 billion hurdles.

CHAPTER SUMMARY AND CONCLUSIONS

There is still a lot of mythology with respect to absolute-return investing; much of it is built on anecdotal evidence, oversimplification, myopia, or simply a misrepresentation of facts. Although hedge funds are often branded as a separate asset class, the point can be made that hedge fund managers are simply asset managers who employ strategies different from those used by relative-return long-only managers. This is not a difference in asset class: It is a difference between the objectives of the two types of asset managers. Hedge funds aim for absolute returns by balancing investment opportunities and risk of financial loss, that is, aiming for some sort of asymmetry between the probability of making money and the probability of losing it. Relative-return managers, by contrast, define their return objective in relative terms. Benchmarked long-only managers aim to win what Charles Ellis [1993] calls a loser's game, that is, to beat the market.

Ellis calls the pursuit of beating a benchmark a loser's game. In a winner's game, the outcome is determined by the winning actions of the winner. In a loser's game, the outcome is determined by the losing behavior of the loser. Ellis makes reference to a book by Simon Ramo, *Extraordinary Tennis for the Ordinary Tennis Player* (New York: Crown Publishers, 1977). Dr Ramo observed that tennis was not one game but two: one played by professionals and a very few gifted amateurs, and the other played by all the rest of us. Professionals win points; the rest lose points. In expert tennis, the ultimate outcome is determined by the actions of the winner. In amateur tennis, the outcome is determined by unforced errors (i.e., the activities of the loser—who defeats himself).

The future path of an economy or stock market is not predictable with any reasonable degree of confidence.* Having a year-end target for the Standard and Poor's (S&P) 500 in January other than for entertainment purposes is similar to having a view on what the weather will be like on Christmas Eve. Both systems (climate as well as the stock market) are extremely complex; this complexity is magnified as the forecasting horizon expands.† The degree of confidence in the forecast decays exponentially with the increase in time. Decision making with respect to the future will always involve uncertainty regardless of the approach used. There will always be risk and uncertainty.

The preceding statement is not as fatuous as it may sound. It raises the question of what a money manager should focus on in the long term: expected return or risk. We advocate the latter. We believe one cannot manage expected return, but one can manage risk. Benjamin Graham is quoted as saying: "The essence of investment management is the management of risks, not the management of returns."[2] Return is the by-product of taking risk. Banks today do not manage portfolios; they manage risk. Their long-term investment strategy is to define the risk they want to be exposed to and manage their exposure accordingly. This implies that banks have an absolute-return focus as opposed to a relative-return focus. Potentially, asset management could be in the process of moving in the direction of banks

---

*Although we can always try: "A severe depression like that of 1920–21 is outside the range of probability."—Harvard Economic Society, weekly letter, November 16, 1929.

†One could argue that the stock market is more complex than the weather. In meteorology cause and effect are distinguishable and the forecaster does not influence the effect. This means a scientific approach makes sense. In a social system with agents being intelligent and capable of adaptation, cause and effect are sometimes reversed and the forecaster influences the effect through the fact that he influences expectations (which then changes the effect).

ELOQUENCE VERSUS MARKETING

We have quoted Karl Popper twice already and are not yet halfway through. One of Popper's main intellectual achievements was his insight into what constitutes genuine "scientific" knowledge. Popper argued that any statement that is not falsifiable cannot count as scientific, because if everything that could possibly happen is compatible with its truth then nothing can be regarded as evidence for it. This breakthrough idea first appeared in his book The Logic of Scientific Discovery, *which was first published in German in 1934 and later in English in 1959. After Popper discovered this idea for the natural sciences, he realized that it also applied to the social sciences.*

Popper also popularized the term open society *in his influential book,* The Open Society and Its Enemies, *published in 1945. In this book, he argues that "certainty" is no more available in politics than it is in science, and that therefore the imposition of any single viewpoint is never justified. This book was a powerful attack on totalitarianism and a defense of liberty. Popper's notion of the open society is based on some form of uncertainty: He states that we, as a society, do not know how to make people happy (the upside). However, we can remove avoidable suffering and handicap (the downside).*

Popper's logic might easily be applied to the investment profession as well: We cannot manage returns (the upside) because they are uncertain. However, we can manage risk (the downside).

Everyone agrees that the term hedge fund *is a misnomer. One could argue that* absolute-return strategy *is a misnomer, too. Perhaps we should—more eloquently—call it* absolute-risk strategy, *as it is risk that is managed, not returns (however, we suspect that calling it an absolute-return strategy is better for marketing purposes, and therefore the probability of the industry's adopting our suggestion is rather slim.)*

and other absolute-return managers such as what we today refer to as hedge funds (i.e., defining risk in absolute terms rather than relative terms). One could also argue that the asset management industry is moving back to an absolute-return orientation. It may turn out that the passionate attachment to market benchmarks was only a brief blip in the industry's evolution.

APPENDIX: ON VOLATILITY AND FAT TAILS

*"Most of academic finance is teaching that you can't earn 40
percent a year without some risk of losing a lot of money. In some
sense, what happened is nicely consistent with what we teach."*
—William Sharpe on LTCM collapse

We believe losing small amounts of money infrequently is—given the
choice—preferable to losing large amounts often. A return distribution
with low standard deviation of returns and negative outliers of around 17
percent can have high excess kurtosis (here used as a measure for fat tails in
especially the left wings of the distribution) while a distribution with high
standard deviation with much more extreme negative outliers of around 42
percent can have low or no excess kurtosis. Why?

The reason is that excess kurtosis is a "relative" measure.* It measures
the existence of outliers relative to the rest of the distribution, that is, the
other returns. Distributions with zero excess kurtosis are called *mesokurtic*.
The most prominent example of a mesokurtic distribution is the normal
distribution. The bell-shaped normal distribution has an *excess kurtosis* of
zero, which equals a *kurtosis* of three. A distribution with positive excess
kurtosis is called *leptokurtic*. In terms of shape, a leptokurtic distribution
has a more acute "peak" around the mean (i.e., a higher probability than
a normally distributed variable of values near the mean) and "fat tails"
(i.e., a higher probability than a normally distributed variable of extreme
values). In finance, a leptokurtic distribution is the most common departure
from the beautifully and titillatingly shaped bell curve.† A distribution
with negative excess kurtosis is called *platykurtic*. In terms of shape, a
platykurtic distribution has a smaller "peak" around the mean (i.e., a
lower probability than a normally distributed variable of values near the
mean) and "thin tails" (i.e., a lower probability than a normally distributed
variable of extreme values). Platykurtic distributions are rare to nonexistent
in finance. Mandelbrot [2004] calls (excess) kurtosis a measure for "spice"

---

*One could easily argue that all risk measures are somewhat "relative" as risk can
be defined in many ways: probability of losing money, not meeting a target return,
falling below a certain threshold, not meeting liabilities, not meeting (quantified)
objectives, underperforming a benchmark, and so on. Balzer [2001] suggests that a
measure for investment risk should be asymmetric, relative to one or more variable
benchmark(s), investor specific, multidimensional, complete (in a specific sense),
numerically positive, and nonlinear. From this catalog of requirements, it becomes
clear that there is no one single measure to capture investment risk.
†We definitely should get out more often.

TABLE 4.1 Excess Kurtosis in U.S. Equity Market

Measurement Frequency	Observation Period	Excess Kurtosis
Daily	1.1969–12.2005	34.7
Weekly (as of Monday)*	1.1969–12.2005	18.2
Weekly (as of Wednesday)*	1.1969–12.2005	3.1
Monthly	1.1800–12.2005	10.6
Monthly	1.1800–12.1899	9.1
Monthly	1.1900–12.2005	8.8

*Most and least extreme excess kurtosis based on weekly returns.
Source: Updated from Ineichen [2004b]; raw data from Global Financial Data and Thomson Financial.

and refers to the excess kurtosis figures for the U.S. stock market (Table 4.1) as "five-alarm chili." Mandelbrot stated:

> *"Statisticians like to condense a lot of confusing information into one clear talking point, and so they have devised a single number to measure what we have been discussing—how closely real data fit the ideal bell curve. They call it kurtosis, from the Greek* kyrtos, *or curved. But we can think of it as how much "spice" is in the statistical broth. A perfect, unseasoned bell curve has a kurtosis of three. A hot, fat-tailed curve of the sort we have been finding [in financial time series] would have a higher spice number, while a curve that had been boiled into a dull paste would have a lower number."*[3]

General wisdom in hedge fund research is that relative value strategies such as, for example, convertible bond (CB) or fixed-income arbitrage have fat tails (and negative skew) and high Sharpe ratios, and that the fat tails (as measured by high excess kurtosis figures) are compensating for risk not picked up by volatility or Sharpe ratios (that leans only on the first two moments of the return distribution). The standard argument goes that, putting it crudely, "You make small amounts of money frequently but every once in a while you lose a lot" (without "a lot" being quantified). The standard aphorism is a comparison to "picking up nickels in front of a steamroller." This is supported by all the research showing how one can game Sharpe ratios using mechanical option strategies.

This standard argument is not necessarily untrue. However, we believe the argument is weak in terms of the absolute magnitude of losses. Our reservations with this line of argument are based on the following: First, the line of argument implies that a long-only strategy that traditionally has lower Sharpe ratios has no or "less" excess kurtosis, that is, less negative optionality or fewer disaster insurance risk properties. We disagree. Second, we believe volatility matters more than excess kurtosis (skew being equal). Excess kurtosis as a risk measure indicates that the distribution deviates from a (Gaussian) normal distribution. The statistic is often used as an indication that there is "higher" probability of a far-from-equilibrium (most often negative) event. However, it does not address the issue of how severe the undesirable event might be; nor does it address the consequences for the investor.

Our first "reservation" against the generally accepted wisdom can easily be countered with Table 4.1. The table shows excess kurtosis of the U.S. stock market (here measured with the S&P 500 index and its predecessors).

We do not need to show drawdown figures to argue that an equity index (here used as a proxy for a long-only buy-and-hold investment strategy where total risk is not managed/controlled) is highly kurtotic, that is, has pretty fat tails when compared to a normal distribution. Assuming a long-only strategy does not have fat tails by examining only a short history or, in the case of the United States, only looking at Wednesday-to-Wednesday returns (Table 4.1) is like feeling safe living in earthquake-prone California or Tokyo. You should know disaster is going to strike, you just do not know the magnitude and timing.

The same higher moment risk statistics as in the United States can be shown if we examine 300 years of U.K. financial market history as opposed to just 200 years of U.S. history. Figure 4.2 shows the frequency distribution of monthly simple returns of the FTSE All-Share Index and its predecessors. Note that the y-axis has been truncated.

Skew and excess kurtosis of the monthly log returns were −0.50 and 56.5, respectively. Mean and standard deviation were 0.12 percent and 3.98 percent. Note that a 50 percent loss followed by a 50 percent gain results in a 25 percent loss. The other way around, a 50 percent gain followed by a 50 percent loss also results in a 25 percent loss. The South Sea Bubble in 1720 resulted in a "regulatory bubble" (actually not unlike today after Enron and the dot-com bubble burst). The piece of legislation was called the *Bubble Act of 1720*. The spike in 1825 was due to the abandoning of the Bubble Act of 1720 and the next bubble, that is, the first railways being built.[4]

Note that some financial professionals play tricks with their captive audiences. One trick is to show a distribution of simple returns and then argue that the distribution is positively skewed, which implies that positive outliers are more likely than negative outliers. We believe more financial professionals should be in prison. Simple returns are log-normally distributed as the left tail is truncated at zero, that is, prices from equities and bonds and most other assets cannot fall below zero. So the left tail is capped at −100 percent but is uncapped on the right-hand side. Regardless

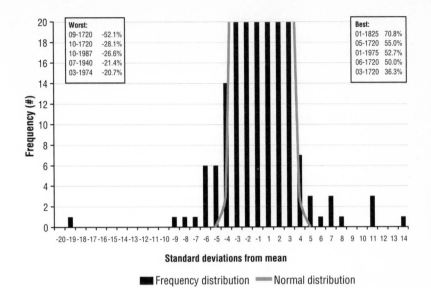

Frequency distribution ▬▬ Normal distribution

FIGURE 4.2 Return Distribution of U.K. Equity Markets (1693 to 2005)
Based on 3,755 monthly nominal log price returns from January 1693 to December 2005. Returns in inserted boxes are simple returns, not log returns.
Source: Updated from Ineichen [2004b]; data from Global Financial Data and Thomson Financial.

of statistical considerations, there are a number of reasons why the normal distribution is much better known than the log-normal distribution. A major one appears to be symmetry, one of the basic principles realized in nature as well as in our culture and thinking. Thus, probability distributions based on symmetry may have more inherent appeal than skewed ones. Two other reasons relate to simplicity. First, man has found addition an easier operation than multiplication, and so it is not surprising that an additive law of errors was the first to be formulated. Second, the established, concise description of a normal sample is handy, well known, and sufficient to represent the underlying distribution, which made it easier to handle normal distributions than to work with log-normal distributions. The normal distribution has been known and applied more than twice as long as its log-normal sister distribution. Finally, the very notion of "normal" conjures more positive associations for nonstatisticians (essentially normal people) than does "log-normal." For all these reasons, the normal or Gaussian distribution is far more familiar than the log-normal distribution is to most people.

Drawing conclusions by examining the tails from historical time series, we believe, has its limitations. A financial time series with excess kurtosis normally means that the underlying series had an accident in its past. A time series with no excess kurtosis in its past simply means that the underlying series has not had an accident yet. However, it does not automatically follow that the probability of an accident is zero or low. The probability of whether the occurrence of an accident is likely or less likely to rock the boat has to be assessed based on reason, not statistics of historical time series. As Lord Bauer, British economist and adviser to Margaret Thatcher, put it: "A safe investment is an investment whose dangers are not at that moment apparent."*

Our second reservation, that volatility is more important than excess kurtosis, needs more elaboration. Imagine an investment strategy with monthly mean returns and standard deviation both equaling 1 percent. A fall of, say, 5 percent in one month is equal to a six-standard-deviation event. This one event will inflate the excess kurtosis figure for as long as it remains in the observation period and/or as long as standard deviations stay low (controlled) at around 1 percent. However, a 5 percent loss is not too bad.

Compare this with an investment strategy that differs from the above with respect to standard deviation. Instead of a standard deviation of 1 percent, the standard deviation is 5 percent. A 5 percent drop would not inflate excess kurtosis at all. Even a 9 percent drop would not influence kurtosis to any significant degree, as it is only a two-standard-deviation event. The effect of large losses would even be small if we assume that the mean return is higher than 1 percent. A 5 percent loss would still not register as excess kurtosis. A six-standard-deviation event in this case is a loss of 29 percent. We believe a 29 percent loss hurts far more than a 5 percent loss.

Table 4.2 shows second, third, and fourth moments of two indices, whereby nonsystematic (idiosyncratic) risk is broadly diversified. We will conceal the first moment of the return distribution (the historical mean return) as well as the nature of the indices, as these would cloud our argument. (There is no champagne bottle awaiting the reader who first figures out what indices are behind investments A and B in Table 4.2. After all we went through so far, it's too easy.)

The worst drawdown from a previous peak for investments A and B in Table 4.2 were −13.9 percent and −44.7 percent, respectively. Note also that, compounding at a fixed rate of 1 percent *per month*, it takes around 15 months to recover from a −13.9 percent drawdown and nearly six years to recover from a −44.7 percent drawdown. We believe that the consequences of 45 percent losses are severe for all investors, while consequences of losses close to single-digit losses are not or to a much lesser extent.

---

*We have found it necessary to repeat this quote, already used once in Chapter 2.

TABLE 4.2 Volatility versus Higher Moments

	Investment A	Investment B
Volatility	5.5	14.4
Skew	-0.4	-0.6
Excess kurtosis	4.8	1.1
Sharpe ratio	High	Low

Source: Author's own calculations; data from Bloomberg and Thomson Financial.

The high excess kurtosis figure of 4.8 in investment A is a function of the fact that volatility was actively controlled. To those of us who think in practical terms, it is investment B that is "short" a disaster put option, not investment A. If volatility is high as well as uncontrolled, a bad outcome is more likely and can easily be disastrous. We agree with Mark Twain on this: "The opposite of hedging is speculating."

We believe that a rational economic agent that is also loss averse* would prefer a high Sharpe ratio/high excess kurtosis investment over a low Sharpe ratio/low excess kurtosis investment (skew being the same). In

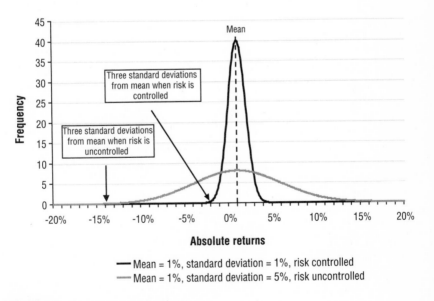

FIGURE 4.3 Log-Normal Distributions

---

*Note that "rational economic agent that is also loss averse" is oxymoronic to the disciple of behavioral finance.

other words, we believe a "rational economic agent that is also loss averse" should prefer investment A to investment B in Table 4.2, irrespective of high excess kurtosis. Investment B is so volatile, that is, the distribution around the expected return so wide, that the *expected* mean return has nearly no relevance. The *realized* mean return in any given month or year could be anywhere (Figure 4.3).

CONCLUSION

If a historical financial time series shows a high excess kurtosis figure, it tells us that there was an accident in the period of observation. Equity returns as well as some absolute-return strategies have high excess kurtosis in their history because there were accidents that were, by definition, unpredictable. A historic time series of a strategy with no excess kurtosis means that the strategy has not yet had an accident, or the time period is too short, or the accident lies in the future. It is unwise to think that an accident is impossible or that the strategy is "safe" in the future just because there is no measurable excess kurtosis in its history. The assessment of risk should be based on thought and insight. Statistics can be helpful as well as misleading.

A high excess kurtosis figure in a return distribution can be misleading. Potentially, the "short disaster put option" talk in hedge fund research has gone too far. An absolute-return manager who manages portfolio volatility diligently and has a volatility of 2 percent and then has a 5 percent drawdown will have high excess kurtosis. A manager who "manages" portfolio volatility recklessly and has a volatility of 9.4 percent* and has a 10 percent drawdown occasionally will have much lower or even no excess kurtosis. We believe that a "rational economic agent that is also loss averse" should have a preference for the former combination over the latter, irrespective of historical excess kurtosis. In other words, we believe losing small amounts of money infrequently is—given the choice—preferable to losing large amounts often. (If you think there is a typo in this last sentence, please read this appendix again.)

---

*A long-only strategy consisting of 60 percent global equities and 40 percent global bonds that was monthly rebalanced from 1990 to 2005 had a volatility of 9.4 percent.

CHAPTER 5

Alpha Is an Option

"Investment is by nature not an exact science."
—Benjamin Graham

We obviously believe there is a case for active money management, or—more precisely and as we prefer to call it—active risk management. There is ample evidence that real-world markets are not perfectly efficient. Different participants in the market have widely differing objectives, time horizons, skill, constraints, and risk tolerances. Market inefficiencies will likely be around for a while, as will bubbles and bursts; consequently, there will be sophisticated and trading-savvy investors who exploit these inefficiencies by hedging unwanted risks. What this means for us is that alpha is not uniformly distributed among the market participants searching for it. Some investors have alpha and know it; others think they have alpha but don't. Other investors do not have it but want it and might or might not get it. In essence, alpha is an option.

In this chapter we make the case for the inefficiency of real-world markets. Obviously, such a broad topic would warrant volumes on its own. We therefore take only a rudimentary look at market efficiency, the theories behind it, and some ideas that reject or challenge it.

INEFFICIENCY OF FINANCIAL MARKETS

Decades ago, Grossman [1976] and Grossman and Stiglitz [1980] proved that, even in theory, markets cannot be fully efficient. Perfectly informationally efficient markets, they argued, are an impossibility, for if markets were perfectly efficient, the return to gathering information would be zero, in which case there would be no reason to conduct research; consequently, trade and markets would soon collapse. After the 1987 crash,

Larry Summers was quoted saying that "the efficient market hypothesis is the most remarkable error in the history of economic theory."

We do not subscribe to the view that markets are efficient just because a majority of "active" managers underperform the benchmark (active here used as in "active long-only"). The view that markets are efficient because the market cannot outperform itself is, we believe, a misunderstanding derived from the "fallacy of composition." *Fallacy* is the general term for reasoning that can seem correct but is really unsound and confusing. The "fallacy of composition" is reasoning that says: Because one person in the crowd can do it, everyone in the crowd can do it. For example, if fire breaks out in a cinema, one person can get out in 30 seconds. However, that does not mean all people can get out in 30 seconds. It is therefore unreasonable to believe that just because a majority of investors underperform, all investors underperform. Not everyone is equally fit. Neither is outperformance, assuming we can measure it properly, a function of randomness. The outcome of a chess tournament or marathon is a function of intellectual or physical fitness in combination with practice and wit, that is, fitness. We believe this to be true for active risk management as well.

Absolute-return managers add value by exploiting market inefficiencies. The high risk–adjusted returns they aim for are a sharp rebuttal to the conventional wisdom that is still taught at business schools and that is still relied upon by many distinguished academics and practitioners—the paradigm that capital markets are efficient. The migration to indexation and core-satellite structures is a consequence of the popular acceptance of this paradigm. However, we believe the pendulum is now swinging back. Today, there is a group of academics as well as practitioners who believe that with a competitive advantage there is the possibility to gain excess returns that can be explained by manager skill. The balance of power between the disciples of the efficient market hypothesis (EMH) and these new heretics is slowly but surely shifting toward the latter.

The EMH and its close relative, the random walk hypothesis, are among the most controversial and hotly contested ideas in all the social sciences. They are disarmingly simple to state, have far-reaching consequences for academic pursuits and business practices, and yet are surprisingly resistant to empirical proof or refutation. Even after three decades of research and literally thousands of journal articles, economists have not yet reached a consensus about whether capital markets are efficient.

Where did it all begin? We could go back as far as the early nineteenth century when the English physicist Robert Brown studied the movement of molecules as they randomly collide with one another as they move in space. This phenomenon later came to be known as *Brownian motion*. Louis Bachelier, a French mathematician, observed in 1900 that if stock prices vary according to the square root of time, they bear remarkable resemblance to Brownian motion. In finance, Brownian motion came to be called the *random walk*, which someone once described as the path a drunk might follow at night in the light of a lamppost.[1]

Other market observers put the start date at 1933 when the founder of *Econometrica*, Alfred Cowles III, answered the question "Can stock market forecasters forecast?" with a three-word abstract: "It is doubtful." Cowles [1933] studied the records of 11 leading financial periodicals and services, over periods varying from 10 to 15.5 years, and found no evidence of the ability to predict successfully the future course of the stock market. Of the 6,904 forecasts recorded during the 15.5-year period, more than four times as many were bullish as bearish, although more than half of the period was occupied by bear markets, and stocks, at the end, were at only about two thirds of their level at the beginning. His analysis concluded that the performance of the stocks analyzed as a whole were negative relative to the performance of the market as a whole. The results could have been achieved through a purely random selection of stocks.

The first formal application of the random walk hypothesis to financial markets can be traced to Paul Samuelson [1965]:

> *"In an information-efficient market—not to be confused with an allocation- or Pareto-efficient market—price changes must be unforecastable if they are properly anticipated, i.e., if they fully incorporate the expectations and information of all market participants."*[2]

Lo and MacKinlay [1999] add:

> *"Unlike the many applications of the random walk hypothesis in the natural and physical sciences in which randomness is assumed almost by default, because of the absence of any natural alternatives, Samuelson believed that randomness is achieved through the active participation of many investors seeking greater wealth. Unable to curtail their greed, an army of investors aggressively pounce on even the smallest informational advantages at their disposal, and in doing so, they incorporate their information into market prices and quickly eliminate the profit opportunities that gave rise to their aggression. If this occurs instantaneously, which it must in an idealized world of "frictionless" markets and costless trading, then prices must always fully reflect all available information and no profits can be garnered from information-based trading (because such profits have already been captured)."*

Fama [1970] argued that "prices fully reflect all available information." Eugene Fama gained a reputation preaching the EMH. According to Fama [1998], market efficiency survives the challenge from the literature on long-term return anomalies. Consistent with the EMH that the anomalies are chance results, apparent overreaction to information is about as common as underreaction, and postevent continuation of preevent abnormal returns is about as frequent as postevent reversal. Most important, consistent with the market efficiency prediction that apparent anomalies can be due to methodology, most long-term return anomalies tend to disappear with reasonable changes in technique.

There Is No Free Lunch Plan

Three and a half decades after the previously quoted statement from Paul Samuelson, Lo and MacKinlay [1999] express the view:

> *"Financial markets are predictable to some degree, but far from being a symptom of inefficiency or irrationality. Predictability is the oil that lubricates the gears of capitalism."*[3]

Campbell, Lo, and MacKinlay [1997] and Lo and MacKinlay [1999] argue that the EMH provides an "anchor" point against which market efficiency can be assessed. In this approach, full or 100 percent market efficiency is just a theoretical concept. This might be a more useful approach than the all-or-nothing view of market efficiency in the traditional literature. The idea is to treat the EMH as an idealization that provides a useful reference point. The advantages of relative efficiency over absolute efficiency are easy to see by way of an analogy. Physical systems are often given an efficiency rating based on the relative proportion of energy or fuel converted to useful work. Therefore, a piston engine may be rated at 60 percent efficiency, meaning that on average 60 percent of the energy contained in the engine's fuel is used to turn the crankshaft, with the remaining 40 percent lost to other forms of work such as heat, light, or noise. No one would ever expect 100 percent efficiency.[4]

The authors also make the point that if one wants to exploit the inefficiencies in a market, he or she must have a competitive advantage of some sort. This could be in the form of information gathering (for instance, by focusing on underresearched small caps or potential short-sell candidates), superior technology, or financial innovation. To be successful in an inefficient market, an active manager therefore has to develop some special area of competency or competitive advantage, that is, an edge of some sort. If this is not the case, the ex-ante alpha is zero (or negative). Any realized excess return, therefore, will be a function not of skill but of chance (or a function of the wrong benchmark against which the excess return is measured). Lo and MacKinlay [1999] argue:

> *"In this version of the Efficient Markets Hypothesis, an occasional free lunch is permitted, but free lunch plans are ruled out."*[5]

Probably one of the most pleasurable activities for academics and practitioners alike is to make fun of erring financial forecasters or financial professionals underperforming a passive benchmark. We fully agree with Robert N. Veres:

> *"Personally, I think everybody who predicts the future with a straight face should be required (by federal law) to change out of the business suit, wrap him/herself in a gypsy shawl, wear one of those pointed wizard's hats with a picture of a crescent moon on it, and make conjuring sounds over a crystal ball. That way, everybody would know exactly what's going on and how much credibility to give the answer."*[6]

There is a possibility that there will always be forecasters in financial markets as there have been seers, prophets, and fortune-tellers throughout the 5,000 years of the documented history of civilization. The inability to forecast market direction in a consistent manner is often used as an argument for market efficiency.* A lot of the entertainment value is derived from the fact that market timers and forecasters view the world as deterministic (as in Newton's view of orbits) as opposed to chaotic (for example, the weather), mad (as in the madness of crowds), or indeterministic and uncertain (as in quantum mechanics). Forecasters trying to assess a complex system will fail by definition because the set of variables and links between these variables is only a small subset of the total dynamic system. Assessing all variables and links in an unbiased fashion is not possible. What is often overlooked, however, is that the only alternative to an intelligent assessment of the future is an unintelligent one. Ignorance and dogma support the latter.

The problem of expert failure can be traced to man's capabilities as an information processor. Every human organism lives in an environment that generates millions of new bits of information every second, but the

---

*Sherden [1998] on forecasting: "Remember the First Law of Economics: For every economist, there is an equal and opposite economist—so for every bullish economist, there is a bearish one. The Second Law of Economics: They are both likely to be wrong."

bottleneck of the perceptual apparatus does not admit more than 1,000 bits per second. We react consciously to only a fraction of the information that is given to us. Then it is up to relative levels of skill, which also vary.

Dozens of studies discrediting experts have made it clear that expert failure extends far beyond the investment scene. And the problems often reside in man's information processing capabilities. Current work indicates that the expert is a serial or sequential processor of data who can handle information reliably in a linear manner—that is, can move from one point to the next in a logical sequence. However, a solution to a complex problem can require configural (or interactive) reasoning. In a configural problem, the forecaster's interpretation of any single piece of information changes, depending on how the individual evaluates many other inputs. The configural relationships of a company or the marketplace itself are extremely complex. In addition, research in configural processing has shown that experts not only can analyze information incorrectly, they can also find relationships that are not there—a phenomenon called *illusionary correlation*.

The complexity of the marketplace naturally leads to an attempt to simplify and rationalize what seems at times to be reality. Often, investors notice things that are simply coincidental, and then come to believe that correlations exist when none are actually present. And if they are rewarded by the investment's going up, the false validity of the practice is further ingrained. The market thus provides an excellent field for illusionary correlation.

UNORTHODOX ECONOMICS AND VOODOO SCIENCE

Introduction

Next to the academic orthodoxy we have discussed so far, there are some alternative ways of thinking about markets. Here, three of them will be discussed very briefly: praxeology, reflexivity, and behavioral finance. These approaches are sometimes considered as "nonscientific" in the academic establishment. Quite often, a derogatory term is used to describe the thought process, for example, *voodoo science,* or something of that order. (Interestingly, orthodox economics was once also branded and perceived as *dismal science* by the scientific establishment.) Note that, over the past couple of years, behavioral finance has become a more or less accepted niche of financial economics. The awarding of the 2002 Nobel Prize in economic sciences to Daniel Kahneman and Vernon Smith will probably further increase the credibility of behavioral economics. Daniel Kahneman received the prize "for having integrated insights from psychological research into economic science, especially concerning human judgment and decision-making under uncertainty" while Vernon Smith was honored "for having established laboratory experiments as a tool in empirical economic analysis, especially in the study of alternative market mechanisms."

Praxeology dates back to the early twentieth century. Its intellectual founder was Ludwig von Mises, a leading proponent of so-called Austrian economics. The defining difference between mainstream and Austrian economics lies in their opposing philosophies toward learning truth. Reflexivity is George Soros's theory on economic affairs.*

Why are these approaches mentioned in connection with inefficient markets and the ability to generate alpha in the form of asymmetric returns? Well, if unorthodox economics has only a small piece of truth and this small piece of truth is fully ignored by the investment establishment, then, by definition, market prices and markets will be biased and, by definition, there will be unorthodox ways for these inefficiencies to be exploited and value extracted.[†] In addition, challenging a contemporary social doctrine cannot be considered a negative per se, irrespective of its authority or broad dissemination. As Sir Sarvepalli Radhakrishnan (1888–1975), Indian statesman, philosopher, and president of India (1962–1967) put it: "It is not God that is worshiped but the group or authority that claims to speak in His name. Sin becomes disobedience to authority, not violation of integrity."

UNORTHODOX HOAX

Many analysts, intellectuals, professionals, market observers, investors, and so on believe that some of the research coming out of academia is nonsense camouflaged as science. The perception is that form *matters more than* content. *Ideas need to be presented in an orthodox way to be published in a scientific magazine. This essentially*

---

*Charles Ellis [2001] on Soros: "Humility is as rare a commodity on Wall Street as customers' yachts. But then George Soros shares little with Wall Street—he's in it, but not *of* it. Soros ignores Wall Street research and has antagonized the major block-trading houses with what many consider an abrasive and arrogant manner. Other observers, however, attribute such criticism to plain jealousy; they say that Soros, to date, has simply been able to outfox the most cunning Wall Street traders."

[†]Note that scholarly economists argue that what is here casually referred to as unorthodox and the acclaimed ignorance is not true. These scholars argue that it is not ignorance but their inability to make economics intelligible to outsiders. That is an elegant self-defense and a fair critique of our critique.

means that practitioners cannot publish in scientific magazines, as they do not have armies of students at their disposal to do the work.

A physicist, Alan Sokal, put this to the test. He wanted to know whether he could write an article that was scientific in form *but was complete nonsense in terms of* content *and then get it published by a reputable scientific magazine. The title of the paper was "Transgressing the Boundaries: Toward a Transformative Hermeneutics of Quantum Gravity." From the conclusions:*

> *". . . the π of Euclid and the G of Newton, formerly thought to be constant and universal, are now perceived in their ineluctable historicity; and the putative observer becomes fatally de-centered, disconnected from any epistemic link to a space-time point that can no longer be defined by geometry alone."[7]*

The rest was in the same vein. The paper was a hoax. (Sometimes we, too, come across a hedge fund paper where we are not sure whether the authors are retesting Sokal's hypothesis by playing a practical joke on the investment community.) The article was accepted and published. Sokal immediately revealed the hoax, provoking a firestorm of reaction in both the popular and academic press. The idea behind the "test" was to show how apparent science is abused. Sokal and Bricmont [1998] argue that the most common tactic is to use scientific (or pseudoscientific) terminology without bothering much about what the words actually mean. Another observation they wanted to illustrate is the current importing of concepts from the natural sciences into the social sciences without giving the slightest conceptual or empirical justification. A big part of research in financial economics and econometrics probably falls into this category.* A further characteristic the authors wanted to demonstrate is the display of superficial sophistication by shamelessly throwing around technical terms in a context where they are

----

**In his Nobel Prize lecture, reprinted in Hayek [1975], Hayek warns about putting excessive reliance on empirical "proofs" in economics at the expense of a coherent theoretical explanation. He argued that economic processes are inherently so complex and constantly changing that the appearance of structural stability is almost always misleading.*

completely irrelevant.* The authors also criticize the use of mathematics in the social sciences. Because mathematical concepts have precise meanings, mathematics is useful primarily when applied to fields in which the concepts likewise have more or less precise meanings. Financial economics is a social science. Data is quite often imprecise or meaningless or both. From this we can safely conclude that many scholarly papers in the field of finance are imprecise or meaningless or both. Sokal and Bricmont also address intellectual inflexibility, adherence to dogma, and ignorance of facts—themes that we touch upon in this book, too:

> *"When ideas are accepted on the basis of fashion or dogma, they are especially sensitive to the exposure even of marginal aspects. For example, geological discoveries in the eighteenth and nineteenth centuries showed that the earth is vastly older than the 5000-or-so years recounted in the Bible; and although these findings directly contradicted only a small part of the Bible, they had the indirect effect of undermining its overall credibility as a factual account of history, so that nowadays few people (except in the United States) believe in the Bible in the literal way that most Europeans did only a few centuries ago. Consider, by contrast, Isaac Newton's work: it is estimated that 90 percent of his writings deal with alchemy or mysticism. But, so what? The rest survives because it is based on solid empirical and rational arguments. Similarly, most of Descartes' physics is false, but some of the philosophical questions he raised are still pertinent today."*[8]

We find this hoax is somewhat applicable to the field of financial economics in general and hedge fund research in particular. The departure from what we perceive as the real world seems huge or—at times—"insurmountable."

---

*We therefore sincerely apologize for talking about excess kurtosis so much. In all our work, we try to follow Einstein's wisdom: "Keep it as simple as possible, but not simpler." This means we try to keep it simple without oversimplifying. Sometimes we fail to do so.

Praxeology

The Austrian school of economics is a very small group of libertarians who oppose mainstream economics. Many of the disciples reject even the scientific method that mainstream economists use, preferring to use instead a prescientific approach that ignores real-world data and scientific tests and is based purely on logical assumptions. It deduces truths from a priori knowledge. Von Mises [1996] stated:

> *"The a priori sciences—logic, mathematics, and praxeology—aim at a knowledge unconditionally valid for all beings endowed with the logical structure of the human mind. The natural sciences aim at a cognition valid for all those beings which are not only endowed with the faculty of human reason but with human senses."*[9]

It is obvious that this does not fit very well with the scientific approach, as it is the method that thousands of religions use when they argue their opposing beliefs and assert the logic of the existence of God. The fact that the world has thousands of religions demonstrates the implausibility of this approach. Theories ungrounded in facts and data are easily spun into any belief a person wants. Initial assumptions and trains of logic may contain inaccuracies so small as to be undetectable, yet will yield entirely different conclusions. The Austrian School of Economics is not as well known as, for example, Keynesianism, mainly because it offered no hope in the face of the crisis of the 1930s. (That said, we observe a mini-renaissance of Austrian economics by perma-bears suggesting we are going back to the pre–Bretton Woods gold standard.)

Some Austrian economists accept the scientific method in principle, but argue that it is more appropriate for hard sciences like physics or chemistry, not the human sciences like sociology or economics. The key difference, they argue, is that humans, unlike electrons, have freedom of choice. Humans are therefore vastly more unpredictable, even if placed in the same situation twice. Austrian economists favor a method called *apriorism*. A priori knowledge is logic, or knowledge that exists in a person's mind prior to, and independent of, empirical experience. For example, the statement "Two plus two equals four" is true regardless of whether a person goes out into the garden and verifies this by counting tomatoes. What this means is that Austrian economists reject the attempt to learn economic laws through experiment or real-world observation. The only true economic laws are those derived from first principles—namely, logic.

To be a science, a school of thought must produce theories that are falsifiable or verifiable. If a theory's correctness or falseness cannot be verified, then it is not scientific. Perhaps it is religion, or metaphysics, or an unsupported claim that must be taken on faith. Austrian economists make claims about the market (such as markets know better than governments), but then deny the tools for verifying those claims (such as statistics):

> *"Statistical figures referring to economic events are historical data. They tell us what happened in a nonrepeatable historical case. Physical events can be interpreted on the ground of our knowledge concerning constant relations established by experiments. Historical events are not open to such an interpretation."*[10]

The point of view that historical data is one of many probable outcomes is a view most investors probably share. The view that the future is uncertain is not unorthodox at all. Most risk managers use a probability distribution of some sort to assess potential future outcomes. In von Mises's words: "Every action refers to an unknown future. It is in this sense always a risky speculation."* As we suggested in Chapter 2, many of the problems in today's risk management processes arise due to an excessive reliance on historical data. Mean-variance optimizations and value at risk (VaR) analysis are generally based on historically observed correlations between asset classes and securities. The problem with this is that the output of the analysis tells us something about risk only under "normal" market conditions. In distressed market conditions, the measured risk under normal market conditions can prove to be useless.

Our discussion of nonorthodox economics in relation to active investment management might appear strange (or unorthodox), to say the least. But we believe the relevance is that it reminds us that orthodox economic thinking is not perfect and its evolution is far from finished. Some of the standard axioms and assumptions have been unchallenged (or the challenges ignored) for too long. The rise of behavioral economics in trying to explain some of the phenomena in financial markets, such as the interaction of buyers and sellers, is most likely a step in the right direction. The current move of taking the behavioral movement to the next level by learning from the neurosciences might just be one further step in the search for truth, that is, how market participants function under uncertainty. The reason why we contrast behavioral finance with praxeology and reflexivity is that the common denominator of the three areas of thought is rather large. Von

---

*Ronald Reagan on von Mises: "Ludwig von Mises was one of the greatest economic thinkers in the history of Western civilization. Through his seminal works, he rekindled the flames of liberty. As a wise and kindly mentor, he encourages all who sought to understand the meaning of freedom. We owe him an incalculable debt." (Source: http://philosophyquotes.com/board/messages/21.html.)

Mises, for example, argued that not connecting an economic theorem to the foundation of real human purposes and plans would be nothing more than a free-floating abstraction unconnected to the world we live in and thus irrelevant as a mental exercise. Disciples of reflexivity and behavioral finance probably would agree.

Reflexivity

George Soros's idea of reflexivity has not received much attention in the academic financial literature.* Financial academics have generally ignored it because it is not based on the scientific approach but partly on "observation and partly on logic,"[11] not unlike praxeology. Reflexivity is discussed in detail in Soros's [1987] *The Alchemy of Finance: Reading the Mind of the Market,* and revised in Soros [2003]. Louis Moore Bacon has described it as the best financial book ever written.[12] In the preface to this book, Soros writes that reflexivity was developed as an abstract philosophical concept before he entered the financial markets: "In other words, I failed as a philosophical speculator before I succeeded as a financial one." Soros also notes in the preface that he probably went too far by claiming that economic theory is false and social science a false metaphor. "Since far-from-equilibrium conditions arise only intermittently, economic theory is only intermittently false."[13] Soros [1998] loses some of his credibility when he says: "I have to confess that I am not familiar with the prevailing theories about efficient and rational expectations. I consider them irrelevant and I never bothered to study them."

Soros argues that market participants are biased. Of course, many behavioral finance theorists have argued that there are biases that affect human judgment and decision making. Soros goes one step further in claiming that not only are there such biases but these biases can have an impact on so-called fundamentals. This reflexive relationship renders the evolution of prices indeterminate and the so-called equilibrium price irrelevant. Money values do not simply mirror the state of affairs in the real world. Valuation is a positive act that makes an impact on the course of events. Monetary and real phenomena are connected in a reflexive

---

*This is actually not entirely true. To capture the idea of reflexivity, theorists have developed models of bandwagons, rational speculative bubbles, fads, second-generation speculative attacks, multiple equilibria, and bank-runs. So academic economists ignore the term *reflexivity* (but not the idea) and deride the notion that it was Soros who came up with the idea first.

fashion; that is, they influence each other mutually. The reflexive relationship manifests itself most clearly in the use and abuse of credit:

> *"It is credit that matters, not money (in other words, monetarism is a false ideology), and the concept of a general equilibrium has no relevance to the real world (in other words, classical economics is an exercise in futility)."*[14]*

Soros argues that the generally accepted view is that markets are always right; that is, market prices tend to discount future developments accurately, even when it is unclear what those developments are. Soros starts with the opposite point of view. He believes that market prices are always wrong in the sense that they present a biased view on the future. The participants' perceptions are inherently flawed, and there is a two-way connection between flawed perceptions and the actual course of events, which results in a lack of correspondence between the two. Soros calls this two-way connection *reflexivity*. Soros also views financial markets as a laboratory for testing hypotheses, albeit not strictly scientific ones: "The truth is, successful investing is a kind of alchemy."[15]

Soros appeals to Hegel's dialectical conception of history, according to which any idea taken to an extreme turns into its opposite. (Soros even warns that this could happen to liberal capitalism unless a deliberate effort is made to prevent it.) The weak link in classic economic theory, according to Soros, is that it does not account for reflexivity. This is due to the fact that classic economic theory was based on Newtonian mechanics. In Newtonian mechanics the object of knowledge is not altered by the act of knowing it. In quantum physics, on the other hand, Heisenberg's uncertainty principle tells us that the object of knowledge is altered by the act of knowing it, or at least of measuring it. In the human sciences, including economics and finance, the object of study is also altered by the act of knowing it, because the object of knowledge is ourselves. Thus, there is a feedback loop uniting the knower with the known. This feedback loop or reflexivity makes for an unstable and unpredictable system.

Soros notes that he first fantasized that his work would be viewed at par with Keynes's *General Theory of Employment, Interest, and Money*, which explained the Great Depression of the 1930s. The general theory of

---

*Given the current (Q2 2006) leverage in the financial system (e.g., U.S. households) and low-risk premiums, we are not the only market participants digging out and rereading Soros's *The Alchemy of Finance* and Austrian theories on the credit cycles and the value of gold.

reflexivity was supposed to explain the great bust of the 1980s. However, the bust did not occur* and George Soros has no general theory.

> *"What I have is an approach that can help to illuminate the present precarious state of our financial system. It cannot explain and predict the course of events in the manner to which we have become accustomed during our long love affair with natural science for the simple reason that reflexive processes cannot be explained and predicted in that manner."*[16]

Soros argues that equilibrium in markets is never reached and is the product of an axiomatic system. The possibility that equilibrium is never reached need not invalidate the logical construction, but when a hypothetical equilibrium is presented as a model of reality, a significant distortion is introduced. The "crowning achievement" of the axiomatic approach, according to Soros, is the theory of perfect competition. The theory holds that, under certain specified circumstances, the unrestrained pursuit of self-interest leads to the optimal allocation of scarce resources. The equilibrium point is reached when each firm produces at a level where its marginal cost equals the market price and each consumer buys an amount whose marginal utility equals the market price. The equilibrium position maximizes the benefit of all participants, provided no individual buyer or seller can influence market prices. It is this line of thinking that results in the current belief of the "magic of the marketplace."

If the assumptions are wrong, what does that tell us of the creditworthiness of the conclusions? Soros notes that it is the assumptions behind the orthodox theories that are wrong.† The main assumptions include perfect knowledge or perfect information, homogeneous and divisible products, and a large enough number of participants so that no single participant can influence the marketplace. However, it is a cardinal principle of scientific method that perfect knowledge is not attainable. Scientists work by constantly testing plausible hypotheses and propounding new ones. If they did not treat conclusions as provisional and subject to improvement, natural science could not have reached its present state of development and it could not progress any further. One could argue that some coincidences are really only scientific truths that have not been discovered yet.

---

*The bust did not occur in the 1980s, but, according to some market pundits, it is now just around the corner.

†Note that Milton Friedman [1953] showed that a theory cannot be refuted by proving that its assumptions are wrong. The only test of the validity of a theory, says Friedman, is the degree of correspondence of its predictions with reality.

Fundamentals lead to a change in price, but price changes can alter the fundamentals. Buy and sell decisions are based on expectations about future prices, and future prices, in turn, are contingent on present buy and sell decisions. Soros argues that to speak of supply and demand as if they were determined by forces that are independent of the market participants' expectations is misleading. The situation is not quite so clear-cut in the case of commodities, where supply is largely dependent on production and demand is dependent on consumption. But the price that determines the amounts produced and consumed is not necessarily the present price. On the contrary, market participants are more likely to be guided by future prices, either as expressed in futures markets or as anticipated by themselves. In either case, it is inappropriate to speak of independently given supply-and-demand curves because both curves incorporate the participants' expectations about future prices.[17]

In 1994, George Soros testified before Congress on the stability of the financial system and was also invited by the late Rudi Dornbusch to present "The Theory of Reflexivity" at the MIT Department of Economics World Economy Laboratory Conference in Washington, D.C., on April 26, 1994. In his presentation to MIT students, Soros started by quoting the beginning of his testimony to Congress:

> *"I must state at the outset that I am in fundamental disagreement with the prevailing wisdom. The generally accepted theory is that financial markets tend towards equilibrium, and on the whole, discount the future correctly. I operate using a different theory, according to which financial markets cannot possibly discount the future correctly because they do not merely discount the future; they help to shape it. In certain circumstances, financial markets can affect the so-called fundamentals which they are supposed to reflect. When that happens, markets enter into a state of dynamic disequilibrium and behave quite differently from what would be considered normal by the theory of efficient markets. Such boom/bust sequences do not arise very often, but when they do, they can be very disruptive, exactly because they affect the fundamentals of the economy."*[18]

Soros went on to say he had not been able to expound his theory before Congress,

> *"... so I am taking advantage of my captive audience to do so now. My apologies for inflicting a very theoretical discussion on you."*[19]

Behavioral Finance

The volume of literature in the field of behavioral finance has grown immensely over the past decade or two. Paul Solvic's [1972] article on individual's misperceptions about risk and Amos Tversky and Daniel Kahneman's papers on heuristic driven decision biases [1974] and decision frames [1979] played a seminal role. Their findings were at variance with the rational, self-interested decision maker posited by traditional finance and economics theory. One could argue that orthodox economics assumes a decision maker, the so-called *Homo economicus,* to behave more like *Star Trek*'s Mr. Spock (or, for younger readers, the android Data), whereas in behavioral finance, decision makers are assumed to be more like *Desperate Housewives.* The field of behavioral finance merges concepts from financial economics and cognitive psychology in an attempt to construct a more detailed model of human behavior in financial markets. The field is seldom far from controversy. Its proponents contend that behavioral finance can explain apparent empirical anomalies in traditional finance theories; its opponents contend that these anomalies merely arise due to faulty testing of existing theory. Apparently, Paul Samuelson defines behavioral finance as "the study of people not doing the most rational thing as judged by assistant professors of finance."[20]

Although several definitions of *behavioral finance* exist, there is considerable agreement among them. Lintner [1998] defines behavioral finance as "the study of how humans interpret and act on information to make informed investment decisions." Thaler [1999] defines behavioral finance as "simply open-minded finance," claiming that "sometimes in order to find the solution to an (financial) empirical puzzle it is necessary to entertain the possibility that some of the agents in the economy behave less than fully rationally some of the time." Olsen [1998] asserts that "behavioral finance does not try to define 'rational' behavior or label decision making as biased or faulty; it seeks to understand and predict systematic financial market implications of psychological decision processes."[21] Olsen [1998] wrote:

> "Behavioral finance is part of science in that it starts from fundamental axioms and asks whether a theory built on these axioms can explain behavior in the financial marketplace. Contrary to some assertions, behavioral finance does not try to define rational behavior or label biased decision-making as biased or faulty; it seeks to understand and predict systematic financial market implications of psychological decision-making processes. In addition, behavioral finance is focused on the application of psychological and economic principles for the improvement of financial decision-making."[22]

Today, the field of behavioral finance is moving into evolutionary biology and the neurosciences. Olsen [1998], for example, quoted the finding of Van Harlow that one's propensity to take risks can be known by measuring the level of a neurochemical called *monoamine oxidase* in one's blood. The due diligence of fund of funds managers does not yet include blood samples when assessing new hedge fund managers. Perhaps it should.

Shefrin [2000] argues that behavioral finance is "the application of psychology to financial behavior—the behavior of practitioners." Behaviorists seek to replace the behaviorally incomplete theory of finance. They seek to understand and predict systematic financial market implications of psychological decision processes, while recognizing that the existing paradigm can be true within specified boundaries. Some suggest that the tenacity and the generality of many human decision attributes indicate that their roots lie in human evolution.

Scott et al. [1999] group the universe of behavioral biases into two main categories: overconfidence and prospect theory.

Overconfidence　As we have noted, behavioral finance has recently gained more academic acceptance than praxeology or reflexivity. The author of *Irrational Exuberance*, Robert Shiller, is one of the leading figures in the field. Given the high degree of acceptance of Shiller's work, as well as Daniel Kahneman's winning the 2002 Nobel Prize, one could easily conclude that behavioral finance is becoming a "mainstream unorthodox" economic discipline. The observation, for example, that excess volatility in the equity market is not based on fundamental uncertainty of future cash flows to investors, which was discussed by Shiller [1981, 1989], is the consensus view by most investors and market observers today.* Kahneman and Tversky's [1979] prospect theory is probably accepted by some economists. However, behavioral finance does not have a unified theory yet. Behavioral finance is more an endeavor. More recent journeys have been into the neurosciences and evolutionary biology. Thomas Malthus and Adam Smith—two of the forefathers of modern economics—were both

---

*Behavioral finance appears to offer an explanation for what observers label excessive stock price volatility as discussed in Shiller [1981, 1989]. Financial economists appear to agree that security price volatility and trading volume should vary directly with the divergence of opinion. At this point, standard finance is unable to explain a wide divergence of opinion except to invoke the concept of asymmetrical information. In public markets for widely traded securities, however, where asymmetries are likely to be small, it seems unlikely that differential information among investors could create the kind of divergence of opinion necessary to account for many instances of high stock-price volatility.

cited by Darwin as inspirations for the principle of natural selection, and analogies between economics and biology have been discussed for more than a century. However, a quantitative foundation for this approach has been slow to develop. Recent research in finance could suggest that this is about to change. Although there are obvious differences between evolution in biological systems and evolution in financial systems, there are also many similarities. The theory of evolution may prove to be as powerful an idea in finance as it has been in biology. (We get somewhat Darwinian when discussing competition in a business context in Chapter 8.) There is no lack of quantitative data, and there are many opportunities for biological principles to be applied to financial interactions. After all, financial institutions are uniquely human inventions that provide an adaptive advantage to our species. This is truly a new frontier whose exploration has just begun.

Economists used to think that idiosyncratic irrationality would not translate into market irrationality because it would take only a few rational investors to offset herd behavior. This economic view is in line with the EMH, which suggests that any irrational trading would soon be corrected through arbitrage and fast money. However, markets do not trade only on available news and rational responses. At times, they reflect investors' irrational impulses. One personality factor influencing financial risk taking is "sensation-seeking."[23] Bernstein [1995] argues that human risk behavior has always been shaped by the environment of the period. Large parts of the 1990s were determined by a fun element—a personal factor influencing financial risk taking, or, as Jonathan Clements in the *Wall Street Journal* puts it:

> *"People get pleasure from it [investing]. It's thrill-seeking behavior. People use investing the way other people go to concerts or to parties."*[24]

The various investment "infotainment" programs on television, essentially discussing noise (statistically speaking), might be an indication that these views are not that far off.*

Today's financial environment has become too complex to the extent that standard theories like the capital asset pricing model (CAPM)† and the

---

*We apologize for making fun of "investainment" programs on television. It's not all bad. We noticed that one broadcaster not only shows the time in hour, minutes, and seconds when displaying a chart, but also has added passing milliseconds in real-time to the time format. This is obviously of great value to all investors.

†Eugene Fama and Kenneth French [2004] on CAPM: "The CAPM, like Markowitz's portfolio model on which it is built, is ... a theoretical tour de

EMH are under attack. Bernstein [1995] pointed out that current classical capital ideas are "suspected of suffering from kurtosis, skewness, and other less familiar malignancies," and that they are under attack by the "nonlinear hypothesis" and "overwhelmed by fears of discontinuity rather than pricing volatilities and factors" and "frequently made irrelevant by exotic new financial instruments that come in unfamiliar shapes and hedge unfamiliar risks." Bernstein added, "As the mathematics that define these risks grow increasingly complex, the dimensions, contours, and limits of risks are becoming correspondingly obscure." He concluded that the effort to abandon the beautiful and coherent logic of classical ideas does not mean that the classical ideas were in some sense "wrong," but rather it reflects on the changing environment in which we live today. In a world that is changing faster than we can grasp, risk seems more difficult to understand and control.

One of the interesting themes (among many) in behavioral finance is the discussion of overconfidence with market participants. Detecting overconfidence in combination with herding behavior and the resulting mean reversion process is probably one of the main goals of contrarians, value investors, and statistical arbitrageurs. It is difficult to imagine that the bubble and burst of the technology sector in the 1960s as well as the 1990s is the function of a random walk.

The classic *In Search of Excellence: Lessons from America's Best Run Corporations* by Peters and Waterman [1982] is not necessarily a guide for investors. The book's authors (business consultants) took a list of companies regarded as innovative by a group of informed businesspeople, and screened them on the following six measures of long-run financial superiority:

1. Rate of growth in corporate assets.
2. Rate of growth in book value.
3. Average ratio of market price to book value.
4. Average return on corporate assets.
5. Average return on book value.
6. Average ratio of net income to sales.

The list of companies they came up with was regarded as fundamentally the best companies. In 1987, an article in the *Financial Analysts Journal*

---

force. We continue to teach the CAPM as an introduction to the fundamentals of portfolio theory and asset pricing ... but we also warn students that, despite its seductive simplicity, the CAPM's empirical problems probably invalidate its use in applications." From Bernstein [2006b], p.1.

by Michelle Clayman was published, in which the analyst tracked the performance of the stocks of these companies for a period following the ranking, 1981 to 1985. These firms had established strong records of performance prior to 1980. By 1980, they had become growth stocks. If the market overreacted and overpriced them, their performance after 1980 should have been poor as the market corrected and the prices of the stocks fell to more reasonable levels.

Clayman [1987] compared the performance of the "excellent" companies with another group she called "unexcellent." These were the 39 companies in the Standard and Poor's (S&P) 500 population that had the worst combination of the six characteristics as of the end of 1980. Between 1981 and the end of 1985 the excellent companies increased by 81.6 percent. However, the unexcellent group rose by 197.5 percent.

Clayman revealed that the stunning characteristics of the excellent companies quickly reverted toward the mean in the years that followed their 1980 screening. Rates of growth in assets and book value nearly halved. Significant reductions were experienced in the other four categories as well. The unexcellent companies also reverted toward the mean. They showed substantial improvement in their median values for all six categories. The market did not anticipate the mean reversion. In Clayman [1994], the author repeats the methodology of her previous work and finds that "excellent" companies again outperformed as a group during 1988 to 1992, with a monthly alpha of 0.38 percent. Financial ratios of both "excellent" and "unexcellent" companies are again found to regress toward the mean. Other research has shown that this phenomenon also exists outside the U.S. stock market. Capaul et al. [1993], for example, looked at annualized return differences among stocks in various international stock markets in the period from January 1982 to June 1992.

For Shefrin [2000], there are two implications of investor overconfidence. First, investors take bad bets because they fail to realize that they are at an information disadvantage. Second, investors trade more frequently than is prudent, which leads to excessive trading volume.

The representativeness heuristic and overconfidence can, to some extent, explain some stock market anomalies. Social scientists and behavioral finance theorists call the phenomenon *representativeness heuristic,* where most investors think that good stocks are the stocks of good companies, although the evidence indicates that the opposite is true. A further consequence of this heuristic is a tendency for people (e.g., chartists, astrologers) to see patterns in data that are truly random. The concept of representativeness heuristic is not new. It goes back to Tversky and Kahneman [1974], who introduced the term in the 1970s with respect to decision making under uncertainty.

Classical economic theory posits the notion of *rational expectation*: People are efficient information processors and act rationally given the information available to them. The classical theory does not assume that people know everything, but it does assume that they make good use of the information they have and that their evaluation of the information is unbiased. Rational economic agents are supposed to make decisions in such a way as to maximize their utility. If the decision outcomes are uncertain, then utility is a random variable, so rational agents act to maximize their expected utility. Empirical evidence suggests, however, that people's judgments are often erroneous—and in a very predictable way. People are generally overconfident.

Loss Aversion and Prospect Theory Prospect theory proposes a descriptive framework for the way people make decisions under conditions of risk and uncertainty and embodies a richer behavioral framework than that of subjective expected utility theory, which underlies many traditional economic models and thinking. The key concepts are loss aversion, regret aversion, mental accounting, and self-control. Whenever we advocate the absolute-return investment philosophy, we keep falling back to the simple notion that losing money hurts. (The cyclical element of this notion is that in bear markets more people seem to agree with us.) Here, we focus only on the concept of loss aversion and prospect theory.

Tversky [1995] stated:

> *"Loss aversion—the greater impact of the downside than the upside—is a fundamental characteristic of the human pleasure machine."*

Loss aversion is based on the idea that the mental penalty associated with a given loss is greater than the mental reward from a gain of the same size. If investors are loss averse, they may be reluctant to realize losses. This can explain the sunk-cost effect whereby decision makers persist in including past costs when evaluating current decision alternatives. Loss aversion need not imply that investors are consistent in their attitude to risk. A key assumption of economic theory is that investors are risk averse. This may not always hold true in the real world. There is evidence that people play safe when protecting gains but are willing to take chances in an attempt to escape from a losing position. As we have alluded earlier, we believe the 2000 to 2002 bear market was the catalyst for the interest in absolute-return strategies and better-diversified portfolios among a wide array of institutional investors. This implies to some extent that institutional investors thought they were risk averse during the good years but found out the hard way that they are also loss averse. We believe this insight is structural (with our line of argument being somewhat perceived as more convincing in bear markets).

Prospect theory differs from expected utility theory. In 1738, Bernoulli suggested that, to evaluate risk, the weighted utility of wealth associated with each possible action is taken into consideration. Expected utility theory came a long way. However, because risk aversion does not hold in all cases, a different model from the classical model is called for. Today, prospect theory (as opposed to the standard model of expected utility) suggests that losses are weighted differently than gains. The S-shaped function of prospect theory has three features that distinguish it from the concave utility function of classical economic analysis:

1. It is defined in terms of gains and losses rather than in terms of asset position, or wealth. This approach reflects the observation that people think of outcomes in terms of gains and losses relative to some reference point, such as the status quo, rather than in terms of final asset position. Because people cannot lose what they do not have, classical economic theory does not address losses. The language of losses presupposes that people evaluate things relative to some reference point.
2. The second feature is that the value function is concave above the reference point and convex below it, which results in the characteristic S shape. This feature means that people are maximally sensitive to changes near the reference point. It also means that people are actually risk-seeking on the downside.
3. The third feature of the value function in prospect theory is that it is asymmetrical. The loss appears larger to most people than a gain of equal size. This characteristic is called *loss aversion.*

Kahneman and Tversky were not the first to challenge utility theory: Friedman and Savage [1948] proposed that the coexistence of the human tendency to gamble and risk avoidance might be explained by utility functions that become concave upward in extremely high range. Savage [1954] showed that the axioms from which expected utility theory is derived are undeniably sensible representations of basic requirements of rationality. Samuelson [1965] explains the violation of expected utility theory. Although it preceded prospect theory, it illustrates the importance of the kink in the value function from Kahneman and Tversky. We believe the findings of prospect theory also apply to institutional investors and not just to students sitting in for a psychological test on campus. Losses and (downside) volatility matter.

CHAPTER SUMMARY AND CONCLUSIONS

There is a case for active money management. Markets are unlikely to be fully efficient. The fact that most active large-cap equity managers underperform the benchmark does not prove that markets are efficient. For example, it is unlikely that lemming effects, consensus hugging, and buying excellent companies (once everyone agrees they are excellent) lead to success. Market inefficiencies will likely be around for a while; consequently, so will sophisticated and trading-savvy market participants who exploit the inefficiencies by hedging unwanted risks. It means that alpha is not symmetrically distributed among market participants searching for it. It is asymmetric. Alpha is an option.

APPENDIX: ON ALPHA, BETA, AND RANDOMNESS

> *"We must believe in luck. For how else can we explain the success of those we don't like?"*
> —Jean Cocteau

There is an ongoing debate as to what alpha really is and, if it exists, who is delivering it and who is getting it. Alpha can be positive as well as negative. Our view in this book and elsewhere is that alpha is the value added of an active investment process involving investment skill that carries a reward in the marketplace and that some investors have alpha in their portfolios net of all fees and all costs and some don't. However, this does not at all mean that all managers who talks about alpha deliver alpha, or that every investor who thinks he has alpha truly has alpha. In addition, we find that alpha is difficult to quantify. In the relative-return world, the value added is quantified by the information ratio. The theory behind the information ratio is well accepted and established. Ex-post the information ratio is calculated by the outperformance of the active manager over the benchmark divided by the tracking risk, that is, the standard deviation of relative returns. We find the logic and idea of the law of active management by Grinold [1989] brilliant and a huge contribution to the investment management profession. However, as the reader must know by now, we do have some difficulties with the denominator of the equation, that is, accepting tracking risk as having anything to do with risk. If Clingons (an extraterrestrial life form) were to attack Earth, most indexed and benchmarked managers would "reduce" risk by moving closer to the benchmark because their risk is defined and perceived as the benchmark. (Note that this is a somewhat extreme example. Clingons would attack

Romulus first.) In any case, finding investment opportunities is one thing, and managing risk in absolute-return space is another. We argue that in absolute-return space, the value added, that is, the alpha, is positive when the manager can create this call-option-like exposure to certain factors in a fairly sustainable and entrepreneurial fashion. This is the asymmetric-risk/return profile we keep falling back to. This is not magic. It does require a large set of variables, though. The process should be sustainable. This does not necessarily mean that alpha is stable. It can vary from year to year. However, if there is serious investment skill involved, the variance of the alpha will be on the positive side. It will not be random, nor should it vary in an erratic symmetrical fashion. Hence our belief that alpha is akin to the payout of an option: higher elasticity (delta) on the upside, lower elasticity on the downside. Some of the aforementioned variables are skill, diligence, intelligence, savvy, and experience. We cannot really quantify all variables in a satisfactory way.

However, there is huge demand for trying to quantify alpha, or more precisely, to separate alpha from beta. Beta today is typically referred to as exposure to a risk premium that more often than not can be captured in a passive, low-cost fashion. The demand for this task is fairly obvious: The rational investor is very happy to pay for alpha but not for beta, if beta is more affordably available elsewhere. Two problems: First, there is no such thing as pure alpha. Most absolute-return strategies involve risk or liquidity premiums in one form or another, that is, include a return element that theoretically could have had been captured in a passive fashion had we just known the factors and their loadings in advance. Second, the real world is very dynamic and complex, perhaps even chaotic. We cannot perfectly isolate and quantify alpha if we do not have an acceptable beta benchmark. We want to, but we can't. The idea of alpha in absolute-return space is somewhat akin to the idea of the EMH. There is no such thing as 100 percent efficiency in markets. The same is true for alpha. There is no such thing as pure alpha. Alpha comes with other risks. Pure alpha is a thought complex, an ideal world to which the real world can be compared. In Chapter 2, we challenged some of the conclusions of the Waring and Siegel [2006] article called "The Myth of the Absolute Return Investor," as the authors claim that there is no such thing as "absolute returns" in investment management. On a certain level they could be right, albeit for the wrong reasons.* Philosophically, one can argue that everything is relative.

One attempt to separate the alpha from the betas is common factor analysis. The idea of factor modeling is essentially to play around with data

---

*We refute their claim that most hedge funds have a "home" or "normal portfolio" they fall back to if their opportunity set falls to zero.

long enough until one finds empirical evidence to prove one's preconception, that is, curve fitting, and then go on and pretend one has found something meaningful, such as cause and effect.* (Note that there are alternative ways to describe factor modeling.[†] An author who can get away with mentioning Clingons in a financial book without immediately losing the reader can probably get away with anything.[‡]) Lars Jaeger [2005] on the topic of factor modeling and alpha:

"If we are humble enough to admit that our models are imperfect, then we should acknowledge that apparent alpha values in factor models are just that—apparent.[§] This means that apparent alpha can derive from any combination of two elements. One element is true alpha—manager skill in generating return without systematic risk—and the other is unmodeled beta, beta that is not captured because of a mis-specified or incomplete model. ... This should make us look at alpha statistics with a healthy degree of scepticism, even after applying the best available regression models."[¶]

The factor model with the highest r-squared we came across in the hedge fund literature is a regression wherein the returns of an equity long/short index minus the risk-free rate are regressed against three factors from Fama and French [1993]. The three factors are the market return minus the risk-free rate (r_m-r_f), small minus big (SMB), and high minus low (HML).[ǁ] SMB is the difference between the return of small-cap stocks and large-cap stocks. There is empirical evidence that small caps outperform large caps in the long term; that is, there is a risk premium for holding small-cap stocks instead of large-cap stocks. High and low refers to high book/price

---

*Note that empirical research is not limited to multiasset-factor models. There are higher forms of curve fitting available.

[†]Lhabitant [2004]: "Factor analysis determines from a statistical perspective the interrelationships among a large number of variables (e.g., fund returns) and expresses these interrelationships in terms of their common underlying dimensions (the factors)."

[‡]We mention extraterrestrials for two reasons: (1) At the very far left-hand side of a fat-tailed distribution, anything is possible. A "worst-case scenario" is never the worst case. (2) The unthinkable actually *does* sometimes occur. In addition, we agree with Oscar Wilde: "Seriousness is the only refuge of the shallow."

[§]This is obviously also true for beta. Apparent beta values in factor models are just that—apparent. Correlation does not prove causality.

[¶]We believe the last sentence is true. However, the sentence is also true if we replace the word *alpha* with *beta*.

[ǁ]Occasionally a factor for momentum is added. However, a momentum factor is typically of much lower statistical significance if significant at all.

TABLE 5.1 Factors from Regression Analysis

	Equity Hedge*			Technology*			Market Neutral**
	4/1997–3/2003	4/1997–3/2000	4/2000–3/2003	4/1997–3/2003	4/1997–3/2000	4/2000–3/2003	4/1997–3/2003
Intercept	0.0067	0.0101	0.0000	0.0086	*0.0111*	-0.0002	*0.0026*
r_m-r_f	0.3214	0.3726	0.2464	0.4169	0.5250	0.3045	0.0341
SMB	0.3653	0.4265	0.3156	0.4101	0.5324	0.2364	0.0882
HML	-0.2081	-0.2467	-0.1549	-0.8599	-0.9790	-0.7448	0.0092

Data: All indices are total return indices in U.S. dollars (USD). Risk-free rate is one-month USD London Interbank Offered Rate (LIBOR). Hedge fund indices: Hedge Fund Research Index (HFRI) Equity Hedge Index, HFRI Sector: Technology Index, HFRI Equity Market Neutral Index. Equity indices: Morgan Stanley Composite Index (MSCI) USA, MSCI USA Value, MSCI USA Growth, MSCI US Large Cap 300, MSCI US Large Cap Growth, MSCI US Large Cap Value, MSCI US Small Cap 1750, MSCI US Small Cap Value, MSCI US Small Cap Growth.
Figures in bold are significant at 99% level, italic at 95% level.
* All regressions have r-squared of 0.83 or higher.
** r-squared of 0.11.
Source: Author's own calculations; raw equity index data from Thomson Financial; hedge fund data from Bloomberg.

ratio (value stocks) and low book/price ratio (essentially growth stocks).* These regressions result in r-squared far higher than 0.80 (which, in the social sciences, is perceived as high) and with all factors having very high statistical significance. These regressions are the mother of all regressions in hedge fund research.

We have also played around with the data. We regressed three hedge fund indices against the three factors mentioned above. We have chosen the six-year period from April 1997 to March 2003. This period allows us to distinguish between two extreme, three-year periods. The first is from April 1997 to March 2000, which arguably was a phase in which growth stocks outperformed value stocks. In the following three years, it was the other way around. Value outperformed growth.

The focus is on the first six columns of Table 5.1, which show two equity long/short indices. The first column shows the regression for the full six-year period, whereas the following two columns show the two three-year

---

*This can cause confusion. Normally, value stocks are shown as having *low* price/book values. However, Fama and French used the reciprocal value, that is, book/price ratio. So a *high* book/price ratio means *low* price/book ratio. *High* here means value stocks. A negative regression coefficient, therefore, means exposure to growth stocks as a positive coefficient would mean exposure to *high* book/price ratio stocks, that is, value stocks. (Yes, we were confused, too.)

periods. We have added factors of a regression with a market-neutral index for the full six-year period to Table 5.1. The motivation for doing so is the occasional casual remark by some market participants that market neutral is the same as equity long/short without the beta, that is, with net market exposure of around zero. We challenge this notion, as we believe market neutral is a separate strategy. The data backs that up to some extent.

The way to read the numbers in the first column as an example is as follows. The intercept of 67 basis points is not explained by the other factors. It is not the risk-free rate, as we have taken the risk-free rate out of the equation. In the attempt to quantify things, the intercept is often referred to as alpha. This would mean that the average equity long/short manager has added 67 basis points of alpha per month to their investor's net of all fees and costs. The 67 basis points are the apparent alpha. Quite often, analysis of this type is used to argue that there is much more beta in the return series than there is alpha. It seems to us that the data is massaged so long until all the alpha can be explained away empirically. The motto often is: If a factor modeling does not work, try principal component analysis. If principal component analysis does not work, try regime-switching models. And so on. To us, this work is actually all very interesting (probably the reason why we should get out more). However, we believe this research sometimes understates the fact that there are good and bad investors as there are good and bad chefs, golfers, entrepreneurs, financial authors, and so on. The researchers are trying too hard to make the data look random, that is, to confirm their preconception of how the world should work. Apart from the data of the empirical analysis being imperfect, there is the even bigger issue of the unlikelihood of the world's being explained by three factors or a couple of principal components.* In addition, there is hindsight bias. These regressions were not in the literature in the 1990s. These regressions appeared after the technology bubble burst, that is, as it became apparent that value and growth stocks could be an important explanatory factor to long/short managers.[†]

---

*We are being somewhat overcritical and simplistic. After all, this is an appendix with reference to extraterrestrials attacking Earth. We obviously regard the search for truth as highly laudable as well as of high importance and value to investors and fiduciaries alike. We just, at times, find the constraints of those in search as too narrow to find full understanding. (Although perhaps it's just that we do not always like their conclusions, especially if they differ from our own, hence our incentive to portray the work as nonsense.)

[†]Here, we are tempted to argue that empirical analysis is for historians, while a deep fundamental understanding of a strategy is for investors. This is obviously not true. Empirical research helps understanding and learning.

The first factor of 0.32 in the first column of Table 5.1 says that a large part of the long/short return above the risk-free rate can be explained by the excess market return (here the total return of MSCI USA minus the risk-free rate). So if the excess return of the U.S. stock market is 10 percent in a given month, the model tells us to expect that 3.2 percent of the return of the average long/short manager is due to being somewhat long the stock market. This is, some argue, bad news. This means that part of the performance fee is based on the return of the stock market that could be captured more cheaply using passive access-instruments such as index funds, exchange-traded funds (ETFs), total return swaps, and so on. However, the 0.32 factor is pretty much consistent with what we believe is the average net exposure of the average equity long/short manager of around 30 percent. At the time of writing (Q2 06), this average net exposure was higher, that is, around 44 percent.

The second factor of 0.37 tells us that a big part of the return is based on capturing the risk premium for small-cap stocks. So if small-cap stocks outperform large-cap stocks by ten percent, we can expect a return of 3.7 percent that is attributable to the outperformance of small caps. This actually is also bad news. An investor does not need to pay $2 + 20$ to capture this premium these days. Passive alternatives are available, especially for institutional investors. The third factor of -0.21 implies a *negative* relationship between the excess return of equity long/short with the excess return of value stocks over growth stocks. (Or a *positive* relationship with growth stocks outperforming value stocks.) This means that long/short managers should lose money when value outperforms growth. In other words, the regressions suggest a long bias toward growth stocks.

The second and third columns of Table 5.1 show the regressions for the two three-year periods ending March 2000 and starting April 2000. We deliberately have chosen this period because, with the benefit of hindsight, we know that the former was an extreme period for growth stocks and the latter for value stocks, in relative performance as well as absolute performance terms, as we will see shortly. The intercept of the growth stocks period was 101 basis points, and the intercept of the value stocks period that followed was zero. Many analysts argue that it is actually the other way around. The argument is that long/short managers were riding the bull market when it was in full swing and then called it a day when the music stopped, that is, went into capital-preservation mode. This is a good marketing one-liner but obviously too simplistic. Risk was not switched from "on" to "off" around March 2000. However, let's have a look at the changes of the three market risk factors. All of them were lower in the second period. This is true for the technology index as well. The technology index shows the performance of a portfolio of long/short managers that invest primarily in technology (growth) stocks. Typically, the net exposure of these managers is higher than the average, more balanced, long/short managers. For instance, the HML factor of the technology index was -0.98 during the dot-com phase. This means nearly full exposure to the growth/value differential.

The reduction in these factors from the first to the second regime means that less of the return is explained by the factors. Our interpretation of this is that risk to the factors was reduced from the first period to the second. This means that for both long/short indices the exposure to the market return, the small/large-cap differential as well as the growth/value stock differential was reduced. The reduction of the first and third factors was a pretty good idea, as the market tanked and value outperformed growth. We call successfully adapting to changing market circumstances *skill* and regard it as of great value to the investor. We think this is part of the alpha. The optionality is that the investor has a call-option-like exposure to factors. If growth works, the risk to growth stocks is increased. If value works, the risk to value stocks is increased. If growth doesn't work anymore, risk is reduced, and so on. This, over time, gives the call-option-like exposure to these factors, which is the main part of this book. The task for having these call-option-like exposures is, we believe, active risk management. Investment skill is required. Choosing exposures at random does not work, as it would not create this call-option-like profile.

Figure 5.1 shows the equity long/short index from April 1997 to March 2003 as well as the discussed model (factors from the first column in Table 5.1). We have added a time series where intercept was set to zero. (Rerunning a zero-intercept regression does not yield largely differing factors than those shown in Table 5.1). We set the time of the regime switch to 100 for presentation purposes. The equity long/short index outperformed the model with zero intercept (no "apparent" alpha) in both regimes.

We hope the reader finds this all very interesting (the part on options, that is). However, we believe there is a more intuitive way of looking at this issue. Panels A and B of Table 5.2 show two return matrixes. We show each nine returns for the three-year period. From top left to bottom right the figures show three-year returns for: small-cap value stocks, all value stocks, large large-cap value stocks, all small-cap stocks, overall U.S. stock market, all large-cap stocks, small-cap growth stocks, all growth stocks, and large-cap growth stocks.

Panel A shows the three-year period from April 1997 to March 2000, and Panel B captures the three-year period from April 2000 to March 2003. So, for example, between April 1997 and March 2000 the absolute total return of the U.S. stock market was 112 percent, whereby small-cap value stocks increased by only 27 percent and large-cap growth stocks

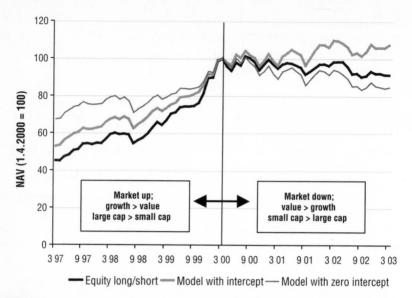

FIGURE 5.1 Equity Long/Short and Factor Model with and without Intercept Equity long/short: HFRI Equity Hedge Index. For model specifications, see text. *Source:* Author's own calculations; hedge fund returns from Bloomberg.

TABLE 5.2 Value/Growth Small-Cap/Large-Cap Return Matrix

Panel A (4/1997–3/2000)				Panel B (4/2000–3/2003)			
(%)	Small Cap	All	Large Cap	(%)	Small Cap	All	Large Cap
Value	27	67	61	Value	19	-33	-21
All	82	112	118	All	-23	-43	-45
Growth	148	164	187	Growth	-52	-53	-62
Equity long/short		128		Equity long/short		-8	
Technology		298		Technology		-47	
Market neutral		31		Market neutral		22	

See table notes of Table 5.1 for details on indices used.
Source: Author's own calculations; raw equity index data from Thomson Financial; hedge fund data from Bloomberg.

mushroomed by 187 percent. A comparison of the two matrixes shows nicely the two extreme regimes. In Panel A the highest number is in the lower-right corner and the lowest number is in the upper-left, as large-cap growth performed best and small-cap value performed worst. In Panel B it is exactly the other way around. We have added three equity-related hedge fund indices to compare performance in the two different regimes. Returns are all total returns in USD and were not annualized.

A long-only investor increased his wealth by 112 percent from April 1997 to March 2000 and then gave back 43 percent from April 2000 to March 2003. This roller coaster ride took the investor from $100 to $212 then back to $120. This results in a compounding rate of return (CARR) of 3.1 percent, assuming dividends were reinvested and not taxed away or spent. However, as alluded in the appendix to Chapter 1, most investors add new money to their investments over time. Investments are someone's savings. Apart from some exceptions, savings accrue over time and are put to work in intervals. A saver investing $100 in March 1997 and adding another $100 in March 2000 would have "compounded" his cash flows at −2.7 percent (internal rate of return [IRR]). Had the investor, instead of investing in the broad market, invested in U.S. small-cap value stocks (upper left-hand corner of the matrix) the CARR would have been 7.1 percent and the IRR 6.7 percent. In other words, the deep-value manager experienced absolute returns in both three-year regimes.* The CARR and IRR for the equity long/short and technology long/short proxies were 13.1 and 9.4 percent for long/short and 13.3 and 6.4 percent for technology long/short. These examples reiterate one important notion made throughout this book, which is that large drawdowns is not good for your financial health and should be avoided if compounding capital positively is a major objective. It seems: The duller the better. The returns of small-cap value stocks look minuscule and dull. However, CARR and especially IRR are superior to the more fascinating long-only alternatives. An absolute-return strategy would try to have a bias toward the southeast corner of the matrix in the first regime and a bias toward the northwest corner in the second regime. A relative-return strategy can do that as well, but only to a limited extent. The marginal contribution to tracking error of Yahoo or Google entering the benchmark is just too large to ignore.

One conclusion from Table 5.2 is that equity long/short is not just about picking stocks in isolation. Regimes such as bull versus bear markets, value versus growth, or small-cap versus large-cap matter, too. If we were to believe all is random, we certainly would need to shy away from an active investment process. However, we believe there is an element of predictability for skilled and experienced investors. This is why we believe that investors who are capable of introducing a bias toward the current regime are producing alpha even though factor modeling tell us that, looking back, it actually was beta. One of the pillars of the EMH is that

---

*Assuming, of course, the value manager managed to stay in business during the dot-com craze.

prices are unpredictable. This is probably true. We would add that prices are unpredictable *to the average investor*. So the notion that prices are unpredictable to the average investor does not foreclose that some investors actually might have an edge over the average investor.

A very common treat in the investment world is that investors see patterns in what is really random. These investors are essentially fooled by randomness.[25] However, the opposite is probably true as well. There are investors who believe a certain market behavior is random, but it is not. Those investors are fooled by randomness, too. Note here that the larger the population of decision-making fools in a marketplace, the less efficient the market and the larger the opportunity set for the nonignorant and skilled investor to capture and sustainably deliver alpha.

Sector long/short specialists are quite often referred to not as stand-alone investments but as an alternative of getting (beta) exposure to a certain sector, essentially an alternative to investing in a long-only sector fund. The alpha argument sits on the notion that these sector specialists have deeper knowledge in the particular sector than generalists. We do not challenge this notion but add that generalist long/short funds can very well be populated by specialist sector desks.

Table 5.2 shows that technology long/short funds have outperformed all the growth indices in all regimes. So in relative-return space they did very well. In absolute-return space they did okay. One hundred dollars went to $398 in the first regime, and then retreated to $211 in the second. However, the drawdowns are too large for most absolute-return investors to accept it as a stand-alone investment. The CARR and IRR of the HFRI Technology Index was 13.3 percent and 6.4 percent. This compares to 1.6 percent and −6.6 percent for the long-only growth stocks investor (lower-right quadrant in Table 5.2).

Market neutral is not entirely unaffected by all of this. In the first three-year period, the return was 31.5 percent and in the second 21.7 percent. This results in a compounding rate of 9.5 percent for the first period and 6.8 percent per year for the second. With the average risk-free rate for the two periods being 5.5 and 3.6 percent, this results in annual excess returns of roughly 4.0 and 3.2 percent per year. Note here that by choosing the six-year period from April 1997 to March 2003, we are showing an example of both an extreme growth period followed by an extreme value period. From an excess return point of view, market neutral seems fairly stable, with only 80 basis points difference between the two regimes. Whether the two returns can be explained by factors or by increased competition in the market-neutral space is open to debate. The annual excess return for the three-year period from April 2003 to March 2006 by comparison was 2.9 percent. This steady decline in returns indicates that there is a structural element responsible for the steady decline, apart from any intermittent cyclical elements. An observation that is difficult to challenge, we find, is the notion that an increase in competition increases market efficiency. The declining excess returns in market neutral could be a case in point. This is one reason we believe manager selection is so important. (Note that by examining hedge fund indices we analyze the performance of the average or median manager. The top decile or top quintile still could be delivering very respectable excess returns. Competition could very well widen, not narrow, the dispersion around the index average. This would support the case repeatedly made in this book that manager selection is key. The wider the dispersion, the larger is the opportunity for the skilled hedge fund picker, but the larger is the risk for the unskilled hedge fund picker.)

BOTTOM LINE

We remember an interview with Ed Thorpe (math professor, author, black-jack player, and hedge fund manager) in either the *Financial Times* or *Wilmott* magazine a couple of years ago. Thorpe was asked whether he thinks markets are efficient or not. His response was something along the lines that markets are not efficient but recommended that most investors should actually behave as if they are. We actually subscribe to that view. Active risk management is difficult and tricky. Alpha is scarce. We believe creating alpha on a sustainable basis is possible and managing risk on an active basis in absolute-return space makes a lot of sense. However, most of investors' capital is excluded from all of this. Let's hope that nothing bad happens.

CHAPTER **6**

Active Risk Management

"The human mind treats a new idea the same way the body treats a strange protein; it rejects it."

—Anatomist P. B. Medawar

"Being ignorant is not so much a shame, as being unwilling to learn."

—Benjamin Franklin

Our interpretation of the idea of "absolute returns" is, in the simplest of terms, about positive compounding of wealth or capital while avoiding negative compounding of wealth or capital. We use the term *asymmetric-return profile*, which goes further than just managing portfolio volatility. If the objective were to reduce portfolio volatility, one could easily just combine any volatile asset class with cash to reduce portfolio volatility. Reducing volatility by adding cash to a risky asset narrows the return distribution in a symmetrical fashion. Both positive and negative returns are lowered, so compounding is lower. However, we believe the idea behind an investment process focusing on absolute returns is to have an idea-generation process for the upside (i.e., the returns) and a risk management process for the downside (i.e., the avoidance of negative absolute returns—especially large ones). The separation of the upside and the downside should result in some form of call-option-like feature, that is, an asymmetry.

In this chapter, we search for the asymmetries available in some absolute-return strategies as compared to passive portfolios with similar volatility characteristics. Before we do so, we discuss issues which make all the difference in active risk management: the applicability and adaptability of skill.

APPLICABILITY AND ADAPTABILITY OF SKILL

Performance in absolute-return space should—in an ideal world—be attributed to skill and not a function of randomness. Another way of putting this is to say that the returns achieved by absolute-return managers should not be attributed to a stochastic process. The original idea of a hedge fund, that is, the Alfred Jones model,* was to have an investment process in which the return is a function of the manager's skill rather than the swings of the equity market. If the investment process is indeed a function of skill, the return is somewhat predictable (as opposed to random), as long as the particular skill is applicable and rewarded in the marketplace (and the bearer of the "skill" doesn't get run over by a bus).

We believe these latter points to be important. Skill is skill, but it might or might not be rewarded in the marketplace; that is, the applicability of skill is subject to change. For example, fundamental stock research was a brilliant idea on the advent of the mutual fund a couple of decades ago. The reward from fundamental stock analysis was huge for the few who rigorously applied the analysis to investment management, as a large proportion of the investment community was ignorant about the valuation of stocks. It was the catalyst for a whole new industry: the professional investment management industry. However, that particular skill got copied *because* it carried a large reward. Consequently, applying simple fundamental stock research today does not carry as high a reward as it used to. In other words, markets become more efficient; that is, they adapt and become somewhat "immune" to the skill. Under competition, the skill gets somewhat "commoditized." This is probably true for many other skills, too. The skills applied in traditional convertible arbitrage (gamma-trading convertible bonds) or merger arbitrage (buying the target and selling the acquirer's stock in an announced merger) do not carry as high a premium as they once did.[†] In other words, if alpha is supposed to be sustainable, the skill must evolve as the opportunity set adapts to the applicability of the skill.

To make matters more complex, there is not only structural change but also cyclical change. So simply buying the convertible and selling the stock short or simply buying the target in a merger and shorting the acquirer might find a decent reward again soon. Determining whether a change of circumstances is cyclical or structural can be difficult (which is why it carries a high price tag).

---

*For literature on hedge fund history, consult: Peltz [1994, 2001], Caldwell and Kirkpatrick [1995], Caldwell [1995], Elden [2001], Anson [2002], Biggs [2006], and Ineichen [2003a].

[†]Note that some investment professionals argue that the variation in a strategy's return is not structural but purely cyclical.

Adaptability versus Style Drift

Many merger arbitrage managers migrated away from the traditional application of the strategy over the past couple of years and moved into other areas, typically by becoming "multi-strategy" and getting involved in corporate restructuring arbitrage, distressed loans, and so on. A negative interpretation of this move is calling it *style drift*. A more positive perspective (and our view) is that those managers evolved, that is, noticed that their skill might not yield as high a reward under changing market conditions and applied their skill elsewhere. In other words, they changed the applicability of the skill set to changes in the opportunity set. To us who believe everything always changes ("change" being the only constant in the universe), this actually makes a lot of sense. Whether the change is cyclical or structural is beside the point. The point is that capital at risk is reduced when the applicability of the skill carries no reward in the marketplace.

Lo [2004] uses the term *maladaptive* to describe an action that once worked but does not work anymore in an environment that has changed. Suboptimal behavior in capital markets, one could argue, is not derived from irrationality but from applying a skill that worked well in a different regime. A long-only buy-and-hold strategy is a case in point. Related to all this, Lo wrote:

> *"The flopping of a fish on dry land may seem strange and unproductive, but underwater, the same motions are capable of propelling the fish away from its predators."*

One Needs to Evolve to Survive   Markets become more efficient over time as "the market" learns and adapts. In other words, markets become "aware" of how pioneers and first-movers exploit market inefficiencies. While skill may remain constant, the reward from applying the skill falls over time. Therefore, one needs to adapt the skill to changing market circumstances; that is, one needs to evolve to survive. It goes without saying that a business model that allows for maneuverability and adaptability is more sustainable than one suffering from the "one-trick-pony" syndrome.

We believe the above to be true. However, one could also argue that there are some "constant" or nondegrading market inefficiencies. For instance, there could be a persistent market malfunction caused by the fact that participants in the market have different utility functions. Convertible arbitrage, one could argue, has been around for decades and has rewarded the arbitrageur handsomely for decades. A large part of the returns is attributed to issuance that is brought to market too cheaply. The reason for bringing the paper to market too cheaply is that the issuer has a different utility function—that is, the benefit of funding through convertibles exceeds the benefit that would be derived by funding through equity or debt, even if the convertibles are priced below "fair" value. The cyclicality in the degree of mispricing stems from shifts in the supply-and-demand imbalances. In 2005, for example, demand for cheap issuance was much larger than supply, so inefficiencies (as in opportunity set) were smaller and returns were therefore below norm. Our point: We believe one can find arguments for both: (1) convertible arbitrage has structurally changed and does not work anymore because the inefficiency was crowded out; or (2) convertible arbitrage was in a cyclical low in 2005.* We lean toward the latter, although we believe convertible arbitrage has to some extent changed structurally in the sense that the rapid expansion of credit derivatives opened new avenues of return for the arbitrageur to exploit. The bottom line for all active pursuits is that one needs to adapt to survive. All strategies change. Standing still is futile. Sir Francis Bacon brought it to the point: "He that will not apply new remedies must expect new evils; for time is the greatest innovator."

THE LAW OF ACTIVE MANAGEMENT

We believe there is a relationship between market inefficiencies and whether an active approach is warranted or not. Furthermore, our interpretation of Grinold's [1989] law of active management is that the value added of an active manager is a function of his skill times the number of independent decisions the manager can make per year (the opportunity set). If one of these two variables (skill or number of opportunities) is zero, the ex-ante value added must be zero, as any number multiplied by zero equals zero. The number of independent decisions can be either zero or positive, while the skill can be a positive as well as a negative figure. It is because of our interpretation of this "law" that we believe the current hedge fund phenomenon is not a short-term phenomenon: If we compare two managers with identical *positive* skills but two different opportunity sets, one is constrained within his area of expertise and the other unconstrained or less constrained; the latter will add more value by definition.

Note that the qualification "within his area of expertise" is quite important. In the early days of the asset management industry, the manager was more or less unconstrained. Over time, traditional managers became more constrained through the introduction of benchmarks. However, hedge fund managers remained only self-constrained. Today, many traditional

---

*By Q2 06, there were strong indications that the opportunity set in convertible arbitrage was recovering, that is, reverting to its mean.

managers are trying to loosen up their constraints to be able to add more value (because their interpretation of "the law" is similar to our own). It is not entirely without irony that hedge funds sometimes seem to be going the other way, that is, becoming more constrained. Part of the impetus for this is that hedge funds that want to cater to institutional investors and want to build franchise value need to become more transparent. This (among other things) means becoming more process driven (as opposed to relying on one single key individual). This leads to a form of self-constraint, as once managers have "sold" themselves to their investors as having a very distinctive niche or focus or approach, they feel compelled to stay within these initial parameters.

There are at least two reasons why investors might exert such pressure on hedge funds managers: (1) They have evaluated the manager on the basis of a particular strategy focus. If that focus changes then they can no longer be sure that the manager is the best available one to implement it, that is there might be another manager who is better suited. So the "gatekeeper," fund of funds manager or consultant, needs to reevaluate the manager given the changed circumstances. (2) Portfolio construction at the fund of fund level presupposes that each manager is providing exposure to certain factors—if the focus of the underlying manager changes then the portfolio construction needs to be changed. Consistency of approach makes life easier for fund of funds manager, or consultant, even if suboptimal in return terms.

We believe that searching for investment skill, finding it, and then constraining it are somewhat paradoxical.* Note that an absolute-return manager is constrained, too, either through his discipline and process (endogenous constraint) or through the investor's mandate (exogenous constraint). One therefore could argue that traditional and alternative asset management are not that far apart, as both managers should be only doing what they have signed up to do with their investors. In other words, the constraint in absolute-return space is somewhat looser (no formal benchmark) and more self-inflicted but not nonexistent.

It is fair to assume that there is a relationship between the degree of efficiency and the opportunity set to add value through an active approach. The more underresearched and/or complex the situation, the higher the potential reward. Note that the strong form of the efficient market hypothesis (EMH) suggests that the price is always right. The whole hedge funds

---

*One could counterargue and say the absence of constraints implies a manager's being able to operate inside as well as outside his core competency. With constraint being paradoxical, we therefore mean constraint in a narrow sense, that is, constraint of the manager's flexibility within his core or related competency.

industry therefore is inconsistent with the strong form of EMH. However, we believe the potential to add value from actively managing assets is positively related to the degree of price inefficiency. The greater the inefficiency, the larger the prospective reward.

LEVERAGE AS A RISK MANAGEMENT TOOL

The use of leverage is important in risk management. Every derivative instrument involves leverage. However, leverage is also a source of confusion as well as misrepresentation. The term *leverage* is often used with a negative connotation. Increasing leverage means increasing risk. This is true, as one can regard leverage as a magnifying glass that increases both positive and negative returns. However, we do not believe leverage is necessarily the best measure of risk for absolute-return strategies and their managers. In fact, we believe a traditional manager has typically higher volatility and investment risk than a long/short hedge fund. The press coverage seems to exacerbate leverage concerns across the market. The general public does not understand that being long Apple and short Microsoft in most cases is less risky than being long Google. The counterargument to that is that leverage increases idiosyncratic risk of the unskilled manager, that is, is somewhat akin to a kid playing with a loaded gun.

It is necessary here to discuss leverage and its relationship to generating alpha before we examine asymmetries in some absolute-return strategies in the remainder of this chapter.

Leverage is often used as a scare tactic when hedge funds are discussed in tabloids. We could call this the *2L syndrome*, as most anti–hedge fund articles use leverage and LTCM (Long-Term Capital Management) as their main argument to attack hedge funds. We understand the use of leverage as a tool to actively manage risk. Generally speaking, and everything else held equal, risk increases as leverage increases and is reduced as leverage decreases. And in the wrong hands, it *can* cause damage.

When market inefficiencies are exploited, leverage is often used because the inefficiencies are too small to be economically meaningful without the use of leverage. The relevant question for the investor is to know which risk factors have been amplified and which have been reduced as a function of the manager's using leverage. The most intuitive way to show the use of leverage appears in Ainslie [1999].

Example   In equity long/short strategies, the net exposure is most often viewed as the main measure when assessing risk. This is probably true to assess portfolio volatility. However, the gross exposure and the ratio between longs and shorts give more insight into the degree of hedging. *Net*

BETA IS BACK

As mentioned earlier, there are some instances of hedge fund managers launching long-only (beta) products. As equities have risen recently, the appetite for equity beta seems to be on the rise, too. There is positive correlation between markets going up (cause) and appetite for that market's assets (effect). Potentially, there are also hedge fund managers and/or investors who question the value added of the short book through the full cycle; that is, they view the short book as just some sort of short-term "volatility dampener." We believe there are two points worth mentioning in this context: one related to risk and one related to the history of hedge funds.

- *Risk: The original idea of a hedge fund was to achieve continuous absolute returns where the return is a function of skill, not market factors. If this can be achieved, the return stream is fairly smooth and revenues a function of success, not luck. This carries a large price tag, as it is more attractive for investors who want to compound capital positively as opposed to being exposed to the market's mood swings naked. If the original idea of creating this asymmetry through active management is abandoned, fees invariably need to fall. An expected 8 percent return with a high degree of conviction in materializing is worth paying for. An expected 8 percent return with a low degree of conviction in materializing is not.*

- *Remember: Hedge funds have already departed from the Alfred Jones model once before. At the end of the 1960s bull market, hedge funds were long and levered. During the two subsequent bear markets (1969 to 1970 and 1973 to 1974), around two thirds closed down. For the 28 largest hedge funds in a Securities and Exchange Commission (SEC) survey from 1968, assets under management declined 70 percent due to losses and withdrawals.*

The near extinction of hedge funds three decades ago was largely explained through managers departing from the idea of hedging certain bets and leveraging up equity market risk. History sometimes has a nasty habit of repeating itself.

TABLE 6.1   Example

	Portfolio A	Portfolio B
Long exposure	150%	75%
Short exposure	-100%	-25%
Net exposure	50%	50%
Long/short ratio	1.5x	3.0x

Source: Ainslie [1999].

exposure indicates what percentage of net assets are net long the market. *Gross exposure,* the sum of long exposure and short exposure, measure capital at risk. However, the *long/short ratio* describes the balance between longs and shorts. It is this ratio, as Ainslie points out, that is a more significant determinant than net exposure of a portfolio's ability to perform in different environments and to produce returns that are not correlated to the market.

Table 6.1 demonstrates the difference. Both portfolios have the same net exposure of 50 percent but differ in terms of the long/short ratio and gross exposure. Portfolio A uses leverage and the gross exposure is 250 percent of principal. Portfolio B is unlevered and therefore has a higher long/short ratio. If the market falls by 15 percent, one can assume both portfolios will lose half of that, according to the net exposure of 50 percent:

Portfolio A $(150\% \times -15) + (-100\% \times -15\%) = -7.5\%$

Portfolio B $(75\% \times -15) + (-25\% \times -15\%) = -7.5\%$

The idea behind equity hedging is stock picking. This means if a manager has stock-picking skill and the market falls by 15 percent, it is possible that the longs fall by only 10 percent, that is, outperform the market, while the shorts can fall by, say, 20 percent, that is, underperform. The two portfolios would display the following return pattern:

Portfolio A $(150\% \times -10) + (-100\% \times -20\%) = +5.0\%$

Portfolio B $(75\% \times -10) + (-25\% \times -20\%) = -2.5\%$

The use of leverage allowed manager A to produce positive returns despite the market's falling 15 percent. The example shows how the skilled manager can leverage his skill, in this case stock picking. Assuming skill is positive, the risk/return profile of the fund is asymmetric. There are more positive returns than negative returns and/or the positive returns are on average larger than the negative returns. This asymmetry would be difficult to implement without the use of leverage. If we apply the logic of the law of active management to all this, it becomes unreasonable why a manager with stock-picking skill should *not* be using leverage. It would be like playing the piano by only using the white keys.

Three Ways to Use Leverage

Leverage can be used in three different ways: to amplify exposure, to diversify exposure, or to hedge exposure. By *exposure,* we mean risk exposure, that is, a financial position that potentially could move against the investor's best (financial) interest. In the following, we give examples for the three different uses of leverage. (None of the three examples contains exposure to idiosyncratic risk.)

Lever Up Assume an investor has an equity base of $100. If the investor has invested $100 in German large-cap stocks and borrows $100 to invest in French large-cap stocks, the investor would be considered levered by 2:1, that is, the gross exposure is 2 or 200 percent, while the equity is 1 or 100 percent. The net exposure would be considered 200 percent, too (i.e., the investor has levered up). The use of leverage has certainly increased the risk exposure. (A purely hypothetical out-of-control bank employee loading up Nikkei futures in a far-away satellite office would also fall in this category.)

Diversify The second example is an investor with the same capital base of $100 invested $50 in U.S. large caps, $50 in a collateralized debt obligation (CDO) of subordinated debt of Chinese bicycle manufacturers, a notional $50 in Kazakh wheat forward contracts, and $50 in a collection of marble sculptures by a series of Icelandic artists. (For the sake of argument, we assume here that the investor's expected return is positive for all four investments and there are no differences in terms of liquidity.) The leverage in this example is 2:1. However, the portfolio is diversified. The portfolio is diversified because the returns are expected to be volatile over time but to be fairly independent of one another. In other words, there should not be a causal relationship between U.S. stocks and Icelandic art (at least not an obvious one).* We believe that the total risk (here defined as the

---

*Correlation and causality are not the same. In what is becoming an infamous example, David Leinweber went searching for random correlations to the S&P 500. Peter Coy described Leinweber's findings in a *BusinessWeek* article entitled "He Who Mines Data May Strike Fool's Gold" (June 16, 1997). The article discussed data mining and the fact that patterns will occur in data by pure chance, particularly

probability of losing large amounts of money) with this portfolio is lower than with a (unlevered) long-only portfolio 100 percent in U.S. stocks. In other words, it is not the leverage per se that tells us something about risk, but the exposure to factor bets,[†] portfolio concentrations, liquidity structure, volatilities, tails, and so on, that have been altered through the use of leverage.[‡] Our point: Additional information (other than leverage) is required to assess risk.

Hedge   The third example is an investor with a capital base of $100, investing $100 in U.K. large-capitalization stocks and short $100 notional Financial Times Stock Exchange (FTSE) 100 futures. The (accounting) leverage is again 2:1, as the gross exposure is 200 percent. However, this investor has used leverage to hedge. The idea of hedging is to find an instrument to mirror-image the original position, in this case U.K. large caps. A short position in FTSE 100 futures has a correlation to a U.K. large-cap portfolio of around −1, while the expected return of the short futures position is negative—that is, the opposite of the long position. The two expected returns cancel each other out—hence the term *hedging*. The difference between hedging and diversifying is that when diversifying, the expected return of all investments is *positive* and the correlation normally between 0 and 1. A hedging instrument, to the contrary, has a *negative* expected return and negative correlation to the asset to be hedged. Note that it is not the use of leverage that has reduced risk, but the reduction of the exposure to a volatile factor (in this case, the stock market). Leverage is just a tool.

---

if one considers many factors. Many cases of data mining are immune to statistical verification or rebuttal. In describing the pitfalls of data mining, Leinweber "sifted through a United Nations CD-ROM and discovered that historically, the single best predictor of the Standard & Poor's 500 stock index was butter production in Bangladesh." The lesson to learn, according to Coy, is that a "formula that happens to fit the data of the past won't necessarily have any predictive value."

[†]Note that the term *bet* in finance is not necessarily equivalent to its colloquial meaning of "gamble." Although we believe the inference of gambling is not correct, it is easily made by the popular press when viewed in the context of financial tools such as derivatives, short selling and leverage. Quite often, these tools are viewed as speculative, whereas we view these tools as mere instruments to actively manage risk efficiently.

[‡]This statement could be challenged: If, for example, extraterrestrials attacked Earth and "nationalized" (or in this case more precisely "extraterrestrialized") all tangible assets, then the investor would owe them money—that is, "risk" could be perceived as higher than if the investor were unlevered in just equities and bonds in an unlevered long-only fashion.

The Art of Generating Alpha

For his statue of David in 1501, Michelangelo used a single block of marble. For Michelangelo, to sculpt meant to take away, not to add, because the sculpture already existed inside the block of marble. The stone was just the covering of a work of art; the sculptor only had to take away the part in excess. The sculptor's hand, guided by skill and experience, could only take out what was already extant inside the block of marble, and needed only to free the "idea" inside from the superfluous matter surrounding it. One could argue that the alpha in capital markets is already there. One just needs to hedge ("take away") all the various unwanted risks in order to carve it out. As markets become more and more efficient, this will be increasingly difficult without using all the risk management tools available. Constraining (positively skilled) managers in their field of expertise and the use of the tools to execute their craft, therefore, cannot be optimal. It's like giving Michelangelo only a hammer. Michelangelo on generating alpha: "If you knew how much work went into it, you wouldn't call it genius."

We believe the term *hedge fund* is a misnomer because there are no hedge funds that hedge all risks. If all risks were hedged, all the returns would be hedged as well. Ex-ante, returns are a function of taking risk. Absolute-return investing implies that the risk-neutral position is cash (i.e., no risky positions at all). Generating alpha, we believe, by definition means to take some risk. However, there are risks that are more likely to carry a reward, and risks that are less likely. This is where the asymmetry comes in again. Some bets follow a Brownian motion; some do not. The process of differentiating the two, the "sculpting," is then a function of intelligence, savvy, effort, experience, and skill.

Hedge funds are involved in all three ways of using leverage discussed above. Given that the three examples differ widely, we find it inappropriate to generalize the use of leverage as universally bad. The realization among many participants in the financial community that there are hedge funds with portfolios that are less risky (because they are well diversified) than, for example, some pension fund portfolios (because risk is highly concentrated) is a change in perception that we believe is structural more than it is cyclical.

ASYMMETRIC RETURNS AND ACTIVE RISK MANAGEMENT

Our claims are simple: First, asymmetric risk/return profiles are attractive. It means nothing else than having a high probability of financial success and survival with a low probability of the opposite. Second, these profiles are not a function of randomness but a function of actively managing risk whereby risk is defined in absolute terms. By *asymmetry,* we actually mean two things: an asymmetry with respect to the *magnitude* of positive versus negative returns as well as an asymmetry with respect to the *frequency* of positive versus negative returns. If our objective is the positive, smooth, and sustainable compounding of capital, one needs a combination of both of these asymmetries. Note that these remarks refer to absolute-return portfolios where single-manager risk (arguably idiosyncratic risk) has been diversified.

In the following sections we discuss asymmetries on a strategy level. This means we examine systematic risk whereby nonsystematic risk (single-manager risk) has been largely eliminated through diversification. We examine some absolute-return strategies across the board, ranging from market neutral to directional, that is, from low volatility to higher volatility. We use these absolute-return strategies as a proxy for what we believe is active risk management.

We compare these strategies with what we believe is passive risk management. For every strategy, we come up with a combination of equity and bonds, equity and cash, or bonds and cash. We calculate portfolios that, assuming monthly rebalancing, have the *same volatility* as the absolute-return strategy. We then take the one that has the highest correlation coefficient from the three. Note that in some low-volatility absolute-return strategies, it is not possible to reduce the volatility by just combining equities and bonds. In these cases we took the combination with the highest correlation from the other two combinations, that is, bonds and cash and equity and cash. The observation period was January 1990 to December 2005 unless stated otherwise.* Equities were based on Morgan Stanley Composite Index (MSCI) World Total Return Index, bonds were based on Global Government Bond Total Return Index, while for cash we used an investment yielding 1-month U.S. Dollar (USD) London Interbank Offered Rate (LIBOR). All analysis is based on monthly USD log returns. We start with a relative value strategy, that is, convertible arbitrage.

Convertible Arbitrage

Figure 6.1 shows the asymmetry versus a symmetric return profile. The bars on the left show the average monthly return when the index was negative while the bars on the right show the average positive returns. The dark bars represent the active risk management strategy in this case convertible

---

*Note that it does not really matter which period we choose. In Ineichen [2000a], we have chosen the period from 1990 to March 2000 (bull market only), and in Ineichen [2004b], the period was from 1998 to August 2003 (full equity cycle). The numbers change somewhat; the story does not.

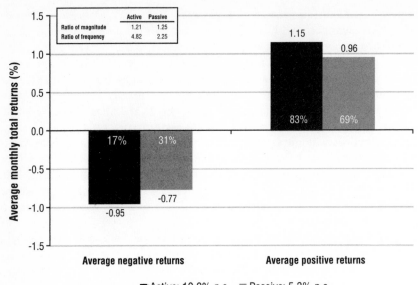

FIGURE 6.1 Asymmetries in Convertible Arbitrage (1990 to 2005)
Active: Hedge Fund Research Performance Index (HFRI) Convertible Arbitrage
Index; Passive: 25 percent MSCI World Total Return Index, 75 percent USD one-
month LIBOR.
Source: Author's own calculations; data from Bloomberg and Thomson Financial.

arbitrage. The light bars measure the long-only portfolio that has the same
volatility and the highest correlation. In this case, this is a portfolio of
25 percent bonds and 75 cash and a volatility of 3.5 percent. Compound
annual rate of return of these two time series are shown in the legend. The
percentages printed in the bars measure the relative frequency of positive
and negative returns. In this graph, we seek an asymmetry in *magnitude*
and an asymmetry in *frequency* or a combination of both. In the inserted
box in the graph, we call the average positive return divided by the average
negative return the *ratio of magnitude*, whereas the percentage of positive
return divided by the percentage of negative returns is the *ratio of frequency*.

   There is very little difference between the two portfolios in terms of
asymmetries with respect to *magnitude*. The two ratios of magnitude are
nearly identical. The difference in average returns is in both portfolios
around 20 basis points, that is, the positive returns are on average around
20 basis points higher than the negative returns. The long-only portfolio is
actually more attractive, as its ratio between positive return and negative

return is 1.25 compared to 1.21 in the case of the absolute-return strategy. However, this difference is minuscule.

The main difference in this case and with many relative-value strategies has to do with an asymmetry with respect to *frequency*. The relationship between positive and negative returns in the case of convertible arbitrage is in ratio terms 4.82 or 83:17. This compares to 2.25, or 69:31 for the passive portfolio with the same volatility. The superior performance of the portfolio where risk was managed actively, therefore, is primarily a function of an asymmetry with respect to frequency and less an asymmetry with respect to magnitude.

Figure 6.2 shows the return distribution of these two portfolios. The vertical axis measures the frequency from a total of 192 monthly returns from January 1990 to December 2005. The horizontal axis categorizes these returns into return buckets of one percentage point. The main difference between the two frequency distributions is that convertible arbitrage

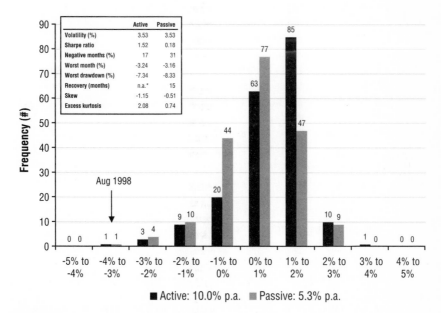

FIGURE 6.2   Return Distribution of Convertible Arbitrage (1990 to 2005)
Active: HFRI Convertible Arbitrage Index; Passive: 25 percent MSCI World Total Return Index, 75 percent USD one-month LIBOR.
*As of December 2005 the strategy had not recovered. The trough was 92.7 percent in May 2005. Convertible arbitrage stood at 97.2 percent at year-end. The October 1998 trough was recovered by the end of that year.
Source: Author's own calculations; data from Bloomberg and Thomson Financial.

has many more observations in the 1 percent to 2 percent absolute-return buckets, while it has only somewhat fewer observations in the 0 percent to 1 percent bucket. The tails also tell a story. Convertible arbitrage has substantially fewer returns in the −1 percent to 0 percent bucket and also fewer in the following two buckets on the left-hand side of the distribution. However, it has more returns in the 2 percent to 3 percent and 3 percent to 4 percent buckets on the right-hand side of the distribution. These subtle differences can explain the extreme difference in the much higher long-term annual compounding rate (shown in the legend of the graph). The outlier on the left is—as one might have guessed—from August 1998. The three outliers in the −3 percent to −2 percent bucket are from March and April 1994 and April 2005.

One of the distribution characteristics of relative-value strategies is fat tails, that is, a fairly inflated statistic for excess kurtosis when compared to long-only portfolios. Many analysts therefore argue that investing in relative-value strategies is like selling out-of-the-money disaster put options or is akin to picking up nickels in front of a steamroller: You do well for a while, but eventually you do not survive the proverbial 100-year storm. Figure 6.2 shows that indeed there are fat tails and the distribution is skewed toward the left-hand side (negative skew). Two points: First, the absolute monthly loss as well as the cumulative loss of the active portfolio with higher excess kurtosis is similar to the passive portfolio. However, excess kurtosis is higher, not necessarily because of fat tails but because the distribution is more "peaked" around the mean.* Both strategies have one outlier on the left due to the Russian default crisis in August 1998. Second, while both portfolios by design have the same standard deviation, the active portfolio has a higher mean return. This results in the worst monthly return of around 3.2 percent in both portfolios being 4.0 standard deviations away from the mean in the case of the active portfolio, while "only" 3.5 standard deviations in the case of the passive portfolio. This difference largely explains the difference in excess kurtosis. While the highest positive return of the active portfolio is higher than the highest return of the passive portfolio (3.3 versus 3.0 percent), these outliers do not contribute to excess kurtosis as much because they are both "only" around 2.5 standard deviations from the mean.

Figure 6.3 shows cumulative performance of these two portfolios. We have included cash as a further reference. The first two time series are portfolios with equal volatility. To the long-term investor, compounding capital at 10.0 percent or 5.3 percent is a big difference.

---

*It is possible for two distributions to have identical fat tails, with one being more peaked by having fewer observations in the section between the peak and the wings.

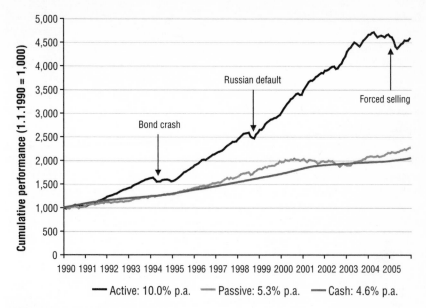

FIGURE 6.3 Cumulative Performance of Convertible Arbitrage (1990 to 2005) Active: HFRI Convertible Arbitrage Index; Passive: 25 percent MSCI World Total Return Index, 75 percent USD one-month LIBOR.
Source: Author's own calculations data from Bloomberg and Thomson Financial.

The graph shows that convertible arbitrage went through a rough period in 2004 to 2005. For a long period, the strategy was the epitome of the marketing slogan "equity-like returns, with bond-like volatility," that is, high Sharpe ratios. This caused the space—putting it mildly—to become somewhat crowded. At one stage, disappointing returns resulted in redemptions, which resulted in forced selling, putting more pressure on prices and subsequently returns, causing more redemptions, that is, a vicious cycle of some sort. As of December 2005 the convertible arbitrage was showing some signs of recovery and the marketplace was certainly healthier after the shake-out. However, as of December 2005, the strategy was still under water.*

---

*Stop press: Losses were recovered by February 2006. Recovery period therefore was nine months, compared to 15 months in the case of the passive portfolio. As of April 2006, convertible arbitrage was 2.4 percent *above* its previous all-time high in April 2004.

Equity Market Neutral

The next strategy we examine is also a relative-value strategy: equity market neutral. This strategy is considered by many—rightly or wrongly—as the purest form of generating alpha. Figure 6.4 shows the asymmetries with respect to magnitude and frequency. In this case, the reference portfolio with the same volatility of 3.1 percent was a combination of 22 percent equities and 78 percent cash.

In equity market neutral we can observe both asymmetries, an asymmetry with respect to magnitude as well as frequency. The ratio between average positive and negative returns (ratio of magnitude) was 2.01, that is, on average positive returns are twice the size that of negative returns (100 basis points versus −50 basis points). This compares with a ratio of 1.25 in case of the reference portfolio with the same volatility (87 basis points versus −69 basis points). The ratio of frequency is also (as was convertible arbitrage) quite large at 4.49. This means that 82 percent of returns were positive. The ratio of frequency for the passive reference portfolio with

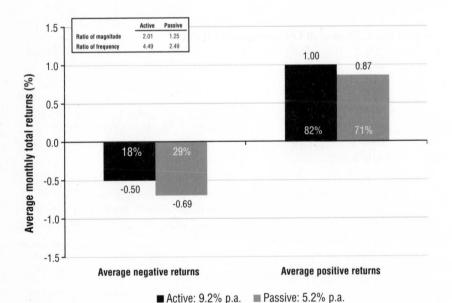

FIGURE 6.4 Asymmetries in Equity Market Neutral (1990 to 2005)
Active: HFRI Equity Market Neutral Index; Passive: 22 percent MSCI World Total Return Index, 78 percent USD one-month LIBOR.
Source: Author's own calculations; data from Bloomberg and Thomson Financial.

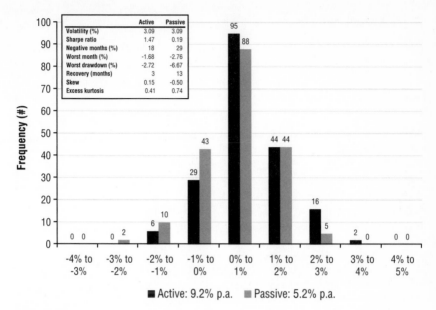

FIGURE 6.5 Return Distribution of Equity Market Neutral (1990 to 2005)
Active: HFRI Equity Market Neutral Index; Passive: 22 percent MSCI World Total
Return Index, 78 percent USD one-month LIBOR.
Source: Author's own calculations; data from Bloomberg and Thomson Financial.

"only" 71 percent positive returns was 2.49. Note that the various statistical biases in single hedge fund indices discussed in the literature reduce the historical compounding rate shown in the graph as well as these two ratios. However, these biases do reduce but not eliminate the asymmetries; neither do the biases change the concept of the two asymmetries, that is, the idea of positive compounding of capital with smaller and fewer negative returns.

Figure 6.5 shows the same story as before: asymmetric returns. The buckets above zero (positive returns) are more heavily populated, while the return buckets to the left of the distribution are of lower frequency and, in this case, of lower magnitude.* Again, it is these asymmetries that allow compounding at 9.2 percent per year instead of 5.2 percent with the same overall portfolio volatility in the case of the passive portfolio. Skew and excess kurtosis are fairly low. The worst drawdown of the strategy was

---

*We would not overrate the fact that there are no negative outliers in equity market neutral. We believe that any financial time series that does not have an accident of some sort in its history probably has an accident waiting somewhere in the future.

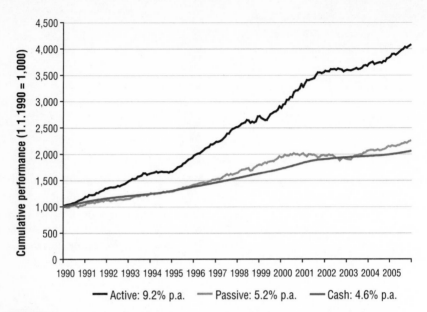

FIGURE 6.6   Cumulative Performance of Equity Market Neutral (1990 to 2005)
Active: HFRI Equity Market Neutral Index; Passive: 22 percent MSCI World Total
Return Index, 78 percent USD one-month LIBOR.
Source: Author's own calculations; data from Bloomberg and Thomson Financial.

only −2.7 percent, from which it took only three months to recover. A
comparable long-only strategy with the same volatility of 3.1 percent had
a maximal drawdown of 6.7 percent, from which it took 13 months to
recover.

Figure 6.6 shows the cumulative performance of a portfolio containing
a good mix of equity-market-neutral manager compared to a portfolio of
equity and cash with the same volatility and with cash with lower volatility.

Distressed Securities

Distressed securities is mostly classified as an event-driven strategy, as
the underlying theme is a corporate event such as a bankruptcy and
the post-bankruptcy recovery. The strategy is most often perceived as
a directional strategy as the long exposure is usually unhedged or only
partially hedged. The directional content is visible in the volatility of the
strategy, around 6.0 percent for a diversified portfolio of distressed securities
managers, which is nearly double the volatility from the two relative-value
strategies discussed above. Most market participants acknowledge that

the strategy is very cyclical. In other words, the opportunity set benefits from corporate bankruptcies and high credit spreads or large discounts of distressed securities depending largely on the stage of the economy in the business cycle. Note that the strategy is very heterogeneous. This means that there is a wide range of substrategies, ranging from very directional to arbitrage. This is the reason why volatility is only around 6 percent, which is obviously low for a strategy with directional exposure. The equity/cash combination, which has the same volatility, is 42 percent equity and 58 percent cash.

Figure 6.7 shows the asymmetries of a diversified distressed securities portfolio with the aforementioned equity/cash combination, with a volatility of around 6 percent.

The previously discussed relative-value strategies showed little asymmetry with respect to magnitude, but pronounced asymmetry with respect to frequency. As the strategies analyzed in this chapter become more directional, the relationship between the two asymmetries changes. In the case of distressed securities, there is a better balance between the two asymmetries,

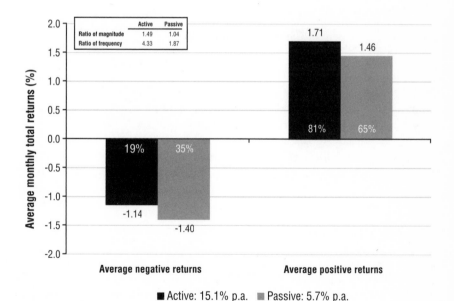

FIGURE 6.7 Asymmetries in Distressed Securities (1990 to 2005)
Active: HFRI Distressed Securities Index; Passive: 42 percent MSCI World Total Return Index, 58 percent USD one-month LIBOR.
Source: Author's own calculations; data from Bloomberg and Thomson Financial.

magnitude *and* frequency. A better balance does not mean it is a better strategy; it's just different from relative value.

The magnitude of returns in the long-only portfolio in Figure 6.7 is fairly balanced, that is, more or less symmetrical. The ratio is 1.04 where 1.0 would indicate perfect symmetry. The ratio in the active portfolio is 1.49. In other words, the average positive return is 49 percent larger than the average negative return. If we think of compounding capital, this is huge. Note that survivorship bias and other biases might have inflated the hedge fund data in use. If we assume the HFRI Distressed Securities Index is inflated by 20 basis points per month (which is a generous assumption), then the return in Figure 6.7 would be 1.51 versus −1.34.* In other words, the asymmetry would be less pronounced but still detectable. Another interesting side remark is fees: The black bars in these graphs are net of one layer of fees. However, fees are asymmetrical. The absolute-return manager gets paid more if he has high and many positive returns. In other words, the absolute-return manager—unlike the relative-return manager—gets paid more if he has these two asymmetries. One therefore could argue that the performance fee is some form of sharing agreement between manager and investor; that is, managers share the value they add with investors by keeping parts of it. Note that the asymmetry of the black bars in Figure 6.7 would probably be more pronounced were we able to show gross returns as higher fees are chopped off positive returns (because of the performance fee).

The asymmetry with respect to frequency is also pronounced in this example. The ratio of frequency was 4.33 for the active risk management portfolio and only 1.87 for the passive portfolio. The 4.33 figure is quite impressive as it is only slightly less than for example equity market neutral that has a volatility which is half that of distressed securities.

Figure 6.8 shows the return distribution of the two portfolios. Same story here, too—more returns in the positive return bucket on the right-hand side of the distribution and smaller and fewer returns on the left-hand side. This combination of returns results in a Sharpe ratio that seems astronomical when compared to a long-only portfolio of equal volatility

---

*If we shave off 20 basis points from the HFRI Distressed Securities Index every month the compound annual rate of return (CARR) falls from 15.1 percent to 12.1 percent. Your author is very much aware of the issues regarding hedge fund data. The poor quality probably reduces the CARR of most time series shown here. However, it does not affect the logic of active risk management, the topic of this book. It also does not affect the logic of asymmetric returns, defining risk as total risk, departing from random exposure to market risk, and thinking more about correlation among portfolio constituents and probabilities of future outcomes rather than historical performance.

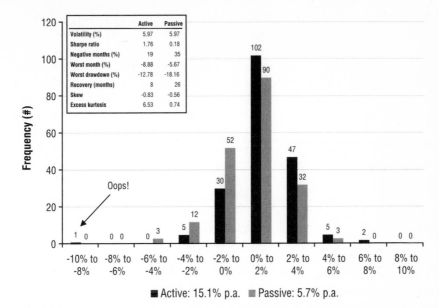

FIGURE 6.8   Return Distribution of Distressed Securities (1990 to 2005)
Active: HFRI Distressed Securities Index; Passive: 42 percent MSCI World Total
Return Index, 58 percent USD one-month LIBOR.
Source: Author's own calculations; data from Bloomberg and Thomson Financial.

(assuming various statistical biases in the data of 20 basis points per month
reduces the Sharpe ratio to 1.26).

Note that excess kurtosis of the active portfolio is huge. The worst
monthly (log) return was −8.9 percent in August 1998. This return was
followed by a −3.6 percent return in September. By October 1998, the
strategy was down 12.8 percent (see inserted table in Figure 6.8). The August
1998 outlier caused excess kurtosis to be inflated drastically. However,
recovery was swift, only eight months.

Some researchers find that absolute-return strategies have autocorrelation (serial correlation) and put their findings in a negative context. This
is hilarious. Autocorrelation means that if we have a positive return today,
the next return is not random. It is a departure from the assumption that
returns are random and follow a bell-curved normal distribution. Positive
autocorrelation means that the next return has a higher probability to be
similar, as opposed to the return's being a function of flipping a coin. The
dogma of the normal distribution and the theory of everything being a function of randomness has clearly been taken too far in the field of finance. If
we have a positive return today, we do not want tomorrow to be a function

of randomness. If the next return is random, we cannot seriously be talking about an active investment process. We want—assuming absolute returns and volatility matter and compounding capital and financial survival is an objective—tomorrow's return to be positive with a likelihood that is higher than random. And the returns in the following month, year, decade, and so on, too. So if you have 80 percent positive returns, autocorrelation is a good thing. (If you are compounding negatively, it isn't.) We believe this departure from randomness to be a function of active risk management. Being exposed to randomness is passive. You need not pay $2 + 20$ to a coin flipper (nor 40 basis points, for that matter).

Often, it is implied that long-only strategies have less autocorrelation. This is not too surprising as the returns are fairly symmetrically distributed around the mean, having a closer resemblance to a normal distribution. Note that the long-only portfolio in Figure 6.8 has a drawdown that is far worse than the active portfolio (-18.2 percent versus -12.8 percent). In addition, it took the passive portfolio 26 months to recover from that loss. It took the active portfolio only eight months to recover. So our view is that, yes, statistically measured autocorrelation is indeed a departure from the normal distribution and the current doctrine in finance. However, we think this is a good thing. When compounding capital, the absolute-return investor wants today's positive return to be followed by a nonrandom positive return. In addition, if the investor finds himself under water after an accident, he wants the recovery not to be a function of randomness but a function of engineering and design, that is, an active investment process. Since these "accidents" in active risk management are often related to liquidity, recovery is not random. Markets and their participants always cool off after market mayhem. Buying when everyone is selling in panic is truly a contrarian and hence active strategy. It is active risk management, that is, the opposite of long-only buy-and-hold, that translates into autocorrelation of positive returns, allowing the investor a swift recovery.

Figure 6.9 shows cumulative performance. We have added a time series that measures the HFRI Distressed Securities Index minus 20 basis points per month. As we mentioned, imperfect data changes the numbers but not the logic.

Event-Driven Multi-strategy

Another strategy in the event-driven space is event-driven multi-strategy funds. The multi-strategy concept has been gaining traction in the last couple of years. The multi-strategy and the multi-fund approach are the two main ways a single hedge fund adviser can grow the business. Therefore, the main reason for the multi-strategy to gain popularity with managers is

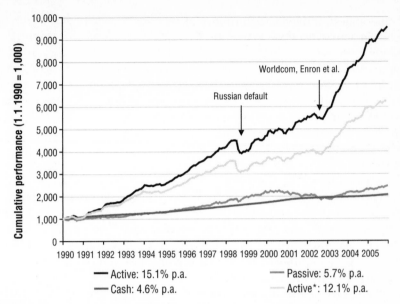

FIGURE 6.9 Cumulative Performance of Distressed Securities (1990 to 2005) Active: HFRI Distressed Securities Index; Passive: 42 percent MSCI World Total Return Index, 58 percent USD one-month LIBOR. Active*: HFRI Distressed Securities Index minus 20 basis points per month.
Source: Author's own calculations; data from Bloomberg and Thomson Financial.

twofold. First, the multi-strategy allows managers to grow their business, as capacity in a single fund is typically constrained. One economic argument for multi-strategy is that the managers are better suited to allocate between event-driven strategies than is the investor. By *better,* we mean smarter (as in savvy), faster, and more efficient. The second motivator for managers is to reduce volatility and business risk. As successful managers grow, they become wealthier, and the demand for some stability and sustainability increases. The typical maturity cycle goes from high-octane start-up entrepreneur to businesspeople running their business. The lower business risk is passed on to the investor. A successful hedge fund manager-turned-large-multi-strategy has a lower probability of default than a smaller single-strategy fund.

Multi-strategy funds are somewhat a hybrid between single-strategy hedge funds and fund of hedge funds. A multi-strategy fund is somewhere in between single-strategy hedge fund and fund of funds with respect to financial and especially operational risk. Today multi-strategy funds are considered a competitor to fund of funds mainly for two reasons. First, the multi-strategy manager charges only one layer of fees, whereas fund of funds have another layer on top of what the hedge funds charge the fund of funds. Second, the investor gets the same diversification as fund of funds. These arguments can be challenged: First, some multi-strategy hedge funds charge fees that are higher than the two layers the investor pays through fund of funds. It is interesting to note that the longer a manager has been around managing risk successfully, the higher the fee structure (and lock-up terms) the manager can get away with. This supports our notion that it takes many data points for the value added to be visible. One could call this a form of "goodwill" that translates into an established reputation and brand and trust in the marketplace. This is a form of alpha that is difficult to quantify because it is intangible. However, the high fees these managers can charge tells us that they must have been doing something right. The second challenge has to do with risk management. One key aspect in risk management is independence. In the case of a multi-strategy fund there is typically one independent risk manager with control authority over all the different trading books. However, there is only one. In the case of fund of funds, the risk management function is spread among *many* independent risk managers. Diversification, therefore, is of a different dimension with fund of funds than it is with multi-strategy funds. We expect this trend from fund of funds to multi-strategy funds to reverse as soon as the first multi-strategy fund blows up.

Figure 6.10 compares average positive returns with average negative returns of an event-driven multi-strategy index with an equity-cash combination with the same volatility of 5.3 percent. The ratio of magnitude is quite small at 1.13 when compared to, for example, distressed securities (1.5) or to the passive portfolio in the graph that has nearly the identical ratio. The big difference between the active and passive portfolio in Figure 6.10 has to do with the other asymmetry, that is, the ratio of return frequency. The ratio of frequency for the active portfolio is 5.0 (83:17). This compares to only 1.9 (65:35) for the passive portfolio. In other words, the huge difference in terms of annual compounding is primarily a function of having fewer negative months than the long-only investor with a portfolio of equal volatility.

Figure 6.11 compares the return distribution of the event-driven multi-strategy index with the passive portfolio with the same volatility. This is a good example of how the skew and excess kurtosis statistic can give a misleading picture for the active strategy. The skew is highly negative and excess kurtosis is high, which is—in isolation—bad. We prefer positive skew over negative skew, and we actually like excess kurtosis as long as the "excess" is on the right-hand side of the distribution (which it is likely to be if the skew is positive). Event-driven multi-strategy displays "bad" characteristics. However, looking deeper we find that the worst drawdown

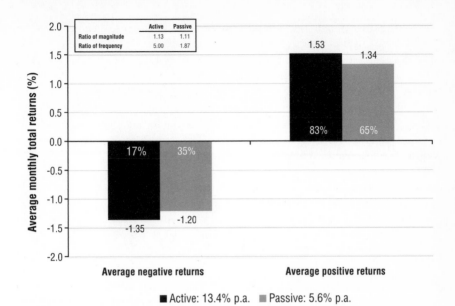

FIGURE 6.10 Asymmetries in Event-Driven Multi-strategy (1990 to 2005)
Source: Author's own calculations; data from Thomson Financial and Center for International Securities and Derivatives Markets (CISDM). Active: CISDM Event-Driven Multi-Strategy Index; Passive: 37 percent MSCI World Total Return Index, 63 percent USD one-month LIBOR.

is only around half that of a long-only portfolio with the same volatility. In addition, the time of recovery was only six months for the active portfolio compared to more than two years in the case of the long-only portfolio. As mentioned before, the recovery in the long-only portfolio is a function of randomness while the recovery in event-driven multi-strategy is more a function of engineering and design, that is, "managed" auto correlation of positive returns in the post-mayhem period. The negative outliers can be explained by exposure to liquidity. Hedge funds can be regarded as liquidity providers, as they often buy when everyone else wants to sell, that is, provide liquidity to the panic-stricken investor running for the exit. After the turbulence of market mayhem, investors tend to take the proverbial cold shower: they cool off somewhat, and markets return to normality with a great deal of mean reversion allowing the swift recovery. The contrarian investor benefits from this recovery. The alpha, however, is not compensation for liquidity. The alpha is in the other buckets. In all buckets except the −8 percent to −6 percent bucket, the active portfolio outperforms the passive portfolio: In the negative buckets there are fewer

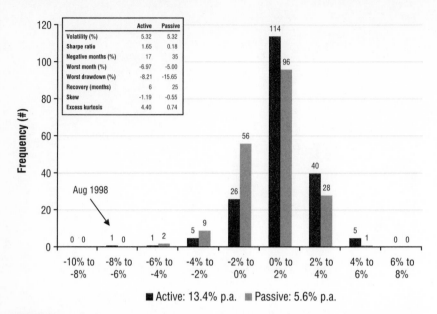

	Active	Passive
Volatility (%)	5.32	5.32
Sharpe ratio	1.65	0.18
Negative months (%)	17	35
Worst month (%)	-6.97	-5.00
Worst drawdown (%)	-8.21	-15.65
Recovery (months)	6	25
Skew	-1.19	-0.55
Excess kurtosis	4.40	0.74

■ Active: 13.4% p.a. ■ Passive: 5.6% p.a.

FIGURE 6.11 Return Distribution of Event-Driven Multi-strategy (1990 to 2005) *Source:* Author's own calculations; data from Thomson Financial and CISDM. Active: CISDM Event-Driven Multi-Strategy Index; Passive: 37 percent MSCI World Total Return Index, 63 percent USD one-month LIBOR.

returns, and in the positive buckets there are more returns. The value added, therefore, is creating this asymmetric-return profile.

Most of the "picking up nickels in front of a steamroller" research focuses on the return buckets on the far left. Let's look at the −2 percent to 0 percent bucket for a change. The active portfolio had 26 observations in this bucket, while the passive long-only portfolio had 56 observations. The sum of the 26 observations was −16.9 percent. The corresponding sum of the 56 observations was −46.3 percent. This is a big difference. The −2 percent to 0 percent return bucket gets no airtime because it is a pretty dull bucket. It's not hot. However, the 29.4 percentage points difference is huge.

Figure 6.12 shows the cumulative performance. The three periods that can explain the hiccups in the cumulative performance are the 1990 recession; the flight-to-quality scenario following the Russian default; and the U.S. accounting scandals, primarily Worldcom. The event-driven space incurred losses when Worldcom went from distressed into bankruptcy.

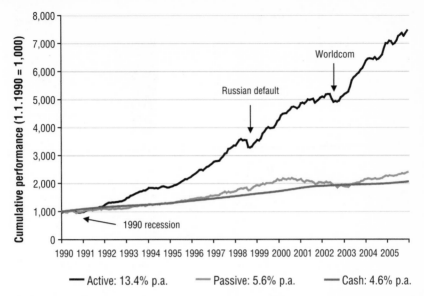

FIGURE 6.12 Cumulative Performance Event-Driven Multi-strategy (1990 to 2005)
Source: Author's own calculations; data from Thomson Financial and CISDM.
Active: CISDM Event-Driven Multi-Strategy Index; Passive: 37 percent MSCI World
Total Return Index, 63 percent USD one-month LIBOR.

Equity Hedge

The next strategy is equity hedge, or equity long/short. Equity hedge is probably the oldest as well as the largest hedge fund strategy and goes back to the Alfred Jones model from 1949. The basic idea is to have one's returns attributed to skill and to a much lesser extent the direction of the stock market. At the most general level, the investor buys stocks he thinks will go up and sells short stocks he thinks will go down. In most cases, this results in the gross exposure being higher than 100 percent of principal, while the net exposure to the stock market is less than 100 percent.

Figure 6.13 shows the asymmetries in equity hedge compared with a passive alternative. The passive alternative with the same volatility of 8.7 percent is 60 percent equities and 40 percent cash. We have added a new set of bars to the graph. It is from a "passive" model portfolio that has very high correlation statistics when regressed with equity hedge. The three factors of this model are from Fama and French [1992] and are (1) the excess return of the market (Standard and Poor's [S&P] 500 return minus risk-free rate), (2) the performance of small stocks versus big stocks (small minus ig [SMB]), and (3) the performance of value stocks relative to growth stocks

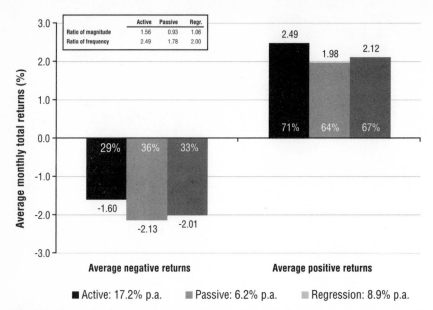

	Active	Passive	Regr.
Ratio of magnitude	1.56	0.93	1.06
Ratio of frequency	2.49	1.78	2.00

Average negative returns **Average positive returns**

■ Active: 17.2% p.a. ■ Passive: 6.2% p.a. ■ Regression: 8.9% p.a.

FIGURE 6.13 Asymmetries in Equity Hedge (1990 to 2005)
Source: Author's own calculations; data from Bloomberg and Thomson Financial. Active: HFRI Equity Hedge Index; Passive: 60 percent MSCI World Total Return Index, 40 percent USD one-month LIBOR; Regression: $0 + 0.40*(r_m - r_f) + 0.27*(SMB) + -0.08*(HML)$ levered by 1.11.

(high minus low [HML] book-to-price). The book-to-price ratio is high for value stocks and low for growth stocks. We have downloaded all three factors from Professor French's Web site.[1] We regressed the excess returns in equity hedge (HFRI Equity Hedge Index returns minus one-month USD LIBOR) with the three aforementioned factors for the period from January 1990 to December 2005. The three variables of this regression were 0.40, 0.27 and −0.08, all highly statistically significant.* The regression assumed an intercept of zero, as we are not trying to prove the existence of alpha but are looking for a passive alternative. The 0.40 factor is essentially the beta to the excess stock market return, and the 0.27 factor is the beta to small-cap stocks, while the −0.08 factor is the beta to value stocks. (Since

---

*These factors differ from those in Table 5.1 in the appendix to Chapter 5 because here we use a longer time period as well as the original factors from Professor Kenneth French's Web site.

the factor is negative, the beta is toward growth stocks.) The r^2 of this regression was 0.65, which is considered high in the field of finance.

The HFRI Equity Hedge Index has been one of the better-performing indices. The compound annual rate of return of the index was 17.2 percent from 1990 to 2005, while volatility was 8.7 percent. The index contains managers who have outperformed the S&P 500 index over the years with volatilities that were lower than that of the index, that is, with net exposures less than 100 percent. Volatility of the index—essentially a proxy for a portfolio of equity long/short managers—is further reduced by combining different managers.

In Figure 6.13 we compare the index, as usual, with a passive portfolio with the same volatility. In this case a combination of 60 percent equities and 40 percent cash has the same volatility of 8.7 percent. In addition we have added the regression that we have levered up by a factor of 1.11 (ignoring financing costs) to have the same volatility as the other two portfolios.

The active portfolio is extreme in both asymmetries, magnitude as well as frequency. One attribute is the skillful use of leverage as briefly discussed at the beginning of this chapter. The ratio of magnitude was 1.56 with the average positive return being 2.5 percent and the average negative return being −1.6 percent per month. This compares to a ratio of less than one in the case of the passive portfolio, that is, the average negative return is larger than the average positive return. The ratio was 0.93. The ratio of frequency was 2.49 in the case of the active portfolio (71:29) which compares to 1.78 (64:36) in the case of the passive portfolio. Equity hedge is another example of both asymmetries resulting in a higher compounding rate of return when compared to long-only portfolios with the same volatility.

The leveraged regression portfolio looks interesting, as it is a much more efficient portfolio than the passive portfolio. The model portfolio has a higher return with the same volatility. There is a slight asymmetry with respect to both magnitude and frequency. Note that the reason for including this regression portfolio in this analysis is that it is probably the most often quoted factor analysis in the hedge fund literature, as well as the regression with the highest statistical significance. However, it should be noted that regression analysis is probably more suitable to historical performance attribution analysis than portfolio construction. We do not know whether these three factors and their loads will result in an efficiency improvement going forward. (We wouldn't be writing books if we did, would we?)

Note that long-only strategies are not perfectly symmetrical. (See Figure 6.14.) Equity long-only strategies are symmetrical with respect to magnitude but slightly asymmetric with respect to frequency over long periods of time when dividends are assumed reinvested. Japan is an exception to this rule; we show only the past 16 years, in most of which

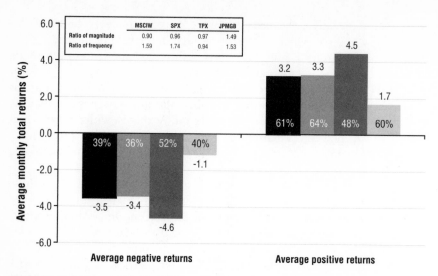

	MSCIW	SPX	TPX	JPMGB
Ratio of magnitude	0.90	0.96	0.97	1.49
Ratio of frequency	1.59	1.74	0.94	1.53

Average negative returns   **Average positive returns**

■MSCI World: 7.3% p.a.■ S&P 500: 10.5% p.a.■ TOPIX: -2.6% p.a. ▪ JPM Global Govt Bonds: 7.2% p.a.

FIGURE 6.14 Asymmetries of Long-Only Strategies (1990 to 2005)
Source: Author's own calculations; data from Thomson Financial. Note: All indices are total return indices in USD, Tokyo Stock Price Index (TOPIX) in Japanese yen (JPY).

Japan compounded negatively. (In Chapter 9, we spend some time on long-term financial market performance.) In other words, negative compounding means having a ratio of magnitude *and* frequency of less than one. In the case of Japan, the average negative return was larger than the average positive return and there were more negative returns than there were positive returns. Bond total return indices are typically asymmetric in terms of both magnitude and frequency when measured against nil percent.

Figure 6.15 shows the return distribution of the HFRI Equity Hedge Index and the passive alternative portfolio with same volatility—same story as above, although the passive portfolio has actually more returns in the 0 to 2 percent bucket. The active portfolio outperforms by having more observations in the buckets beyond 2 percent (and, of course, fewer negative returns). Note that the worst peak-to-trough drawdown of the passive portfolio is nearly three times as large as with the active portfolio, while the recovery period is 3.4 times that of the active portfolio.

Long/short managers occasionally pride themselves of having fat tails in their return distribution, then pausing for the information to sink in, and then adding that their fat tails are actually on the upside, that is, the right-hand side of the distribution. While this might not be the ultimate

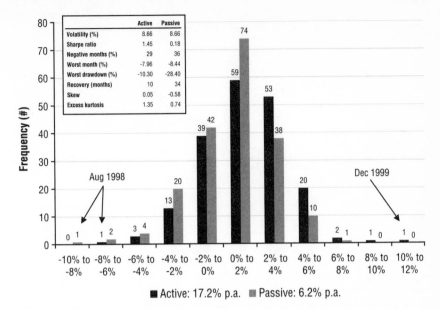

FIGURE 6.15 Return Distribution of Equity Hedge (1990 to 2005)
Source: Author's own calculations; data from Bloomberg and Thomson Financial. Active: HFRI Equity Hedge Index; Passive: 60 percent MSCI World Total Return Index, 40 percent USD one-month LIBOR.

demonstration of their humility, Figure 6.15 shows to some extent that the notion is not entirely without merit. Occasionally, net exposure jumps for a short market rally, and the alpha-beta balance changes briefly toward the latter. Or does it? In December 1999, many equity hedge managers increased their net exposure and benefited from the year-end rally. The critics cried foul, claiming this is beta and not alpha. Is this true? We are not so sure. We believe there is still debate on what is true alpha and what is beta. When alpha is defined as fundamental stock-picking skill, then the December 1999 return is beta and not alpha. However, we lean toward the argument that it is these asymmetries in the return distribution that is the alpha. In other words, one single month is not alpha or beta. That—we believe—is a myopic view of the world. It is somewhat akin the shareholders focusing only on earnings of the next quarter. This is short-term and hardly optimal, neither for management nor for shareholders. The same is probably true when assessing hedge funds. We need more than one or two data points to assess whether there is alpha. If a manager changes his net exposure and the result is an asymmetric return distribution similar to the one above, we are inclined to argue that it is alpha, that is, largely skill based. Note also that

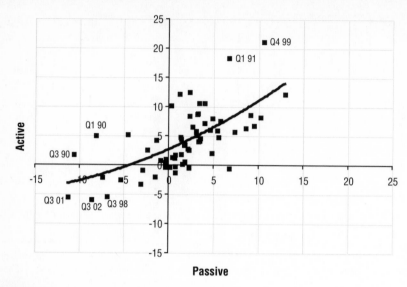

FIGURE 6.16 Quarterly Returns (1990 to 2005)
Active: HFRI Equity Hedge Index; Passive: 60 percent MSCI World Total Return
Index, 40 percent USD one-month LIBOR.
Source: Author's own calculations; data from Bloomberg and Thomson Financial.

the worst return in both time series is from August 1998 where the 60:40
equity-cash mix lost more. In other words, the best and worst returns are
highly correlated to the stock market. This does not mean that the returns
are pure beta. The asymmetries are the alpha.

There are many different ways in which these asymmetries can be
presented. Figure 6.16 shows an alternative way of capturing the above-
mentioned asymmetry. The chart shows all quarterly total returns of the
passive equity-cash portfolio from 1990 to 2005 and the corresponding
quarterly total return in the HFRI Equity Hedge Index. The graph visualizes
the two asymmetries.

Correlation between equities and equity long/short is clearly positive.
The correlation coefficient between the two time series (based on monthly
log returns) was 0.66 for the period from 1990 to 2005, 0.80 for the
period from 1995 to 2005, and 0.82 for the period from 2000 to 2005.
However, a correlation coefficient does not pick up the call-option-like
feature (sometimes referred to as a *hockey stick*) displayed in the graph. If
the causality is asymmetric, the correlation coefficient can be a misleading
or even erroneous tool to prove or measure causality.

The graph shows that the asymmetry is a function of losing less money
or even generating positive returns in difficult market environments, for

example, in Q1 90, Q3 90, Q3 98, Q3 01, and Q3 02, and outperforming during the good times, for example, during Q1 91 (Desert Storm) and Q4 99 (year-end rally). One of the criticisms of hedge funds is that they use leverage. Quite often when long/short managers outperform the stock market during good market conditions, critics argue that they have levered up stock market beta risk. If this were true, then a large fall in the market would need to result in an even larger loss for equity long/short. Leverage by itself does not create the asymmetry. Using leverage to amplify market beta risk results in the risk—measured, for example, by the volatility of returns—being increased in a symmetrical fashion. If managers were just a leveraged play on the stock market, their returns would be larger when markets fall. However, they are not. In other words, it is true that hedge funds use leverage. However, the use of leverage is part of Michelangelo's aforementioned toolkit, that is, leverage in the hands of a skilled group of managers can result in an attractive asymmetric risk/return payoff.

Figure 6.17 is yet another way to make a similar point. The graph shows the underwater perspective (index level as a percentage of all-time high) of the active portfolio and the passive long-only portfolio. A line at

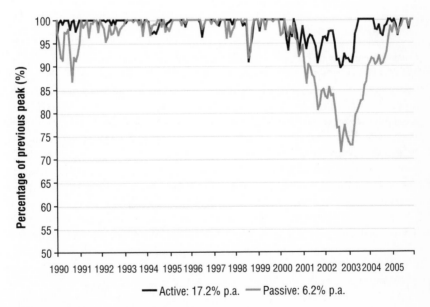

FIGURE 6.17 Underwater-Perspective Equity Hedge (1990 to 2005)
Active: HFRI Equity Hedge Index; Passive: 60 percent MSCI World Total Return Index, 40 percent USD one-month LIBOR.
Source: Author's own calculations; data from Bloomberg and Thomson Financial.

100 percent means new profits are being generated. The worst drawdown (largest percentage under water) in the active portfolio was 10.3 percent, which compares to 28.4 percent for the passive portfolio. (As hedge fund marketers know, this way of presenting data works great in bear markets, as it applies the concept of loss aversion when the pain from losing money is fresh.) The special case here is that correlation between the two is high. So the two portfolios reach the trough at the same time, at the end of September 2002. However, the two differ widely in terms of magnitude of the drawdown and the recovery, despite both portfolios having the same volatility. The HFRI Equity Hedge Index had recovered, that is, reached its previous all-time high after 10 months by July 2003. The long-only alternative took 34 months to recover. It had recovered by July 2005.* The overall duration of being under water was 40 months, in the case of the active portfolio, and 64 months (more than half a decade), in the case of the long-only portfolio. Note that the high-water-mark feature of hedge funds is designed to give the manager an incentive for both, avoiding large losses as well as recovering swiftly from losses to be able to generate new profits. So arguing against equity hedge because it has high correlation to long-only benchmarks is missing the point, to say the least.

Sector Specialists

Sector specialists are a special case in the equity hedge universe. Typically, these managers, as the name implies, specialize in one sector of the equity market. The great advantage of these managers is the extreme focus and high degree of specialization on only a small part of the overall market. So these managers are positioned toward the left-hand side of the spectrum of Figure 4.1 in Chapter 4. The great disadvantage, one could argue, is that the portfolios are far from efficient. This means to most investors that these funds are not stand-alone investments but are a small part of an absolute return portfolio. The criticism of sector specialists is that there is more beta than alpha—a notion that is difficult to reject. However, if we were able to detect asymmetries net of fees, it becomes difficult to reject the notion that there is indeed alpha there, too. We look at the technology sector as an example. These hedge fund managers focus on stocks in the technology space such as multimedia, networking, PC producers, retailers, semiconductors, software, and telecommunications.

---

*Assuming no fees were paid (as we are using passive indices gross of fees) and assuming dividends were reinvested and not taxed (as we are using total return indices).

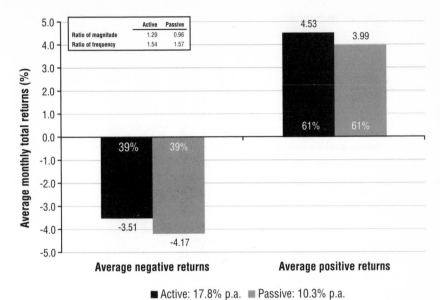

FIGURE 6.18 Asymmetries in Technology (1991 to 2005)
Active: HFRI Sector: Technology Index; Passive: 73 percent NASDAQ (National Association of Securities Dealers Automated Quotation system) Composite Index, 27 percent USD one-month LIBOR.
Source: Author's own calculations; data from Bloomberg and Thomson Financial.

Figure 6.18 shows the asymmetries of the HFRI Technology Index with a portfolio that consists of 73 percent NASDAQ Composite and 27 percent cash. Both portfolios have a volatility of 18.5 percent. The correlation between the two time series was very high at 0.89. The observation period in this case is from 1991 to 2005, that is, one year shorter than the previous examples due to the HFRI Technology Index's not being available until 1991. The ratio of frequency of the two portfolios was nearly identical at around 1.5. There is a "small" difference with respect to the ratio of magnitude. The active portfolio had a ratio of 1.29 that compares to 0.96 for the passive portfolio. However, this small difference in the ratio of magnitude explains whether the investor compounds at 17.8 percent or 10.3 percent—in essence, a small difference with big effect.

Figure 6.19 shows the two return distributions. We have added the normal distribution to the frequency distribution for comparability purposes. Note that the two normal distributions are identical in shape because the volatility in both cases is 18.5 percent, but the normal distribution of the active portfolio has its mean further to the right, as the average return is

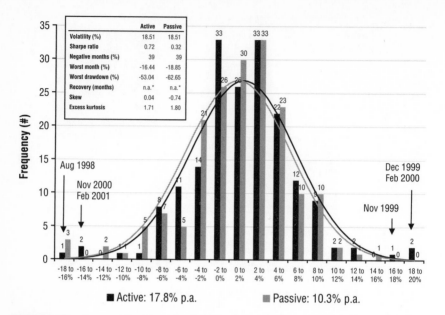

FIGURE 6.19   Return Distribution of Technology (1991 to 2005)
Active: HFRI Sector: Technology Index; Passive: 73 percent NASDAQ Composite
Index, 27 percent USD one-month LIBOR. * As of December 2005, not yet recovered
from September 2002 low.
Source: Author's own calculations; data from Bloomberg and Thomson Financial.

higher than the average return of the passive portfolio. The two frequency
distributions are indeed very similar, hence the high correlation coefficient.
There is some variation in the tail return buckets. The active portfolio has
one observation in the left tail and three in the right tail. The passive portfolio has three in the left tail and zero in the right tail. Interestingly, then,
excess kurtosis of the two portfolios is nearly identical. Both portfolios have
drawdowns in excess of 50 percent, which is not that surprising for a portfolio with a volatility as high as 18.5 percent. A volatility of 18.5 percent is
clearly in the long-only equity portfolio volatility territory.

Interestingly, the percentage of negative returns is nearly identical: The
active portfolio had 71 and the passive portfolio 70 negative returns. The
active portfolio was much heavier in the −2 percent to −0 percent return
bucket, but lighter in the next bucket, that is, returns between −4 percent
and −2 percent. The active portfolio also had more returns in the −6 percent
to −4 percent bucket but less in the rest of the left tail, that is, below −6
percent.

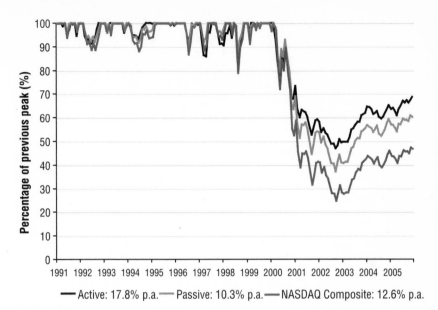

FIGURE 6.20 Underwater Perspective of Technology (1991 to 2005)
Active: HFRI Sector: Technology Index; Passive: 73 percent NASDAQ Composite
Index, 27 percent USD one-month LIBOR.
Source: Author's own calculations; data from Bloomberg and Thomson Financial.

We do not think conventional methodology is able to pick up these
subtle differences. However, these "subtle" differences can have a large
impact on the rate at which capital compounds.

Figure 6.20 shows the underwater perspective of the two portfolios
with the same volatility of 18.5 percent. We have added the NASDAQ
Composite Index, which had a volatility of 25.3 percent. The graph shows
that neither portfolio is particularly suited for the loss-averse investor.
However, the graph does not display the differences very well; neither does
the compounding rate in the legend of the graph. Table 6.2 might help.

The table shows the annual returns of these three portfolios and some
risk and return statistics. We show three different ways to calculate returns.
The first is just a simple arithmetic average of the annual returns shown in the
table. This method does not link the years together. The second return is the
compound annual rate of return (CARR). This return is somewhat more
relevant to the investor. It shows the annual return assuming the investor
invested at the beginning of 1991 and left the investment unchanged until
the end of 2005. The CARR shows the rate at which the buy-and-hold
investor compounded capital over the 15-year period. However, equally

TABLE 6.2 Different Ways to Calculate Investors' Returns

(%)	Active	Passive	NASDAQ
1991	19.0	41.3	56.9
1992	30.7	12.2	15.5
1993	30.6	11.5	14.7
1994	10.0	-1.2	-3.2
1995	50.9	29.9	39.9
1996	30.6	17.8	22.7
1997	6.9	17.2	21.6
1998	28.5	29.6	39.6
1999	124.3	59.3	85.6
2000	-15.3	-29.3	-39.3
2001	-12.8	-14.9	-21.1
2002	-16.5	-23.8	-31.5
2003	25.4	34.9	50.0
2004	5.4	6.6	8.6
2005	5.1	1.9	1.4
Volatility	18.5	18.5	25.3
Sharpe ratio	0.72	0.32	0.29
Sortino ratio	1.01	0.36	0.37
Worst drawdown	-53.0	-62.6	-75.0
Average return	21.5	12.9	17.4
CARR*	17.8	10.3	12.6
IRR**	15.4	7.2	8.7

*CARR: Compound annual rate of return.
**IRR: Internal rate of return assuming equal annual investments.
Source: Author's own calculations; data from Bloomberg and Thomson Financial.

relevant or even more relevant is the internal rate of return (IRR). Here, we assumed that the investor invests 100 at the beginning of every year. In other words, the saver makes 15 installments of 100 each year. The IRR shows at which fixed rate these investments/cash flows compounded. One could easily argue that this method is more relevant, as investors (private investors, pensions funds, etc.) add new money to their capital stock/savings in regular or irregular intervals.

The IRR shows the differences between the active portfolio and the other two portfolios very well. It's why volatility matters. The small differences that are hardly visible by examining the return distribution become quite clear when examining the IRR. The IRR of the active portfolio is more than double the IRR of the passive portfolio. Losing 15 percent, 30 percent, or 40 percent in the year 2000 is a very big difference. An investment that has a very high correlation to an index such as the NASDAQ but limits the downside is—we believe—of great value.

The bottom line is that sector funds can add value. Their funds are probably not a stand-alone investment for most investors. However, if these funds have high correlation to a market benchmark with limited downside—and therefore higher IRR—then these funds are a substitute for the underlying benchmark. Why buy the sector outright?

Macro

We discussed macro in some detail in Chapter 3 in connection with whether the investor should pay a fee for macro. The conclusions were affirmative. The following analysis backs up that conclusion. Again, we compare two portfolios with the same volatility, in this case a volatility of 8.1 percent. The passive portfolio with highest correlation to the active portfolio consisted of 48 percent global equities and 52 percent global government bonds, monthly rebalanced.

Figure 6.21 shows the asymmetries. The value added of a diversified portfolio of macro managers is a good mix between an asymmetry with respect to magnitude as well as frequency. The average positive returns were higher than the negative returns by a factor of 1.77. This compares with a ratio of 1.02 in the case of an equity-bond combination with the same volatility. The ratio of frequency is 2.37, which is slightly higher than the 1.82 of the long-only passive portfolio. So the bottom line is that the active portfolio had higher positive returns and lower negative returns and has more of the former and less of the latter.

Figure 6.22 examines the two return distributions. Interestingly, the return distribution of the active portfolio does not materially depart from a normal distribution. Skew and excess kurtosis are fairly low in both portfolios. Somewhat surprising was that the worst drawdown in the passive portfolio was nearly double that of the active portfolio, but the recovery period for both portfolios were the same. The active portfolio had its trough of −10.7 percent from April 1994 to July 1995. (Note that the attrition rate around that period was high. We discuss idiosyncratic risk in

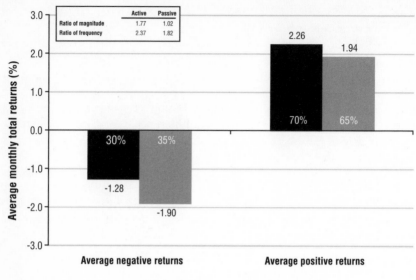

FIGURE 6.21   Asymmetries in Macro (1990 to 2005)
Active: HFRI Equity Hedge Index; Passive: 48 percent MSCI World Total Return
Index, 52 percent JPM Global Government Bond Total Return Index.
Source: Author's own calculations; data from Bloomberg and Thomson Financial.

the next chapter.) The passive portfolio lost −19.9 percent as of September
2002 and had recovered by December 2003. The active portfolio fell by
10.7 percent by April 1994 and had recovered by July of the following year.
To spot the difference we need to examine the time under water. The passive
portfolio was under water by 47 months compared to only 18 months in
the case of the active portfolio. The difference between the two was that
in the case of macro there was a shock to the system and a sharp drop
followed by a swift recovery, at least for the majority of funds that did not
throw in the towel after the bond crash in 1994. In the case of the equity-
bond combination, there was negative compounding from March 2000 to
September 2002 to the maximum drawdown of −19.9 percent, followed by
a 15-month recovery. Note that the active strategy has significantly fewer
observations in the two return buckets from −6 percent to −2 percent.

Figure 6.23 shows the fairly steady rise of a diversified portfolio. As
mentioned in Chapter 3, these portfolios have an element of trend-following
and typically give some profits back coming into the trend reversal, that is,
money is lost at turning points and regime shifts. One example is the Internet
bubble wherein managers entered or got out too late or went short too early.

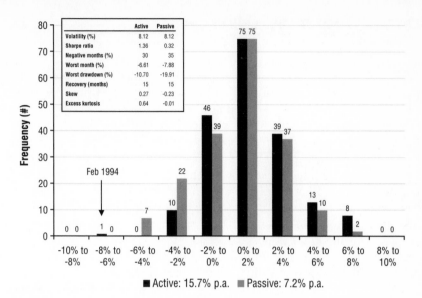

FIGURE 6.22 Return Distribution of Macro (1990 to 2005)
Active: HFRI Equity Hedge Index; Passive: 48 percent MSCI World Total Return
Index, 52 percent JPM Global Government Bond Total Return Index.
Source: Author's own calculations; data from Bloomberg and Thomson Financial.

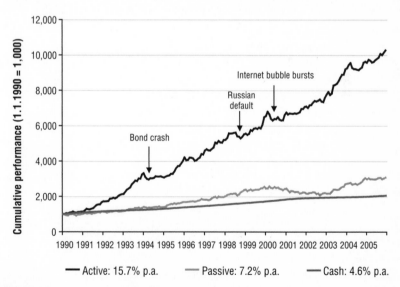

FIGURE 6.23 Cumulative Performance of Macro (1990 to 2005)
Active: HFRI Equity Hedge Index; Passive: 48 percent MSCI World Total Return
Index, 52 percent JPM Global Government Bond Total Return Index.
Source: Author's own calculations data from Bloomberg and Thomson Financial.

CHAPTER SUMMARY AND CONCLUSIONS

We believe that in active asset management it is important to apply a skill that carries a reward in the marketplace within an opportunity set where the risk/reward trade-off is skewed in favor of the risk taker. What we keep referring to as a structural change in the asset management industry is about finding skill (which is difficult enough), as well as the optimal setup for that skill to be operational in a value-added fashion. In terms of applying skill, we believe there is a trade-off between transparency and standardization on the one hand, and entrepreneurial maneuverability on the other. Interestingly, traditional asset managers are becoming somewhat more entrepreneurial by venturing into the absolute-return space, while hedge funds by and large are moving in the opposite direction, that is, they are becoming more transparent (as in self-constrained, disciplined, and process driven) to cater more to high-quality (quite often institutional) investors.

We believe this to be consistent with our story of hedge fund land merging with traditional asset management land. In other words, from now on, we should be talking about product differentiation in asset management—that is, distinguishing between *active* and *passive* risk management—and not between hedge funds and non-hedge funds.

Table 6.3 summarizes the two asymmetries discussed in this chapter, for what we believe is active risk management as well as a passive alternative portfolio. The last two sections of Table 6.3 shows a ranking of the 14 strategies by Sharpe ratio and by the sum of the two asymmetries (magnitude and frequency). The rankings are not identical but close. The active strategy in all cases has a higher ranking than the passive portfolio.

TABLE 6.3 Summary of Asymmetries

	Portfolio Volatility	Sharpe Ratio		Ratio of Magnitude		Ratio of Frequency		Rank Sharpe Ratio		Rank Asymmetry	
	(%)	Active	Passive	Active	Passive	Active	Passive	Active	Passive	Active	Passive
Convertible arbitrage	3.53	1.52	0.18	1.21	1.25	4.82	2.25	3	14	3	8
Equity market neutral	3.09	1.47	0.19	2.01	1.25	4.49	2.49	4	10	1	7
Distressed securities	5.97	1.76	0.18	1.49	1.04	4.33	1.87	1	12	4	10
Event-driven multistrategy	5.32	1.65	0.18	1.13	1.11	5.00	1.87	2	13	2	9
Equity hedge	8.66	1.45	0.18	1.56	0.93	2.49	1.78	5	11	6	13
Sector (technology)	18.51	0.72	0.32	1.29	0.96	1.54	1.57	7	9	12	14
Macro	8.12	1.36	0.32	1.77	1.02	2.37	1.82	6	8	5	11

Source: Author's own calculations.

APPENDIX

The Random Approach to Manager Selection*

"It would be foolish, in forming our expectations, to attach great weight to matters which are very uncertain."
—John Maynard Keynes

Many research papers on hedge funds coming out of academia focus on the survivorship bias issue in hedge fund data, while the media has a field day every time a hedge fund blows up. While both are very interesting, does it matter to the investor? In this appendix we show a simulation that we understand as a response to the overemphasis on bad data by academia and the overemphasis on blow-ups by the popular press.

The goal of this simulation was to find out whether survivorship bias matters to the investor with no manager-selection skill and no portfolio-construction skill. In other words, the simulation shows the random approach to hedge fund manager selection. Our line of argument is that single-manager risk is idiosyncratic risk and hence should be diversified. We apply the same logic for hedge fund investments as we do for stocks: Occasionally, a listed company goes bankrupt and the company's stock becomes worthless. Accidents happen. The way investors manage that risk is by not holding one stock but many. The same is true for hedge funds. At the end of the day, absolute-return managers are entrepreneurs. Some occasionally fail. This is unfortunate but the risk of single managers defaulting is easily controllable through diversification, as is default risk in the stock or corporate bond market.

For this simulation we were able to examine what we believe was high-quality hedge fund data. The data was based on European hedge funds only and included failed hedge funds. The advantage of using European hedge funds only is that the representation of the data is much higher than any comparable database on U.S. hedge funds would be. The European hedge fund scene is much younger and has fewer hedge funds. Most hedge funds are located in London and are registered with the local regulatory body. Also, the data provider, Eurohedge, has been around since the dawn of European hedge funds. These advantages make us believe that we are working with a sample that is perhaps 90 percent of the entire population. Commercially available databases on U.S. hedge funds hardly exceed 40 percent representation. One disadvantage of examining European hedge

---

*This simulation was first published in Ineichen [2004b]. Herein we show a shorter version of the whole analysis.

funds is that the data does not include frauds, primarily because there are hardly any. We can adjust for that in a simulation. The reason why hedge fund fraud is predominantly a U.S. phenomenon is all very interesting but beyond the scope of this book.

SIMULATION

Assume the following:

- Two thousand independent investors randomly select 2,000 different portfolios comprising European hedge funds on January 1, 1995.
- All portfolios consist of 15 different hedge funds.
- The 15 hedge funds are equally weighted on January 1, 1995.
- If a fund drops out (due to termination in the database), a substitute is randomly selected from all funds available at the time (the portfolio is not rebalanced to equal weighting).
- The 2,000 investors, who do not know each other and are entirely immune to fads, start investing on January 1, 1995, and examine their portfolio on August 31, 2003.

Figure 6.24 shows the frequency distribution of the 2,000 simple returns generated by the randomizer. The line shows the log normal distribution with the given mean and standard deviation of the simulation. The left box in the graph shows some statistics of the simulation. The right box shows some statistics of the most extreme portfolios of the 2,000 runs.

- The average return of the 2,000 portfolios was 15.25 percent. As a source of reference, the compound annual rate of return of the MSCI Europe Total Return Index and the JPM European Government Bond Total Return Index in the same time period was 7.65 percent and 8.56 percent, respectively.
- The range of compound annual rates of return of the simulation was wide, from 10.1 percent for the worst of the 2,000 portfolios to 21.1 percent for the best. In other words, the worst possible combination of hedge funds has beaten a long-only buy-and-hold investment style handsomely. The 90 percent range was much narrower, that is, from 13.5 percent to 17.0 percent. Note that by 90 percent range, we mean that 5 percent of all portfolios had a return of 17.0 percent or better, while 5 percent had a return of 13.5 percent or worse. In other words, 90 percent of the portfolios were in that, statistically speaking, "90 percent range."

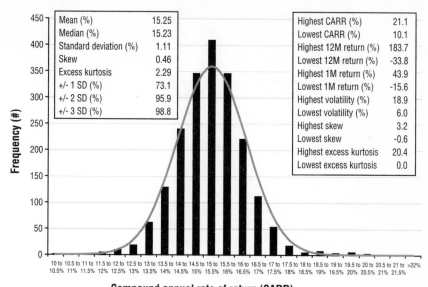

FIGURE 6.24 Return Distribution of 2,000 Randomly Selected Hedge Fund Portfolios
Distribution includes live as well as terminated funds. No fund was represented twice in a portfolio. Bars show frequency distribution, line shows log-normal distribution with given mean and standard deviation.
Source: Ineichen [2004b]; raw monthly returns from Eurohedge.

- The median portfolio volatility was 8.6 percent, with the extremes at 6.0 percent and 18.9 percent. The 90 percent range was from 7.0 percent to 10.0 percent. In other words, an investor with no asset allocation skill and no manager selection skill had around a 50:50 chance of achieving a Sharpe ratio of around 1.2 by simply following only one rule: diversifying single manager risk.

- The standard deviation of the return distribution of the whole simulation was 1.11 percent. We were surprised by such a low figure. Intuitively, we had expected the standard deviation to be higher because of the influence of the terminated funds. However, as we did not rebalance, poor-performing funds decreased in portfolio weight over time. In the original simulation in Ineichen [2004b] we reran this simulation with different starting points. The numbers changed. However, the conclusions did not. In one of the simulations, we altered the data. For every fund that stopped reporting, to the data provided we added another last return of −100 percent. In other words, we assumed that every fund that stopped reporting went bust. The results of this arguably extreme simulation were as follows: The mean CARR was 12.0 percent, that is, more than 300 basis points lower than the simulation shown here. Interestingly, 300 basis points is a figure that many researchers find is the average sum of all the biases that inflate hedge fund data. The standard deviation was substantially higher, at 1.83 compared to 1.11 in this simulation. Interestingly, the excess kurtosis was much lower, at 0.66, compared with 2.29 in this simulation shown here. Actually, this is not that interesting for the reader who did not skip the appendix to Chapter 4: The higher excess kurtosis in the shown simulation is a function of the standard deviation's being so much lower.

■ Overall, the distribution was fairly normal, with skew and excess kurtosis slightly inflated. There were 73.1 percent of observations within one standard deviation of the mean (of 15.25 percent). There were 21 positive outliers higher than three standard deviations from the mean, and only four below three standard deviations on the left-hand side of the distribution. In other words, the outliers were positively skewed. The outliers largely explain positive skew for the whole distribution as well as the excess kurtosis (left inserted box in Figure 6.24).

■ The worst drawdown of all 2,000 portfolios over one and twelve months was 15.6 percent and 33.8 percent, respectively. Note that a fund of hedge funds with drawdowns of this magnitude is, we believe, unlikely to remain in business for very long. We therefore do not recommend that fund of hedge fund managers start selecting hedge funds randomly.

We wondered what the distribution would look like if we had randomly chosen European stocks instead of hedge funds back in 1995. At first sight, comparing hedge fund portfolios with stock portfolios seems to be comparing apples with oranges. However, the common denominator between the two is that both hedge funds and stocks are businesses with idiosyncratic risk that requires diversification in a portfolio context.

The next simulation (Figure 6.25) is based on DAX stock constituents (instead of European hedge funds). We have chosen the Deutscher Aktien Index (DAX—German stock index) for two reasons. First, the number of constituents as of 1995 is similar to the number of available European hedge funds at the time; that is, there were around 30 European hedge funds at the beginning of 1995. Second, we know all index changes with the exact date since 1995. Choosing the DAX is an extreme example, as the DAX was heavy on new economy stocks that got hammered during the observation period. Had we chosen a more balanced index instead of the DAX, the clusters would have looked slightly different. The conclusions we

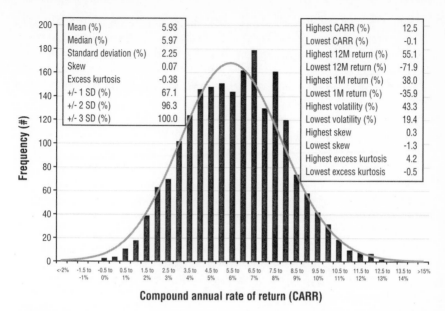

Compound annual rate of return (CARR)

FIGURE 6.25 Return Distribution of 2,000 Randomly Selected Stock Portfolios Distribution includes live as well as terminated stocks. No stock was represented twice in a portfolio. Bars show frequency distribution, line shows log-normal distribution with given mean and standard deviation.
Source: Ineichen [2004b]; raw monthly returns from Thomson Financial.

draw from the analysis, however, are not at all dependent on which index we chose.

The simulation is based on the same assumptions as the first simulation:

- Two thousand independent investors randomly select 2,000 different portfolios comprising DAX 30 constituents on January 1, 1995.
- All portfolios consist of 15 different stocks.
- The 15 stocks are equally weighted on January 1, 1995.
- If a stock drops out (due to index deletion or merger), a substitute is randomly selected from all DAX constituents available at the time (the portfolio is not rebalanced to equal weighting).
- The median of the distribution was 5.97 percent. (The compound annual rate of return of the DAX 30 index in the same period was 5.99 percent.) This compares with 15.25 for the hedge fund simulation. Note that in both simulations we included near defaults. Note further that the hedge fund simulation is based on net returns, while the stock simulation does not include transaction costs or fees.

- Standard deviation was 2.25 percent and was much higher than the 1.11 percent in the previous simulation. Given the high standard deviation, excess kurtosis is low for reasons discussed in the appendix to Chapter 4. The highest excess kurtosis from all 2,000 simulations was only 4.2, that is, much lower than with the previous simulation based on hedge funds data.
- Analyzing time series of hedge fund indices, one can often find that skew is negative. An alternative (albeit unorthodox) way of looking at skew is comparing the highest and lowest returns. The highest/lowest 12-month return of the hedge fund simulation was 183.7 percent and −33.8 percent respectively (inserted right box in Figure 6.24). This would suggest positive skew (as the highest return is much higher than the lowest return is low). The best and worst 12-month return in the DAX simulation was 55.1 percent and −71.9 percent, respectively (Figure 6.25). This would suggest negative skew (as the lowest return is much lower than the highest return is high). These conclusions do not change if we look at the 90 percent range only. This is another way of looking at the asymmetries we have been pounding about in this book.

Figure 6.26 and Figure 6.27 each compare the two simulations. Figure 6.26 compares the portfolio return with the portfolio volatility of the 4,000 simulations. Figure 6.27 contrasts the maximal drawdown with portfolio volatility. Former Harvard president Derek Bok was once quoted as saying: "If you think education is expensive, try ignorance." By examining these two graphs, we could rephrase and argue: "If you think hedge funds are risky, try stocks."

In the past, randomly selected hedge fund portfolios had a "high-return/low-volatility/high-kurtosis" pattern, while equity or equity-biased portfolios had, by comparison, more of a "low-return/high-volatility/low-kurtosis" pattern, that is, the opposite. We believe the current large capital inflows into hedge funds is based on the changed perception in the market-place that the former pattern is more attractive than the latter—especially for "economic agents that are also loss averse." It is more attractive to lose small amounts of money infrequently than it is to large amounts often.

Our central hypothesis is that the asset management industry (in its active form) is moving toward an absolute-return approach (as outlined in Ineichen [2001; 2003a, c; 2004a] and reiterated in this book). This would mean that an active manager would have the increased flexibility to create an asymmetric-return profile, that is, manage total risk to avoid large losses or, worse, negative compounding. The previous three charts show that randomly selected stock portfolios have volatilities of around 19.4 percent

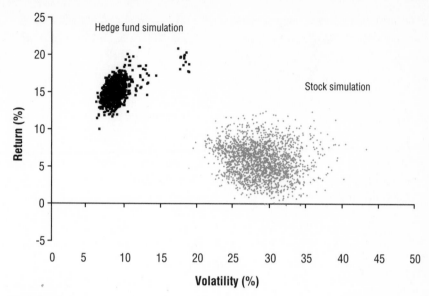

FIGURE 6.26 Return versus Volatility
Source: Ineichen [2004b].

and 43.3 percent, whereas randomly selected hedge fund portfolios have volatilities of around 6.0 percent and 18.9 percent. Assuming mean annual returns of randomly selected stock portfolios and randomly selected hedge fund portfolios are the same going forward (which is a possibility), the low-volatility/high-kurtosis combination, we believe, is still much more attractive than the high-volatility/low-kurtosis combination. The reason is, as outlined in this book and elsewhere, the impact of large absolute losses or negative compounding on the long-term rate of compounding capital.

Figure 6.27 reveals a very important aspect of investment life, potentially the most important fact of portfolio construction: correlation among portfolio constituents. Correlation among stocks is high, especially when markets fall. Not only is correlation high, but the volatility of correlation is also high. All randomly selected portfolios of stocks had massive drawdowns, as there is no combination of stocks that has capital preservation characteristics. (Note that we are showing an extreme example. Had we chosen global stocks instead of DAX constituents, the cluster of the stock simulation would move somewhat to the northwest. However, economic logic as well as our conclusions do not change when using different data.)

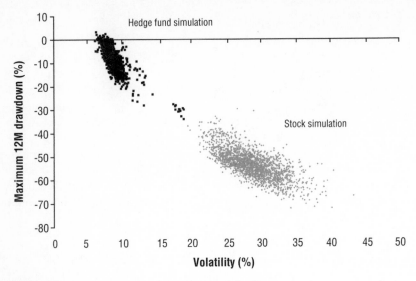

FIGURE 6.27 Maximum Drawdown versus Volatility
Source: Ineichen [2004b].

Large drawdowns due to sharp increases in correlation among hedge fund portfolio constituents is less extreme. Correlation among single hedge funds can be low as well as fairly stable.* With the hedge fund simulation, the cluster of drawdowns starts at zero or in some cases even above zero.[†] This means that there are combinations of portfolio constituents that eliminate or substantially reduce downside volatility. Hedge fund allocators construct portfolios by combining constituents to form a portfolio that has these capital-preservation characteristics. Correlation is, we believe, the key variable in portfolio construction. Phrasing it more boldly: In a random combination of hedge funds, there is some probability that drawdowns will be only single digit. In a random combination of stocks, this probability is close to zero.

---

*Note that intuition as well as anecdotal evidence suggests that correlation among hedge funds can also jump toward one under certain circumstances. However, this intuition is not backed by data. The dispersion of returns across the various strategies and locations is simply too large for correlation among *all* funds to jump.

[†]Some analysts show drawdown as a positive number, implying that the term *drawdown* already indicates a minus sign. We prefer showing drawdowns with the minus sign as there are portfolios (simulated as well as in the real world) where the worst 12-month return, that is, the "maximum 12-month drawdown," is actually a positive return.

Bottom Line

If we compare random stock portfolios with random hedge fund portfolios and define investment risk as either volatility or maximal drawdowns, random hedge fund portfolios, in the past, had higher returns with less risk. The extreme heterogeneity and diversity in the absolute return strategies allows investors to pick portfolio constituents that are largely independent (or, more precisely, less dependent than for example stocks). The low, and by comparison, fairly stable correlation of portfolio constituents allows construction of conservative portfolios. In the past, randomly selected portfolios of hedge funds most often had volatilities of less than 10 percent and maximum 12-month drawdowns of less than 30 percent. We believe these risk levels, available to the *naïve* investor, can largely be improved by the *intelligent* investor.

CONCLUSIONS

Businesses (hedge funds, as well as stocks) are risky. The feature that allows combination of risky businesses to form a conservative portfolio is correlation and its inertia. Low and inert (stable) correlation among different portfolio constituents allows the construction of conservative portfolios. High and unstable correlation among portfolio constituents does not.

We believe constructing portfolios with low compound annual returns, high volatility, and high probability of large drawdowns is easy. Constructing portfolios with high compound annual returns, low volatility, and low probability of large drawdowns is not. We therefore recommend an active approach for the latter. For the former, a random or passive approach suffices.

CHAPTER 7

Asymmetry of Single-Manager Risk

"To build may have to be the slow and laborious task of years. To destroy can be the thoughtless act of a single day."
—Sir Winston Churchill

In this chapter, we examine asymmetries relating to nonsystematic, that is, idiosyncratic risk. The previous chapter dealt with portfolios in which idiosyncratic risk was eliminated through diversification. In the absolute-return world, idiosyncratic risk means primarily the risk borne by the hedge fund investor that the hedge fund "blows up." Under normal circumstances, hedge funds should not blow up. However, in the real world, accidents happen. Circumstances change.

In examining single-manager risk, the objective is to get some idea of the probability of losing all or a significant part of one's capital due to extreme situations. We will examine a large data set that includes discontinued funds. However, even by including dead funds in the analysis, we still cannot be certain whether the last return in the database was really the last return for the investor. We also cannot be certain whether our data captures all investment possibilities to the investor. The imperfections of hedge fund data have been extensively written about in the academic literature so we will not repeat these points here. See Chan et al. [2005] for a comprehensive and recent update on the hedge fund literature. Nevertheless, this section will give at least some idea of idiosyncratic risk when investing in hedge funds. Again we search for asymmetries.

We examine single-manager risk for two strategies: convertible arbitrage and global macro. We believe that two examples are sufficient to bring home our points regarding idiosyncratic risk. We have chosen these particular strategies for two reasons: First, convertible arbitrage is a some-what narrowly defined strategy (at least by comparison), whereas global macro is not. A convertible arbitrage fund is a fund in which the main part of the portfolio has to do with convertibles-type risk whereby in most cases directional market and credit risks are fully or partly hedged. Once a convertible arbitrage manager grows and becomes multi-strategy, it typically is removed from the convertible arbitrage category to event-driven multi-strategy. Global macro, however, is not narrowly defined. It could involve nearly anything. Second, convertible arbitrage is a relative-value strategy that is typical of low volatility due to limited market risk, that is, is nondirectional. Conversely, global macro is considered directional.*

CONVERTIBLE ARBITRAGE

By analyzing convertible arbitrage, we are looking at a strategy that—when compared to other absolute-return strategies—can be narrowly defined. However, the dispersion of the returns achieved by managers still can be large. Figure 7.1 shows all monthly returns of managers classified as convertible arbitrage from a large database from 1990 to 2005. The database included current as well as dead funds. Returns are in U.S. dollars (USD) and net of fees. Every tick is a monthly return of a fund. The graph is designed to show the wideness of return dispersion in a given month. It shows that a comment such as "CB arbitrage is up 1.2 percent this month" does not really mean a lot, as the dispersion around that 1.2 percent can be extremely wide; even in an apparently narrowly defined strategy. Returns are all over the place.

Examining a large set of single-manager data, such as Figure 7.1, allows us to get a better feel for the true risk of investing in absolute returns, that is, hedge funds (the one big caveat being that the analysis is backward looking). This analysis highlights some of the less pleasant asymmetries of absolute-return investing—asymmetries that are typically not noticed when diversified portfolios of hedge funds are examined. The good news for the investor is that these extreme event–type risks are primarily idiosyncratic. This means that these risks can largely be eliminated by diversification.

Figure 7.2 shows single-manager returns for the full year of 2005, which arguably was one of the worst years for convertible arbitrage. Every dark tick measures a fund's monthly net return, while the gray line shows the return of the Hedge Fund Research Inc. (HFRI) Convertible Arbitrage Index.

---

*We have questioned the use of ambiguous sector classifications in Ineichen [2000a, 2003a] and do not need to repeat the critique here.

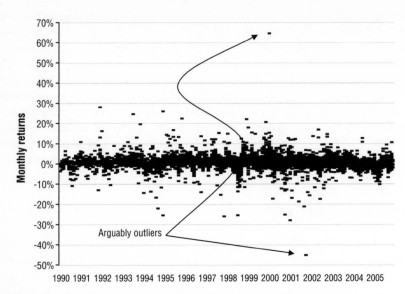

FIGURE 7.1   Monthly Returns in Convertible Arbitrage (1990 to 2005)
Source: Author's own calculations; data from Alternative Investment Solutions.

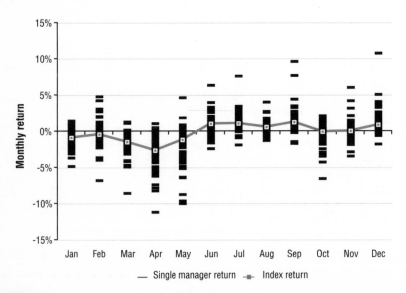

FIGURE 7.2   Convertible Arbitrage Managers in 2005
Source: Author's own calculations; single-manager returns from Alternative Investment Solutions; index data from Bloomberg.

Figure 7.2 shows that a majority of the observations are within 300 to 400 basis points of the median or the index. However, from a risk management point of view, it is the other observations and the probability thereof that are the focus of attention. The difficult months of 2005 were April, May, and October. Figure 7.2 shows that not all funds did equally well. Dispersion of returns increases in difficult market situations, especially on the downside. This is an asymmetry that would suggest that skew is negative. The graph also shows that not all funds lost money in these difficult months. This goes to show that even in a strategy that is fairly narrowly defined, such as convertible arbitrage, there are diversification benefits by not holding only one fund. This is important in the light of tail risk and the spreading (and flawed) idea that one needs only 15 funds for an efficient portfolio of hedge funds. Not fully utilizing the large spectrum of weakly correlated return streams that are one of the major characteristics of the hedge fund industry essentially means leaving money on the table.

Figure 7.3 shows the performance of Funds A and B from two different managers and the HFRI Convertible Arbitrage Index for the three years to 2005. All three time series were indexed to 1,000 for comparability. Both

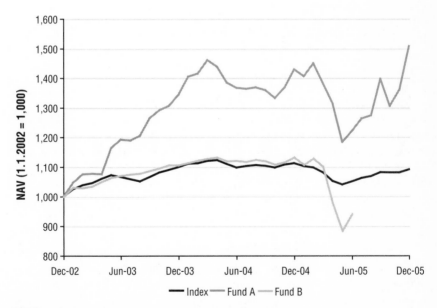

FIGURE 7.3 Example of Two CB Arbitrage Managers
Source: Author's own calculations; single-manager returns from Alternative Investment Solutions; index data from Bloomberg.

funds display a somewhat "typical" profile in a stress scenario. (The caveat here is that, in the hedge fund space, "typical" is not always easy to define with any precision, as discussed above.)

Fund A was a large, well-known fund that has performed well for years. The fund was established in the marketplace and launched by a credible alternatives shop with a good reputation in the market. However, in March and April 2005, it suffered larger losses than its peers. It came into the death-spiral of being a large part of a tight market in combination with investor redemptions, liquidity drying up, and the market having gotten wind of the semiforced selling. However, due to its reputation and brand value, it survived the storm. Recovery was swift, as the market recovered. Losses were recovered within months, as Figure 7.3 shows.

Fund B was small and not well known. The fund was not part of a larger, reputable alternatives shop, but a boutique. The fund was struggling to reach critical mass. Performance was mediocre in absolute-return terms, that is, performing along the lines of the median manager or the index. This manager also was hit by losses that were, similarly to Fund A, large in percentage terms. However, this fund did not survive the storm. It threw in the towel after heavy losses, giving money back to investors. The fund's losses for March, April, and May 2005 were 2.4 percent, 11.2 percent, and 9.6 percent, respectively, which was heavy underperformance relative to peers. Sharpe ratios at one stage of the fund were close to 3.0, that is, very impressive in terms of risk-adjusted returns. At the time of closing, Fund B was only down around 5 percent, relative to inception from a couple of years before. A fund that has not built up a great deal of investor confidence in the run-up to the losses (i.e., goodwill) does not survive an accident of this magnitude if its peers do not suffer a similar magnitude of losses. This is a major difference to Fund A, which had similar losses but survived the storm. This is one of the reasons why business and investment issues are interlinked and why business issues get a lot of attention in this book. Alpha is not simply the intercept of a regression.

This comparison shows that alpha probably has an intangible element to it. If a firm builds up goodwill with its investors over many years, it is better positioned to weather the storm that is going to appear sooner or later. Furthermore, it can pick its own investor base, that is, replace trigger-happy return chasers with serious investors. These intangible elements are obviously difficult to quantify. In Chapter 5, we argued that alpha is an option from the investors' perspective. Applying that logic to this example, we could say that the "option" of Fund A was deeper in-the-money, while Fund B was a tiny option. Obviously, the former is more valuable than the latter.

We have a tendency to argue that, though accidents do happen, idiosyncratic risk does not matter that much because it can be controlled/eliminated through diversification. However, in the real world, idiosyncratic risk matters, as idiosyncratic risks can be correlated and become systematic risk, or worse, the perfect storm. In addition, not all investors hold portfolios wherein single-manager or single-entity risk is fully diversified. In other words, these investors are exposed to accidents akin to a stock or corporate bond portfolio consisting of only a couple of names. The mayhem around the debacles of Enron and LTCM somewhat supports this argument.

If idiosyncratic risk matters, then probability of accidents or large idiosyncratic losses and concentrations thereof matters to the investor. Figure 7.4 is an attempt to get an idea of the probability of failure in convertible arbitrage. (We will take a look at another strategy later, but the main messages remain unchanged.) Some of the caveats are as follows: (1) We derive a distribution from the past. This means the data could be unrepresentative (too good or too bad) of the universe. (2) The future might be different than the past. (3) One could argue that an absolute-return strategy changes over time, morphing into something that is different from a couple of years earlier. Nevertheless, while fundamental analysis

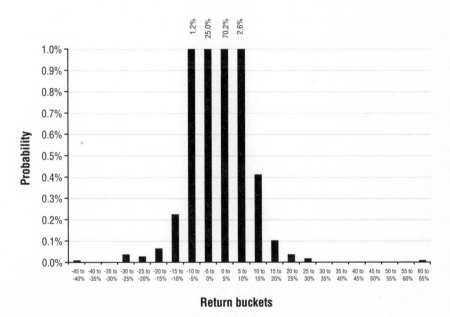

FIGURE 7.4 Convertible Arbitrage Manager Return Distribution (1990 to 2005) *Source:* Author's own calculations; data from Alternative Investment Solutions.

of investment strategy and manager operational due diligence is more important, examining the past allows us to have some reference.

Figure 7.4 shows the return distribution of all monthly net returns of all funds (survivors and nonsurvivors) that were available to us. Such a return distribution is vastly different from a distribution drawn from a hedge fund index that captures the performance and risk of a diversified hedge fund portfolio. The vertical axis has been truncated to visualize the outliers of the sample. The four percentage figures at the top of the graph are the percentages of the observations within the respective return bucket. In this case we examined simple returns, not log returns.

The two most extreme returns were −44.9 percent and 64.8 percent (also visible in Figure 7.1). One of the differences between the two returns is that the former was probably in the news, while the latter was not. Note that more than 70 percent, that is, more than two thirds of the returns, were in the 0 percent to 5 percent return bucket. This is net of fees. In other words, in more than two out of three months, convertible arbitrage managers made between 0 percent (the special case where the gross return equals fees) and 5 percent. There were 73.4 percent positive returns, that is, in roughly three out of four months, convertible arbitrage managers made money for their investors, net of fees and including the funds that are not among us anymore. In other words, the proverbial chimpanzee throwing darts on a big list of convertible arbitrage managers would have done pretty well.

Let's turn to the left-hand side of the return distribution. The first negative return bucket is also strongly populated −25.0 percent of all returns were between −5 percent and zero (in other words, 95.2 percent of observations were between −5 and 5 percent), and 1.2 percent of returns were between −10 and −5 percent. A total of 26.6 percent of returns were negative. The 73.4:26.6 ratio (of positive versus negative returns) is quite an asymmetry when compared to the risk-uncontrolled world, that is, the long-only space. Recall that the ratio between positive and negative returns measured by the HFRI Convertible Arbitrage Index in Chapter 6 was 83 percent to 17 percent. So the ratio is lower when measured with single-manager returns. However, the asymmetry is still there and measurable.

One way of looking at tail risk is by examining observations beyond a certain threshold. The percentage of occurrences below −10 percent and −20 percent were 0.37 percent and 0.07 percent, respectively. This means that if history is any guide and we hold only one convertible arbitrage manager in our portfolio, we can expect to lose more than 10 percent in any given month every 23 years and more than 20 percent every 111 years.* So losing 20 percent or more of one's capital with a convertible arbitrage manager is literally the proverbial "100-year flood," as only very few managers have experienced this kind of drawdowns in any given month. How do these loss probabilities compare to the stock market? Companies can fail in the stock market, too. Accidents happen. This is idiosyncratic risk.

Figure 7.5 compares the left tail of the distribution of monthly returns in convertible arbitrage with the left tail of monthly returns of the constituents of the Standard and Poor's (S&P) 500 and Russell 3000 indices. The Russell 3000 index represents approximately 98 percent of the U.S. stock market. We show only returns smaller than −20 percent. We have again truncated the vertical axis to visualize the outliers. By way of comparison, if we hold only one Russell 3000 stock in our portfolio, we can expect to lose more than 10 percent every four months and more than 20 percent every 13 months.

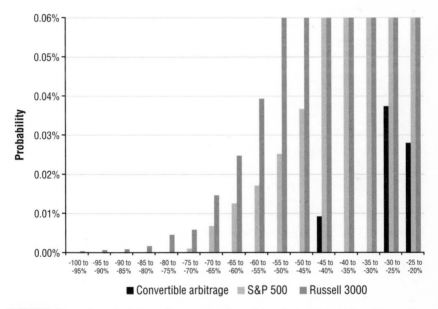

FIGURE 7.5   Left Tail of CB Arbitrage Funds and Stocks in S&P 500 and Russell 3000
Source: Author's own calculations; hedge fund data from Alternative Investment Solutions; stock prices from Thomson Financial.

---

*Note that losing a total of 20 percent over three consecutive months is much higher than once every 111 years.

The graph more or less speaks for itself. The probability of losing a large percentage of capital in the stock market in a month is several times the probability of losing the same percentage with a hedge fund. It is comparisons like these that raise some questions:

- What are some academics actually trying to tell us when they speak about the danger of fat tails in hedge fund space? These scholarly papers coming from the hedge-fund-bashing fraternity of academia could easily be perceived as misleading the investor when the fat tails in hedge funds are compared with the stock market. Note that we have been placid to long-only stock investors. We show only the tail risk of current constituents in the S&P 500 and Russell 3000. This introduces a positive bias. The left tail of the distribution would look worse had we included stocks that were excluded from the index during the period 1990 to 2005 (as we did for hedge funds). In other words, the Worldcoms and Enrons are not in the graph. The graph shows only current constituents as of December 2005, that is, survivors.

- What do regulators actually mean when they advocate that retail investors need protection? From what? Allowing retail investors to buy stocks but not hedge funds does not make sense. If the marketplace needs protection of the retail investors, it should potentially be the other way around.* Both stocks and hedge funds can go to zero. Retail investors have lost far more money due to mismanagement and fraud in the corporate world than investors have lost money through hedge funds. Investors lost hundred of *millions* through hedge fund fraud. Investors lost hundred of *billions* through corporate fraud (actually some argue it's a trillion and not a couple of hundred billion).† A somewhat ironic twist to this is that some hedge fund investors actually benefited from corporate fraud, as hedge funds are permitted to sell stock short. (According to *Conspiracy of Fools*,[1] it was short-sellers asking the tough questions at Enron's investor conference calls.) So the increase in market efficiency that is caused by hedge funds (in terms of liquidity and dissemination of information) results in wealth being

---

*This is obviously a contentious point that is here exaggeratedly stated. If we compare hedge funds with mutual funds, which many investors arguably do, then the story is, of course, different.

†According to one estimate, investors lost US$435 billion due to Worldcom, Tyco, Global Crossing, and Enron alone. A hedge fund fraud spread sheet that we maintain that contains around 80 frauds with estimates and guesstimates of how much investors lost due to fraud indicate that the aggregate loss due to hedge fund fraud could have been around US$6.3 billion from 1994 to spring 2006.

transferred from losers to winners, that is, from retail investors holding corporate frauds in their 401ks to high-net-worth individuals and institutions investing in hedge funds. The irony is that the restriction of retail investors is causing losers to remain losers. The regulatory regime is denying the retail investor an option. Options always have an economic value.

There are some explanations for both questions. Scholars like to create a laboratory environment where hypothesis can be scientifically tested, preferably using standard quantitative tools. The laboratory environment is created by assuming, among other things, perfect markets. (Nothing designed by man is perfect, certainly not the competitive interactions of humans for profit, i.e., financial markets.) The tools are typically some data and a set of theories heavily biased toward the two variables explaining a normal distribution (return and standard deviation of returns) and skew and kurtosis to explain deviations from the normal distribution.

The normal distribution is symmetrical. In many situations studied in the natural and social sciences, a normal distribution, that is, the bell-curved probability distribution, works pretty well. It works well, for example, if we are looking at the heights of people in the population. If we think of 220 people in an airplane where the average height is 5.5 feet and one standard deviation is 10 inches, a normal distribution will give us a pretty good estimate of the body heights of the 220 passengers. The normal distribution has thin tails, which is applicable in this case. It is very unlikely that there is a passenger that is either 10 inches short or 10 fathoms tall. Most of our tool kit in finance—sigma, variance, standard deviation, correlation, r-squared, Sharpe ratios, and so on—are all directly linked to the normal distribution. However, in the world of finance, a distribution with fat tails is much more applicable than a distribution with thin tailes. In addition to this, the distributions should allow for asymmetries, as asymmetries are not just a topic of a Wiley Finance book, but are part of the real world.*

We hope the reader finds this all very interesting. After all, empirical analysis such as the above shows what happened. However, empirical analysis shows us only the effect, not the cause. Often, we find an erroneous conclusion—sometimes implicit, sometimes explicit—that correlation proves causality between cause and effect. It does not. Looking

---

*Recommended reading on the subject: Taleb [2004a], Mandelbrot and Hudson [2004], and Buchanan [2000].

at historical time series is somewhat a desperate escapist activity. Ideally, we would instead want to examine positions. However, in hedge fund space, this is rather difficult for various reasons. The positions today tell us something about the risk at this very moment looking forward. Backing out a guess of what risk was from comparing a couple of time series is very much inferior, but in most cases it is all that an analyst can do. The following example was chosen to show that we could also identify asymmetries when examining positions. Meaning: Our asymmetries with respect to magnitude and frequency are not just something we casually found in data. Ex-ante managers are looking for high-profit-potential/lower-risk situations, or situations where the probability of gaining x is much higher then losing x. We believe the whole absolute-return investment philosophy is designed around these asymmetries.

Example The manager in this example was long a convertible on a stock from the transport sector (of which one driving factor is fuel prices). The convertible had a varying amount of warrants attached, which rapidly augments the instrument's delta as the underlying equity moves up and decreases the delta on the way down. To fully exploit this instrument, the manager was overhedged on this position. The reason for this overhedged position was twofold. First, the analysis of the stock led the manager to the conclusion that the stock was reaching a valuation level that was unsustainable. However, consensus earnings growth from 2006 to 2007 assumed fuel costs to be 25 percent less than prevalent levels. Assuming flat fuel costs, organic earnings-per-share growth would have had been much less attractive. Additionally, the manager felt that the stocks' valuation did not factor in potential changes in demand due to either economic or weather-related conditions. The key point was that the stock was trading at valuation levels that can be supported only by assuming a best-case scenario going forward. This is like an option of some sort: little upside potential, bigger downside potential.

The convertible instrument provided an ideal way to exploit the manager's belief that the equity was already pricing in a large part of any upside that the stock could reap from an improving fuel cost and/or consumer environment. By placing a bearish hedge on the position, the fund was positioned to benefit significantly on a downside move in the stock, while the negative exposure on an upside move would be mitigated by the rapidly increasing delta of the convertible instrument as the attached warrants came into play. In other words, the manager's view was asymmetric and his positions in the marketplace were a reflection of this asymmetry.

In the end, the fund benefited as the company eventually lowered guidance for the year. The underlying equity sold off heavily and the manager made money.

GLOBAL MACRO

The second strategy we look at is global macro. We have chosen global macro because it is perceived as being at the opposite end of the spectrum to relative value strategies such as convertible arbitrage. (This could be debated, as many macro managers morphed into multi-strategy vehicles, including relative-value strategies that materially can improve portfolio efficiency, as the return source is mostly different from directional macro bets.)

Figure 7.6 shows the distribution from 1990 to 2005 of all returns of current and dead funds that carry the global macro moniker. Note that the x-axis must be expanded on both sides when compared to convertible arbitrage.

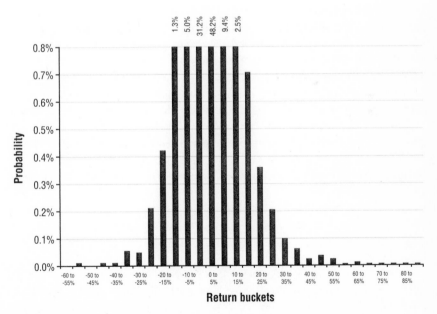

FIGURE 7.6 Global Macro Manager Return Distribution (1990 to 2005)
Source: Author's own calculations; data from Alternative Investment Solutions.

The returns are spread across a wider spectrum than relative-value strategies. Empirical research also finds a relationship between the volatility and/or directionality of the strategy and the attrition rate. This is fairly intuitive: *Directional* generally means higher market risk. Higher market risk generally means higher probability of a large drawdown. Large drawdowns decrease survival probability.

The frequency of positive to negative returns was 62 percent to 38 percent for global macro funds as compared to 73 percent to 27 percent for convertible arbitrage. As highlighted in the previous chapter, every strategy shows a different combination of the two asymmetries—an asymmetry with respect to magnitude and an asymmetry with respect to frequency. With low-volatility strategies, the asymmetry with respect to magnitude is smaller and the asymmetry with respect to frequency is higher. With directional strategies, such as global macro shown here, the asymmetry with respect to frequency is lower while the asymmetry with respect to magnitude is higher. However, the asymmetry with respect to magnitude is not as high as suggested in Chapter 6, where we examined *index data*. The average monthly return of all positive returns (survivors and nonsurvivors) from the sample of *single-manager data* was 3.50 percent, and the average negative return was −3.14 percent. At first sight, this implies an asymmetry. However, the asymmetry is small. The asymmetry disappears if we do not take a zero return as reference, that is, distinguish between positive and negative returns, but take the risk-free rate as reference. The average monthly risk-free rate between 1990 and 2005 was around 37 basis points. This means the average excess return above the risk-free rate is smaller than the average return below the risk-free rate. This small but relevant detail is not picked up by examining index data. It means that picking macro managers at random probably does not add value in terms of incremental alpha. An active approach with positive selection skill is required.

Figure 7.7 shows the left tail of the single-macro-manager return distribution, again compared with stocks from the S&P 500 and Russell 3000 for the period 1990 to 2005. We have left both axes the same as the previous graph (Figure 7.5), which showed the left tail in convertible arbitrage for comparative purposes. Note that we are comparing distributions with largely different sample sizes. The macro distribution is based on 16,159 returns, whereas the other two distributions are based on 87,006 returns and 385,765 returns, respectively. The three outliers on the left of global macro are based on two observations, each of which results in an outlier of 0.012 percent. In other words, if there were 385,000 data points in global macro, the difference between global macro and the Russell 3000 would most likely still be large, but not as extreme as implied by the graph.

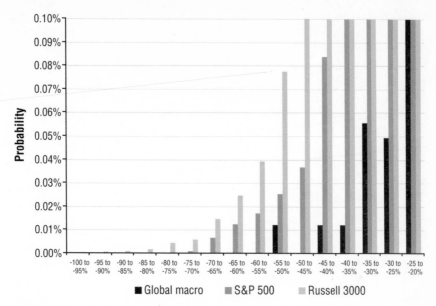

FIGURE 7.7 Left Tail of Global Macro Funds and Stocks in S&P 500 and Russell 3000
Source: Author's own calculations; hedge fund data from Alternative Investment Solutions; stock prices from Thomson Financial.

The left tail in global macro, when compared to a relative-value strategy, is more densely populated. This is not very surprising, as—generalizing somewhat and as mentioned before—portfolios of global macro managers are of higher market risk than portfolios of relative-value funds. Higher market risk translates into higher portfolio volatility. Higher volatility translates into a higher probability of a double-digit drawdown. A higher probability of a large drawdown translates into a higher attrition rate over time. If we compare the left tail in global macro with stocks in the stock market, we are reminded of our favorite saying in this book: "If you think hedge funds are risky, try stocks." The probability of suffering a large loss from investing in a stock is many times larger than the probability of experiencing a large loss from investing in a global macro manager.

The previous two graphs fail to pick up the extreme dispersion of returns among hedge funds, in general, and global macro, in particular. Figure 7.8 looks at cumulative returns of two managers with opposing success compared to the HFRI Macro Index from 1997 to 2005. Fund A had a good start and outperformed the index, albeit with a higher volatility. Then things started to go in the wrong direction. The fund started at 1,000,

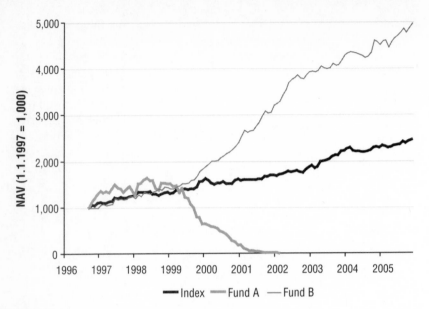

FIGURE 7.8 Example of Two Global Macro Managers
Source: Author's own calculations; single-manager data from Alternative Investment Solutions; index data from Bloomberg.

increased to 1,635, and from there went to 6 to close shop for a loss from inception to closing of 94 percent or from peak to closing of 99.6 percent. Manager B compounded at 19.7 percent from 1997 to 2005, while the index returned 9.5 percent per year in the same period. The investors' response to such divergence is manager-selection skill. This extreme dispersion of returns is both a risk *and* an opportunity. For an investor who has no manager-selection skill or who picks managers at random (essentially an investor who thinks he has selection skill but does not), the width of performance is a risk. However, for an investor who has the skill (essentially an investor who thinks he has selection skill and does), processes, and infrastructure to separate the wheat from the chaff, this wide dispersion is a great field of opportunities to add value.

The graphs in this chapter so far have hopefully demonstrated that single-manager risk is not zero but relatively small when compared to stocks. We keep falling back on comparing hedge funds with stocks because there are still so many people around who think investing in hedge funds is risky while investing in stocks is not. The next step in portfolio construction is correlation. The fact that single portfolio constituents can fall in price is unfortunate. However, modern portfolio theory is primarily about combining different constituents to a portfolio whereby the portfolio is of lower volatility than the weighted average volatility would suggest. The third variable after expected return and expected risk is expected correlation, that is, the relationship between the portfolio constituents. One of the amazing features in macro, as mentioned earlier, is that the single managers can be "high risk" but that a combination of these managers can still result in a "low-risk" portfolio. The variable that ties all this together is correlation. If correlations between portfolio constituents are high, then one can expect that they will fall in a synchronized fashion if something unpleasant happens. However, if correlation is low, chances are that some constituents might fall if something unpleasant happens but some might rise. To get a feel for this, we examine a correlation matrix.

Figure 7.9 shows a correlation matrix of 30 global macro funds over the period 2003 to 2005. We have selected 30 funds by alphabet where we had three years of return data. By *alphabet,* we mean we sorted the list by fund name and then picked the first 30 whereby we had three years of continuous data. We picked 30 for presentation purposes. We avoided picking two funds from the same organization. Selecting funds by alphabet is pretty much random, which was intended.* We have applied some color-coding.

The last row of Figure 7.9 shows off-diagonal correlation of the 30 constituents. By off-diagonal correlation, we mean the average correlation of a fund with all the other funds in the matrix, that is, the average correlation with all funds except oneself (which is one by definition). The range of off-diagonal correlation was between −0.06 and 0.33, which we believe is very low. The average off-diagonal correlation was 0.18. It is this low correlation that allows constructing conservative portfolios. How does this compare to stocks?

The black line labeled "Global Macro" in Figure 7.10 shows off-diagonal correlation of 30 randomly chosen global macro funds, that is, the last row from Figure 7.9, sorted in ascending order. We compare these correlations with off-diagonal correlation for the stocks in the Dow Jones Industrial Average and a random selection of 30 stocks from the S&P 500 (first 30 by alphabet). We were somewhat surprised to see that the difference between

---

*The first letter of a fund name should have no explanatory power with respect to the fund's risk-adjusted performance. However, if empiricists continue massaging the data, they indeed might find that funds starting with "A" for alpha outperform those that start with "B" for beta. The hedge-fund-bashing part of academia is already recommending passive strategies based on past return patterns. Potentially, it's only a small step in introducing the alphabet to their analysis.

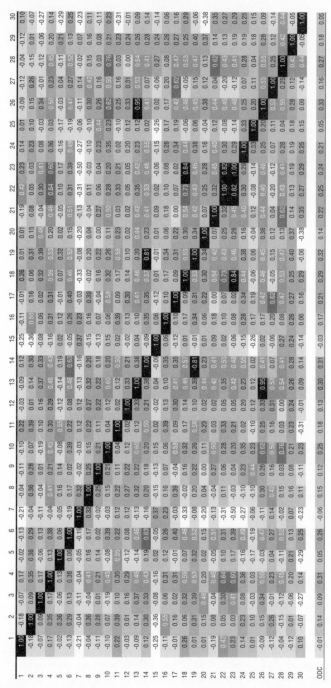

FIGURE 7.9 Correlation Matrix Global Macro Managers (2003 to 2005)
Source: Author's own calculations; hedge fund data from Alternative Investment Solutions. ODC = off-diagonal correlation.

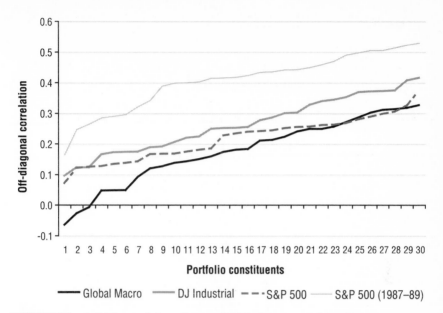

FIGURE 7.10 Off-Diagonal Correlation of Global Macro and Stocks
Based on monthly returns from 2003 to 2005, unless stated otherwise.
Source: Author's own own calculations; hedge fund data from Alternative Investment
Solutions; stock prices from Thomson Financial.

the global macro line and the two stock correlations was so small. When
we did this for the first time a couple of years ago, the difference was
much larger. The reason is that when we did this a couple of years ago, we
were looking at stock correlations in a bear market (stocks in free fall). In
other words, correlations among stocks is not only higher than correlations
among absolute return funds, the *volatility of correlation* is higher too.
To show this we have added the off-diagonal correlation of 30 randomly
chosen stocks for the S&P 500 from 1987 to 1989, that is, covering the
1987 crash. Stock correlation was much higher. That is exactly the problem
with what we called *uncontrolled risk* in Chapter 2. Correlation jumps
up in an out-of-control fashion during market mayhem. This phenomenon
can be controlled by paying attention to correlation of the single portfolio
constituents. (It doesn't always work, though.)

Figure 7.11 shows an extreme example of two funds whereby the wings
of the distribution were negatively correlated. The graph shows NAVs
(net asset values) from 1996 to 2001 whereby values of July 31, 1998
(the last date before the 1998 trouble started), were indexed to 1,000 for
presentation purposes. Fund 1 follows a relative-value strategy, whereas

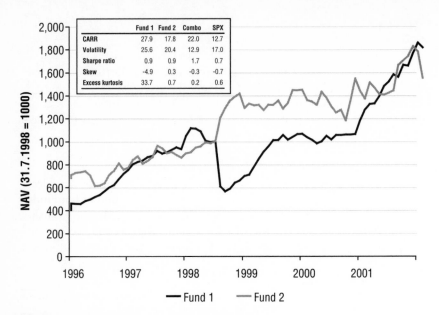

FIGURE 7.11 Negative Correlation of the Wings
CARR: Compound annual rate of return. Combo: Portfolio containing Funds 1 and 2, equal weighting, monthly rebalanced. SPX: S&P 500 Total Return Index. Sharpe ratio was based on an average risk free rate of 5.35 percent.
Source: Author's own calculations; data from Alternative Investment Solutions.

Fund 2 is a systematic trading fund. The inserted table in Figure 7.11 shows some statistics for the two funds from 1996 to 2001 as well as a portfolio containing the two funds (Combo) and the S&P 500 Total Return Index (SPX). The portfolio was equally weighted with monthly rebalancing.

The example shows how two funds can have a (positive) certain correlation under normal market conditions but display negative correlation during market stress. The statistics in the inserted table show the dramatic impact the negative correlation of the wings can have on risk-adjusted return measures. The Sharpe ratios of the single funds were around 0.9 in both cases. (The two Sharpe ratios for the first period from 1994 to July 1998 were 2.0 and 0.4.) The 1998 incident caused Fund 1 to have high negative skew and extreme excess kurtosis. However, the two-fund portfolio (Combo) has a fairly high Sharpe ratio with skew and excess kurtosis lower than the S&P 500 index. Note that a portfolio of two hand-picked portfolio constituents—in this case, hedge funds—can be of lower volatility than a portfolio of 500 U.S. large-cap stocks.*

We believe this is the one most important item that the general public and popular press gets wrong: The notion that risky portfolio constituents (hedge funds) using risky tools (derivatives, leverage, and short selling) can, when intelligently designed, result in a portfolio that has a fraction of downside risk that the general public and popular press is generally used to (long-only investments).

Note that Figure 7.11 shows a somewhat idealized world. In the hedge fund world correlation can also erratically increase (essentially as in any other human activity†). Table 7.1 shows a performance update of a selection of hedge fund indices, ranging from composite indices, fund of fund indices, to single-strategy indices. Looking from left to right, the first section shows monthly returns from July 2005 to June 2006. The second section shows four quarterly returns from Q3 2005 to Q2 2006. The last part on the right shows returns for the first half of 2006, 12-month period to June 2006 as well as annual returns in 2005 and 2004. We have applied a color code to visualize returns that are worse than one standard deviation *below* the 10-year mean (black) as well as returns that were better than one standard deviation *above* the mean (gray).

Table 7.1 shows that there are periods where correlation among strategies is high, both on the upside as well as on the downside. October 2005 and May 2006 were notable for an increase in correlation on the downside. Many strategies suffered losses that were higher than one standard deviation from the mean. January 2006 is a case in point where correlation was high on the upside. All strategies except dedicated short sellers had positive returns. Many of those returns were between 1 and 2 standard deviations above the mean. January and May 2006 performance resulted in Q1 2006 being well above average while Q2 2006 was way below average. (Interestingly, this resulted in H1 2006 performance being very "normal.")

Table 7.1 reveals another interesting aspect of hedge fund investing: The 2004 and 2005 annual performance for some strategies were worse than one standard deviation below average but still registered—given circumstances—decent positive absolute returns. This is not the case in the stock market. Assuming an average return for the S&P 500 of 8 percent and

---

*The caveat here is that we hand-picked Funds 1 and 2 based on their performance, that is, by pure hindsight. However, a deep understanding of the optionalities (asymmetries) of the various strategies and styles allows the experienced investor to construct portfolios where the effect is similar to Figure 7.11 on a forward-looking basis.

†This was ably put in Gustave Le Bon's *The Crowd*.

TABLE 7.1 Recent Hedge Fund Performance

Category	Index	Jul 05	Aug	Sep	Oct	Nov	Dec	Jan 06	Feb	Mar	Apr	May	Jun	Q3 05	Q4 05	Q1 06	Q2 06	H1 06	12M	2005	2004
HF Composites	HFRI Fund Weighted Composite Index	2.30	0.82	1.93	-1.41	1.66	1.82	3.49	0.45	1.95	1.88	1.57	-0.21	5.13	2.05	5.98	0.07	6.06	13.78	9.27	9.05
	CS Tremont Hedge Fund Index	1.92	0.89	1.63	-1.46	1.48	1.61	3.23	0.34	1.82	2.22	-1.30	-0.11	4.50	1.61	5.46	0.78	6.29	12.86	5.90	9.64
	Eurekahedge Hedge Fund Index	1.73	0.86	2.10	-1.17	2.11	2.07	3.24	0.29	1.99	1.98	-1.60	-0.48	4.76	3.00	5.60	-0.12	5.46	13.80	10.08	9.27
	Eurekahedge North American HF Index	2.04	0.52	1.24	-1.09	1.45	1.33	3.18	0.13	1.98	1.39	-0.86	-0.05	3.84	1.69	5.36	0.47	5.85	11.77	6.72	9.83
	Eurekahedge European Hedge Fund Index	2.24	1.33	2.25	-2.02	1.76	2.20	3.27	1.53	1.93	1.50	-2.26	-0.60	5.93	1.89	6.87	-1.40	5.37	13.74	12.80	8.72
	Eurekahedge Asian Hedge Fund Index	1.75	0.98	3.05	-1.01	2.85	4.44	3.27	-0.01	3.13	1.80	-2.39	-0.84	5.88	6.33	6.50	-1.46	4.94	18.15	15.96	9.79
	Eurekahedge Japan Hedge Fund Index	1.37	1.91	4.29	1.41	2.75	6.01	0.81	-2.47	1.98	-0.59	-3.22	-0.66	7.74	10.46	0.27	-4.42	-4.16	14.05	23.68	9.20
FoHF	HFRI Fund of Funds: Composite Index	1.74	0.84	1.55	-1.45	1.68	1.98	2.88	0.35	1.70	1.76	-1.89	-0.61	4.18	2.19	5.00	-0.77	4.18	10.92	7.50	6.87
	HFRI Fund of Funds: Conservative Index	1.35	0.58	1.05	-0.75	0.89	1.32	2.09	0.56	1.23	1.36	-0.68	0.05	3.01	1.46	3.92	0.72	4.67	9.39	5.16	5.82
	HFRI Fund of Funds: Diversified Index	1.80	0.85	1.53	-1.51	1.70	2.01	2.84	0.35	0.00	1.70	-1.94	-0.65	4.24	2.18	4.91	-0.92	3.95	10.71	7.47	7.19
	HFRI Fund of Funds: Market Defensive Index	0.38	0.53	1.51	-0.49	2.57	1.06	2.94	-0.67	1.74	2.92	-1.30	-0.70	2.44	3.15	4.03	0.87	4.94	10.88	5.87	3.27
	HFRI Fund of Funds: Strategic Index	2.28	1.15	2.08	-2.18	2.24	2.69	3.62	0.32	2.17	1.99	-2.92	-1.08	5.61	2.70	6.21	-2.06	4.02	12.82	10.29	8.38
Relative-value	HFRI Relative Value Arbitrage Index	1.34	0.69	1.18	-0.36	0.82	1.48	2.20	0.62	1.33	1.12	0.17	0.61	3.24	1.94	4.20	1.91	6.19	11.77	6.03	5.58
	HFRI Equity Market Neutral Index	0.82	0.56	0.95	-0.30	0.54	0.54	1.45	0.27	0.91	1.32	0.05	0.64	2.35	0.80	2.65	1.92	4.62	7.93	6.23	4.15
	HFRI Statistical Arbitrage Index	0.78	-0.48	0.76	-0.12	1.82	0.75	1.40	0.91	2.49	1.23	0.47	0.70	1.06	2.46	4.87	2.42	7.41	11.21	5.28	4.00
	HFRI Convertible Arbitrage Index	1.08	0.58	1.27	-0.07	0.04	0.91	2.40	1.17	1.04	0.62	0.81	0.07	2.96	0.88	4.68	1.51	6.25	10.36	-1.86	1.18
	HFRI Fixed Income: Arbitrage Index	0.97	0.39	0.82	0.46	0.15	0.52	0.73	0.74	0.38	1.03	0.58	0.48	2.19	1.13	1.86	2.10	4.02	7.49	5.61	5.99
Event	HFRI Event-Driven Index	2.35	0.89	1.00	-1.80	1.29	1.57	3.32	0.97	2.48	1.64	-0.59	-0.03	4.29	1.03	6.91	0.95	7.92	13.72	7.30	15.02
	HFRI Distressed Securities Index	1.65	1.32	1.10	-0.49	0.91	0.94	2.56	0.61	2.00	1.96	0.87	-0.03	4.12	1.36	5.25	2.82	8.21	14.21	8.25	18.89
	HFRI Merger Arbitrage Index	1.12	0.71	0.63	-1.57	1.29	1.82	3.12	1.16	1.97	1.41	-0.08	0.84	2.48	1.51	6.37	2.18	8.69	13.07	6.26	4.08
Equities	HFRI Equity Hedge Index	2.95	0.74	2.25	-1.87	2.14	2.32	3.95	0.02	2.55	1.76	-2.32	-0.56	6.05	2.56	6.62	-1.16	5.39	14.61	10.61	7.69
	HFRI Equity Non-Hedge Index	4.10	-0.11	2.25	-2.88	3.34	1.72	5.81	-0.25	2.56	2.29	-4.15	-0.96	6.20	2.09	8.25	-2.90	5.11	13.96	9.93	13.31
	HFRI Sector: Health Care/Biotech Index	4.54	0.59	0.49	-2.18	1.64	1.69	3.90	2.20	1.63	-1.57	-1.85	0.46	5.67	1.10	7.92	-2.95	4.74	11.90	4.73	7.96
	HFRI Sector: Real Estate Index	2.22	-1.52	0.60	-1.20	1.85	1.19	2.14	1.40	2.33	0.81	-0.62	1.00	1.27	1.83	5.98	1.19	7.24	10.59	5.37	18.43
	HFRI Sector: Technology Index	3.23	-0.91	1.25	-1.56	1.62	2.37	4.90	0.92	2.79	0.77	-5.16	0.44	3.57	2.41	8.82	-4.01	4.46	10.79	5.54	5.35
	HFRI Short Selling Index	-2.78	2.73	1.44	1.42	-2.41	-0.15	-1.34	0.14	-0.60	-0.34	3.03	1.11	1.31	-1.17	-1.79	3.82	1.96	2.08	7.26	-3.84
Other directional	HFRI Macro Index	0.74	0.73	2.11	-0.63	1.46	1.28	2.40	-0.47	1.15	2.72	-1.22	-0.52	3.62	2.11	3.09	0.94	4.06	10.10	6.81	4.64
	CS Tremont Managed Futures Index	0.78	-0.88	1.38	-1.97	4.17	-2.53	2.71	-2.62	4.09	2.92	-2.70	-2.04	1.27	-0.47	4.11	-1.90	2.13	2.95	2.49	5.96
	Barclays CTA Index	-0.54	0.87	0.36	-0.14	2.85	-0.43	1.32	-1.63	1.51	3.64	-0.73	-1.29	0.68	2.27	1.17	1.56	2.75	5.79	1.71	3.30
	Barclays Discretionary Traders	-0.76	0.86	0.71	0.44	1.58	1.29	0.63	0.63	1.20	1.02	-0.98	1.66	0.80	1.88	3.15	0.14	3.29	6.08	7.55	8.69
	Barclays Systematic Traders	-0.45	1.04	0.33	-0.19	3.22	-0.82	1.56	-1.94	1.53	4.01	-0.92	-1.36	0.92	2.18	1.11	1.66	2.79	6.00	0.95	0.54
	HFRI Emerging Markets (Total) Index	2.94	1.99	4.82	-2.59	3.27	3.74	5.75	2.26	1.87	4.55	-4.17	-0.87	10.05	4.36	10.16	-0.68	9.41	25.65	21.04	18.42

Source: Alternative Investment Solutions, data from Thomson Financial and Bloomberg.

236

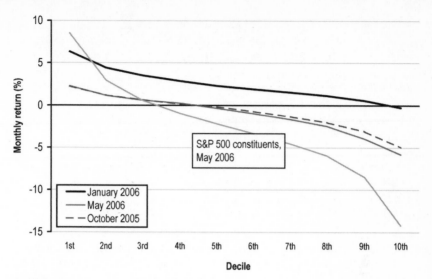

FIGURE 7.12 Manager Returns by Decile
Source: Author's own calculations; data from Alternative Investment Solutions.

a volatility of 15 percent, one standard deviation below average results in an absolute return of −7 percent (8−15). Contrast this with the HFRI Relative Arbitrage Index. The average return over the past 10 years was 9.3 percent while volatility was 3.2 percent. This means returns below 6.1 percent are further away from the mean than one standard deviation. This means more positive returns relative to negative returns over time, that is, an asymmetric return profile (asymmetry with respect to frequency). This means higher (as well as less stressful) compounding of capital over time.

Figure 7.12 adds some color as to what happened in May 2006 and October 2005. The graph was designed to show extreme months in terms of manager returns irrespective of strategy and location. Figure 7.12 shows average manager returns across all strategies by decile for two bad months as well as one extremely good month (January 2006) taken from a large universe of global hedge funds. In other words, most "normal" months are somewhere in between these two extremes.

In January 2006 the average return of the worst decile was barely negative at −0.25 percent. Only around 6 percent of managers had a negative month. In May 2006, by contrast, the four best deciles had small but positive returns while the six worst deciles had negative returns (which was quite similar to October 2005). In October 2005 and May 2006, the percentage of managers reporting negative returns was 57 and 61 percent, respectively.

The fourth line in Figure 7.12 shows the 10 deciles in terms of average stock returns for the 500 stocks in the S&P 500 index (taking into account dividends). We have added this line for comparative purposes. Only the three upper deciles managed positive returns in May 2006, 72 percent of stocks ended the month in negative territory. The average return of the worst decile was −14.2 percent which compares with −5.8 with hedge funds in May 2006. In September 2002, 84 percent of stocks in the S&P 500 had a negative return with the worst decile yielding −30.8 percent.

As we elaborated extensively throughout this book: accidents happen, both in long-only as well as in absolute-return space. During a stress period, correlation typically increases. The differences between hedged and long-only portfolios are subtle but are visible in graphs such as the one in Figure 7.12 (or some of the graphs in the appendix of Chapter 6). These subtle differences have a material impact on the rate at which capital compounds. It's the difference between what we called *controlled risk* and *uncontrolled risk*. It's not only volatility that matters, correlation and the volatility or inertia of correlation matters, too.

CHAPTER SUMMARY AND CONCLUSIONS

Any investment bears risk. As Alan Greenspan put it: "Risk, to state the obvious, is inherent in all business and financial activity." Some of this risk is systematic, and some is nonsystematic, that is, idiosyncratic to a single entity such as a company or hedge fund. Even an investment in the so-called risk-free rate bears risk. The risk-free rate to a U.S. investor and the risk-free rate to an Icelandic investor, however, are not the same. The common denominator that allows a comparison of the U.S. government defaulting on its obligations and the Icelandic government not being able to meet its liabilities is probability. The same is true for single-stock risk or single–hedge fund risk.

We could casually remark that idiosyncratic risk does not matter, as it should be diversified away in the first place. In other words, one could argue that an investor who is exposed to idiosyncratic risk is stupid because idiosyncratic risk is unnecessary risk that bears no risk premium. If a stock or a hedge fund defaults, to finish this argument, the stupid investor should not complain, as he has only himself to blame. In a sense, Enron and LTCM are nonevents from the perspective of the investor, as these two entities should have been such a small part of an investor's portfolio that a full loss would not cause negative utility. However, the real world—to state the obvious—does not work like that. The demise of Enron and LTCM are by no means nonevents. Idiosyncratic risk matters to most investors (and—it seems—regulatory bodies).

The reasons for this can be manifold. First, a total loss is always painful. Second, in the institutional investor landscape, there is considerable reputation risk (i.e., newspaper headline risk) and career risk associated with single–hedge fund default. There is a (somewhat dated) Wall Street saying that "no one was ever sacked for owning IBM." This means play it safe and you will be fine, as the probability of IBM's defaulting (at the time of the saying) was perceived as low. Third, the analytics of the investment process are called into question with total losses. At the end of the day, exposure to default is a low probability event but of high economic and especially behavioral impact.

The metric to compare differences in idiosyncratic risk is probability. In this chapter, we attempted to counterbalance the fuss that is often made with respect to tail risk caused by defaulting hedge funds. When we compare the probability of large losses from hedge funds with the probability of large losses from stocks, we find that the former is minuscule. An investor who holds a randomly picked convertible arbitrage fund in his portfolio can expect to lose 20 percent or more in any given month once every 111 years. The investor holding one randomly picked global macro fund can expect to lose 20 percent or more in any given month once in around 24 years. By comparison, an investor randomly picking one S&P 500 stock will find that, on average, a loss of 20 percent or larger occurs every four years. When one randomly picks stocks from the Russell 3000, such a loss occurs roughly every 23 months. It is interesting, then, that U.S. private investors can hold single-stock risk in their 401k plans but not hedge funds. The notion that it is probability of loss that allows comparisons between (systematic as well as nonsystematic) risks has not yet fully sunk in with all regulators and all investors. One claim of this book is that it will—eventually.

CHAPTER 8

Asymmetric Returns as a Business

"Entertainment is our biz. Luck is yours."
—Print advertisement of European casino operator

INTRODUCTION

We believe hedge funds are not a separate asset class, in that characteristics of the average or index return may be different from those expected of any one fund. Normally, there is wide dispersion of returns among funds, following the same strategy. Moreover, there is no "risk premium" associated with hedge funds in the classic economic sense. In the traditional asset classes, such as equities or bonds, there is an economic rationale for why investors might expect a positive return from their investment. But for hedge funds there is no equivalent economic theory. In fact, in the case of hedge funds, returns are achieved by the manager's ability to exploit inefficiencies left behind by other (less informed, less intelligent, less savvy, ignorant, or uneconomically motivated) investors in what is largely considered a zero- or negative-sum game.

As we will point out in this section, predictability (herein used as the opposite of randomness) of some sort is important when a favorably skewed risk/reward trade-off is the objective. What causes the predictable market behavior does not really matter: It might be different central banks trying to adhere to a multiple set of conflicting objectives, asset managers indexing to their particular asset benchmarks, liability managers immunizing duration risk according to a particular liability profile, regulatory/accounting changes, or outright foolishness causing predictable market behavior. All investors could be acting rationally relative to their particular set of objectives, the information available to them, and incentive structures under which they are operating. However, an uneconomic, suboptimal, or unrealistic set of objectives can be the cause of uneconomic behavior in the marketplace. In a zero-sum game, the predictability stems from the roles of predator and prey being fairly straightforward. In this chapter, we discuss issues regarding the coexistence of frogs and snakes from a business perspective.

Figure 8.1 contrasts assets with investors. The first bar is an estimate of equity and debt, the second bar an estimate of who owns these assets, that is, the investors. The two bars should be of the same size. If assets grow by x percent, all investors' capital grows by x percent, too. If an investor grows at 2x, someone else or a group of other investors got less than x. (Whether the 2x are a function of skill or luck or leverage is beside the point at this stage.)

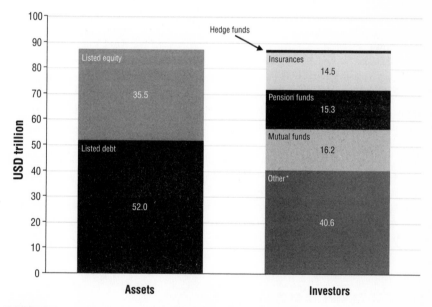

FIGURE 8.1   Global Asset Base versus Investor Base (2004)
*Other: Mainly governmental (supranational) bodies, corporate treasuries, banks, and private investors investing directly. The $40.6 trillion was assumed for the two bars to be the same size. Note that in this graph we have ignored investments related to property, commodities, currencies, art, wine, and so on.
Source: UBS Hedge Fund Research Inc. (HFRI), Investment Company Institute (ICI), Organization for Economic Cooperation and Development (OECD), PricewaterhouseCoopers.

When presenting the data like this, one is inclined to ask what the fuss over hedge funds is all about. When compared to the aggregate asset base or other investors, the hedge funds industry, with around $1.3 trillion assets under management, seems still rather minuscule.

If, for example, equities halve from $36 trillion to $18 trillion, someone is going to lose that kind of capital or wealth. Not all investors can be hedged; only some can. Essentially, those investors can be hedged who transfer that risk to other investors, presumably—or ideally—to those consciously indifferent to short-term market swings.

If the Sharpe ratio were a good measure for risk-adjusted returns, the analysis of hedge funds would be rather simple. A majority of hedge funds have Sharpe ratios in excess of 1.0, while equity and bond portfolios (as a proxy for long-only strategies) do not.* We believe that Sharpe ratios (and brethren measures) are, at best, a good measure for the *investment* risk of a portfolio. However, an investor investing in a hedge fund is also exposed to *operational* or *business* risk. Sharpe ratios are not designed to measure business risk.

An airline company's stock, for example, is exposed to various types of risk, some of which are measured by volatility of its stock price. However, equity volatility might not be a good measure to assess default probability of its bonds. A credit rating by a neutral agency conducting due diligence and analyzing balance sheet dynamics is probably more appropriate. The same logic should apply to assessing risk of hedge funds. The investment risk should be assessed differently than the business risk, despite the two being interrelated.

We believe a (well-balanced) market-neutral or a long/short investment style (both of which use leverage) is less risky than a (well-balanced) long-only investment style, almost by definition. However, while a market-neutral investment style is of little "risk," it does not follow that an investment in a market-neutral *fund* is safe. At the end of the day, a hedge fund is a business. Occasionally, businesses fail. Accidents happen. This is true in the stock market and the corporate bond market, as well as hedge funds.

THE BEST BUSINESS MODEL—EVER

Every business carries risk. Every business model is based on some assumptions or expectations about the future, which may turn out to be right or

---

*Comparing Sharpe ratios of two investments with different liquidity characteristics is somewhat unfair, as returns are often smoothed in the case of the less liquid investment. See, for example, Getmansky, Lo, and Makarov [2003].

wrong. Assessing hedge fund investments has a lot to do with assessing the business models of the investment manager.

What is the best business model—ever?

We believe the best business is to run a lottery. Running a lottery is an ultra-high-margin business in which the margins are more or less stable and sustainable and therefore predictable. The provider of a lottery sells lottery tickets whereby the economic value (fair value) of the ticket is a fraction of the price the buyer pays. As a matter of fact, running a lottery, as a business, is so attractive that very often governments keep this privilege for themselves, hence the multitude of "state" lotteries and the restrictions of "private" ones.

Ask yourself the following question: If you sell lottery tickets for $1 per ticket whereby every one millionth ticket pays out $100,000 to one lucky winner, how many tickets, as an entrepreneur, do you want to sell? Answer: as many as possible. This is statistical arbitrage at its best: For every round, you take in (on average) $1 million (roughly your gross earnings) and pay out $100,000 (your cost). That's a high-margin operation. Occasionally, there will be outliers. For example, it is possible that you sell 11 $100,000 winning tickets in one round. This would result in a loss (paying out $1.1 million and taking in only $1 million). Statistically, the $100,000 loss would be a far-from-equilibrium event, that is, a statistical outlier on the wrong side of the return or cash flow distribution. The reason for it to be "far from equilibrium" is not that $100,000 is a lot of money but that the equilibrium (mean cash flow or mean return) is so high and the volatility around the mean is so low. Empiricists, analyzing your business model with highly sophisticated quantitative techniques borrowed from the natural sciences on your cash flow stream (read: historical returns), would—finding an inflated excess kurtosis statistic—probably come to the conclusion that you are doomed because you are picking up nickels in front of a steamroller.

A lot of the hedge fund research stresses that some relative-value strategies are informationless and that managers are selling far-out-of-the-money or disaster put options, that is, picking up nickels in front of a steamroller. Note that risk measurement and risk management are not the same. (See Chapter 2.) Robert Gumerlock, a former head of risk at Swiss Bank Corporation and O'Connor, stated:

> *"When O'Connor set up in London at Big Bang, I built an option risk control system incorporating all the Greek letters—deltas, gammas, vegas, thetas and even some higher order ones as well (the delta of the gamma and the gamma of the vega). And I'll tell you that during the crash it was about as useful as a US theme park on the outskirts of Paris."*[1]

There are three points that are important: stability, sustainability, and predictability of earnings or returns or cash flows or revenues. The three are interrelated. A purely quantitative-driven process might or might not add value. MIT professor and hedge fund manager Andrew Lo, in an acceptance speech for the 1997 Paul A. Samuelson Award for Outstanding Scholarly Writing on Lifelong Financial Security on the practicability of quantitative finance, said:

> *"It's a happy coincidence that some of the most rigorous and mathematically sophisticated models of economics—financial models—also happen to be the most practically relevant ones as well. Indeed, practical relevance has been rather forcefully demonstrated by the recent success of Long-Term Capital Management."*[2]

The date of the speech was January 4, 1998.*

Departing from Randomness

The more a business generates its revenues from a predictable, nonrandom source, the better. Running a lottery is an extreme example. To understand why a lottery has stable cash flows that are sustainable over time and, therefore, are predictable, we need to understand the fundamentals of the trade (as opposed to examining historical time series with the help of a computer). The reason a lottery works is that there are so many fools. From a neoclassical economic perspective, the buyer of a lottery ticket is a fool in the market. He spends $1 for something that is worth, say, $0.001. The beauty of the business model is that the buyer often knows that the value is not even close to $1 but still continues to spend $1 or more per week on lottery tickets.[†]

The reason the cash flows are stable is that the sample of fools buying lottery tickets is fairly stable. There might be some cyclical variation in their spending habits due to changing economic conditions. However, these variations are not huge. Hope for "more" probably always sells well. The

---

*We are inclined to argue that brilliant quantitative finance with humility results in unbelievable riches whereas brilliant quantitative finance with hubris sooner or later results in disaster.

[†]Behavioralists try to explain the utility of the lottery ticket buyer hedonistically, that is, in nonfinancial terms. Perhaps (your author wouldn't know) the ticket buyer's utility from briefly thinking of what one would say to his boss when handing in one's resignation makes up for the $0.999 difference per ticket. Note that one could also explain the rationale for buying a lottery ticket with a utility function with an extraordinary preference for skewness.

reason why the cash flows are sustainable is that the world is not going to run out of fools any time soon—again, purely economically speaking. Neither will the buyers smarten up, as they already (presumably) know that their purchase is uneconomical from a probability-weighted expected return (rational expectations) point of view. Given that the entrepreneur's returns are stable and sustainable, they are fairly predictable (especially in the absence of competition). The cash flows of a provider running a lottery operation do not follow a random walk.* A license to run a lottery is a license to print money. If there is such a thing as a benchmark in the absolute-return world, it is running a lottery operation. (Note that we have ignored social/ethical considerations while discussing lotteries. Lotteries are potentially controlled to mitigate cash flowing from a loser [the gambler] to a winner [the entrepreneur]. Given that active asset management is a zero-sum game, that is, a transfer of cash flow from losers to winners, active asset management could one day be banned, too.)

What is the second best business model? Running a casino must rank pretty high on the scale of attractive business models. Donald Trump was possibly on to something when he said:

> *"People think I'm a gambler. I've never gambled in my life. To me, a gambler is someone who plays slot machines. I prefer to own slot machines."*

The idea is the same as that of running a lottery. The prerequisite for success is that some agents must behave uneconomically. Someone has to give (read: lose). One could argue, as with active management, it's a zero-sum game, as resources (in this case, money) are simply transferred from losers to winners.

Note that we could easily counter this argument: In theory we could assume that all investors could "win" if we assume that "winning" means perfectly matching objectives with outcome. In a sense, we could assume that the casino gambler is not a loser because he has utility from losing money in the form of entertainment and sensation. The same could apply to asset management: We could argue that, for example, a pension fund with a relative-return perspective causing market inefficiencies has utility from losing money in the form of perfectly immunizing duration risk. In other words, everyone could be happy—the gambler, as he has sensation; the liability-benchmarking pension fund, as he has a perfect match between

---

*It goes without saying that the statistical tools and techniques that were designed to assess distributions of random variables are inappropriate to assess the attractiveness of a business where cash flows (returns) are not randomly distributed.

assets and liabilities (i.e., no risk for the sponsor); and the absolute return investor, as he has, well, absolute returns.

Assume a casino has 10 roulette wheels. Every roulette wheel has 36 numbers and one zero (sometimes even two zeros). The gambler's gain is 36 times his capital at risk by betting on a number or 100 percent in the case of betting on a color (red or black). The casino gets all the capital at risk if the ball stops at zero. The casino, on average, makes nothing in 36 out of 37 spins of the wheel. However, every thirty-seventh spin it wins. This relationship is stable; the cash flow is sustainable and fairly predictable.*

Positive Compounding as a Major Business Objective

Empiricists analyzing the business model on the cash flow stream would, finding a negative skew statistic, probably come to the conclusion that the strategy is highly unattractive, missing the point entirely. They cannot be blamed. One of the standard assumptions in finance is the random walk and the notion that returns are distributed normally. However, the tools and techniques from standard financial theory might not capture the essence of what is going on, that is, the objective to create and run a business where fairly predictable positive compounding is the major purpose. If positive compounding is an objective, randomness needs to be curtailed and controlled.

Speaking of randomness, in the appendix to this chapter we try to predict the year-end value of the Standard and Poor's (S&P) 500—primarily for entertainment purposes. Investors who take year-end point-forecasts seriously are advised to skip this appendix.

There is also the potential for excess kurtosis in the preceding casino example. For example, a gambler who is betting with above-average sums could get lucky and win 36 times his capital. It is also possible that a gambler wins a couple of times in a row (and the casino unfortunate enough to only have one or two roulette tables [read: concentration of risk]). However, the business is still attractive. The cash flows are still sustainable and predictable and, if well diversified, stable as well. This means the cash flow pattern after a large drawdown is not random, but predictably mean reverting, most likely, the next day. A large drawdown in the stock market, for example, is (one could argue) also mean reverting. The difference is that one does not know if it halves before it mean reverts and by when the mean reversion will

---

*The last time your author thought it was attractive to run a casino was during a recent (and first) visit to the casino in Monte Carlo. More than one player was playing roulette and taking notes on the sequence of numbers. What a great business, indeed. (Or, depending on your point of view, what a cruel world it is.)

have been completed. We find this distinction to be material. Highlanders (as in Christopher Lambert) might disagree though.

A random recovery from a loss and a predictable recovery from a loss are, we believe, very different. Figures 8.2 and 8.3 show the underwater perspective (index as percentage of previous all-time high) of the Tokyo Stock Exchange Price Index (TOPIX) that was under water by 33.7 percent at the end of February 2006. In both figures, we have run a bootstrapping approach, that is, the nonparametric generation of random scenarios by drawing historical returns with replacement, to simulate 200 possible paths of recovery. Figure 8.2 shows the potential TOPIX recovery by resampling TOPIX total returns from 1973 to February 2006. This methodology assumes that we know that the TOPIX will continue to tick (a reasonable assumption) and that the future will "pick" returns from a distribution that resembles the distribution of the past. This allows us to get a feel for what is possible. (It does not give us a feel for the unthinkable, though.)

Figure 8.2 indicates that recovery could be swift. In the best of 200 scenarios, the TOPIX will have recovered by October 2006, that is, before

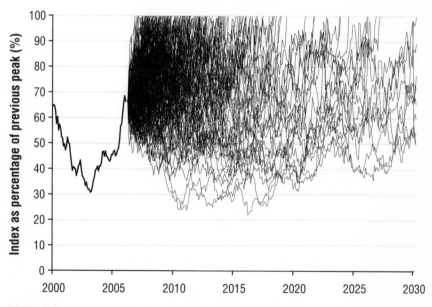

FIGURE 8.2 TOPIX Recovery with Resampled TOPIX Returns
Graph shows TOPIX from January 2000 to February 2006 and 200 randomly created paths using TOPIX total returns in JPY from March 1973 to February 2006. *Source:* Author's own calculations; raw data from Thomson Financial.

this book hits the shelves. However, chances are that the TOPIX will still be under water long after the book has been read (and/or binned) and—eventually—become obsolete. The median scenario was a recovery by May 2010. In six out of 200 scenarios, the TOPIX will not have recovered by 2030. This is one good reason why volatility matters to mortals.

Figure 8.3 shows 200 potential recoveries using (what we believe are) nonrandom returns of the HFRI Fund of Funds Composite Index. These returns are "engineered," that is, the result of active risk management on two levels, the hedge fund and fund of funds level. We believe the two figures visualize what we referred to as *very different*. (The situation does not even change if we normalize the mean returns of the two indices, that is, lower the average return for the fund of hedge fund index.) Essentially, what we are doing here is showing that an asymmetric return profile is more attractive than a symmetric return profile, such as the raw exposure to the return profile of a stock market. It's active versus passive. Note that we are not comparing like for like. Recovery in Figure 8.2 is based

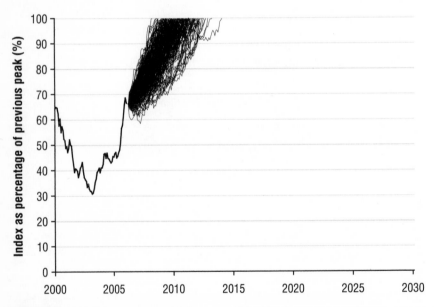

FIGURE 8.3   TOPIX Recovery with Resampled HFRI Fund of Hedge Fund Returns
Graph shows TOPIX from January 2000 to February 2006 and 200 randomly created paths using HFRI Fund of Funds Composite total returns in USD from January 1990 to February 2006.
Source: Author's own calculations; raw data from Thomson Financial.

on gross returns, while sampled returns in Figure 8.3 are net of two layers of fees.

- Both recoveries have positive mean returns; that is, both samples are upwardly biased (as the return distributions from which we draw returns have, historically, a positive mean).
- Figure 8.2 shows that recovery simulated with volatile returns can be short and gradual (akin to post-1987) as well as long and choppy (akin to post-1929).*
- Note that there is always light at the end of the tunnel. Figure 8.2 just somewhat implies that there is uncertainty as to whether the light stems from daylight at the end of the tunnel or from another train's headlights coming toward you.

Assuming statistical arbitrage is attractive because cash flows are stable, sustainable, and predictable, what is the next best business model? We believe it is running a bank. The original business model of running a lending bank was statistical arbitrage. The idea is to take in money and pay a low return and lend money and charge a higher return. (It is therefore not too surprising that some hedge funds are involved in the loan market.) Probability of default of creditors can easily be managed through diversification, as it is idiosyncratic risk. Insurers, too, were early players in statistical arbitrage. The idea is to structure the policies so that, on average, the cash inflows are larger than cash outflow; one just needs to get ones statistics right.†

There is a problem with all this. The banking business, insurers, and any other form of statistical arbitrage are not necessarily lottery-like businesses. The problem can be summarized in one word: competition.

---

*Note that we could have designed Figure 8.2 to look much worse than it presently does, for example by using price returns instead of total returns or by selecting a shorter time span than 1973 to 2006. (We have chosen the period from 1973 to 2006 due to the availability of the total return index series.) Selecting a shorter period would have resulted in the mean being lower (because the bear market would be more heavily weighted). This would have resulted in the average steepness of the lines being lower, that is, the average recovery being longer. However, we think Figure 8.2 is sufficient as it is to show the possible "recovery" of a long-only investor currently under water or the outright exposure to the "elements," that is, uncontrolled risk.

†Which is obviously easier said than done. In the past couple of years, mortality rates have declined at a faster pace than anticipated and 100-year floods seem to happen almost annually.

HONEY, I'VE SHRUNK THE MARGINS

Competition Puts Pressure on Margins

During the equity bull market, insurers generated returns from having invested assets in the stock market but not necessarily from statistical arbitrage, that is, their core business. The fact that there are many insurers with more or less homogeneous products competing with each other means that margins have shrunk. Buyers' demand, in combination with positive margins, falling production costs, and falling barriers to entry, increase suppliers' competition and put margins under pressure. It is unlikely that an industry or subindustry is exempt from this mechanism. Note that in this section we use the term *margin* for fees as opposed to spreads, fully aware that in hedge fund space the two have evolved in diametrically opposite directions: Spreads have narrowed while fees have risen.

Figure 8.4 shows different possible positions, with respect to margins (as in fees) and value added (somewhat adopting and modifying Boston Consulting Group's growth/market share matrix).

The gray area shows normal business activity, whereby those who add value command a high margin and those who offer a commoditized product do not. Normal business activity should be within that area. The exceptions are high-margin/low-value-added (essentially a seller's paradise) and

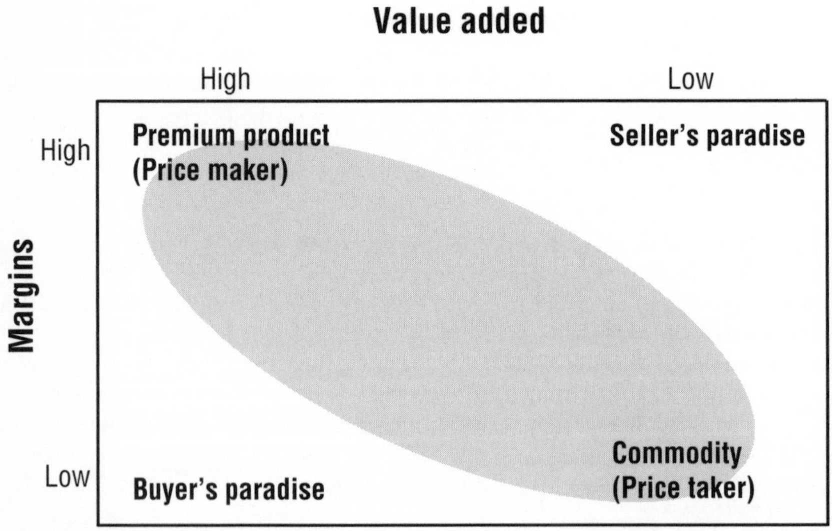

FIGURE 8.4 Buyer/Seller Paradise
Source: Ineichen [2005].

low-margin/high-value-added combinations (arguably a buyer's paradise). An example of a seller's paradise is designer ball pens. Production costs are low (how much can it cost to produce a ball pen these days?), the product homogeneous and easily replaceable. A cheaper alternative can always be found quickly. It can command a premium because it (we assume) inflates the self-confidence or perceived social status of the buyer (displaying the pen visibly). (In marketing this is known as the *snob effect*.) Running a lottery, as pointed out earlier, is also a seller's paradise. An example of a buyer's paradise would be airline tickets. Competition has forced margins close to zero, while the service is of great value to the buyer. A London–New York airline ticket costs a couple of hundred dollars and takes a few hours. The next alternative costs either much more (private jet) or takes much longer (taking a boat, swimming, etc.).

How are products in the asset management industry positioned in this matrix? Potentially, most products have a tendency to start in the upper-left, migrate to the upper-right and then fall to the lower-right-hand corner. Active large-cap long-only products were in the upper-left when a research-driven process was new and the reward from simple fundamental securities analysis was high, that is, the reward from applying that particular skill was high and the product was an innovation. Over time, competition pushed the product to the right as the reward from applying the skill got reduced or even crowded out. The upper-right-hand corner in Figure 8.4 is unlikely to be a sustainable position unless market forces are artificially and/or uneconomically disturbed, such as in lotteries (government essentially running a monopoly) or premium pens (snobs remaining snobs). The product's journey continued south, accelerated through cheaper alternatives (competition) and potentially the equity bear market (sudden reality kick among investors and change in risk perception). In institutional investment management, there is a good chance that active long-only products are going to stay in the lower-right-hand corner, as there are cheaper alternatives and the potential value added is sometimes considered to be fairly random, that is, rarely sustainable and hardly predictable. Long-only beta is not scarce and access, therefore, does not carry or warrant a huge premium.

In defense of the traditional asset management industry, note here that one could easily argue that an active long-only fund is still of great value when compared with the portfolio of the average private investor rather than a market benchmark. Empirical research suggests that on average active large-cap long-only funds do not beat the benchmark net of fees, missing the benchmark by a couple of basis points. However, Barber and Odean [2000] demonstrate that private investors underperform by much more than a "couple of basis points." In theory, private investors could invest in exchange-traded funds (ETFs) or other indexed vehicles and, "theoretically," be better off economically. In practice, which might or might not be a relief to the reader, only a small minority want their wealth compound on "auto-pilot." In other words, many private investors would be better off if they invested in actively managed long-only funds than trying to do it themselves.*

How are hedge funds positioned in the matrix?[†] It is not entirely unthinkable that hedge funds will go the same way as mutual funds, just delayed by a couple of decades. We believe hedge funds today capture large parts of the upper part of the matrix; that is, margins (as in fees) are high. There are hedge funds that are adding value and charging high fees as well as hedge funds that are not adding value but still are charging high fees. (Note that with "high fees" we account for the general perception that fees in hedge fund space are high. Based on the concept of dead weight, it is quite easy—if need be—to make the point that hedge funds charge low fees while traditional active long-only managers charge high fees.[‡]) Potentially, all products have a tendency to meet in the lower-right-hand corner of Figure 8.4. How is one to escape?

The Role of Innovation and Marketing

Schumpeter's [1937] creative destruction suggests that competition erodes the entrepreneurs' margins over time. It is extremely unlikely that hedge funds are exempt from this law (despite the past couple of years of hedge funds history suggesting otherwise). We could call it a "gravitational force" pulling products to the lower part of our margin/value-added matrix. There are probably two legal ways to stop this "natural" force: innovation and marketing.

- **Innovation:** Innovative products can command a premium, that is, higher margins, as there temporarily is no cheaper alternative. Innovation can come in various forms: new products creating their own new

---

*Note that popular all-out criticism of the whole asset management industry has a tendency to miss this crucial point: Indeed, private investors would be better off if they invested in ETFs and leave the investment untouched for decades. However, many follow a do-it-yourself approach, which empirically underperforms professionally managed long-only funds significantly.

[†]Note here (again) that we do not perceive hedge funds as a separate asset class. We view hedge funds as asset management companies that launch products that, in the past, have differed widely from traditional products. We believe, in five years' time, product differentiation will be key and not, as today, differentiation of regulatory status of the provider.

[‡]See Ineichen [2000a], p. 63 or Ineichen (2003a), pp. 130–131.

demand, product improvement, new design, new distribution channel, and so on.

- **Marketing:** Good product marketing gives the buyer the illusion of a premium product, that is, some form of feel-good factor or snob effect, allowing the provider to withstand gravity in the margin/value added matrix for a finite amount of time.* Continuous marketing can keep product demand positive.† With a commoditized product, increasing market share is key. (In most cases, increasing profitable market share is probably more advisable than increasing market share for its own sake.) In some countries, mutual fund TV advertisements are broadcast next to ads for laundry detergent, suggesting a fairly commoditized consumer product.

Alpha versus Access Innovation in the hedge funds industry can mean two things: the search for new sources of returns for the fund as well as the search for new sources of revenue for the business. The two are obviously correlated but far from being synonymous.

- **Returns:** We believe that innovation with respect to new strategies or new nuances within existing strategies is an imperative. Market ineffi- ciencies do not last forever; some inefficiencies are cyclical, while others are one-off opportunities. In any case, adapting to changing market circumstances is important, as the infusion of capital always changes circumstances, that is, the risk/reward relationship of the opportunity set. (In capital markets, feedback loops and the greater fool theory have wide application.)
- **Revenues:** We believe that the hedge fund business model is not as easily scalable as that of a traditional manager, as maximizing assets is normally not an optimal strategy. Some hedge fund managers scale their business by migrating from a core strategy to a multi-strategy approach. An alternative to this is the multi-product approach, where new strategies are put into separate vehicles as opposed to a master fund (thereby changing performance characteristics, that is, reducing volatility as well as, in most cases, returns). An interesting recent

---

*Although if you are "betamax" in a "VHS" world, all the marketing in the world will not help. We recently came across the phrase "being betamaxed," implying a business idea or model that has run its course. We have not yet come across the phrase "being alphamaxed." (Note that betamax was largely considered as technically the better format.)

†One observant colleague of ours recently pointed out to us that many hedge fund marketers are female and gorgeous. As we hadn't noticed ourselves, we thought that was quite interesting.

development within the hedge funds industry in this respect is the launch of long-only vehicles by some managers. Typically, this is done by taking the long book out of the long/short portfolio and launching it as a separate fund. This is attractive from the manager's point of view for two reasons. First, a long-only fund is more scalable than a long/short fund. Second, with a new fund, the manager can leverage the existing brand value (where it exists) at low incremental cost.

Performance Attribution and Fees

In Ineichen [2001], we phrased changes in the investment management industry as follows. In Figure 8.5 we classified the most active and most passive investment styles into a two-dimensional grid, where the vertical axis is the level of fees and the horizontal axis the performance attribution. Absolute-return strategies are in quadrant I: Fees are high and performance is, in theory and to some extent practice, determined by the manager's skill. The other extreme is quadrant III, where margins are low and performance is attributed to the market.

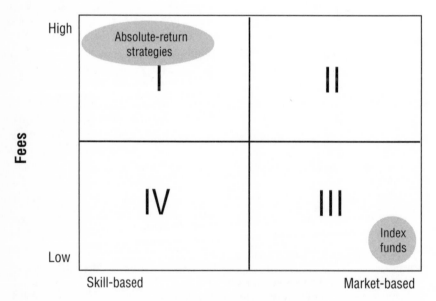

FIGURE 8.5 Different Business Models
Source: Ineichen [2001].

In Ineichen [2001], we wrote (footnotes from original):

"Alpha-generating strategies are normally skill-based strategies. If the flexibility of the manager is reduced to zero, the ex-ante alpha is zero as a result. However, as with every other industry, the asset management as well as the hedge fund industry will most likely transform (or converge) over time. A possible future scenario is that those asset managers with a competitive advantage will be offering skill-based strategies.* One of the pillars supporting this belief is that a competitive advantage, to some extent, is determinable in advance whereas the path of a market is not.[†] A firm with prudent, intelligent, experienced and hardworking managers will have an advantage over a firm with fraudulent, uneducated hooligans."[‡]

Today, the bifurcation between alpha and beta is undeniable. However, this is also a temporary phase in financial history. Just because it (combining indexing with active overlay) is currently happening and more and more investors seem to be doing/talking about it, it does not automatically follow that it's the pinnacle of investment wisdom for all times. We still believe that indexing and benchmarking is, putting it mildly, not the last word on how institutional investors manage their assets. Until very recently in the United Kingdom, for example, pension funds had roughly 75 percent of their assets in equities, of which most was either benchmarked or indexed to the Financial Times Stock Exchange (FTSE) All-Share Index. A couple of years ago, one particular stock was roughly 13 percent of the index. In other words, U.K. pensioners had quite a concentrated exposure to one stock. (Note that modern portfolio theory suggests that nonsystematic risk should be properly diversified, as its exposure does not carry a risk premium. Note too, however, the problem solved itself to some extent on its own, as the stock lost 80 percent of its value and, therefore, by underperforming

---

*Note that the subindustry for indexed investment products is oligopolistic, that is, there are only a few large organizations dominating the market. These companies, today, most likely have a competitive advantage over other asset managers. In the United Kingdom, some traditionally active managers have already departed the passive investment arena. This could mean that the positioning of asset managers into separate quadrants in the chart is in the process of unfolding. In other words, the specialization in investment management mentioned earlier is simply continuing.
†We assumed here that the future is uncertain and that there are no market participants with a model with an r^2 of 1.0. We apologize to all those readers who know the level at which the NASDAQ will end the year.
‡However, if both are long-only, the latter can outperform the former due to luck.

the average, became a smaller proportion of the index and, hence, of U.K. pensioners' portfolios).*

Alpha? What Alpha?

We believe it is pretty safe to say that not all that is marketed as alpha is alpha, neither in the hedge fund industry nor elsewhere. Clifford Asness [2004a, b] recommends we should distinguish not between alpha and beta but between traditional betas, hedge fund betas, and true alpha. Traditional beta and true alpha are at opposing ends of the spectrum. Traditional beta refers to the traditional asset classes where a long-only strategy is sufficient to capture the yield or risk premium. True alpha (as opposed to marketing alpha or promised alpha), then, is a source of return that is entirely explained by the managers' investment skill and is not compensation for any systematic risk. Hedge fund beta is something in between the two extremes. Hedge fund betas are systematic risk premiums that require a slightly more sophisticated strategy than a long-only strategy. Skilled investors can pick up the risk premiums (while unskilled investors cannot). In other words, the premiums are compensation for some form of systematic risk (i.e., not risk free). It is distinguished from traditional beta in the sense that it requires a higher degree of sophistication than the pursuit of a long-only style to capture the premium.

In a related context, Lars Jaeger [2002] uses the terms *risk premium strategies* and *complexity premium*. What he means is that there are risk premiums that are easily captured and others that are not so easily captured. The equity risk premium, for example, can easily be picked up through a long-only buy-and-hold strategy. However, picking up a premium around systematically mispriced stocks after an announced merger requires other, more complex strategies.† As Jaeger puts it:

> "I believe that many AIS [alternative investment strategies] earn
> their return by assuming risk in a risk averse financial world, rather
> than from the identification of market inefficiencies. By taking
> these risks the investor is compensated with an expected return,
> the risk premium. I therefore refer to these strategies as 'risk pre-
> mium strategies.' ... premiums in financial markets are positive
> expected returns that exceed the risk free interest rate in exchange

---

*Stocks from the European peer group fell by between 90 percent and 95 percent. In other words, U.K. pensioners were lucky (in relative-return space, that is).
†Mitchell and Pulvino [2001], for example, suggest that there is a premium for putting on every announced deal passively.

*for accepting the possibility of a financial loss. Over time, risk pre-
miums provide an inherent and permanent positive expected return,
the source of which does not disappear if spotted by other investors
(although it can fluctuate over time). The nature of its underlying
risk premium is directly related to a strategy's risk profile. The
risks and premiums vary among different strategies. It is important
to understand the economic rationales for the premiums of each
individual strategy sector. ... For 'risk premium strategies,' manager skill primarily expresses itself through premium identification,
proper timing and the appropriate risk management."*

In our previous research, we only distinguished between alpha and beta.
We are very sympathetic to the way Asness and Jaeger put it. However,
we also still believe that "manager skill" that spots the premium, times the
premium, and manages risk appropriately is essentially alpha, at least in
a wider sense. What else? First, the proverbial dart-throwing chimpanzee
cannot do it. There is no passive alternative, that is, a purely nonadaptive
way to capture the premium. Both the "premium" and the proper skill to
exploit the varying premium change over time. Second, someone else is on
the other side of the trade losing out.

INTELLECTUAL PROPERTY VERSUS ADAPTABILITY OF SKILL*

We suspect that the belief and confidence in a purely mechanical, nonadaptive way to make money is potentially disastrous, as circumstances always
change (initial opportunity changing due to increased attention, feedback
loops, etc.).† As Warren Weaver, author of *Lady Luck: The Theory of
Probability* put it: "The best way to lose your shirt is to think that you have
discovered a pattern in a game of chance."[3] Potentially, raw intelligence
without some form of market-savvy is probably as short an out-of-the-
money put option as the opposite, that is, an unintelligent, ignorant trader.
In the pursuit of pure and sustainable alpha, as well as survival probability, a balance between the two—intellectual property and adaptability—is
probably best.

Figure 8.6 systematizes the investment management landscape with
regard to intellectual property and adaptability in an ever-changing market

---

*This section benefited greatly from discussions with Charlotte Burkeman, UBS
Investment Bank.
†Unless you have a monopoly to run lotteries, that is.

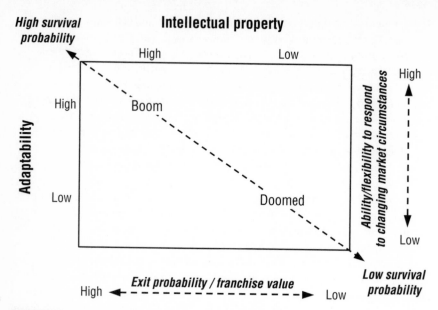

FIGURE 8.6 Intellectual Property versus Adaptability
Source: Ineichen [2005].

environment. By intellectual property, we mean an investment process that is based on some form of research as opposed to pure intuition. By adaptability, we mean the ability and flexibility to respond to change, as outlined in the first section of Chapter 6. (Note that "overadaptedness" is also a risk to survival. A species of birds for example might have fended off predators in its natural habitat and survived because, over generations, they grew a large beak. However, at one stage the beak might become so heavy that they cannot fly anymore. If flying to the next island for food is a prerequisite for survival, they die and become extinct. In other words, the beak was an advantage in one regime but a disadvantage in another. Variation in the gene pool, which allows rapid innovation and mutation of disciplines, forms the building blocks of survival. The parallel to the asset management industry is that, potentially, many investment companies have overadapted themselves to rising stock markets, the equity risk premium puzzle, and the doctrine of relative returns. They now cannot fly to the next island.)

Ranking high on intellectual property as well as adaptability is the best of all worlds. As a matter of fact, we believe what we call *active risk management* and *asymmetric-return profile* arrives from not being ignorant about one of the two (or both), that is, having a fundamental understanding of what is going on as well as understanding short-term relevancies and market dynamics. Long-term investors need to pay attention to the short term, and short-term investors need to pay attention to the long term. We do not suggest that combining the two is easy. The spread of differing personalities executing different crafts is—in our experience and putting it politely—wide. However, the rewards for investment firms that foster a culture of excellence as well as continuous improvement could be high.

The worst process is probably where both intellectual property and adaptability are low, as, for example, with most day-traders: Survival is low and most likely a function of randomness (and how deep the pockets were at the beginning of the activity). There is no such thing as building franchise value. (Suffering from the "one-trick-pony" syndrome essentially means dying when the pony dies. See Ineichen [2000a or 2003a] for an obituary on the relative-return approach.)

The term *hedge fund* was never a good term, as mentioned earlier, but it is becoming even less useful as time passes. We believe one does not need the legal structure of hedge funds to occupy the upper-left-hand corner of Figure 8.6. However, we do find the ability and flexibility to respond to changing market circumstances, that is, manage total risk, rather crucial if longevity (or an exit price tag) is a business objective.

For a business to have a valuation, there must be some form of continuity of the revenue drivers, that is, sustainability of some sort. In addition, the drivers need to be transferable; otherwise, the business is not scalable and cannot grow. High-quality earnings are perceived as earnings with lower volatility. In other words, earnings that are continuously reoccurring are preferred over erratically random earnings, and hence deserve a higher multiple. (In the late 1990s banks could increase their price-to-earnings ratio by getting rid of volatile earnings from trading activity. Judging from corporate transactions in the mid-2000s, banks now want those earnings back.) Departing from randomness and migrating toward a value proposition built on the idea of sustainable earnings could be key. This brings us back to alpha, the ultimate value proposition in active investment management.

If it requires skill to unlock the value of "hedge fund beta," then calling it "beta" might not be appropriate. Your author's mother-in-law would not be able to identify the "beta," find an optimal entry point, manage risk over the duration of the trade, find an optimal exit, and, at the same time, keep transaction costs low.* We believe investment skill is required to do that.

---

*Although this is more or less what the "do-it-yourself fraternity" among researchers suggest our mothers-in-law should be doing.

The identification and distinction of the "random bit" and the predictable part is, we believe, a function of investment skill, savvy, or, most likely, a combination of the two. Whether we should call these skills "alpha" is, we believe, open to debate.

Jaeger [2002] argues that "risk premiums provide an inherent and permanent positive expected return, the source of which does not disappear if spotted by other investors (although it can fluctuate over time)." We are not convinced that there is such a thing as a permanent risk premium* that does not go away when spotted by other investors. We believe there must always be crowding-out effects and feedback loops. And if the premium fluctuates over time, some investors will try hard to find nonrandomness by trying to optimize entry as well as exit points, a task unadvisable in the absence of any form of skill related to investment management. (Note that large historical returns do not prove investment skill. Some people call the relationship between financial success and randomness, that is, making a lot of money in the absence of talent, the "Spice Girls effect.")

So, in the end, we might be left with just alpha and beta after all. Alpha depends on skill, the scarcity of skill, and how the skill is rewarded in the marketplace. Alpha is then also about finding the optimal business structure to create an asymmetric risk/reward profile. If the skill to achieve all this becomes commoditized, it turns into beta. Overall, we find talking about alpha much easier than generating it.

Difference between Generating Alpha and Talking about It

We believe the task of marketers in active asset management is to sell alpha, irrespective of whether it is true alpha or not. We also believe that hedge funds have benefited hugely from various factors over the past couple of years. One is that these hedge fund betas (assuming we want to call these time-varying risk premiums that) are not perfectly correlated with traditional beta, that is, addition to a traditional portfolio adds value on a portfolio level by definition. (This is the reason why we believe ignoring hedge funds altogether is or soon will be considered imprudent from the

---

*The "risk" part of the term *risk premium* means that there is the risk that you might not get the premium but lose out. U.S. investors in the past decades, for example, picked up an equity risk premium over bonds, while Portuguese equity investors in the 1970s or Argentine investors in the 1950s (or Imperial Russian, Chinese, Egyptian, German investors, etc.) did not. Survivors garner the "premium," while nonsurvivors get the "risk," hence the term *risk premium*. Survival is a prerequisite.

perspective of an institutional investor with fiduciary responsibility, that is, an economic agent managing someone else's money and subject to the prudent expert rule. It is not entirely unthinkable that one day, perhaps soon, we will be in an environment where a fiduciary who does not exploit or at least considers all avenues of portfolio efficiency will be perceived as imprudent. History shows that there is not always a happy end to sticking with the status quo. Sometimes you really do need to fly to the next island.)

In Figure 8.7 we have another go at describing how the asset management industry is changing. First we distinguish between the upside, that is, the search for yield and returns, and the downside, that is, risk control. Then we distinguish between an active and a passive approach. The reason for this distinction is that our previous verbiage occasionally landed us in trouble with active asset managers (which we classified as passive). An active manager sees himself as active when compared to an index fund. This is fair. However, an "active" long-only manager is still passive when compared to an absolute-return manager, that is, when controlling total risk (as opposed to tracking risk) is concerned. The mandate to control total

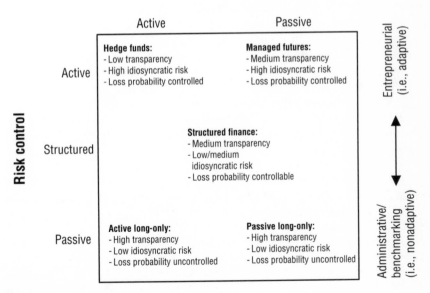

FIGURE 8.7   Return Seeking/Risk Control Matrix
Source: Ineichen [2005].

risk in traditional active asset management still sits with the end investor, not with the manager.

We believe there is something in between actively managing risk and passively managing risk. In Figure 8.7, we have added another layer. We highlighted this in Chapter 3, where we compared hedge fund portfolios with capital guaranteed structures on equity indices that also give the investor an asymmetric return profile: Normal volatility on the upside and lower or controlled volatility on the downside. We continue to believe that current transformation of the asset management industry is really a merger between the traditional asset management industry and what is largely called the *risk management business*, that is, the business of trading and structured products. Note that some financial organizations have combined two extremes, the lower-right-hand corner with the upper-left—quite successfully, one might add.

We believe the traditional asset management industry can be active or passive with respect to seeking returns but is passive with respect to controlling total risk (as mentioned in Chapters 1 and 2). The products are characterized by a high degree of transparency and low idiosyncratic risk (whereby we mean default risk of the manager and losses for operational, that is, noninvestment reasons). The manager does not control loss probability. The maximum loss is (somewhat theoretical) 100 percent of capital. Note that there are many advantages to the benchmarking approach, that is, what we called the *second stage of asset management*. (The benchmarking paradigm is well documented in Siegel [2003].)

Hedge funds are in the upper left of Figure 8.7. Compared to mutual funds, hedge funds are of lower transparency, while idiosyncratic risk, that is, the probability of default, is typically higher* (while investment risk might or might not be higher). The maximum potential loss to the investor is limited to 100 percent of capital (same as with mutual funds and most other investments).[†] The main difference is that the loss probability of the portfolio is actively controlled by the manager, in the case of absolute-return managers, while it is not in relative-return space.

---

*Note that the spread in credit (difference between most and least creditable) in the hedge fund industry is huge. There are high-quality organizations where default probability is low. There's also the opposite.

[†]Here, we are comparing an investment where systematic risk is the main risk to the investor (mutual funds), with investment vehicles where credit risk (which is idiosyncratic, i.e., nonsystematic risk) is the main risk to the investor (hedge funds). We therefore sometimes prefer comparing hedge funds to stocks or corporate bonds rather then mutual funds, from an idiosyncratic-risk-to-the-investor point of view (as, for example, in the previous chapter).

We have put managed futures (i.e., systematic trend-followers or directional trading systems) into the upper-right-hand corner of Figure 8.7. The return-seeking process is nondiscretionary, systems driven, and perhaps similar to an index fund, except that in the case of trend-following it is not the beta that is captured at lowest possible costs but a series of trends or trend reversals (essentially time-varying beta). The idea is to create a system that can minimize loss exposure, yet exploit profitable trends. The value added is in actively managing risk through improving systems (improving pattern recognition, entry signals, exit signals, execution, etc.).

In Chapter 3, we compared the asymmetric-return profile of well-balanced hedge funds portfolios with products coming out of structured finance. In the return/risk matrix (Figure 8.7), we classify structured finance somewhere in the middle. The return-seeking process is probably more passive than active, as the future payout is most often predetermined and/or rule based (although in the recent past there have been structures on actively managed absolute- as well as relative-return portfolios). We consider structured finance more entrepreneurial than benchmarking because innovation and adapting to changing market conditions plays an important role (innovation and adapting to change being, in some ways, the opposite of benchmarking). Different market conditions warrant different structures, exposures, and strategies. Transparency, on the other hand, is probably lower than with mutual funds. We believe that to be the case because there are many moving parts in a structure that are inexplicable to the options theory illiterate. (In the past, sellers of structures were *wrongly* accused of malpractice because the buyer *did not* understand all the moving parts of the structure and the interaction thereof. In other cases, sellers of structures were *rightly* accused of malpractice because the buyer *did* understand all the moving parts of the structure and the interaction thereof.)

Structured finance seeks to provide a return distribution that differs from a symmetrical return distribution accessible through a purely passive investment approach. Risk control in structured finance is different from hedge funds as well as traditional asset management. The difference between hedge funds and long-only asset management is that managing total risk is active with the former and passive with the latter. Structured finance is something in between. Risk is somewhat predefined. The maximum loss in a capital-guaranteed structure, for example, can be determined in advance (the guarantee being as good as the structurer being credible, that is, default probability of the structurer is never zero). One could argue, for example, that the buyer of a capital-guaranteed product on an equity index is exposed to randomness on the upside, and predictability, that is, predefined controlled risk, on the downside.

Are Benchmarking and Financial Innovation Opposites?

We called the current seismic shift rippling through the investment management industry a paradigm shift or structural change in the industry. We also noted that this shift is the second shift after the introduction of market indices as benchmarks, some 30 years ago. However, it is reasonable to assume that change and innovation will not stop here, that is, they will continue to change the investment management landscape going forward. To some long-term hedge fund investors, the topic of what we call asymmetric-return profile is, apart from being vastly obvious all along, already outdated. What's next?

Financial textbook theory might or might not be any help. Financial theory, essentially a subcategory of economics, is only roughly 60 years old* and economics dates back only around 250 years. It is not entirely absurd to assume that the current line of thinking is subject to paradigm shifts, too. In financial theory we are still working with the first set of theories (modern portfolio theory [MPT], arbitrage pricing theory [APT], capital asset pricing model [CAPM], efficient market hypothesis [EMH], etc.). The product coming out of this work is essentially the index fund. The index fund, we believe, is most consistent with the Bachelier-Brown-Savage-Fama line of thinking. Taleb [2004b] commented:

> *"Finance academia, unlike the physics establishment, seems to work like a religion rather than an empirical science with beliefs that have resisted any amount of empirical evidence. Financial theory being a fad, not a science, it may take a fad, and not necessarily a science, to unseat its current set of beliefs."*

Hedge funds are somewhat an antithesis to what has been taught at the finance faculties of business schools in the past. Until very recently (around 1999) the financial literature on the subject of hedge funds has been quite thin. (However, one could also counter this by arguing that hedge funds weren't fit for institutional involvement before that date.)

There has obviously been a lot of fine-tuning going on with respect to the first generation of financial theory. More interesting, there also is a body of research (behavioral finance) that (in essence) stipulates that the theory

---

*The inaugural issue of the *Financial Analysts Journal* was January 1945. The inaugural issue of the *Journal of Finance* was 1946 and was largely ignored by the economics community. Milton Friedman, sitting on the examination committee of the University of Chicago's economics department, was apparently averse to granting Harry Markowitz a doctorate in economics, as his thesis was not economics; neither was it business administration. From Holton [2004] referring to Bernstein [1992].

is wrong, or, phrasing it less extremely, to the extent that the assumptions are unrealistic, the theory is of little practical use. (However, unrealistic assumptions do not refute theory.) Behavioralists combine economics with psychology to formulate their attacks on orthodox financial theory, essentially arguing that one of the standard assumptions in economics (that of the "rational economic man" behaves rationally in a neoclassical, that is, probability-weighted utility-maximizing sense) is wrong (or too far from reality to be of any practical use).* While we believe behavioralists have interesting things to say and a strong case to make, they still do not have a better theory. One could easily argue that the most intelligent course of action is to go with the best theory at hand. While combining economics with psychology might not yield a new theory (it certainly increases the entertainment value of economics), combining economics with physics (known as "econophysics") or evolutionary biology ("evolutionary finance") might.

Econophysicists for example use power-law distributions to predict markets or assess risk. (Mathematician Benoit Mandelbrot and Chicago economist Eugene Fama found in the 1960s that markets are better described by power-law distributions than normal distributions. Big jumps in market value are more common in power-law systems than normal distributions.) The claim is that markets were not random after all, as fat tails, that is, high-standard-deviation events, follow a power-law distribution and are clustered. In other words, there is predictive value in studying historical return distributions. The irony is that technical analysis, that is, the attempt to predict future market movement from past market movement, that, to EMH purists and CAPM huggers is utter nonsense, might have merit after all.

Evolutionary finance tries to explain seemingly irrational behavior from a survival-seeking perspective. See, for example, Andrew Lo's adaptive markets hypothesis (AMH). Lo [2004] said:

> *"Competition, cooperation, market-making behavior, general equilibrium, and disequilibrium dynamics are all adaptations designed to address certain environmental challenges for the human species, and by viewing them through the lens of evolutionary biology, we can better understand the apparent contradictions between the EMH and the presence and persistence of behavioral biases. Specifically, the AMH can be viewed as a new version of the EMH, derived*

---

*Economist Vilfredo Pareto (and later Ludwig von Mises) thought that much of human activity was driven not by logical action, but rather by nonlogical action. On this, of course, economics has nothing to say—which is why, ultimately, economics will always fail empirically.

from evolutionary principles. Prices reflect as much information as dictated by the combination of environmental conditions and the number and nature of 'species' in the economy or, to use a more appropriate biological term, the ecology."

One of the dynamic factors in active asset management, we believe, is the crowding-out effect. Inefficiencies do not persist. Frogs are not indefinitely safe in their habitat; they're intermittently safe at best. In other words, adapting to changing market circumstances and innovating, that is, finding new opportunities, new business models, recognizing when the old in inapplicable, and so on, is part of active asset management. As Heraclitus put it: "There is nothing permanent except change." We have a tendency to view adapting to changing market circumstances and innovating somewhat as the opposite of benchmarking. (Hence, the two are on opposite ends in Figure 8.7.)

CHAPTER SUMMARY AND CONCLUSIONS

The current period in financial history could be viewed as being akin to the period of Enlightenment in Western thought. The period of Enlightenment too was characterized by an abandoning of long-held beliefs and intellectually constraining doctrines. The period was the gateway for a period of innovation, technical as well as sociological. Immanuel Kant's *The Critique of Pure Reason* was one of the markers signaling this important inflection point.* Peter Bernstein's [2003, 2004] five inflection points† and Andrew Lo's [2004] *Adaptive Markets Hypothesis* could be equivalent signposts in contemporary investment management and finance.

Comparing the current spreading of institutional interest in alternative investment strategies with Kant et al. is probably a tick over the top. However, we believe a lot of the recent change in ideas and business models is structural in nature. There is no way back. It is unlikely that commoditized products and services suddenly trade at a premium or that

---

*If we were to run fantasy wild, we could easily find further parallels between Kant and current developments in the active asset management industry: Some of Kant's work didn't fit into the prevailing governing body. Furthermore, it was important for Kant to stress what was knowable and what was not. This is advisable in investment management space, too.

†Bernstein discusses five changes in perception. In order of appearance, these points of inflection touch on: the independence of research, the limitations of indexing, the sins of benchmarking, the absurdity of a long-only constraint, and the open-end format as an antiquity.

indexing and benchmarking are again perceived as the pinnacle of investment wisdom. Potentially, viewing from a business perspective, we are not, today, witnessing the beginning of the end but have just experienced the end of the beginning. Kuhn [1962] probably was right when he argued that "mere disconfirmation or challenge never dislodges a dominant paradigm: Only a better alternative does." Managers defining risk as total risk and managing it through an active investment process might be this "better alternative."

Sustainable wealth is not derived from speculation (here defined as a bet on a random variable) but from entrepreneurialism, that is, setting up businesses, adapting to change in the face of competition, innovation, and hard work, that is, building a capital base. It is unreasonable to expect that highly talented and motivated individuals would build wealth for others while not materially participating in the venture themselves: This is true in the investment management industry as well as elsewhere. To us, absolute-return investing means balancing risk and return and trying to be exposed to nonrandomness, at least to some degree, that is, fairly predictable positive compounding of some sort. It's about levering an edge under competition in an entrepreneurial, adaptive way. A business exposed to large random swings is unlikely to be sustainable. How could it? A business where positive cash flows are stable, sustainable, and, hence, predictable, is likely to be the better business.

In 2001 and 2002, there was the fear that money would be pulled from the hedge fund industry as soon as the equity market started to rise again. However, in 2003 and 2004, when equity markets rose, we experienced a first indication that this is, in fact, unlikely to happen in institutional investment management. Not only did large parts of the 2001 to 2002 inflows remain in absolute-return space, new money followed, eventually, resulting in the spike of capital inflow in the fourth quarter of 2003 (Q4 03) and the first quarter of 2004 (Q1 04). This was despite equity markets rallying. We believe large parts of this capital buys into the absolute-return investment philosophy and not, or to a lesser extent, into historical returns. If investors were buying historical returns, we would argue that the growth is more cyclical and less structural. We believe, however, that the main driver of the growth is a sustainable change in investors' perception of risk. In other words, growth is driven by investors' enlightenment that short-term volatility, and therefore risk-adjusted returns, now matter to the long-term investor.

We could be wrong. The absolute-return phenomenon in institutional investment management is new and could turn out to be short lived. Regulatory ignorance and/or incompetence is a sword of Damocles dangling over the whole industry. (Referring to active shareholders as *locusts* is a case in point.*) Furthermore, a series of negative events could dent or reverse investors' newly found and therefore un-stress-tested confidence for all times. (The proverbial "weak hand" could be running for the exit, similarly to the way late-comers to private equity ran for the doors post the Internet bubble bursting, that is, essentially at the first sign of double-digit negative returns.) Hedge funds could fall back to tailoring to private investors, as they have in the past, and could come to be considered as not suitable for institutional investors and their fiduciaries. A potential tipping point in this regard could be the realization and subsequent consensus-forming that alpha exists but can be reliably captured only by the few, not the many—in other words, an awakening that pure alpha (net of fees) can be picked up only by the most sophisticated and nimble among institutional investors, that is, first-movers and early-adapters, but not latecomers and copycats. This would need to rest on the belief that the average investor does not get any alpha on a sustainable basis. This would mean that the search for alpha occurs at a net cost to the below-average, as well as the average, institutional investor. For this enlightenment to materialize, say 90 percent of all institutional investors giving up on the search for alpha, investors needed to overcome what behavioralists call overconfidence, a heuristic bias that skews decision making under uncertainty away from the von Neumann–Morgenstern/Savages' maximization of expected utility doctrine. All investors know that the search for alpha is a zero-sum or negative-sum game after fees. In addition, many investors doubt the sustainability of pure alpha. So why do they play the game? It could be because they perceive themselves as above-average; that is, many investors are probably overconfident with respect to capturing alpha and/or picking alpha-generating managers. Only few investors probably view themselves as below-average or just average investors. (And if they did, they probably wouldn't tell their sponsor and exit the game.) Institutional investors acknowledging this could be a structural change in itself, reverting the shift we have been witnessing over the past five years. It would set a milestone in institutional investment management. Hedge funds would fall back to lull private investors (most of whom never really cared about relative performance anyhow).

We do not believe in the course of events described in the preceding paragraph. We believe some of the current changes in relation to absolute returns and risk-adjusted returns in investment management are structural, as opposed to a passing fad. This means the current transformation of hedge

---

*We wonder what Aldous Huxley would have said to an overgeneralization of human action referenced to the fauna. Probably something a long the lines: "Single-mindedness is all very well in cows or baboons; in an animal claiming to belong to the same species as Shakespeare it is simply disgraceful."

funds turning their maverick entrepreneurialism into more institutional entrepreneurialism is not going to reverse but will continue to evolve. At the same time, traditional asset management is not sitting on the sidelines watching the fees go elsewhere. The two will probably meet somewhere in the middle. Nevertheless, not all ideas and business models will win and survive. Innovation is a process of renewal as well as destruction. Some frogs *do* end up in the snake's food chain.

APPENDIX: PREDICTING THE FUTURE OF THE S&P 500

> *"Jan, the bottom line is, before the end of the year, the NASDAQ and Dow will be at new record highs."*
> —Myron Kandel, CNN, April 2000*

In this appendix, we show a couple of attempts to predict the future path of the S&P 500. This appendix was not designed to demonstrate that we have no clue where the S&P 500 is going but to re-iterate that volatility matters.

In Figure 8.8, we show the S&P 500 and Nikkei 225, both logged. We have brought the latter forward for the all-time high to overlay with the all-time high in the S&P 500 index. We then truncated the two vertical axes for visual effect. This could be viewed as a "history repeats itself" method. We could also call the illustration the "gravity graph," as the idea behind the logic is that "what goes up must come down." It worked for years. Perma-bears around the world have been using this graph for ages. Only in the recent past has the U.S. stock market shown a departure from copying Japan's destiny of the 1990s. True bears, however, stick with the story and argue that the current rally is the longest bear market rally in financial history and that the S&P 500 will hit lows similar to Japan's. The graph suggests lows of 720 and 500 should the S&P 500 move back, tracking the Nikkei 225.

In Figure 8.9, we have run a bootstrapping approach, that is, the nonparametric generation of random scenarios by drawing returns with replacement whereby a series of possible future paths are simulated by randomly picking monthly returns from the past. For Figure 8.9 we used 1,272 monthly total returns for the 106-year period from January 1900 to December 2005. In other words, we are randomly picking historical returns

---

*Quoted in Covel, Michael (2004). "Trend Following," Upper Saddle River, NJ: Prentice Hall.

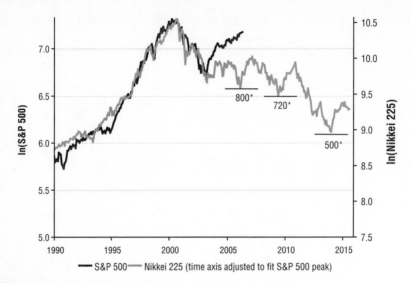

FIGURE 8.8 The Gravity Graph
Nikkei 225 (rhs) was brought forward for an all-time high based on monthly data (1.1.1990) to match the all-time high of S&P 500 (1.9.2000). Both axes were truncated for visual effect. April 2006 inclusive.
*S&P 500 equivalent lows as measured by assuming that drawdowns from the all-time high are equal to those in the Nikkei 225.
Source: Author's own calculations; data from Thomson Financial.

from the recent distribution of U.S. history, that is, including the 1929 period. This gives us a range of possibilities and paths for the next x years, in this case 200 predictions for the S&P 500 until the end of 2015 assuming reinvestment of dividends (all total returns).

Figure 8.9 assumes that all returns are independent and random (and we know from which distribution to pick returns). To get an idea of the future, then, we just need to resample historical returns to get a distribution for future returns. The chart shows 200 possible scenarios, given these assumptions. The best and worst of these runs indicate a compounding rate of 29.8 percent* and −8.0 percent, respectively. Both scenarios are thinkable. However, both scenarios are very unlikely. The range in which 90 percent of all scenarios fall was 23.2 percent and

---

*Note that we used nominal (not real) total returns for this analysis. This means compounding at 30 percent could still be a bad thing in a hyperinflation scenario, that is, if dropping greenbacks from helicopters is perceived as a good idea.

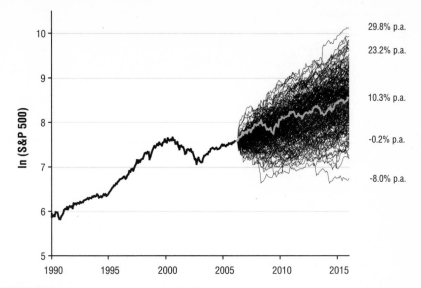

FIGURE 8.9 S&P 500 with Resampled U.S. Returns
Historical line (1.1990 to 02.2006) shows log of S&P 500 Total Return Index.
Bootstrapping method is based on total returns from S&P 500 and predecessor
indices from January 1900 to December 2005. Based on 200 runs with replacement.
Bold light-gray line shows the median scenario. The five returns at the right show
the full range of possible compounding rates as of 2015, the 90 percent range as
well as the median.
Source: Author's own calculations; data from Thomson Financial and Global
Financial Data.

−0.2 percent, respectively. The median scenario returned 10.3 percent,
which is pretty much the average historical returns for the U.S. stock
market, including dividends. This is the most likely prediction. However,
this analysis shows what exposure to uncontrolled volatility really means
over a 10-year period. It means that 10-year outcomes could be all over
the place. (Volatilities of the 200 simulated portfolios ranged between 12
and 25 percent. The median portfolio in Figure 8.9 had a volatility of
14.4 percent.)

We could combine the historical with the statistical method. The bootstrapping method in Figure 8.9 uses returns over the past 106 years of U.S.
history. One could argue that the past 106 years of U.S. history are not
a good indication for the next 10 (i.e., the analysis is upwardly biased).
From an evolutionary point of view, the United States came out on top
in a competitive game of survival of the fittest. A historical perspective,
however, suggests that at some stage complacency kicks in and the fittest

becomes the second fittest, third fittest, and so on. (If in doubt, ask an Englishman, an Austro-Hungarian, or—if you know one—an Ottoman.)*
A more realistic return set, one could therefore argue, is the return series of postbubble Japan (or any other return distribution with a lower mean than a distribution from the U.S. stock market). Figure 8.10 shows the

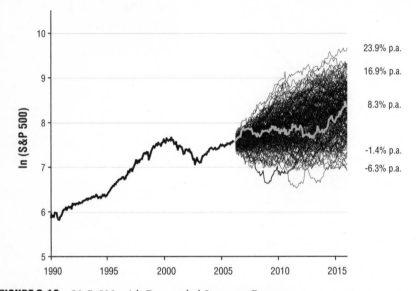

FIGURE 8.10   S&P 500 with Resampled Japanese Returns
Historical line (1.1990 to 02.2006) shows log of S&P 500 Total Return Index. Bootstrapping method is based on total returns from MSCI Japan from January 1970 to February 2006. Based on 200 runs with replacement. Bold light gray line shows the median scenario. The five returns at the right show the full range of possible compounding rates as of 2015, the 90 percent range as well as the median. *Source:* Author's own calculations; data from Thomson Financial.

---

*In 1910, the market capitalization of Swiss stocks was smaller than that of U.K. stocks in Swiss francs by a factor of 22.5 and smaller than Austria-Hungary by a factor of 3.8. By the end of 2004, Swiss market capitalization was still smaller than that of U.K. stocks. However, the factor was 3.4, while Swiss market capitalization was seven times the market cap of Austria and Hungary combined. Lacking the ambition to build an empire might be dull (and might or might not rob its citizens of a sound sense of humor), as discussed in the appendix to Chapter 1. However, dullness (read: stability, sustainability, and predictability) is potentially good when compounding capital on a sustainable basis is a major objective. (Data for these calculations are from Thomson Financial and Goetzmann [2004], quoting Lenin [1917].)

same bootstrapping analysis where we replaced the U.S. total returns from 1900 to 2005 with total returns from the Japanese index from January 1970 to February 2006. This is not as entirely unreasonable as it initially sounds. We do not know today from which distribution destiny will pick its returns. It could be a distribution with high mean and outliers on the upside (peace dividend) or a distribution with low mean with outliers on the downside (war).

The whole distribution of potential paths was less wide when we resampled total returns from the MSCI Japan instead of total returns from the U.S. stock market. The best and median portfolios were lower, while the worst portfolio was higher. This is intuitive, as the Japanese stock market had a tougher 35 years than the U.S. stock market over the past 106 years. Which of the two versions is more realistic? It depends on whether one believes in history repeating itself or in mean reversion. If the past 106 years of U.S. history are a good indication of the next 10 years, then the first analysis is more relevant. If we believe in mean reversion and the notion that outperformance can result in underperformance and vice versa, then the second analysis might be more relevant. Who cares, anyway? The point of this exercise is to demonstrate that we should know what we don't know. In the case of predicting the S&P 500 over the next 10 years, we not only do not know the mean return, we do not even know from which distribution to pick returns. So we do not know the range of possibilities with any reasonable degree of confidence either. The only thing we know is that volatility is high. High volatility translates into a wide range of possible scenarios by 2015.

Another (alternative) way of trying to predict the future path is by comparing it to some tangible assets, for example, oil and gold, both of which are expressed in the same currency as the U.S. stock index. Figure 8.11 shows how many barrels of oil it takes to buy one S&P 500 price index.

- On average (1861 to 2005), it took 15.8 barrels of oil to buy one S&P 500 index. At the end of 2005, this relationship was 20.5. If mean reversion brings the ratio to its long-term average, the S&P 500 could move to 964 (from 1,250) with oil remaining at $61 per barrel.
- If the ratio falls to its 1970s low of 3.6 in 1979, the S&P 500 could fall to 220, assuming constant oil prices of $61, or to 360 index points if oil rises to $100 per barrel. The 3.6 ratio from 1979 implies an oil price of $347, assuming the S&P 500 remains at 1,250. If the ratio falls to its all-time low of 0.48... well, you probably don't want to know.

Figure 8.12 shows how many ounces of gold it takes to buy one stock index. We simply divided the S&P 500 index by the oil and gold price to get a ratio. The idea behind this "methodology" is that we are measuring

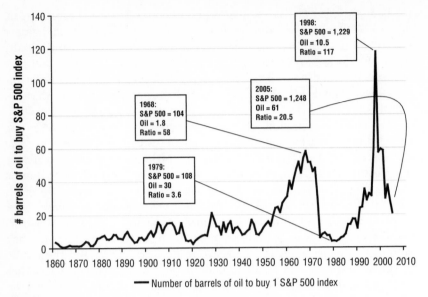

— Number of barrels of oil to buy 1 S&P 500 index

FIGURE 8.11 Barrels of Oil to Buy One S&P 500 Index
Source: Author's own calculations; data from Thomson Financial and Global Financial Data; oil data from 1861 to 1981 from British Petroleum (BP).

the stock index with a different base. Instead of U.S. dollars, that is, fiat money, we show the index in a tangible asset. Gold as a reserve currency has a longer track record than the U.S. dollar. The idea of fiat money is potentially un-stress-tested. These displays obviously are designed to scare and are often used by perma-bears and alarmists. For us, this is just one more way to show the extreme volatility in capital markets, especially the stock market.

- On average (1939 to 2005), it took 1.4 ounces of gold to buy one S&P 500 index. At the end of 2005 it took 2.4 ounces to buy one S&P 500 index. Mean reversion would suggest an S&P 500 of around 718 at a constant gold price of $513 or a gold price of $1,747 at a constant S&P 500 of 1,248 (or a combination somewhere in between).
- The 1979 low of the ratio of 0.21 would imply an S&P 500 price of 108 at constant gold prices or a gold price of $5,943 per ounce at constant S&P 500 prices. (Note that we used annual year-end data. Based on year-end data, gold peaked in 1980 at 589.5; based on daily data, it peaked on January 18, 1980, at 835.0. On that day, it took only 0.133 ounces to buy one S&P 500.)

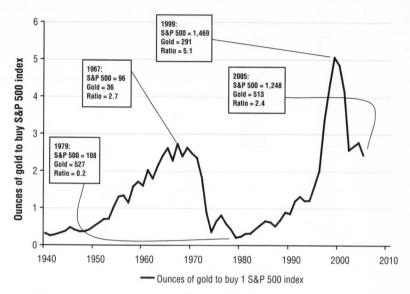

FIGURE 8.12 Ounces of Gold to Buy S&P 500 Index
Source: Author's own calculations; data from Thomson Financial; gold data from 1939 to 1968 from Global Financial Data.

Marc Faber—investor, author, prognosticator, and arguably a gold bull—in an interview, answered the question as to what his view on the stock market was right now (May 2006) this way:

> *"I think we are in a bear market for financial assets. There's a bear market where the Dow Jones, say, would go from here −11,000 to 33,000. It would go up in dollar terms but the dollar would collapse against, say, gold or foreign currencies. That's what I think will happen with Mr. Bernanke at the Fed because he has written papers and he has pronounced speeches in which he clearly says that the danger for the economy would be to have not deflation in the price of a fax machine or PC, but deflation in asset prices. And so I believe that he is a money printer. If I had been a university professor, I would not have let him pass his exams to become an economist. I would have said, 'Learn an apprenticeship as a money printer.'"*[4]

In the long term, valuations are the primary driver of returns. Jeremy Grantham, chairman of GMO, breaks down historic price/earnings (P/E) ratios into quintiles (Figure 8.13). The first quintile represents the 20 percent of years in which the P/E ratio was lowest and shows the subsequent average

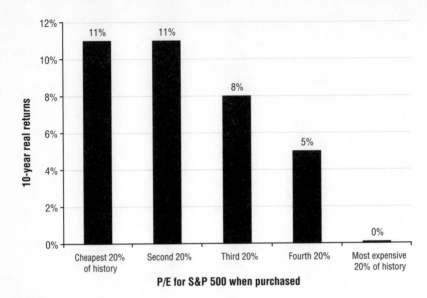

FIGURE 8.13 Quintiles of Market Average P/E to Predict 10-Year Returns
Source: Mauldin [2006], GMO, Standard & Poor's. Based on return data from 1925 to 2001.

annual real return over the following 10 years. The last quintile shows the opposite, that is, the most expensive 20 percent of years and the subsequent annual real 10-year return. The graph suggests that investors can expect double-digit real returns over 10 years if they buy when the market is histori-cally cheap and more or less nothing if they buy when markets are expensive.

Mauldin [2006] argues correctly that the numbers are subject to torture, and analysts can fiddle around with them until they say just about anything. Based on historical P/E ratios from Thomson Financial Datastream from January 1968 to April 2006, the S&P 500 at 1,300 was in the fourth quintile. Based on data and methodology from Professor Robert Shiller (using monthly data from January 1871 to December 2005), the index was in the fifth quintile at year-end 2005. (Shiller [2000] divides the index in real terms by average 10-year inflation-adjusted earnings. See Figure 9.11 in the next chapter.) If we use Shiller's data[5] and create a time series by dividing the real index by real earnings (as opposed to 10-year average that introduces a lag), the S&P 500 index has moved from the fifth quintile into the fourth around September 2005. So at the time of writing we were either in the fourth or fifth quintile.

Perma-bears typically argue that valuations do not revert to the mean but overshoot on the downside. Any argument to the contrary must give a good reason why "this time it's different." As John Mauldin—referencing *Dirty Harry*—put it:

> *"Secular bear markets have never ended when the markets go to average P/E ratios. They have always overshot in the past. Could it be different this time? Want to bet your portfolio? Do you feel lucky, punk?"*[6]

BOTTOM LINE

All these comments and graphs—enlightening and entertaining or not—strengthen our confidence that long-term investors cannot be indifferent to short-term volatility. We believe the percentage of investors agreeing with this notion is increasing, but that the percentage is also somewhat path- and volatility-dependent: The faster markets fall, the more people seem to agree.

CHAPTER 9

The Past, the Present, and the Unpredictable

"The less a man knows about the past and the present, the more insecure must be his judgement of the future."

—Sigmund Freud

IS IT A BUBBLE?

The hedge fund industry surpassed the $1 trillion mark in 2004 or 2005 and is today (Q2 06) a $1.2 to $1.5 trillion industry in terms of assets under management, depending on which survey one puts one's faith in. This compares to a global equity market capitalization (listed equity) of around $44.0 trillion, global mutual funds of around $16.2 trillion, and global pension fund assets of around $15.3 trillion. The annual growth rate of the hedge fund industry from 1990 to 2005 was around 23 percent, based on data from Hedge Fund Research Inc. (HFRI) (assuming the industry is $1.5 trillion and continues to grow at 23 percent, and assuming listed global equities and bonds are valued at around $90 trillion and growing at 5 percent, hedge funds would become "the market" by around 2031). Given the current strong demand for hedge fund exposure and the industry resembling a typical seller's market (where the seller dictates the terms and the buyer willingly accepts), it is quite difficult to argue against the financial community's getting a little too excited about an old idea too fast. We believe it makes sense to take a step back and examine what is going on, especially in the light of some hedge fund managers themselves calling the growth of the hedge fund industry a bubble.

At the most general level, we believe there is always change. "Change" was the major theme in Chapter 2. If the world were static, sticking to the current doctrine would actually make a lot of sense. However, it is not. The response to *change* by survival-seeking agents is *adapting* to change. As Benjamin Franklin put it: "When you are finished changing, you're finished." We believe this to be true for frogs when a frog-eating snake enters their habitat, as well as investors exposed to change—that is, risk.

With respect to change within an industry such as the investment management industry, as with any other industry, one could distinguish between structural and cyclical change. By structural change, we mean permanent change—evolutionary, progressive jumps, where outdated ideas and approaches are replaced with new and improved ones, that is, progress. A classical example of an industrial evolutionary jump was the well-deserved retirement of the horse and the switch to the automobile in the individual transport industry. Although the car has not entirely superseded the horse-powered coach, the latter today represents only a small part of the individual transport industry. By cyclical change, we mean some form of cyclical swing or mean reversion—ups and downs, good times and bad times, expansion and contraction, easing and tightening, or, in its most erratic form, bubbles and bursts. Our work is focused on structural change. Our appeals to caution are somewhat related to cyclical change.

Cyclical versus Structural Change

In April 2004, we heard someone say at a conference: "Whenever Main Street falls in love with what Wall Street has to sell, there is a correction within 12 to 36 months." There are some anecdotal indications that this thought is not entirely without merit. At the time of writing, we are 24 months into this prediction.

Under normal circumstances, there is a balance between buyers and sellers—what economists refer to as *equilibrium*. If there are more buyers than sellers, then prices go up a little (i.e., the marginal buyer outweighs the marginal seller). If there are more sellers than buyers, prices go down a little. However, every now and then, the "caveat emptor" rule is abandoned, and herd instinct results in contagion, which then results in some form of hysteria or mania. A bubble builds. Then, at some stage, quite often out of the blue, size causes the bubble to burst.* (Note that size is the cause for the

---

*Note that those who predict bubbles are normally too early. Robert Shiller and Alan Greenspan, for example, were referring to the "irrational exuberance" in U.S. equities markets around December 1996. Their reasoning, based on historical overvaluation, was sound. However, the index roughly doubled in the years after the argument. Others spent the whole of the 1990s arguing that U.S. equities were overpriced.

burst. However, it is a random event that is the catalyst. After the burst, it is often this random event that is perceived as the cause. Think of sand piles.*) This is roughly the pattern of popping asset bubbles.

Bubble or not, the current (arguably Darwinian) developments are certainly an amazing phase in the evolution of the investment management industry. We believe the main characteristic of a bubble is mispriced assets. With respect to hedge funds, this seems not to be the case. Hedge funds are asset managers, not assets. However, as we are probably not necessarily considered the most bearish market observer of the absolute-returns industry, we would like to reiterate some of our observations, arguments, and thoughts in this matter and discuss whether the current enthusiasm for hedge funds shows some bubble-like symptoms. Apart from the swing from the "hedge-funds-are-for-the-financially-suicidal" approach of only a couple of years ago to the current, shall we say, "optimism" being an amazing phase in financial history, there are, we believe, also some red flags popping up. Some of these symptoms are shown in Table 9.1. In the table, we list some bubble symptoms and assess whether they are applicable in the case of hedge funds. Note that we believe overzealous regulatory activity is not a bubble symptom but a postbubble phenomenon.

This Time It's Different   Sir John Templeton was once quoted as saying: "The four most expensive words in the English language are 'this time it's different.'" We believe that the introduction of active risk management in absolute returns and seeking asymmetric-return profiles is a paradigm shift in the investment management industry, that is, a structural change, not a cyclical one. Because of our verbiage of paradigm shifts, and so on, we could be perceived as belonging in the "this time it's different" camp. This is, of course, very unfortunate. The "this time it's different" notion should send a chill down any literate investment professional's spine. Certain things never change. Human mass behavior/enthusiasm is probably one of these "things" that never change. As Jim Rogers [2000] puts it:

> *"In the laws of economics, in the laws of history, in the laws of politics, and in the laws of society, it's **never** different this time. The law of gravity isn't ever suspended for someone's convenience, and*

---

*Add one grain of sand to a pile of sand. Then another. The pile will get bigger and bigger. At one stage, size has caused the sand pile to become very unstable. One grain of sand can result in the collapse of the whole sand pile. The last grain of sand is unpredictable—it's random. However, the causality between size and the instability of the system and the laws that govern the collapse might not be. See Buchanan [2000].

TABLE 9.1 Bubble Symptoms

Bubble Symptom	Trueor False?
Mispriced assets	False. Hedge funds might occasionally act as marginal buyers or sellers of an asset or asset class, but that does not imply mispriced assets. We believe that, more often than not, active asset management increases liquidity of the marketplace and reduces marke t inefficiencies.
Excessive leverage	False. Average leverage per fund is lower than it was before 1998. However, aggregate leverage of the whole industry is higher due to massive growth of the industry. Net exposures with equity long/short managers has increased from the 20s (20 percent net long) in Q1 03 to the mid 40s in Q1 06.
Massive growth	True.
Excessive M&A activity	False. M&A activity has just begun recently. Traditional asset managment shops have woken up to the idea of absolute returns. Some build in-house, others buy. However, M&A activity is not excessive yet.
Institutional involvement	True. (There is the notion/belief that institutional investors are last movers by design as their decision-making process, involving consultants, trustees, etc., is slowest.)
Excessive hiring	True.
Rookies coming to the party	True.
Space getting crowded	True. Spreads have fallen across the board. (Interestingly, but perhaps not too surprisingly, margins [as in fees] for the average hedge fund manager have gone up due to an imbalance between supply and demand.)
Excited media coverage	False. Media coverage has increased quantitatively but is, in our view, balanced to still slightly negative; in some cases still outright ignorant of basic facts and characteristics.
Investor selection overconfidence	False (probably with some exceptions). Most new investors invest through fund of hedge funds.
Return expectations too high	Potentially true (but certainly on the way down).
People saying "this time it's different"	True. (Humble analysts writing books tooting paradigms shifts might or might not fall into this category.)
Fashionable	True.
Expert hairdresser recommending hedge funds	False. (Not yet.)

Adapted from Ineichen [2005].

these laws are just as rigorous, though more subtle and complex. If they weren't universal, we wouldn't call them laws."

We agree. However, our line of defense goes as follows: An asset bubble is not the same as the current inflows into hedge funds. We see hedge funds as money managers with a different set of objectives, investment philosophy, and risk management culture when compared to traditional long-only managers. Hedge funds seek absolute returns while managing risk actively. Their definition of *risk* is different: The risk-neutral position is cash, not a benchmark as is the case in traditional asset management. The absence of a benchmark results in more flexibility, that is, a superior framework for adapting to an ever-changing market environment.

All Investors Are Loss Averse   Historical returns sell. However, past returns might not be a good indicator of future returns. An investment philosophy and risk management process, however, tells us today how risk will be managed in the future. As for the future of active asset management, we believe the superior investment philosophy has a lot to do with "absolute returns" as discussed in, well, *Absolute Returns,* and the most promising risk management process is one whereby the manager tries to achieve "asymmetric returns."

The aim of an absolute-return investment philosophy is to have a fairly constant positive return stream, ideally irrespective of stock market direction. The absolute-return investment philosophy is targeted at loss-averse investors, that is, investors who are not indifferent to downside volatility. Our central hypothesis, as stated in Ineichen (2001; 2003a, c), is that some form of an absolute-return investment philosophy will become the norm in the field of investment management, as all investors—private as well as institutional—are loss-averse in one form or another. This forecast is heavily biased toward the behavioral concepts of prospect theory and loss aversion (Chapter 5), as well as what some practitioners call *negative compounding*. The term essentially means that losing money in the *short term* is not good for your financial health in the *long term*. In other words, volatility matters. Time does not diversify risk, at least not as much as thought throughout the 1990s. In addition, it is the *consequences* of loss that matter, not the *probability* of loss. As Peter Bernstein [1975] put it: "The determining question in structuring a portfolio is the consequence of loss; this is far more important than the chance of loss."

Humorist Will Rogers (1879 to 1935) was probably a loss-averse investor, preferring absolute returns over relative returns, and an asymmetric return distribution over a symmetric one:

> *"I'm more concerned about the return of my money than with the return on my money."*

Magical Thinking—Investors' Placebo Effect Typically, people use magic to attempt to explain things that science has not yet explained, or to attempt to control things that science cannot. Many articles on neuroscience have shown that the human brain excels at pattern matching, but that humans do not have a good filter for distinguishing between perceived patterns and actual patterns. Thus, people often are led to see "relationships" between actions that do not actually exist, creating a magical belief. Behavioralists call this phenomenon *magical thinking*.

A further bubble symptom not yet mentioned refers to a headline where a pension fund manager was quoted saying something along the lines of "We don't believe in equities and bonds; we invest in hedge funds." This goes too far even for our reckoning. We fear that this implies that hedge fund managers are magicians who deliver returns out of the hat without taking risk. This to some extent also implies a somewhat fuddled understanding of risk. We believe the benefits of hedge funds to the institutional portfolio are primarily complementary to the other moving parts in the portfolio.

Trying to introduce an asymmetry to various risk factors and diversifying portfolio risk by adding alternative sources of return are certainly laudable. However, we would not go as far as abandoning the other parts in their entirety. Many absolute-return strategies are difficult to execute and, more often than not, involve some form of skill. However, that's probably the only commonality with magicians.

Bottom Line　Expectations of future hedge fund returns could be—as possibly with every other investment (real estate, equities, tulip bulbs, etc.)—too high, and potentially a source of disappointment. Some investors thought of the 180-basis-point fall in hedge funds in Q2 04 as a catastrophe. (This fall was the sixth worst quarter over the past 15 years for a diversified hedge funds portfolio as measured by the HFRI Fund of Funds Composite Index.) If a 180-basis-point loss is referred to as a catastrophe, then there is certainly room for disappointment going forward. (What we found interesting was that a 180-basis-point loss in the traditional portfolio is perceived as "just another day at the office." Potentially, there is some serious mental accounting going on with investors new to hedge funds, where confidence in the recently made investment decision is low.)

We believe the search for alpha, risk-adjusted returns and diversification—that is, absolute-return managers seeking asymmetric returns—is progress in the field of institutional investment management. However, progress is not a gradual endeavor. Rather, progress is erratically jumpy and dotted with setbacks. The current movement into hedge funds is unlikely to depart from this norm. Temporary setbacks are a possibility.

Myron Scholes [2004] commented on the future for hedge funds:

> *"The models hedge funds and financial institutions use to manage risk are still in their infancy. The next decade will produce a revolution in how risk is measured and controlled. The components that must evolve include such diverse issues as how to aggregate risks, how to optimise holdings, how to plan for shocks, how to create a feedback system to learn from outcomes, how to provide information to superiors and investors, in effect, how to define transparency, how to build an appropriate capital structure given the dynamics of the asset mix, and how to compensate employees to mitigate risks. The future for hedge fund investing is exciting, dynamic, and challenging."*

In a sense, the absolute-return phenomenon is unlikely a bubble about to burst, but rather progress in the investment management industry. However, we are not quite sure whether we (the financial community) are at the beginning of the beginning or the end of the beginning.

RETURN EXPECTATIONS REVISITED

In Ineichen [1999], we discussed equity volatility in the twentieth century; we analyzed U.K. stock market volatility since 1694 and U.S. stock market volatility since 1800. One of the conclusions was that volatility at the end of the 1990s was more or less the norm in a long-term context. It was the below-average volatility of the mid-1990s that was the exception. At the time of writing these lines (April 2006), volatilities were just off the mid-1990s lows.

We also examined volatility in U.K. consumer prices since the thirteenth century in the 1999 report. At the time we thought that covering 700 years of history was sufficient to claim having a long-term view. We were short-sighted, one could argue, as the history of civilization goes back roughly 5,000 years. In our December 1999 report, therefore, we were covering only the medium term (700 years) and the short term (100 to 300 years). We would like to rectify this and look at the long-term as well.

In Chapter 2, we defined risk as exposure to change. This definition holds pretty well the test of time. Table 9.2 shows the largest cities over time. Faber [2002] uses the size of a city as a rough proxy for its prosperity.

TABLE 9.2   Cities that Have Been Largest

City	Year	City	Year
Memphis	from 3100 B.C.	Cordoba	935 A.D.
Akkad	2240	Kaifeng	1013
Lagash	2075	Constantinople	1127
Ur	2030	Merv	1145
Thebes	1980	Constantinople	1153
Babylon	1770	Fez	1170
Avaris	1670	Hangzhou	1180
Memphis	1557	Cairo	1315
Thebes	1400	Hangzhou	1348
Nineveh	668	Nanjing	1358
Babylon	612 (first over 200,000)	Beijing	1425
Alexandria	320	Constantinople	1650
Patna	300	Beijing	1710
Chang'an	195	London	1825 (first over 5 million)
Rome	25	New York	1925 (first over 10 million)
Constantinople	340 A.D.	Tokyo	1965 (first over 20 million)
Ctesiphone	570		
Chang'an	637		
Baghdad	775 (first over 1 million)		

Faber [2002] based on Chandler [1987].

Marc Faber uses this table to make the point that things (as, for example, prosperity) change. The size of a city is somewhat related to its prosperity. Most cities in Table 9.2 flourished at the time when they were the largest city in the world (give or take 100 to 150 years). However, prosperity comes and goes. One needs either an extremely short memory or a complete lack of history to assume that matters do not change. As the late John Kenneth Galbraith put it: "There can be few fields of human endeavor in which history counts for so little as in the world of finance."

What Happened to the Long Term?

We believe the paradigm of long-only equity investment is continuing its dissemination process. More and more investors are realizing that being too long can be suboptimal. The belief that being long for the long term and safe at the same time is being proven wrong if long term is not defined properly and disutility is experienced from interim losses. Investors are not indifferent to volatility (an absolute measure for risk). One could even go one step further and argue that an overweight in equities is a paradox: The reason equities outperform bonds is that they are more risky. However, if they are more risky, then the probability that they go in the wrong direction is higher. If that were not true, then equities would not be more risky. (We briefly discussed the time diversification controversy in Chapter 4. The bottom line was that you do not experience the long term if you die in the interim.)

The consensus view is that equities outperform bonds in the long term. Dimson et al. [2002], Fama and French [2002], and Ibbotson and Chen [2002] all put the expected equity-bond risk premium for the U.S. stock market after adjusting for the positively upward biased sample period at around 4 percent. We do not have a counterclaim. The point made here is that we do not know how long *long term* really is, and that disutility can be experienced from volatility before the long term materializes. Figure 9.1 shows rolling annualized 10-year real total returns for U.S. stocks, bonds, and bills from 1800 (equities from 1802, bills from 1835) to 2005 ("real total returns" means returns adjusted for inflation and including the reinvestment of any distributions). The compound annual rate of return (CARR) for the real total return time series of equities, bonds, and bills from the start to 2005 was 6.1 percent, 3.4 percent, and 2.9 percent, respectively. The annualized 10-year total real return at the end of 2005 for U.S. equities, bonds, and bills stood at 9.6 percent, 5.9 percent, and 1.5 percent, respectively.

Figure 9.1 shows that even over 10-year periods, annual returns of a long-only portfolio can be negative in real terms. In addition, the black line can fall below the gray line; that is, equities can also underperform

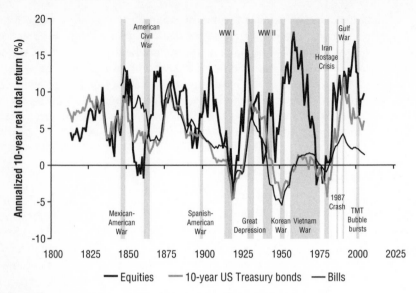

FIGURE 9.1   Rolling Annualized 10-Year Real Total Returns of U.S. Stocks, Treasuries, and Bills
Source: Author's own calculations; data from Global Financial Data and Thomson Financial.

bonds. Believers in time diversification must argue that this all is not too bad because over 20- or 30-year periods, annual real returns are positive and black lines hover over gray lines in displays such as the one in Figure 9.1.

Here's the challenge: Imagine a pension fund compounding negatively over many successive years. Will the pension fund board say, "Well, all right, we have destroyed capital, but in the long term, returns will be positive"? This is unlikely. The pressure that built up in the periods from 2000 to 2002 was immense. We believe it is unreasonable to argue that time reduces risk in the real world, that is, including the behavioral treats and constraints of institutional investors. Institutional investors are unlikely to be indifferent to volatility despite the idea that everything will turn out okay in the long term. Volatility matters. (For example: If the French go on national strike for weeks because of a small amendment in the labor law, imagine the mayhem in the streets of Paris when Mme. and M. Toulemonde's pensions start compounding negatively over a period of a couple of years. Risk management is a financial discipline. However, the lack of it might also have socioeconomic ramifications one day.) The current institutional investor's move into alternative investments is about managing volatility more actively. One of the main tools of the risk manager is correlation.

Correlation can be managed actively. The best way to do it is to understand the different sources of return streams in the portfolio, that is, how the investments are related to each other. Correlation of portfolio constituents is the key variable when managing volatility.

Figure 9.2 shows a return distribution by decade for a balanced U.S. portfolio. The portfolio is invested 60 percent in equities and 40 percent in 10-year U.S. government bonds, annually rebalanced. Both Figure 9.1 and Figure 9.2 show that correlation between equities and bonds can be positive for a while. In a two-asset-class portfolio, there is negative compounding if the two assets move in tandem. Negative compounding is less likely with a properly diversified portfolio.

We believe two-asset-class portfolios such as the one showed in Figure 9.2 are somewhat outdated. They stem from a time when investors and their agents did not have sufficient understanding about risk, which is now being rectified in the marketplace. We believe the expansion into absolute-return strategies, private equity, real estate, emerging markets, commodities, infrastructure, and so on, to last a little longer and to be more structural in nature than cyclical. Figure 9.3 shows the same distribution

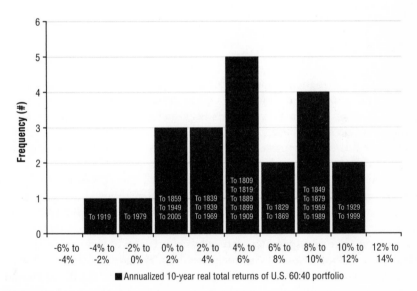

FIGURE 9.2 Distribution of Annualized 10-Year Real Total Returns of U.S. Portfolio from 1800 to 2005
Note: 1802 to 1809 and 2000 to 2005 are less than 10 years.
Source: Author's own calculations; data from Global Financial Data and Thomson Financial.

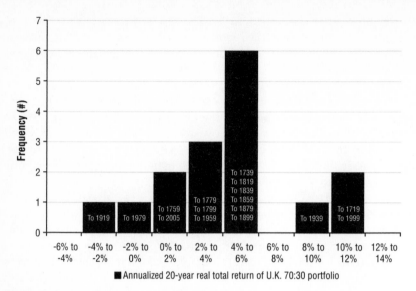

FIGURE 9.3   Distribution of Annualized 20-Year Real Total Returns of U.K. Portfolio from 1700 to 2005
Note: 2000 to 2005 is less than 20 years.
Source: Author's own calculations; data from Global Financial Data and Thomson Financial.

as Figure 9.2 but for a balanced U.K. portfolio. We have chosen a 70:30 mix, as the allocation to long-only equities in the United Kingdom over the past decade or two traditionally has been higher than in the United States. Note that this graph shows annualized 20-year real total returns instead of annualized 10-year returns (as the data covers 306 years instead of only 206, as in the case of the United States).

Figure 9.3 illustrates a couple of points: First, it seems the United Kingdom had a pretty prosperous and stable nineteenth century. The whole century was is in the 4 percent to 6 percent real total return bucket. It must have been dull—as in prosperous. (Winning Waterloo probably helped, too.) Second, once again we can show that the assumptions of returns being normally distributed can be misleading. Perhaps it is just us, but the returns in Figure 9.3 do not look normally distributed. Third, we thought it was interesting to note how the tails between the two portfolio return distributions (United States and United Kingdom) were correlated, on both the right- and left-hand sides. This despite annualizing 10-year returns in the U.S. example and 20-year returns in the U.K. example. The graph also shows that the periods to 1999 were extreme outliers. It is exactly this extraordinary period that has framed most of the beliefs that prevail in institutional asset management today.

Figure 9.4 shows the annual real total returns for the U.K stock market from 1700 to 2005, as well as the single years for the eight 20-percentage-point ranges.

The 1970s contributed three outliers. This illustrates nicely the clustering properties of equity market volatility. There are some mean-reversion patterns with respect to the outliers. The worst negative outlier (1974) was followed by the best (1975). A bet on mean reversion can be risky, though. Such a bet would have worked in 1974 but would have been disastrous in 1973, which had the second worst outlier. We believe a fair assessment of the current situation is that we do not know whether we are in a situation similar to 1973 or one similar to 1974. We never know.* Campbell and Shiller [2001] stated:

> *"The very fact that ratios have moved so far outside their historical range poses a challenge however, both to the traditional view that stock prices reflect rational expectations of future cash flows, and to our view that they are substantially driven by mean reversion. Observers of either persuasion must face the fact that something extremely unusual has occurred. In this situation a broad judgement of our position in history, of the uniqueness of recent technological advances and investment patterns, and of the state of market psychology assumes more than usual importance in judging the outlook for the stock market. There is no purely statistical method to resolve finally whether the data indicate that we have entered a new era, invalidating old relations, or whether we are still in a regime where ratios will revert to old levels. In our personal judgment, while we do not expect a complete return to traditional valuation levels, we still interpret the broad variety of evidence as suggesting a poor long-term outlook for the stock market."*

By historical standards, the U.K. stocks, bonds, and bills have seen lower levels. Figure 9.5 shows the rolling 20-year real total returns. The compound annual rate of return for the three total real return time series from 1700 to 2005 was 4.6 percent for equities, 3.2 percent for bonds, and

---

*This should not imply that we should not try and predict stock markets other than for entertainment purposes. It's just that the forecast is not manageable and reliance upon it can be futile. However, the distribution around the forecast is manageable, and active management thereof can materially increase prosperity and survival probability.

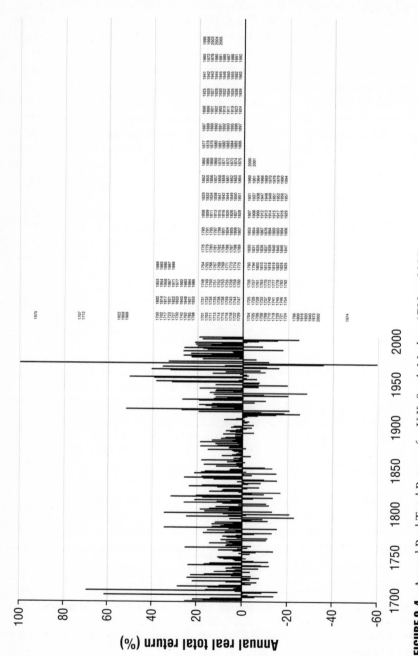

FIGURE 9.4 Annual Real Total Returns for U.K. Stock Market, 1700 to 2005

Note: x-axis was truncated for presentation purposes: 1975 real total return was 101.7 percent; 1974 return was −59.4 percent; 1973 return was −35.6 percent.

Source: Author's own calculations; data from Global Financial Data and Thomson Financial.

2.3 percent for bills (1800 to 2005). The annualized 20-year total real return at the end of 2005 for U.K. stocks, bonds, and bills stood at 8.3 percent, 8.8 percent, and 4.1 percent, respectively. Note that the bold black line (stocks) can fall below the gray line (bonds) even over a 20-year period.

Do high equity valuations imply that "this time it's different" or are they based on an imperfect understanding of history? Figure 9.5 is one of these "the-party-is-over" graphs. We (the financial community) would all be better off if the party continued, that is, if equity markets went on compounding at 20 percent per year. However, history suggests otherwise. The important message of Figure 9.5 is that there could be extended periods where value is destroyed. As Dimson et al. [2002] put it:

> *"The most fundamental question of all is: Do investors realise that returns are likely to revert to more normal levels, or do current valuations embody exaggerated expectations based on imperfect understanding of history?"*

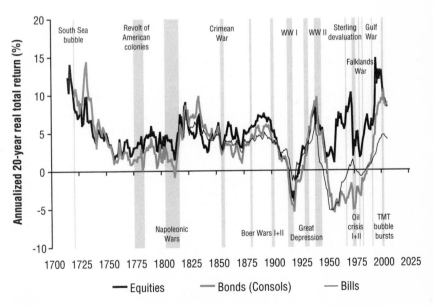

FIGURE 9.5   Rolling Annualized 20-Year Real Total Returns of U.K. Stocks, Bonds, and Bills
Source: Author's own calculations; data from Global Financial Data and Thomson Financial.

Some pension funds (primarily in continental Europe) just started to have meaningful allocation to long-only equity around the mid- and late 1990s. This underlines two previously made notions: (1) A flexible entrepreneurial approach (absolute yardstick for risk) is probably superior to a static administrative investment process when dealing with uncertainty, and (2) investing and risk management is like musical chairs: Someone slow is always left without a chair.

One purpose of the risk management function is to avoid disasters. The *musical chair effect* suggests that having good ideas too late can be disastrous. A more formal description of the musical chair effect is the distinction between a trend-following and a contrarian investment strategy. In terms of financial risk (as opposed to for example newspaper headline risk or career risk), a trend-following strategy has a high probability of failure, if one is the last to jump on the trend. In the United Kingdom, for example, we could be witnessing another practical example of the musical chair effect: In the mid-1990s, actuaries and consultants in the United Kingdom pushed equity weightings to above 75 percent. At least with some actuaries the new idea is now about the adoption of a liability benchmark portfolio, split between fixed interest and index-linked bonds. This means that actuaries recommended 75 percent equities around the peak of the equity market, and now that bonds have peaked (as interest rates were recently at their lowest for more than a generation), the recommendation is a bond-heavy portfolio. We would not necessarily describe this as a contrarian approach to investment management.

Some of our assertions are based on our belief that a contrarian, dynamic, flexible, and market-oriented approach to risk management is superior to a trend-following, static, administrative, and dogmatic approach. This, of course, is a matter of perspective.

Japan has had a different history than the United States and the United Kingdom. Figure 9.6 shows rolling annualized five-year real total returns for long-only equities, bonds, and bills in Japan. This is the third graph of its kind in this chapter. We have chosen different periods for annualizing returns. For the United States we used a 10-year period, for the United Kingdom a 20-year period, and for Japan a 5-year period. The reason for this is that there is a longer equity history in the United Kingdom. In addition, these differences in periods also allow us to compare the differences of the vertical axis that can be used as a proxy for volatility. The larger the return span, the larger the variation. So the variability over 20 years is smaller than over 5 years. We wanted to show that negative compounding can occur over 5, 10, and 20 years as well as that equities can underperform bonds over 5, 10, and 20 years. Figure 9.6 shows the negative compounding

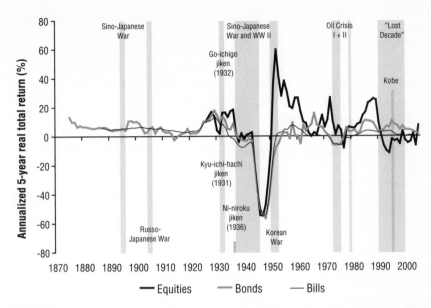

FIGURE 9.6 Rolling Annualized Five-Year Real Total Returns of Japanese Stocks, Bonds, and Bills
Note: Inflation data starts 1920. For the period from 1870 to 1919, we assumed an annual rate of inflation of 1.6 percent, which is the average from 1920 to 1944.
Source: Author's own calculations; data from Global Financial Data.

of Japanese assets during World War II. Note that negative compounding of −50 percent over five years results in a fall from $100 to $3.

One of the positive properties of absolute-return strategies is that they seem to recover from drawdowns swiftly when compared to long-only strategies due to mean reversion. One could argue that equities also have this attractive feature when compared to bonds. The distribution of equity returns is symmetrical. An investor participates in the full upside as well as downside. Bonds are occasionally considered as being akin to a short put strategy because the investor has limited upside (essentially the coupon) but the full downside in case of default. So bonds are in a sense asymmetrical, too. However, they are asymmetrical in the wrong direction, that is, limited upside, unlimited downside. The other way around is more attractive.

Figure 9.7 shows the underwater perspective (index of previous all-time high) of Japanese equities and bonds based on annual real total returns. Equities and bonds had a fairly synchronized drawdown of more than 98 percent as of 1947, in the case of equities, and of more than 99 percent as of 1953, in the case of bonds. (Note that vendors of long-only strategies

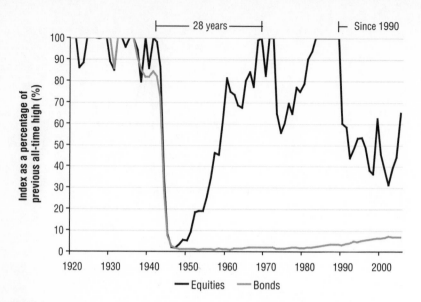

FIGURE 9.7   Underwater Perspective of Japanese Equity and Bond Market (1920 to 2005)
Based on annual real total returns.
Source: Author's own calculations, data from Global Financial Data Graph shows index as percentage of previous all time high in percent.

never present the empirical facts like we do here. Most research supporting a long-only investment style suffers from survivorship bias, as only return streams from surviving markets such as the United States, United Kingdom, Sweden, and Switzerland are shown.) Equities reached the high-water mark by 1969; that is, it took equity investors 28 years to recover from this drawdown. Bond investors are not quite there yet. According to the data that is available to us, long-term bond investors are still under water by some 93 percent. Assuming a real total return of 2 percent per year, bond investors will have recovered from this drawdown by the year 2141. (So equities actually *do* outperform bonds. It is interesting, then, that disciples of liability benchmarking are suggesting bond-heavy portfolios.)

By contrasting Japan with the United Kingdom and the United States, we also want to show different distributions of returns. Figure 9.6 shows well the properties of the fact that correlation across asset classes can be high for a long time. We also wanted to show that the notion of equities outperforming bonds in the long term is true in probably most cases (Table 9.3) but it strongly depends on how *long term* is defined. In the United Kingdom, equities have outperformed bonds in 22 out of

TABLE 9.3 Long-Term Real Total Returns (1700 to 2004)

(%) Asset / Currency	U.S. Equity USD*	U.S. Bonds USD*	U.S. Bills USD*	U.K. Equity GBP	U.K. Bonds GBP	U.K. Bills GBP	Japan Equity JPY	Japan Bonds JPY	Japan Bills JPY	Germany Equity DEM/EUR	Germany Bonds DEM/EUR	Germany Bills DEM/EUR	World Equity USD*	Europe Equity USD*	EAFE Equity USD*	Commodities Index*** USD*	Commodities Gold USD*	Commodities Oil USD*
Long term																		
1699–2004				4.8	4.8	3.4												
1799–2004**	6.4	6.1	3.4	4.8	4.8	2.8												
1899–2004	7.0	1.5	0.8	4.6	1.4	1.1											4.0	
1925–2004		2.2	0.8	6.2	2.4	1.1	3.5	-2.0	-3.7	5.2	1.4	-1.0	5.9	5.3	5.2	3.2	4.0	4.2
By century																		
1699–1799				4.8	4.6												0.1	
1799–1899**	5.7	5.5		4.9	4.2	4.0											2.7	3.7
1899–1999	7.0	1.3	-1.3	5.1	1.3	1.0										3.0		
By decade																		
1699–1709				9.0	6.4													
1709–1719				10.9	16.5													
1719–1729				2.8	5.5													
1729–1739				6.3	5.9													
1739–1749				2.6	2.1													
1749–1759				1.1	0.5													
1759–1769				6.3	3.2													
1769–1779				0.2	-0.1													
1779–1789				9.8	6.9													
1789–1799				0.1	-0.4													
1799–1809**	1.3	3.0		7.3	2.7	1.7											0.0	
1809–1819	3.9	7.7		2.5	5.0	5.9											0.0	
1819–1829	7.9	8.5		6.3	9.7	6.4											0.0	
1829–1839	2.4	3.4		1.2	2.6	3.1											0.7	
1839–1849	9.7	8.2	11.4	7.5	5.8	5.7											0.0	
1849–1859	-1.1	3.8	7.4	3.5	1.7	2.3										1.0	2.0	
1859–1869	11.1	1.9	2.4	4.2	2.5	4.0										1.0	-1.9	-5.3
1869–1879	10.1	8.5	8.8	5.6	4.1	3.3										-2.0	0.0	-12.7
1879–1889	5.7	3.9	4.7	8.2	5.5	5.2										-0.6	0.0	-1.2
1889–1899	5.2	4.4	3.6	3.0	0.1	2.3										1.7	0.0	4.6
1899–1909	7.4	-0.6	2.3	-0.3	-9.3	2.3										11.9	0.0	-1.1
1909–1919	-2.9	-4.4	-2.5	-6.3	8.4	-4.9										-7.0	0.0	16.3
1919–1929	16.0	6.4	4.9	10.5	5.8	7.6										0.4	0.0	-6.2
1929–1939	1.4	6.0	2.7	6.0	0.8	0.8	10.4	4.0	-0.6	6.5	9.4	6.3	2.5	3.9	4.6	8.6	5.4	-3.5
1939–1949	3.2	-2.8	-4.6	13.4	-2.5	-1.9	-25.7	-35.2	-33.1	-9.5	-20.4	-21.9	-2.6	-10.5	-9.6	0.1	1.5	9.7
1949–1959	16.7	-1.5	-0.2	4.5	-2.9	-0.4	27.5	0.5	5.3	23.1	2.8	1.1	16.6	18.5	18.2	2.6	-2.4	1.5
1959–1969	5.1	-0.2	1.5	-2.6	-3.3	1.9	8.5	6.2	0.5	3.5	3.2	0.9	4.4	2.1	2.5		0.1	0.8
1969–1979	-1.4	-1.3	-0.8			-3.3	3.5	-2.0	-3.3	-2.6	3.0	0.2	-0.4	1.1	2.5	15.5	30.6	24.5
1979–1989	11.9	7.5	3.8	15.9	5.7	4.6	19.0	6.8	2.7	12.8	5.3	3.3	14.1	12.7	16.8	-0.3	-1.3	-2.7
1989–1999	14.8	4.9	2.0	11.0	11.9	4.1	-5.0	6.1	1.5	9.6	6.2	3.1	8.8	11.2	4.3	-1.1	-3.2	1.6
1999–2004	-4.7	5.8	0.2	-5.4	4.3	2.1	-6.3	2.1	0.8	-9.4	5.6	1.6	-4.4	-2.0	-3.2	4.1	8.6	11.1

EAFE = Europe, Australia and Far East. *In USD and adjusted for U.S. inflation. **United States from 1802. ***The Economist. *Source:* Global Financial Data.

30 full decades between 1700 and 1999 for an average risk premium by decade of 1.60 percent. The range of extreme relative performance by decade was 15.9 percent outperformance in the 1950s and 5.6 percent underperformance in the 1710s. The average risk premium and range is not calculated by decade but by year and not until 2004 but including 2005 was 1.64 percent, 95.2 percent outperformance in 1975, and 37.2 percent underperformance in 2002, whereby equities outperformed bonds in 178 out of 306 years.

In the United States, equities have outperformed bonds in 13 out of 20 full decades for an average risk premium by decade of 3.1 percent. The range of relative performance was 18.2 percent outperformance in the 1950s and 4.9 percent underperformance in the 1850s. By year, the risk premium averaged 3.95 percent, while relative performance ranged from 55.4 percent outperformance in 1933 to 46.5 percent underperformance in 1931. Equities outperformed bonds in 114 out of the 203 years to 2005.

In Japan, equities have outperformed bonds in five out of eight full decades since 1920 for an average risk premium by decade of 5.5 percent. (Excluding the 1950s rebound, the equity risk premium was 1.9 percent when measured by decade and in real total return terms.) The range of relative performance was 30.9 percent outperformance in the 1950s and 9.8 percent underperformance in the 1990s. By year, the risk premium averaged 8.6 percent, while relative performance ranged from 127.6 percent outperformance in 1948 to 49.1 percent underperformance in 1962. Equities outperformed bonds in 48 out of the 84 years to 2005.

Another way of looking at the data is by examining annualized 30-year real total returns. Table 9.4 shows annualized 30-year real total returns for a selection of regions for stocks, bonds, bills and a 50:50 portfolio of stocks and bonds. The illustration supports the notion that equities outperform bonds in the long term. (It also shows how easy it is to spin a story by how data is presented. In Table 9.4, the equity risk premium in the United States is 6.1 percent.) The table also shows that many regions had their 30-year high in real total return terms in 2004 (data in Table 9.4 does not include 2005). We do not believe that everything that goes up must come down. However, history somewhat hints that there is such a thing as mean reversion.

Note that examining long-term return data is very interesting. However, there are no investors who have an isolated 30-year investment horizon. Decisions are made in the interim. Most investors, private as well institutional, will have their focus on annual performance statistics and make decisions based on annual returns.

Figure 9.8 shows the distribution of a 50:50 Japanese portfolio (50 percent equities, 50 percent bonds, annually rebalanced). The return buckets

TABLE 9.4 Annualized 30-Year Real Total Returns (1925 to 2004)

	Stocks	Bonds	Bills	50/50*		Stocks	Bonds	Bills	50/50*		Stocks	Bonds	Bills	50/50*
World in USD					**US**					**Germany**				
Average	5.77	0.87	0.31	3.32	Average	7.00	0.87	0.31	3.93	Average	6.27	-0.25	-2.20	3.01
Standard deviation	0.91	1.70	1.16	0.99	Standard deviation	1.76	1.70	1.16	1.04	Standard deviation	1.83	4.40	4.43	2.21
Maximum	8.03	4.43	1.76	6.17	Maximum	10.49	4.43	1.76	6.68	Maximum	11.64	4.57	2.72	7.29
Year	1961	2004	2004	2004	Year	1961	2004	2004	2004	Year	1978	1987	2004	1978
Minimum	4.24	-1.49	-1.58	1.69	Minimum	4.35	-1.49	-1.58	2.07	Minimum	2.64	-5.93	-7.34	-0.78
Year	1958	1969	1962	1974	Year	1994	1969	1962	1981	Year	1990	1973	1973	1974
Europe in USD					**UK**					**France**				
Average	4.58	0.87	0.31	2.72	Average	6.29	1.41	0.34	3.85	Average	3.77	-2.31	-2.82	0.73
Standard deviation	2.18	1.70	1.16	1.78	Standard deviation	1.43	1.41	1.06	1.23	Standard deviation	2.05	5.50	5.29	3.50
Maximum	9.19	4.43	1.76	6.81	Maximum	10.70	5.02	2.49	7.86	Maximum	8.95	5.97	3.08	8.20
Year	2004	2004	2004	2004	Year	2004	2004	2004	2004	Year	2004	2004	2004	2004
Minimum	1.36	-1.49	-1.58	0.18	Minimum	2.30	-0.95	-1.09	0.88	Minimum	0.05	-9.63	-10.55	-3.92
Year	1974	1969	1962	1970	Year	1974	1976	1962	1974	Year	1972	1964	1965	1972
EAFE in USD					**Japan**					**Australia**				
Average	5.10	0.87	0.31	2.98	Average	4.60	-3.86	-5.00	0.37	Average	6.31	0.61	-0.02	3.46
Standard deviation	2.09	1.70	1.16	1.65	Standard deviation	4.72	7.41	5.79	5.66	Standard deviation	1.16	2.17	2.20	1.32
Maximum	8.49	4.43	1.76	6.21	Maximum	14.43	3.97	0.85	8.22	Maximum	9.46	5.36	3.32	7.41
Year	1988	2004	2004	2004	Year	1977	1991	1978	1978	Year	2004	2004	2004	2004
Minimum	1.69	-1.49	-1.58	0.39	Minimum	-0.96	-13.24	-12.10	-6.81	Minimum	4.08	-2.33	-2.84	1.00
Year	1966	1969	1962	1970	Year	1963	1961	1961	1964	Year	1974	1976	1963	1976

EAFE = Europe, Australia, and Far East World, Europe, and EAFE in USD and adjusted for U.S. inflation; countries in local currencies adjusted for local inflation.
*Portfolio 50 percent stocks, 50 percent bonds, annually rebalanced.
Source: Global Financial Data.

measure the frequency of annualized five-year real total portfolio returns. The idea of comparing this distribution with the previous two is twofold. First, the normal distribution might hold in some financial instruments in the short term. The normal distribution is a pretty good and elegant assumption when experimenting with financial data under laboratory conditions. However, for the long-term investor, it has no relevance. Accidents happen, and we do not know when and where they happen; neither do we know their magnitude. We can only learn about them and manage risk according to our disutility from them. Second, long-term return distributions can look vastly different. The one shown in Figure 9.8 is very different from the previous ones. So we also have no clue from what kind of distribution the future will pick its returns. We do not know whether the U.S. stock market will have a return distribution over the next 80 years that looks like Figure 9.8. Showing long-term cumulative performance of the U.S., U.K., Swedish, or Swiss stock market (all of them—so far—surviving markets) and arguing that time diversifies risk is at best a highly misleading marketing one-liner, and at worst intellectual fraud. As we elaborated in Chapter 2, there is uncertainty on top of risk. We believe the wisest course of action is to manage risk and uncertainty. This will increase the cost of the investment process. However, ignorance could be costlier.

The previous six figures showed the three largest single-country economies in the world: the United States, the United Kingdom, and Japan.

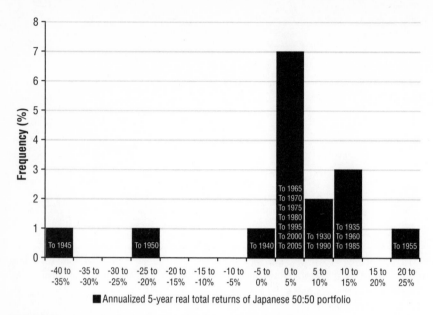

FIGURE 9.8 Distribution of Annualized Five-Year Real Total Returns of Japanese Portfolio from 1925 to 2005
Source: Author's own calculations; data from Global Financial Data.

Going forward, this will obviously change, unless, of course, China decides to try out another flawed social idea, putting it again—economically speaking—into the backyard of the global economy (which seems unlikely from today's perspective; but then so did the probability of Egypt's being taken over by the Nubians prior to 750 B.C., given that they themselves had been conquered by Egypt several time before*). One of the points of all this is that we should learn to know what we don't know. Rightly or wrongly, the stock market is often regarded as a proxy for economic prowess. Figure 9.9 compares a famous chart comparing the Dow Jones Industrial Average Index with the Nikkei 225 Index of Japan. Note that the chart is not that meaningful, as both indices are price-weighted indices (as opposed to capitalization-weighted), which is largely considered an inferior index methodology, and the chart is based on *nominal price* returns instead of *real total* returns; the two indices are not necessarily representative of their home markets, as they cover only a limited number of stocks when compared to the market total. However, this display regularly comes into fame

---

*This analogy also works with Romans and Barbarians.

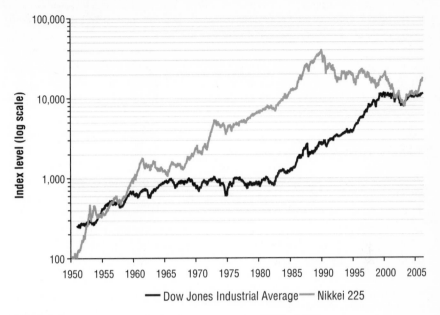

FIGURE 9.9 Dow Jones Industrial Average versus Nikkei 225
Source: Thomson Financial.

at crossing points of the two indices. Japan benefited greatly from World War II recovery (somewhat a base effect) and especially the Korean War (economically speaking). The Nikkei 225 overtook the Dow in October 1952, only to be overtaken by the Dow in June 1954. The two indices went back and forth. Then Japan unfolded its economic miracle and took off, leaving the Dow Jones behind, starting in August 1957. In early 1990, at an index level close to 40,000, the Nikkei 225 was more than 14 times the price of the Dow, then in the mid-2500s. During the "lost decade," it fell back and crossed the Dow a tick below 10,000 in February 2002 and between 8,000 and 9,000 during April to June 2003. With a new bull market starting in 2005, the Nikkei is again far and above the Dow, at 17,222; on April 1, 2006, that compares to 11,114 with the Dow Jones Industrial.

They will meet again, we're sure. We just don't know when and where. Can we be really sure? Will they ever cross again? We actually do not know that either with any degree of confidence.

We believe some of these illustrations underline the necessity for a paradigm shift with respect to risk management. The asset management industry is potentially at a crossroad. In our view, the belief that returns are manageable must be relaxed. Risk is manageable, but not returns. Returns from passive exposure to asset classes, such as equities and bonds, are given by the market and by history. Returns are not forecastable, as the returns are influenced by the forecast. Returns are not a pure function of fundamentals, as the fundamentals are influenced by the expectations of the fundamentals; that is, cause and effect are not distinct, as is the case in the natural sciences. Risk as well as the consequences of a negative market move, however, can be assessed and managed.

Markets Will Continue to Fluctuate

The equity market will be either higher or lower in one, three, five, or twenty years from now. (The often quoted observation that the year-end close of the Dow Jones Industrial Average in 1964 [874.13] was the same as 1981 [875.00] is a coincidence as well as not very meaningful because it is based on nominal price returns and not real total returns.) In the following, we briefly discuss the bull case, the bear case, and the objective case. It has probably been a long time since the views of the bulls differed so much from the views of the bears. It seems to us that the bears are much more bearish than the bulls are bullish. We conclude this section with the "alternative case."

Bull and Bear Cases Most market forecasters were bullish at the beginning of 2000. Markets fell in 2000. In 2001 and 2002, most market forecasters suggested that there is light at the end of the tunnel. In March 2003, equity markets eventually started to reverse. What seemed like a bear market rally, at first, turned into a new bull market. Fears of inflation were balanced by fears of deflation. The U.S. deficit is not really an issue for the bulls. (The bears recommend moving into the mountains and owning gold physically.) After all, the U.S. dollar was up during 2005 (contrary to what most investors and pundits had predicted). Oil at $70 per barrel is not really an issue either; after all, there are tar sands in Canada, and if that's not enough, we can convert more sugar into ethanol. Emerging markets are booming as if there is no tomorrow. As of this writing, the yield differential of emerging-market bonds over U.S. Treasury bonds was less than 200 basis points (Figure 9.10). We have overlaid the bond spreads with the Volatility Index (VIX), which shows short-term implied volatility of S&P 500 options. Both measures are frequently used as a proxy for the appetite for risky assets. Low means appetite is high; that is, risk is perceived as low.

The bear case is less discussed in sell-side research but is regularly brought up by a minority of pundits and journalists as well as alarmists. The three most often described scenarios are a credit crunch, deflation, and Keynes's liquidity trap, or a combination thereof. The general belief

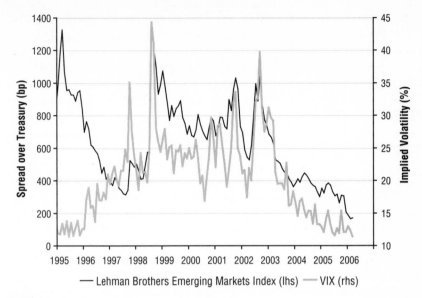

FIGURE 9.10 Emerging Market Yield Differential to U.S. Treasury and VIX
Source: Lehman Brothers, Thomson Financial.

of the bears is that Alan Greenspan was right in referring to the equity market as "irrationally exuberant" in December 1996 but turned from a bull market critic to a bull market cheerleader in the aftermath of these remarks in December 1996. Most bears weight the impact of debt on the economy more strongly than do the bulls. In addition, they believe that central bankers' intervention in the monetary system has a positive short-term impact, with dire, negative long-term side effects, as fighting market forces, they believe, works in the short term but not in the long term. Bears, generally speaking, do not ignore some of the claims of Austrian economics ("It's credit that matters, not money"), whereas everyone else in the financial industry, by and large, does. The argument is that monetary easing in the United States from 2001 to 2003 resulted in corporate balance sheets being repaired but risk being shifted from corporate balance sheets to the consumer and their household balance sheet. One could argue that these risks have been magnified in the past couple of years as the overall level of U.S. debt to gross domestic product (GDP) has continued to accelerate since 2002. One view is that—from here onward—all depends on the U.S. consumer.

If there is one characteristic that typifies Americans, so the argument goes, it's optimism. Even in difficult circumstances, Americans prefer to look on the bright side. According to this argument, we (the global economy) now depend on the sunny outlook of the U.S. consumer. The economic growth of the past has been propelled largely by the insatiable consumption of U.S. households. Their hunger for gadgets is one of the engines of China's growth story and has increased living standards elsewhere. But U.S. consumers only spend so lavishly because of their blithe assumption that it's fine to save nothing and borrow up to the hilt—things will turn out right in the end. Asset inflation, especially houses, is the new way of saving. The U.S. personal savings rate has dropped from around 8 percent of income in the 1980s to below nil today. With U.S. interest rates and energy prices rising, however, it's unclear how long even American optimism can survive.

Figures 9.11 and 9.12 show two similar valuation methods for the U.S. stock market from 1900 to 2005. As both methods have stock market prices in the numerator, the two graphs look alike. Figure 9.11 shows cyclically adjusted P/E for the S&P 500 index and is from Robert Shiller's *Irrational Exuberance* [2000], and Figure 9.12 shows Smithers and Wright's "q" [2000]. "q" refers Nobel Laureate James Tobin's "q." Smithers and Wright define "q" (or "equity q") as the ratio between the value of companies according to the stock market and their net worth measured at replacement cost. Tobin's q includes corporate debt.

At an S&P 500 level of around 1,248.3 at the end of December 2005, the U.S. stock market was still valued above its long-term average based on these two metrics. Assume investors holding U.S. stock decide that not its current valuation but a P/E of 10 times is more appropriate (which, historically as well as statistically, is a possibility). Assuming $75 is a reasonable estimate for the index constituents aggregate earnings per share including all adjustments for options and pension fund deficits, the S&P 500 could fall to 750, as the index did in autumn 2002. For an investor experiencing great disutility from an index level of 750, the notion that equities outperform bonds in the long term is not that relevant. Interim volatility is largely influenced by valuation swings. These swings, we believe, are difficult or impossible to forecast. However, the risk is manageable.

The late Leon Levy refers to the 2000 to 2002 erosion of $7 trillion in market value as a Shakespearean drama with five acts, whereby by 2002 we were in the third:

> *"My instincts, refined by fifty years of experience in finance, tell me that we are in but the third act of a five-act Shakespearean drama that portends a bad ending. Stock prices may have plummeted from their dizzying heights, but neither consumers nor investors have yet realized the perils of the suffocating pall of debt hanging over the financial world. Nor have they reckoned with the increasing*

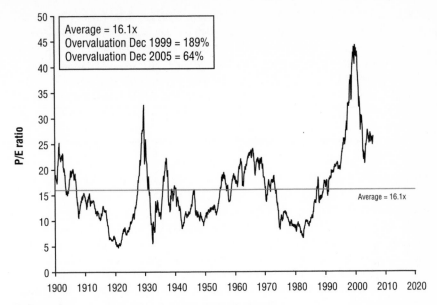

FIGURE 9.11   Cyclically Adjusted PE (1900 to 2005)
Source: Shiller [2000]. Update from http://aida.econ.yale.edu/~shiller/. Based on monthly data.

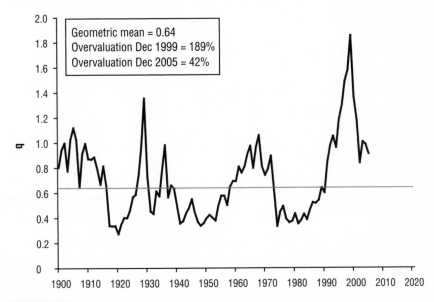

FIGURE 9.12   Equity q, 1900 to 2005
Source: Smithers and Wright [2000]. Update from www.smithers.co.uk. Based on annual data.

difficulty of competing in a global market burdened with excess capacity and idled workers in almost every industry. Even at today's discounted prices, the markets have yet to digest that the massive tide of foreign money that flowed into the markets in the past decade is ebbing and may begin to flow out, and consumers have only just begun to save more and spend less (a nearly inevitable result of harder times that will drive the last act of this drama)."[1]

The quote refers to the fall in 2002. Potentially we are now (April 2006) at the end of the fourth act.

The Objective Case   There is an objective case. The objective case is what a rational investor can expect of equities based on an estimate for bonds plus a premium for holding equities or a notional expected return based on inflation plus dividend and earnings growth. The aforementioned bull and bear cases are subjective. However, one could quite easily argue that there is no objective case as any case is based on the assumptions and beliefs of the observer assessing the situation. As William A. Sherden, author of *Fortune Sellers* [1998], puts it: "Remember the First Law of Economics: For every economist, there is an equal and opposite economist—so for every bullish economist, there is a bearish one. The Second Law of Economics: They are both likely to be wrong."

Ibbotson and Chen [2002] show an illustrative decomposition of equity market return components from 1926 to 2000 for the U.S. stock market (Figure 9.13). Feasible long-term equity returns are a sum of dividend yield and a long-run earnings growth rate. Ibbotson and Chen decompose the realized 75-year average compound U.S. stock market return of 10.7 percent into supply and demand. Demanded return is decomposed into 5.2 percent nominal Treasury bond return plus 5.2 percent ex-post equity risk premium plus small interaction/reinvestment terms. Supplied return is decomposed in 3.1 percent inflation plus 4.3 percent dividend yield plus 1.8 percent real earnings growth rate plus 1.3 percent repricing effect plus small interaction/reinvestment terms. The third bar removes the unexpected pricing effect. The paper concludes that investors required an average nominal equity market return of 9.4 percent between 1926 and 2000.

We believe the most important word in the last sentence is *average*. The fourth bar in Figure 9.13 is an illustrative way of showing an expected average for the future. The figure derived from the model is the objective return expectation for the next 75 years (or whatever one defines as the long term).* Any other estimate would be subjective at best or heretic at worst.

---

*Two pre-Worldcom surveys of different U.S. experts (finance and economics professors by Welch [2000, 2001] and CFOs and treasurers by Graham and Harvey

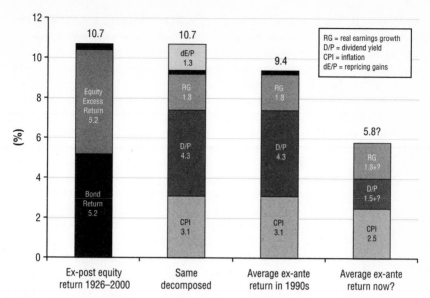

FIGURE 9.13 Decomposition of 1926 to 2000 Equity Market Returns
Source: Ilmanen [2003] based on Ibbotson and Chen [2002].

However, how relevant is the estimate for the practitioner who needs to make financial decisions?

Potentially, it is not that relevant, as it is perceived by a majority of investors. It is certainly a blessing if we know with a high degree of confidence that equities will outperform bonds by a couple of percentage points in the long run going forward. However, these long-run expectations are not manageable. If there is disutility from interim volatility, the objective

---

[2001]) resulted in long-run equity return expectations of 8 percent to 9 percent and stock-bond risk premium estimates of 3.5 percent to 4.5 percent. The equity return forecast in the CFO survey has stabilized at around 8.2 percent to 8.3 percent in 2002. A survey of global investors by Ilmanen [2003] from April 2002 comes up with the most cautious views on future equity market returns. The mean forecast for next decade average equity market return is 7.6 percent for the United States. Compared with bond yields of around 5.2 percent, these forecasts imply a stock-bond risk premium of 2.4 percent. From Ilmanen [2003]. This goes to show that the "objective case" is somewhat of a misnomer. A vast array of models, and differing views on model input variables such as growth rates and risk premiums, result in a wide range of solutions. Relying ones' financial health on one of the outputs is, we believe, speculative and unlikely to be optimal for most investors.

long-term return expectation loses its practical relevance for most or even all investors. We believe that the prolonged bull market has led to the asset management industry's focusing more heavily than normal on the forecast (which is not manageable) as opposed to the probability distribution around the forecast (which is manageable).

We do not claim the absence of the equity risk premium. Our point is that a risk manager facing uncertainty has to make financial decisions irrespective of differing views and school of thought. The debate about the equity risk premium continues to be a puzzle.* Mehra and Prescott [1985] initiated the equity premium puzzle over 20 years ago. Academics and practitioners alike have proposed various solutions to the equity premium puzzle (alternative utility functions, market imperfections, etc.), but there is limited agreement on the topic. More recently, Mehra [2003] discusses the challenges the claim from 1985 battled over the years. The current debate is about the *expected* equity premium's being different from the past premium. Mehra argues that before the equity premium is dismissed, researchers with opposing views need a plausible explanation why the future should be different from the past. In the absence of such an explanation, Mehra ends his 2003 article by making the following claim:

> *"Over the long term, the equity premium is likely to be similar to what it has been in the past and returns to investment in equity will continue to substantially dominate returns to investment in T-bills for investors with a long planning horizon."*

We challenge the practicability of "long term" and "long planning horizon" in preceding quote. Today, it should be clear that relying on "the long term" story could result in an underestimation of volatility and its subsequent disutility with respect to financial objectives. Volatility was not perceived as much of a problem during the 1990s bull market—for plan sponsors, trustees, consultants, and private investors alike. However, the game has now changed. Most investors now have a different perspective than they had five years ago. Our observations surrounding the debate on the equity premium is not necessarily an economic counterclaim. However, we note that the term *long term* is very vague. Potentially, the term is too vague for most investors to have practical application in an uncertain and ever-changing world. Once we overheard a cynic saying that "a long-term investment is a short-term investment that went wrong."

---

*A good compilation of articles on the debate and links to further material can be found at http://www.aimrpubs.org/ap/issues/v2002n1/toc.html.

While there is uncertainty with respect to the expectation (model uncertainty as well as uncertainty with respect to the return components), we believe the greater contribution to ex-ante volatility is derived from changes in valuation, that is, profits and losses from repricing. This volatility, we believe, is not forecastable with any degree of confidence or sustainability (although, as stated earlier, risk can be assessed in a historical context and managed accordingly). We do not know whether valuation will fall through its long-term averages (the horizontal lines in Figures 9.11 and 9.12) over the next three years. If history is any guide we can assume that there is some probability that they will (unless the claim "this time it's different" in this special case has merit). However, what we do know with (by comparison) a high degree of confidence is that price as well as valuations will fluctuate (read: change) for the foreseeable future. If there is disutility from losses, a long-only buy-and-hold strategy (where volatility is not managed through either an absolute-return strategy or derivatives or other hedging techniques) might not be ideal.

Probabilistic, Dynamic, and Flexible Approach

The notion that asset allocation is important is pretty solid. Having a strategic target, therefore, has merit. Or does it? Having a strategic target biases the investment process toward a deterministic and/or dogmatic view of the world as it heavily relies on return expectations. We believe that the reliance on return expectations is admirable, as it focuses on the long term. However, most return expectations are heavily biased toward historical returns. In addition, it also exposes the portfolio to interim volatility and disutility thereof. In this book, we try to make the case that, when dealing with uncertainty, a probabilistic, dynamic, and flexible approach is probably superior to a dogmatic, static, and inflexible one.

A "probabilistic approach" implies that there are no axioms in the social sciences (everything is uncertain) and that reliance on beliefs and dogmas might help administer large portfolios but also can be dangerous with respect to managing risk. It means that what we believe today is either true, false, or currently a good idea but is subject to change. It means, putting it simply, that we do not know what we do not know (as opposed to the dogmatic approach that assumes and relies upon "we know"). A probabilistic approach suggests that one treats beliefs as beliefs and exercises humility by respecting that the only constant is change. If we define *risk* as "exposure to change," then risk management (as opposed to asset allocation) is the discipline that relies on little else than that the status quo will change. An asset allocator with a 75:25 equity-bond mix can become complacent with respect to risk during a bull market, especially when equity-bond correlation is high by coincidence. The risk manager, however, is always aware that circumstances could change and that the capital could be exposed to excessive or undesirable risk.

By "dynamic and flexible approach," we refer to the observation that absolute-return managers try to protect the capital with which they were entrusted by their investors and are flexible to react to changes in the market environment. The absence of a proper wealth preservation incentive and lack of flexibility on the part of the manager under the relative return paradigm results in the asset management function's being rather administrative and static in nature as opposed to dynamic, entrepreneurial, and flexible. Many layers of administration might protect the investor, but not necessarily his money.

A dynamic and flexible approach is more risky than a static and administrative approach. However, the reason we feel strongly that the paradigm should change is that the increased risk from a flexible and entrepreneurial approach is primarily idiosyncratic in nature; that is, single-manager risk can be nearly fully eliminated through diversification alone. Diversification is indeed the only free lunch in economics. It is now for the fee-paying investor base to enforce change. (The fee-receiving part of the financial industry will supply whatever there is demand for.)

FUTURE OPPORTUNITY SET FOR ACTIVE RISK MANAGERS

Absolute-return managers search for imbalances in supply and demand.* Searching for imbalances in supply and demand might be considered one of the few common denominators of all active managers. In other words, putting it crudely, active managers require a great supply of fools (economically speaking) to exercise their craft. If all investors acted purely on objective economic criteria, supply-and-demand imbalances would not exist

---

*Supply/demand imbalances, one could argue, are also inefficiencies. However, a convertible bond trading at an implied volatility of 25 percent while stock options are at 30 percent is an objective mispricing. The economic relationship is defined by a mathematical formula, that is, the strategy is a fairly pure form of arbitrage. A stock market trading at a P/E of 80 or gold at a 20-year low are not objective mispricings, but imbalances of overly excited buyers or overly disappointed (or forced) sellers. The analysis of the situation is subjective. Conversion and the timing of the conversion are uncertain, as there is no expiry date (as in the case of convertibles).

(or only to a much lesser extent). Market inefficiencies exist because some market participants do something that is uneconomic. That does not mean uneconomic market participants are irrational. These market participants might be incentivized to do what they do. This means their "economics" is different to what would be considered as objectively economic. In other words, their behavior might be fully rational when considered against their *subjective* economics but irrational when compared with *objective* economic criteria.* For instance, many actuaries, after the turbulence of the 2000 to 2002 period and the continuously falling discount rates (increasing present value of liabilities), from their subjective perspective, may find indexing assets to liabilities the currently most economic thing to do.

However, the current observable move from "asset benchmarks" to "liability benchmarks" might supply yet another massive and long-lasting market imbalance (or investment opportunity from the absolute-return manager's point of view). The reason is that benchmarking, irrespective of benchmarking against assets or liabilities, means that the actions of the benchmarker (or his agent) are determined or at least heavily influenced by *subjective* economic criteria (the economics of the principal and his agent) and not *objective* economic criteria (the economics of the marketplace).[†] Buying and selling of liquid assets by the benchmarker are determined by changes in the benchmark or his idiosyncratic economic circumstances, and not by changes in the market place or economic reasoning in the absolute-return space, that is, the real world. In addition, the measurement process of the principal interferes with the investment process of the agent, as it determines his (subjective) economics through the agent's incentive structure. The risk-neutral position, for example, for an agent with a benchmark is the benchmark itself, irrespective of market conditions. To us as observers, it seems—potentially—that every balanced system requires frogs as well as snakes. If the frogs do something silly, the snakes could be

---

*A variant of what we call *subjective economics* could be the purchase of assets because of excess liquidity (instead of the risk/reward trade-off's being attractive) or levering up the corporates' balance sheet because financing is cheap (instead of the risk/reward trade-off's being attractive), and so on.

[†]Note that one of the ideas of the 1990s was that the long-term investor can stomach and/or ignore short-term market volatility. The belief was that it is the mean return that matters, not the distribution around the mean. We believe it is the other way around. The mean of a distribution cannot be managed. The distribution (and the consequences thereof), however, can be managed, hence our manifesto for active risk management. Exploiting Marx somewhat: "Pension beneficiaries in the world unite; you have nothing to lose but your claims."

all over them. As Mark Twain put it: "Let us be thankful for the fools. But for them, the rest of us could not succeed."

Liability benchmarking in equity-heavy institutional portfolios implies, generally speaking, more bonds and higher duration relative to the status quo. We do not, unfortunately, have an edge in forecasting interest rates and bond prices. We therefore have to leave it to the reader to decide whether (ex-ante) bond risk is upwardly or downwardly skewed, given that:

- Interest rates are just off multigenerational lows.*
- Public and private debt levels are historically high (and still rising).†
- Savings-age population ratios (especially in the United States)‡ are falling and are thought of as negatively correlated to yields and inflation.
- Past GDP growth is more a function of leverage (cheap financing) than innovation and productivity gains.
- There is competitive currency devaluation and rising protectionism.

Ryan [2003], an advocate of using liability indices, commented on some of the more behavioral issues in the investment management industry:

> *"We are all sheep in this business. Here's what happens. If you made a lot of money doing the wrong things, would you call up a client and say: "By the way, I want to change the way I do things." Consultants tend to have the keys to the kingdom ... They are the ones who told their clients to be heavily skewed to equities because over every 10-year period they would beat bonds. It is hard for these consultants to turn around and say, 'By the way, that doesn't work.'"§*

---

*Edward Chancellor [2004] on low interest rates: "Keep the Fed funds rate at 1% for long enough and even the defunct dot-com bubble comes back to life." With the benefit of hindsight, that comment was spot on.

†According to some estimates, in the United States household and corporate borrowing for the acquisition of financial assets has climbed to around 85 percent of all credit activity, while total new borrowing is at record levels. Chancellor [2004] stated: "In Britain, much of the household debt taken on in the past few years has also gone into buying financial assets. In the twenty-first century, it seems, every man's home is his hedge fund."

‡In the United States, the inflection point of the growth rate (i.e., the point when the ratio started to fall) of the 35- to 54-year-olds to population (savings-age population) was around 2001. In Europe, this inflection point is thought of as being later, as Europeans, for whatever reason, had slower birth growth and, therefore, later growth reversal in baby boomers.

TABLE 9.5 Historical Returns (1990 to Q1 2006)

	1990	1991	1992	1993	1994	1995	1996	1997	1998	1999	2000	2001	2002	2003	2004	2005	Q1 06
	Hedge Funds 17.5%	Global Equities 19.0%	Hedge Funds 12.3%	Hedge Funds 26.3%	Risk-free rate 6.0%	Global Equities 21.3%	Hedge Funds 14.4%	Hedge Funds 18.0%	Global Equities 24.8%	Hedge Funds 26.5%	Comm. 11.5%	Hedge Funds 2.8%	Comm. 23.0%	Global Equities 33.8%	Global Equities 15.2%	Comm. 22.5%	Global Equities 6.7%
	Global Bonds 11.8%	Global Bonds 15.5%	Global Bonds 4.6%	Global Equities 23.1%	Global Equities 5.6%	Global Equities 19.3%	Global Equities 14.0%	Global Equities 16.2%	Global Bonds 15.3%	Global Equities 25.3%	Risk-free rate 6.6%	Risk-free rate 1.9%	Global Bonds 19.4%	Global Bonds 14.5%	Comm. 11.2%	Global Equities 10.0%	Hedge Funds 4.7%
	Risk-free rate 7.6%	Hedge Funds 14.5%	Risk-free rate 3.3%	Global Bonds 12.3%	Comm. 4.6%	Hedge Funds 11.1%	Risk-free rate 5.5%	Risk-free rate 5.7%	Risk-free rate 5.1%	Comm. 6.8%	Hedge Funds 4.1%	Global Bonds -0.8%	Risk-free rate 1.4%	Hedge Funds 11.6%	Global Bonds 10.1%	Hedge Funds 7.5%	Comm. 4.0%
	Comm. -3.2%	Risk-free rate 4.3%	Comm. -2.6%	Comm. 11.6%	Global Bonds 1.3%	Risk-free rate 5.7%	Global Bonds 4.4%	Global Bonds 1.4%	Hedge Funds -5.1%	Risk-free rate 5.8%	Global Bonds 2.3%	Comm. -16.3%	Hedge Funds 1.0%	Comm. 8.9%	Hedge Funds 6.9%	Risk-free rate 4.4%	Risk-free rate 1.2%
	Global Equities -16.5%	Comm. -6.5%	Global Equities -4.7%	Risk-free rate 3.3%	Hedge Funds -3.5%	Comm. 2.8%	Comm. -1.5%	Comm. -4.4%	Comm. -16.5%	Global Bonds -5.1%	Global Equities -12.9%	Global Equities -16.5%	Global Equities -19.5%	Risk-free rate 1.1%	Risk-free rate 2.4%	Global Bonds -6.5%	Global Bonds -0.4%

Hedge Funds: HFRI Fund of Funds Composite Index; Global Bonds: JPM Global Government Bond Total Return Index; Risk-free rate: Year-end reading of USD one-month LIBOR; Comm.: CRB Commodity Price Index; Global Equities: MSCI World Total Return Index.
Source: Author's own calculations; data from Bloomberg and Thomson Financial.

Bottom Line Active money management is a competition and is said to be a zero-sum game (or a negative-sum game after fees). This is probably true. However, this notion does not imply the absence of winners and losers, nor that the outcome of the competition is purely a function of randomness. The notion is also based on the assumption that all market participants are playing the same game. In a game of tennis, for example, if one player is nimble, reactive as well as proactive, and adapts to changing circumstances, while the other player benchmarks his forehand to the right-hand corner, the outcome of the game is unlikely to be a function of randomness. The nimble competitor will soon find himself in the position of having an edge. Benchmarking means that the action of one player becomes predictable to the other competitors; that is, the benchmarked investor is essentially showing his hand to the other players. It is therefore not entirely inappropriate to argue that absolute-return investors are not really *generating* alpha, they are just capturing the negative alpha left behind by the benchmarked, that is, economically constrained, investor.

RETURN UPDATE AND OUTLOOK

What is our take on future returns in the absolute-return space? History suggests equity-like positive returns with bond-like drawdowns. This is

---

§First part of answer to the question "Why aren't more pension funds moving to your approach of using a custom liability index?" Ryan [2003], p. 59.

what we refer to as *asymmetric-return profile* and claim to be a function of active risk management. We believe the asymmetry to persist going forward. We believe a diversified portfolio of absolute-return investment strategies over the next 5 to 10 years will compound in line with equities and bonds, that is, 300 to 500 basis points above the risk-free rate, with a much lower probability of the investors' capital being wiped out in the interim. Note that this last remark is quite important. Potentially, some investors' return expectations for long-only equities and diversified hedge fund portfolios net of two layers of fees are the same, that is, a nominal return of around 8 percent. However, the expectation for the risk-adjusted return is not the same, as diversified hedge fund portfolios are much less volatile than long-only investments.

Table 9.5 shows historical annual returns from a diversified hedge funds portfolio net of two layers of fees compared to global equities, global bonds, commodities, and the year-end USD one-month risk-free rate. Annual returns were ranked in descending order and color-coded. The table reveals both: an element of randomness in some cases as well as cyclicality in others.

Diversified hedge fund portfolios rank first in 7 out of 17 readings (Table 9.5) and rank last only once (the asymmetry). A negative absolute return occurred twice (1994 and 1998). Global equities ranked first six times, while ranking last five times (the symmetry*). A negative absolute return occurred five times. Global bonds never rank first and only four times ranked last, which is primarily a function of lower volatility (also an asymmetry, but tilted toward the wrong side). A negative absolute return occurred four times. Presenting the data like this shows the autocorrelation properties in equities in 2000 to 2002 and commodities in 1996 to 1998, that is, what we herein call *negative compounding*. Hedge funds show the opposite effect: mean reversion. A negative return year is followed by a rebound. The logic of this, as discussed in previous chapters, is that a negative return is typically associated with an accident of some sort, resulting in a market dislocation of some sort. The reason for the mean reversion is that the opportunity set is extremely attractive in such a panic scenario. When the market panics, it pays to be contrarian.[†]

---

*This is probably why academia is hooked on the coin-flipping analogy: heads, market is up, tails, market is down for the year. However, if there is no performance fee (i.e., only management fee), the perspective of the investment manager versus the client is: heads, I win, tails, you lose.

[†]Barton Biggs on being a contrarian: "Being a contrarian is very chic. The only trouble is that now everyone is a contrarian. Even Wall Street economists are

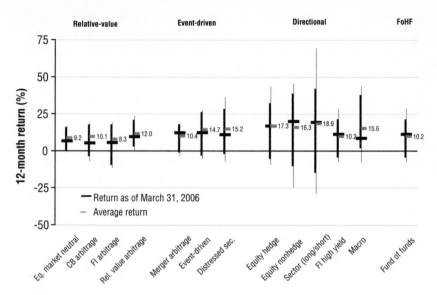

FIGURE 9.14 Twelve-Month Returns for a Selection of Hedge Fund Strategies Based on HFRI indices in USD from January 1990 to March 2006.
Source: Author's own calculations; data from Bloomberg.

Commodities gained traction in recent years. One reason is recent historical performance. Another is apparent negative correlation with equities. At first sight of Table 9.5, it seems that whenever equities fall by a double-digit percentage, commodities have a positive double-digit return and vice versa. This worked well in 1998, 2000, and 2002. However, it did not in 1990 and 2001. This means such "rules" derived from past performance are dangerous. Note that bonds always had a positive return when equities had a negative double-digit year, except 2001 where bonds were more or less unchanged. Hedge funds always had a positive absolute return in those years. Again, we are skeptical of such empirical findings. It's not that these observations are not enlightening; our skepticism is founded on the notion that the causality is spurious and the relationship might therefore not hold in the future.

Figure 9.14 shows 12-month returns by strategy as of March 2006 compared with its own history. The large dark horizontal tick shows the 12-month return as of March 31, 2006. The small gray horizontal tick measures

now contrarians. ... Therefore, instead of being contrarians, perhaps we should be contracontrarians." From Biggs [2006], p. 143.

the average 12-month return for the full period from January 1990 to March 2006. The thin vertical line measures the trading range of 12-month returns. The bolder vertical line shows the 90 percent range (cutting off 5 percent of the observations on each end of the distribution). The graph allows us to observe three things for the full universe of strategies at the same time: (1) current absolute performance, (2) performance relative to average return and return distribution (i.e., range of returns), and (3) whether strategies move in sync, that is, are correlated. For instance, when equity hedge was at its low of −8.7 percent in September 2001, equity market neutral and convertible arbitrage were around their mean while the relative-value strategies as well as the event-driven strategies were between their mean and nil. This means that while one strategy was losing money, other strategies still were generating positive absolute returns for the 12-month period.

Most strategies were around their long-term averages in March 2006. Convertible arbitrage had just recovered from an all-time-low of −6.5 percent as of April 2005. This mean-reversion feature works quite often (at least for the surviving funds).

CLOSING REMARKS

There is little evidence to suggest that absolute-return investing (hedge funds) is not a growth story. Growth in absolute-return space is a mix of capital inflow and capital gains. It has been high over the past decade, and accelerated since equity markets peaked in 2000 and temporarily spiked in 2004. Three important questions are whether the stark growth is "healthy," whether there is a potential disaster in the making, and whether the nature of growth is cyclical or structural.

For the time being, we stick with our view of a paradigm shift in the investment management industry. Our confidence in the structural element's outweighing the cyclical element is based primarily on reason (which, unfortunately, is rather subjective) but is also supported by an observation made in 2003.

In 2001 and 2002, there was the fear that money would be pulled from the hedge fund industry as soon as the equity market started to rise again. However, in 2003, we experienced a first indication that this is in fact unlikely to happen. Not only did large parts of the 2001 to 2002 inflows remain in absolute-return space, new money followed, eventually, resulting in the spike of capital inflow in 2004. This was despite equity markets rallying. We believe large parts of this capital buys into the absolute return investment philosophy and not, or to a lesser extent, into historical returns. The continual high inflows into hedge funds despite strong gains in the equity market suggest that underlying factors are structural in nature. We believe that the main driver of the growth is a sustainable change in the perception of risk. In other words, short-term volatility now matters to the long-term investor and exposure to an asymmetric return profile is more attractive than naked exposure to the whims of history and randomness.

We could be wrong. Over the past six years, we were given the opportunity to speak at a vast number of events on the subject of absolute-return investing. The audience has normally been investment professionals. Today (Q2 06), we feel there is some sort of link between the direction of stock markets (stock markets are all heavily correlated these days) and the number of heads nodding in agreement with our comments in the audience. When equity markets were in free fall in 2001 and 2002, the number of heads nodding vertically in agreement with our line of argument was higher than it is today.* Far from being statistically significant, it allows us to hypothesize that future growth of absolute-return investing is indeed correlated with equity markets. Hence, there is a structural as well as a cyclical element to the growth: We expect the growth of absolute-return investing to decrease if equity markets continue to compound at 30 percent per year, as they did, for example, in 2003. In addition, our forecast of the idea of absolute-return investing being "bigger" than hedge funds (a new paradigm) would turn out to be incorrect if equity markets were to compound at 30 percent forever. If equities do compound at 30 percent, we would, at infinity, have to accept intellectual defeat. Conversely, we expect the number of nodding heads to increase again should the recent rise in the equity markets reverse or, worse, turn out to be a bear market rally (albeit a long one).

It is entirely reasonable to assume that most market participants are heavily biased toward the most recent past. How else can we explain the reversion of risk perception toward hedge funds in only a couple of years? We believe graphs such as some shown in this chapter help explain why fiduciaries, actuaries, consultants, managers, analysts, and so on, believed long-only strategies and relative returns were conceptually good ideas. It's because they worked in the most recent 20 years. In a broader historical context, however, the functionality of long-only is not the rule, but the exception to the rule. Statistically speaking, the 20-year period ending in

---

*A more passive audience today could also imply that our line of argument is presented to the already converted or that the argument is old and now obvious and that we failed to challenge our audience with something new that they do not already know. A passive audience, of course, could also be a function of a lack of personality (as in dull) on our part and the appreciative nodding heads in 2001 and 2002 purely a product of our imagination.

December 1999 was an outlier, a historical aberration. Unfortunately, we believe it is this aberration that formed many beliefs and perceptions and supports many (potentially outdated and dangerous) investment approaches today.

Another observation supporting our view of a paradigm shift is the widely discussed phenomenon of brain-drain in the investment management industry. Generally speaking, the term *brain-drain* implies that talent moves from old/large businesses into new/lean businesses. What we find interesting is that the drain is only one way. (Otherwise, it probably would not be called *drain*.) There are numerous investment professionals leaving existing money management (primarily traditional asset management, trading, research, and financial advisory) to set up or join a hedge fund. However, there is not a single *successful* hedge fund manager (to our knowledge) who, after thinking things through, has decided that the long-only, buy-and-hold investment style is a superior means of managing money. (In Warren Buffett's parlance, it is probably "like going back to holding hands"). We believe this observation to be based on the change of perspective that investment management is really about managing risk, not returns. According to this changed perception, active money management means that the active manager not only has a mandate to find and enter investment opportunities, but also has the flexibility and authority to exit the opportunity, once the risk/reward relationship has changed unfavorably. In other words, the alpha in active money management is largely attributable to balancing risk with potential reward, that is, risk management skill. From the investor's perspective, this is an option on the potential reward without the full downside exposure.

One question we are asked regularly is whether an episode such as in 1998 can happen again. Can there be a situation again where one large fund sets off a chain reaction that puts the whole financial system at risk? Our response is always: "Of course." Nothing designed by the human hand is perfect. Markets are, therefore, not perfect. We agree with Oscar Wilde: "To expect the unexpected shows a thoroughly modern intellect." In any (social) ecosystem, there will be far-from-equilibrium events and accidents. We might not know where and when they will happen or the magnitude of the shock, but we believe it would be unreasonable to think that the probability of a crisis rattling the foundations of our financial system is zero. The relevance for the investor is not the *probability* of the event but the *consequences* of the event. Shocks to the financial system might be similar to earthquakes. Every day, small pieces of rock crumble in the Earth's crust. These unremarkable minor rearrangements of the Earth's crust happen in response to the stresses that build up slowly as the continental plates, creeping over the planet's surface, rub against one another. In the morning hours of January 17, 1995, for example, 20 kilometers southwest of Kobe, some small rocks on the ocean floor suddenly crumbled. The crumbling of those first rocks altered the stresses on others nearby, causing them also to break apart. In just 15 seconds, the earth ripped apart along a line 50 kilometers long, just "because" a couple of rocks crumbled.[2]

A hedge fund is a business. Occasionally, businesses fold. Infrequently, one small event triggers other small events, and disaster results. The initial small event causing the whole chain reaction can be determined only with the benefit of hindsight (if at all). Knowing with foresight the inaugural micro event that triggers a chain reaction is impossible. In the next financial disaster, which is inevitable, a hedge fund may or may not be the rock that starts to crumble, setting off a chain reaction. It could also be a pension fund, government authority, or any other market participant.

If disasters are impossible to predict on a macro level, the focus of attention should be biased toward the micro level. And if the probability of a disastrous event is impossible to determine, the focus of attention should be biased toward the investors' consequences from the event. We believe intelligent, prudent, diligent, and indefatigable evaluation of the micro variables (portfolio constituents) and the characteristics of their interrelationships (correlation) is probably the best way to anticipate and minimize the adverse consequences of a disaster. Ignorance (with respect to new ideas), vanity (as in overconfidence), inertia (as in the "musical chairs" effect), dogmatisms (as in the "it always has been like this around here" effect) and benchmarking (as in the "just following orders" syndrome and "equities outperform bonds in the long term" marketing one-liner) are probably the worst.

The evolution of an industry is comparable with the evolution of a species. A population of frogs, for example, may grow unchallenged and reach a peak on the fitness curve. But if a snake that eats frogs suddenly comes into the area, the frogs' fitness might change. The frog population may well evolve, develop, camouflage, and adapt to the change. However, it might also end up as snake food.

Notes

CHAPTER 1

1. See Asness [2004a,b].
2. See Bernstein [2003, 2004].
3. Berkshire Hathaway, annual report, 2003.
4. See Ineichen [2003a].
5. *CFA Magazine*, AIMR, inaugural issue, January/February 2003.
6. http://www.investopedia.com/terms/c/coppockcurve.asp.
7. From Graham [1985], p. 1. This quote was originally from Graham's classic *Security Analysis*, first published in 1934.
8. Heilbroner, Robert (1999). *The Worldly Philosophers: The Lives, Times, and Ideas of the Great Economic Thinkers*, 7th rev. ed. Westport, CT: Touchstone.

CHAPTER 2

1. Greenwich Associates [2003], "The Alternative Balancing Act," Greenwich Report.
2. From Mengle [2003], p. 5.
3. From Parker [2005], p. 291.
4. From Bernstein [1996], p. 336.
5. From Jaeger [2005], page 272. Italics in original.
6. From Warwick, Ben [2000]. *Searching for Alpha: The Quest for Exceptional Investment Performance*. New York: John Wiley. We have also seen this quote credited to Daniel Kahneman.
7. From Ashley [2003], p. 98.
8. *Institutional Investor*, September 2001.
9. See, for example, Bookstaber [1997].
10. From Waring and Siegel [2006].
11. Ibid.
12. Create/KPMG [2005], p. 74.
13. Speech by SEC Commissioner Cynthia A. Glassman: Remarks Before the Tenth Annual Conference on SEC Regulation Outside the United States, London, February 23, 2006. http://www.exchange-handbook.co.uk/news_story.cfm?id=57826.
14. "SEC Commissioner Criticizes Hedge Fund Rule," *Boston Globe,* March 31, 2006.
15. Reproduced by permission of RiskMetrics Group, Inc. © 1998–2006 RiskMetrics Group, Inc. All rights reserved.

CHAPTER 3

1. *Financial Times*, from March 31, 2003.
2. From Bernstein [1996], p. 299.
3. From Yang and Faux [1999].
4. From Cerrahoglu and Mukherjee [2003].
5. Presentation by Richard Spurgin, "Next-Generation Commodity Indexes," First Annual Switzerland Member Roundtable, CAIA Association, Zurich, May 4, 2006.
6. Julie Rohrer, "The Red-Hot World of Julian Robertson," *Institutional Investor*, May 1986.
7. From Caldwell and Kirkpatrick [1995].
8. From Ahl [2001].
9. From Campbell [2000].

CHAPTER 4

1. From Lighthouse Partners' Funds, March 2006 estimates.
2. Quote from presentation by Rob Arnott.
3. From Mandelbrot [2004], p. 96.
4. As discussed in Ineichen [1999, 2000b] in more detail.

CHAPTER 5

1. From Bernstein [1992].
2. From Lo and MacKinlay [1999], p. 3.
3. From Lo and MacKinlay [1999], p. 4.
4. From Campbell, Lo, and MacKinlay [1997], p. 24.
5. From Lo and MacKinlay [1999], p. 7.
6. From Sherden [1998].
7. From Sokal and Bricmont [1998], p. 2.
8. Ibid., p. 8.
9. From von Mises [1996], p. 57.
10. Ibid., p. 56.
11. From Soros [1995], p. 72.
12. Keynote speech at the 2000 Hedge Fund Symposium (EIM/EuroHedge/SFI), "Can Institutions Afford to Ignore Hedge Funds?" April 27, London.
13. From Soros [1987], p. 9.
14. Ibid., p. 20.
15. Ibid., p. 14.
16. Ibid., p. 21.
17. Ibid., p. 29.
18. From Soros [1994].
19. Ibid.
20. From Bernstein [2006a].
21. From Brabazon [2000].

22. From Olsen [1998].
23. See, for example, Leong et al. [2002].
24. Clements, Jonathan (1997). "Market Exuberance Isn't Too Rational? Sometimes, Investors Just Do It for Fun," *Wall Street Journal,* July 15, p. C1.
25. See Taleb [2004a].

CHAPTER 6

1. http://mba.tuck.dartmouth.edu/pages/faculty/ken.french/data_library.html.

CHAPTER 7

1. Eichenwald, Kurt (2005). *Conspiracy of Fools: A True Story.* New York: Broadway Books.

CHAPTER 8

1. Found in Alexander, Carol (1996). *The Handbook of Risk Management and Analysis.* Chichester: John Wiley & Sons.
2. http://www.tiaa-crefinstitute.org/research/speeches/docs/0104b98.pdf.
3. Weaver, Warren (1963). *Lady Luck: The Theory of Probability.* New York: Doubleday/Anchor.
4. http://www.abc.net.au/insidebusiness/content/2006/s1632456.htm.
5. http://www.econ.yale.edu/~shiller/data.htm.
6. From Mauldin [2006].

CHAPTER 9

1. Levy [2002], p. 2.
2. From Buchanan [2000].

References

Adams, John (2002). *Risk*. London: Routledge. First published in 1995 by UCL Press.

Ahl, Peter (2001). "Global Macro Funds—What Lies Ahead?" *The Capital Guide to Alternative Investment*, ISI publications, 2001 edition.

Ainslie III, Lee S. (1999). "Hedged Equity Investing," in Ronald A. Lake, ed., *Evaluating and Implementing Hedge Fund Strategies: The Experience of Managers and Investors*, 2nd ed. London: Euromoney Books.

Anson, Mark J.P. (2002). *Handbook of Alternative Assets*, The Frank J. Fabozzi Series. New York: John Wiley & Sons.

Ashley, Gerald (2003). *Uncertainty and Expectation: Strategies for the Trading of Risk*. Chichester: John Wiley & Sons.

Asness, Clifford (2004a). "An Alternative Future," *Journal of Portfolio Management*, 30th anniversary issue, pp. 94–103.

Asness, Clifford (2004b). "An Alternative Future: Part II," *Journal of Portfolio Management*, Vol. 31, No. 1 (Fall), pp. 8–23.

Balzer, Leslie A. (2001). "Investment Risk: A Unified Approach to Upside and Downside Returns," in Frank Sortino and Stephen Satchell, eds., *Managing Downside Risk in Financial Markets*. Oxford: Butterworth Heinemann.

Barber, Brad M., and Terrance Odean (2000). "Trading Is Hazardous to Your Wealth: The Common Stock Investment Performance of Individual Investors," *Journal of Finance*, Vol. LV, No. 2 (April), pp. 773–806.

Bergstresser, Daniel, Mihir A. Desai, and Joshua Rauh (2004). "Earnings Manipulation and Managerial Investment Decisions: Evidence from Sponsored Pension Plans." NBER working paper, No. 10543.

Bernstein, Peter L. (1975). "Management of Individual Portfolios," in Sumner N. Levine, ed. *The Financial Analyst's Handbook*. Homewood, IL: Dow Jones-Irwin, Inc.

Bernstein, Peter L. (1992). *Capital Ideas: The Improbable Origins of Modern Wall Street*. New York: Free Press.

Bernstein, Peter L. (1995). "Risk as a History of Ideas," *Financial Analysts Journal*, Vol. 51, No. 1 (January/February), pp. 7–11.

Bernstein, Peter L. (1996). *Against the Gods: The Remarkable Story of Risk*. New York: John Wiley & Sons.

Bernstein, Peter L. (2003). "Points of Inflection: Investment Management Tomorrow," *Financial Analysts Journal*, Vol. 59, No. 4 (July/August), pp. 18–23.

Bernstein, Peter L. (2004). "Overview: A Fifth Point of Inflection," CFA Institute Conference Proceedings, Points of Inflection: New Directions for Portfolio Management.

Bernstein, Peter L. (2006a). "The Paradox of the Efficient Market," *Journal of Portfolio Management*, Vol. 32, No. 2 (Winter), p. 1.

Bernstein, Peter L. (2006b). "The Great Alpha Merry-Go-Round," *Journal of Portfolio Management*, Vol. 32, No. 3 (Spring), p. 1.

Biggs, Barton (2006). *Hedgehogging*. Hoboken, NJ: John Wiley & Sons.

Black, Fisher (1986). "Noise," *Journal of Finance*, Vol. 41, pp. 529–544.

Black, Fisher and Myron Scholes (1973). "The Pricing of Options and Corporate Liabilities," *Journal of Political Economy*, Vol. 81, pp. 637–654.

Bookstaber, Richard (1997). "Global Risk Management: Are We Missing the Point?" *Journal of Portfolio Management*, Vol. 23, No. 3 (Spring), pp. 102–107.

Bookstaber, Richard (2003). "Hedge Fund Existential." *Financial Analysts Journal*, Vol. 59, (September/October), pp. 19–23.

Brabazon, Tony (2000). "Behavioural Finance: A New Sunrise or a False Dawn?" University of Limerick, August–September.

Brinson, Gary P., L. Randolph Hood, and Gilbert L. Beebower (1986). "Determinants of Portfolio Performance," *Financial Analysts Journal*, Vol. 42, No. 4 (July/August), pp. 39–44.

Brulhart, Todd, and Peter Klein (2005). "Problems with Extreme Hedge Fund Returns," AIMA, Winter.

Brunnermeier, Markus K., and Stefan Nagel (2003). "Hedge Funds and the Technology Bubble," AFA 2004 San Diego Meetings; EFA 2003 Annual Conference Paper No. 446.

Buchanan, Mark (2000). Ubiquity: Why Catastrophes Happen. New York: Three Rivers Press.

Caldwell, Ted. (1995). "Introduction: The Model for Superior Performance," in Jess Lederman and Robert A. Klein, eds., *Hedge Funds*. New York: McGraw-Hill.

Caldwell, Ted, and Tom Kirkpatrick (1995). "A Primer on Hedge Funds." Courtesy of Lookout Mountain Capital, Inc.

Campbell, John Y. (2000). "Asset Pricing at the Millennium." *Journal of Finance*, Vol. 55, No. 4 (August), pp. 1557–1568.

Campbell, John Y., and Robert J. Shiller (2001). "Valuation Ratios and the Long-Run Stock Market Outlook: An Update." NBER working paper, No. 8221.

Campbell, John Y., Andrew W. Lo, and A. Craig MacKinlay (1997). *The Econometrics of Financial Markets*. Princeton: Princeton University Press.

Capaul, Carlo, Ian Rowley, and William F. Sharpe (1993). "International Value and Growth Stock Returns," *Financial Analysts Journal*, Vol. 49, No. 1 (January/February), pp. 10–23.

Capco (2003). "Understanding and Mitigating Operational Risk in Hedge Fund Investments," Capco White Paper, March.

Chan, Nicholas, Mila Getmansky, Shane M. Haas, and Andrew W. Lo (2005). "Systematic Risk and Hedge Funds." Working paper, August.

Chancellor, Edward (2004). "Inefficient Markets: John Bull's Market," *Breaking Views*, March 18.

Chandler, Tertius (1987). *Four Thousand Years of Urban Growth*. New York: Edwin Mellen Press.

Cerrahoglu, Burak, and Barsendu Mukherjee (2003). "The Benefits of Commodity Investing," Working Paper, University of Massachusetts, March.

Clayman, Michelle (1987). "In Search of Excellence: The Investor's Viewpoint," *Financial Analysts Journal*, Vol. 43, No. 3 (May/June), pp. 54–64.

Clayman, Michelle (1994). "Excellence Revisited," *Financial Analysts Journal*, Vol. 50, No. 3 (May/June), pp. 61–65.

Cowles, Alfred (1933). "Can Stock Market Forecasters Forecast?" *Econometrica*, Vol. 1 (July), pp. 309–324.

Create/KPMG (2005). "Hedge Funds: A Catalyst Reshaping Global Investment." by Professor Amin Rajan, CREATE et al. Survey with participation of over 550 executives from hedge funds, fund of funds, long-only funds, administrators, and pension funds from 35 countries.

Dimson, Elroy, Paul Marsh, and Mike Staunton (2002). *Triumph of the Optimists: 101 Years of Global Investment Returns.* Princeton: Princeton University Press.

Edwards, Franklin R., and James Park (1996). "Do Managed Futures Make Good Investments," *The Journal of Futures Markets*, Vol. 16, No. 5, pp. 475–517.

Elden, Richard (2001). "The Evolution of the Hedge Fund Industry," *Journal of Global Financial Markets*, Vol. 2, No. 4 (Winter), pp. 47–54.

Ellis, Charles D. (1993). *Investment Policy: How to Win the Loser's Game,* 2nd ed. Homewood, IL: Business One Irwin.

Ellis, Charles D., with James R. Vertin (2001). *Wall Street People: True Stories of Today's Masters and Moguls.* New York: John Wiley & Sons.

Ellsberg, Daniel (1961). "Risk, Ambiguity, and the Savage Axioms," *Quarterly Journal of Economics*, 75, pp. 643–669.

Elton, Edwin, Martin Gruber, and Joel Rentzler (1987). "Professionally Managed, Publicly Traded Commodity Funds," *Journal of Business*, Vol. 60, No. 2, pp. 175–199.

Elton, Edwin, Martin Gruber, and Joel Rentzler (1990). "The Performance of Publicly Offered Commodity Funds," *Financial Analysts Journal*, Vol. 46, No. 4 (July–August), pp. 23–30.

Faber, Marc (2002). *Tomorrow's Gold: Asia's Age of Discovery.* Hong Kong: CLSA Books.

Fama, Eugene F. (1965) "The Behaviour of Stock Prices," *Journal of Business*, Vol. 38, pp. 34–105.

Fama, Eugene F. (1970). "Efficient Capital Markets: A Review of Theory and Empirical Work," *Journal of Finance*, Vol. 25, pp. 383–417.

Fama, Eugene F. (1998). "Market Efficiency, Long-Term Returns, and Behavioral Finance," *Journal of Financial Economics*, Vol. 49, No. 3, pp. 283–306.

Fama, Eugene F., and Kenneth R. French (1992). "The Cross-Section of Expected Stock Returns," *Journal of Finance*, Vol. 47, pp. 427–465.

Fama, Eugene F., and Kenneth R. French (1993). "Common Risk Factors in the Returns on Stocks and Bonds," *Journal of Financial Economics*, Vol. 33, pp. 3–56.

Fama, Eugene F., and Kenneth R. French (2002). "The Equity Premium," *Journal of Finance*, Vol. 57, April.

Fama, Eugene F., and Kenneth R. French (2004). "The Capital Asset Pricing Model: Theory and Evidence," *Journal of Economic Perspectives*, Vol. 18, No. 3 (Summer), pp. 25–46.

Friedman, Milton (1953). "The Methodology of Positive Economics," in *Essays in Positive Economics*. Chicago: University Press.

Friedman, Milton, and Leonard Jimmy Savage (1948). "The Utility Analysis of Choices Involving Risk," *Journal of Political Economy*, Vol. 56, pp. 279–304.

Fung, William, and David A. Hsieh (1997). "Empirical Characteristics of Dynamic Trading Strategies: The Case of Hedge Funds," *Review of Financial Studies*, Vol. 10, No. 2, pp. 275–302.

Getmansky, Mila, Andrew W. Lo, and Igor Makarov (2003). "An Econometric Model of Serial Correlation and Illiquidity in Hedge Fund Returns." MIT Sloan working paper No. 4288–03; MIT Laboratory for Financial Engineering working paper No. LFE-1041A-03; EFMA 2003 Helsinki Meetings, March.

Goetzmann, William N. (2004). "Will History Rhyme? The Past as Financial Future," *Journal of Portfolio Management*, 30th anniversary issue, pp. 34–41.

Graham, Benjamin (1985). "The Intelligent Investor," 4th rev. ed., New York: HarperCollins.

Graham, John R., and Cambell R. Harvey (2001). "Expectations of Equity Risk Premia, Volatility and Asymmetry from a Corporate Finance Perspective." NBER working paper.

Grinold, Richard C. (1989). "The Fundamental Law of Active Management," *Journal of Portfolio Management*, Vol. 15, No. 3 (Spring), pp. 30–37.

Grinold, Richard C., and Ronald N. Kahn (2000). *Active Portfolio Management: A Quantitative Approach for Producing Superior Returns and Controlling Risk*, 2nd ed. New York: McGraw-Hill.

Grossman, Sanford J. (1976). "On the Efficiency of Competitive Stock Markets Where Trades Have Diverse Information," *Journal of Finance*, Vol. 31, pp. 573–585.

Grossman, Sanford J., and Joseph E. Stiglitz (1980). "On the Impossibility of Informationally Efficient Markets," *American Economic Review*, Vol. 70, pp. 393–408.

Hagstrom, Robert G., Jr. (1994). *The Warren Buffett Way: Investment Strategies of the World's Greatest Investor*. New York: John Wiley & Sons.

Hayek, Friedrich August (1975). "Full Employment at Any Price?" The Institute of Economic Affairs, Occasional Paper 45, London.

Holton, Glyn A. (2004). "Defining Risk," *Financial Analysts Journal*, Vol. 60, No. 6 (November/December), pp. 19–25.

Ibbotson, Roger, and Peng Chen (2002). "Stock Market Returns in the Long Run: Participating in the Real Economy," *Financial Analysts Journal*, Vol. 59, No. 1 (January/February), pp. 88–98.

Ilmanen, Antti (2003). "Expected Returns on Stocks and Bonds," *Journal of Portfolio Management*, Vol. 29, No. 2 (Winter), pp. 7–27.

Ineichen, Alexander M. (1999). "20th Century Volatility." Warburg Dillon Read, Global Equity Research, December.

Ineichen, Alexander M. (2000a). "In Search of Alpha: Investing in Hedge Funds," Global Equity Research, UBS Warburg, October.

Ineichen, Alexander M. (2000b). "Twentieth Century Volatility—A Review of Stock Market Volatility in the Twentieth Century," *Journal of Portfolio Management*, Vol. 27, No. 1 (Fall), pp. 93–101.

Ineichen, Alexander M. (2001). "The Search for Alpha Continues: Do Fund of Hedge Funds Managers Add Value?" Global Equity Research, UBS Warburg, September.

Ineichen, Alexander M. (2002a) "Lemmings and Pioneers," Global Equity Research, UBS Warburg, October 18.

Ineichen, Alexander M. (2002b). "Managing the Curve:—Improving Risk-Adjusted Returns," Global Equity Research, UBS Warburg, September.

Ineichen, Alexander M. (2003a). *Absolute Returns: The Risk and Opportunities of Hedge Fund Investing.*" New York: John Wiley & Sons.

Ineichen, Alexander M. (2003b). "Asymmetric Returns and Sector Specialists," *Journal of Alternative Investments*, Vol. 5, No. 4 (Spring), pp. 31–40.

Ineichen, Alexander M. (2003c). "Fireflies before the Storm," Global Equity Research, UBS Warburg, June.

Ineichen, Alexander M. (2004a) "Absolute Returns: The Future of Wealth Management?" *Journal of Wealth Management*, Vol. 7, No. 1, pp. 64–74.

Ineichen, Alexander M. (2004b). "European Rainmakers," Global Equity Research, UBS Investment Bank, April.

Ineichen, Alexander M. (2005). "The Critique of Pure Alpha," Global Equity Research, UBS Investment Bank, June.

Irwin, Scott, and B. Wade Brorsen (1985). "Public Futures Funds," *Journal of Futures Markets*, Vol. 5, No. 3, pp. 463–485.

Irwin, Scott, Terry Krukemyer, and Carl Zulauf (1990). "Investment Performance of Public Commodity Pools: 1979–1990," *Journal of Futures Markets*, Vol. 13, No. 7, pp. 799–819.

Jaeger, Lars (2002). *Managing Risk in Alternative Investment Strategies: Successful Investing in Hedge Funds and Managed Futures.* London: Prentice Hall.

Jaeger, Lars (2005). *Through the Alpha Smoke Screens: A Guide to Hedge Fund Return Sources.* New York: Institutional Investor Books.

Jaeger, Robert A. (2005). "Risk: Defining It, Measuring It, and Managing It," in Virginia Reynolds Parker, ed., *Managing Hedge Fund Risk—Strategies and Insights from Investors, Counterparties, Hedge Funds and Regulators,* 2nd ed. London: Risk Books.

Jorion, Philippe (2005). *Financial Risk Manager Handbook,* 3rd ed. New York: John Wiley & Sons.

Kahneman, Daniel, and Amos Tversky (1979). "Prospect Theory: An Analysis of Decision under Risk," *Econometrica*, Vol. 47, No. 2, pp. 263–291.

Kat, Harry M., and Helder P. Palaro (2005). "Who Needs Hedge Funds? A Copula-Based Approach to Hedge Fund Return Replication," City University working paper.

Keynes, John M. (1921). *A Treatise on Probability.* London: Macmillan.

Knight, Frank H. (1921). *Risk, Uncertainty, and Profit.* Boston: Houghton Mifflin.

Kritzman, Mark P. (2000). *Puzzles of Finance: Six Practical Problems and Their Remarkable Solutions.* New York: John Wiley & Sons.

Kuhn, Thomas (1962). *The Structure of Scientific Revolutions.* Chicago: University of Chicago Press.

Kurz, Mordecai (1994). "On the Structure and Diversity of Rational Beliefs," *Economic Theory,* Vol. 4, pp. 877–900.

Kurz, Mordecai (1997). "Endogenous Economic Fluctuations and Rational Beliefs: A General Perspective," Chapter 1 in Mordecai Kurz, ed., *Endogenous Economic Fluctuations: Studies in the Theory of Rational Belief* (monograph). Springer Series in Economic Theory, No. 6, August.

Le Bon, Gustave (1982). *The Crowd: A Study of the Popular Mind,* 2nd ed. Atlanta: Cherokee Publishing Company. First published 1896. New York: Macmillan.

Lenin, Vladimir I. (1917). *Imperialism: The Highest Stage of Capitalism.* New York: International Publishing Company reprint, 1969.

Leong, Clint, Tan Chee, Michael J. Seiler, and Mark Lane (2002). "Explaining Apparent Stock Market Anomalies: Irrational Exuberance or Archetypal Human Psychology?" *Journal of Wealth Management,* Vol. 4, No. 4 (Spring), pp. 8–23.

Levy, Leon, with Eugene Linden (2002). *The Mind of Wall Street: A Legendary Financier on the Perils of Greed and the Mysteries of the Market.* New York: Public Affairs.

Lhabitant, François-Serge (2004) *Hedge Funds—Quantitative Insights.* Chichester: John Wiley & Sons.

Liang, Bing (2003). "On the Performance of Alternative Investments: CTAs, Hedge Funds, and Funds-of-Funds," Working Paper, University of Massachusetts, November.

Lintner, G. (1998). "Behavioral Finance: Why Investors Make Bad Decisions," *The Planner,* Vol. 13, No. 1, pp. 7–8.

Litzenberger, R., and N. Rabinowitz (1995). "Backwardation in Oil Futures Markets: Theory and Empirical Evidence," *Journal of Finance,* Vol. 50, No. 5 (December), pp. 1517–1545.

Lo, Andrew (2004). "The Adaptive Markets Hypothesis: Market Efficiency from an Evolutionary Perspective," *Journal of Portfolio Management,* 30th anniversary issue, pp. 15–29.

Lo, Andrew, and Craig MacKinlay (1999). *The Non-Random Walk Down Wall Street.* Princeton: Princeton University Press.

Mandelbrot, Benoit, and Richard L. Hudson (2004). *The (Mis) Behavior of Markets: A Fractal View of Risk, Ruin, and Reward.* New York: Basic Books.

Markowitz, Harry M. (1952). "Portfolio Selection," *Journal of Finance,* Vol. 7, No. 1 (March), pp. 77–91.

Markowitz, Harry M. (1959). *Portfolio Selection: Efficient Diversification of Investments.* New York: John Wiley & Sons.

Mauldin, John (2006). "It's Value Time Again," *Thoughts from the Frontline,* John Mauldin's Weekly e-Letter, Investors Insight Publishing, Inc., May 5, 2006.

May, Irenee D. (2005). "Managing Hedge Fund Risk from the Dealer's Perspective," in Virginia Reynolds Parker, ed., *Managing Hedge Fund Risk: Strategies and*

Insights from Investors, Counterparties, Hedge Funds and Regulators, 2nd ed. London: Risk Books.

McCarthy, David, Thomas Schneeweis, and Richard Spurgin (1996). "Investment Through CTAs: An Alternative Managed Futures Investment," *Journal of Derivatives,* Vol. 3, No. 4, pp. 36–47.

Mehra, Rajnish (2003). "The Equity Premium: Why Is It a Puzzle?" *Financial Analysts Journal,* Vol. 59, No. 1 (January/February), pp. 54–69.

Mehra, Rajnish, and Edward C. Prescott (1985). "The Equity Premium: A Puzzle," *Journal of Monetary Economics,* Vol. 15, No. 2 (March), pp. 145–161.

Mengle, David (2003). "Risk Management as a Process," in Peter Field, ed., *Modern Risk Management: A History.* London: Risk Books.

Mitchell, Mark, and Todd Pulvino (2001). "Characteristics of Risk and Return in Risk Arbitrage," *Journal of Finance,* Vol. 56, No. 6 (June), pp. 2135–2175.

Olsen, Robert A. (1998). "Behavioral Finance and Its Implications for Stock Price Volatility," *Financial Analysts Journal,* Vol. 54, No. 2 (March/April), pp. 10–18.

Parker, Virginia Reynolds (2005). "Integrating Risk Management into the Portfolio Management Process for Effective Fund-of-Hedge-Funds Risk Management and Performance Measurement," in Virginia Reynolds Parker, ed., *Managing Hedge Fund Risk: Strategies and Insights from Investors, Counterparties, Hedge Funds and Regulators,* 2nd ed. London: Risk Books.

Peltz, Lois (1994). "A Look Back—and Forward—at the Hedge Fund Community," in Ronald A. Lake, ed., *Evaluating and Implementing Hedge Funds Strategies: The Experience of Managers and Investors,* 2nd ed. London: Euromoney Books.

Peltz, Lois (2001). *The New Investment Superstars: 13 Great Investors and Their Strategies for Superior Returns.* New York: John Wiley & Sons.

Peters, T.J., and R.H. Waterman (1982). *In Search of Excellence: Lessons from America's Best Run Corporations.* New York: HarperCollins.

Rahl, Leslie (2003). *Hedge Fund Risk Transparency: Unraveling the Complex and Controversial Debate.* London: Risk Books.

Rogers, Jim (2000). *Investment Biker: Around the World with Jim Rogers.* Chichester: John Wiley & Sons. First published 1994 by Beeland Interest, Inc.

Roy, A.D. (1952). "Safety First and the Holding of Assets," *Econometrica,* Vol. 20, No. 3 (July), pp. 431–449.

Ryan, Ronald A. (2003). "Pension Fund Management: Addressing the Problem of Asset/Liability Mismatch," AIMR Conference Proceedings, *Improving the Investment Process through Risk Management,* No. 4, pp. 52–61.

Samuelson, Paul A. (1965). "Proof that Properly Anticipated Prices Fluctuate Randomly," *Industrial Management Review,* Vol. 6 (Spring), pp. 41–49.

Savage, Leonard J. (1954). "The Sure-Thing Principle," in *The Foundations of Statistics.* New York: John Wiley & Sons.

Scholes, Myron S. (2004) "The Future of Hedge Funds," The Nobel Laureate View, *Journal of Financial Transformation,* Alternative Investments, The Capco Institute, Vol. 10, April.

Schneeweis, Thomas, Uttama Savanayana, and David McCarthy (1991). "Alternative Commodity Trading Vehicles: A Performance Analysis," *Journal of Futures Markets*, Vol. 11, No. 4, pp. 475–487.

Schumpeter, Joseph (1937). *Business Cycles: A Theoretical, Historical, and Statistical Analysis of the Capitalist Process.* New York: McGraw-Hill.

Scott, James, Mark Stumpp, and Peter Xu (1999). "Behavioral Bias, Valuation, and Active Management," *Financial Analysts Journal*, Vol. 55, No. 4 (July/August), pp. 49–57.

Seifert, Werner G. (2006). *Invasion der Heuschrecken.* mit Hans-Jochim Voth, Berlin: Econ.

Shefrin, Hersh (2000). *Beyond Greed and Fear.* Boston: Harvard Business School Press.

Sherden, William A. (1998). *The Fortune Sellers: The Big Business of Buying and Selling Predictions.* New York: John Wiley & Sons.

Shiller, Robert J. (1981). "Do Stock Prices Move Too Much to Be Justified by Subsequent Movements in Dividends?" *American Economic Review*, Vol. 71, No. 3, pp. 421–436.

Shiller, Robert J. (1989). *Market Volatility.* Cambridge, MA: MIT Press.

Shiller, Robert J. (1994). *Macro Markets: Creating Institutions for Managing Society's Largest Economic Risks.* Oxford: Oxford University Press.

Shiller, Robert J. (2000). *Irrational Exuberance.* Princeton: Princeton University Press.

Shiller, Robert J. (2003). *The New Financial Order: Risk in the 21st Century.* Princeton: Princeton University Press.

Siegel, Laurence B. (2003). *Benchmarks and Investment Management* (monograph). Charlottesville, VA: The Research Foundation of CFA Institute, August.

Smithers, Andrew, and Stephen Wright (2000). *Valuing Wall Street: Protecting Wealth in Turbulent Markets.* New York: McGraw-Hill.

Sokal, Alan, and Jean Bricmont (1998). *Fashionable Nonsense: Postmodern Intellectuals' Abuse of Science.* New York: Picador USA.

Solvic, Paul (1972). "Psychological Study of Human Judgement: Implications for Investment Decision Making," *Journal of Finance,* Vol. 27, pp. 779–801.

Soros, George (1987). *The Alchemy of Finance: Reading the Mind of the Market.* New York: John Wiley & Sons.

Soros, George (1994). "The Theory of Reflexivity," MIT Department of Economics World Economy Laboratory Conference, Washington DC, April 26.

Soros, George, with Byron Wien and Krisztina Koenen (1995). *Soros on Soros: Staying Ahead of the Curve.* New York: John Wiley & Sons.

Soros, George (1998). *The Crisis of Global Capitalism.* New York: Public Affairs.

Soros, George (2003). *The Alchemy of Finance,* 2nd ed. New York: John Wiley & Sons.

Summers, Lawrence H. (1985). "On Economics and Finance," *Journal of Finance,* Vol. 40, pp. 633–635.

Taleb, Nassim N. (2004a). *Fooled by Randomness: The Hidden Role of Chance in Life and in the Markets,* 2nd ed. London: Texere.

Taleb, Nassim N. (2004b). Book review of *The (Mis)Behavior of Markets: A Fractal View of Risk, Ruin, and Reward,* by Benoit Mandelbrot and Richard Hudson. New York: Basic Books, 2004; www.fooledbyrandomness.com.

Thaler, Richard H. (1999). "The End of Behavioral Finance," *Financial Analysts Journal,* Vol. 55, pp. 12–17.

Tinbergen, Jan (1962) "Voorspellingen in politiek, economic en sociologie," (Forecasts in Politics, Economics and Sociology), Nederlands Tijdschrift voor de Psychologie en haar Grensgebieden, XVII, pp. 193–197.

Tversky, Amos (1995). "The Psychology of Decision Making," *Behavioral Finance and Decision Theory in Investment Management,* AIMR, No. 7.

Tversky, Amos, and Daniel Kahneman (1974). "Judgement under Uncertainty: Heuristics and Biases," *Science,* Vol. 185, pp. 1124–1131.

von Mises, Ludwig (1996). *Human Action: A Treatise on Economics,* 4th ed. San Francisco: Fox & Wilkes. First published 1949 by Yale University.

Von Neumann, J. V., and O. Morgenstern (1947) *Theory of Games and Economic Behavior.* Princeton: Princeton University Press.

Waring, M. Barton, and Laurence B. Siegel (2006). "The Myth of the Absolute-Return Investor," *Financial Analysts Journal,* Vol. 62, No. 2 (March/April), pp. 14–21.

Welch, Ivo (2000). "Views of Financial Economists on the Equity Risk Premium and on Financial Controversies," *Journal of Business*, October.

Welch, Ivo (2001). "The Equity Premium Consensus Forecast Revisited," Discussion paper, Cowles Foundation.Yang, Philip L. Jr., and Richard G. Faux, Jr. (1999). "Managed Futures—The Convergence with Hedge Funds." In Ronald A. Lake, ed., *Evaluating and Implementing Hedge Funds Strategies: The Experience of Managers and Investors,* 2nd ed., London: Euromoney Books.

Alexander M. Ineichen, CFA, CAIA, is managing director and senior investment officer for the Alternative Investment Solutions team, itself a business with UBS Global Asset Management. In October 2000, Ineichen authored *In Search of Alpha: Investing in Hedge Funds*, which has become the most often printed research publication in the documented history of UBS Investment Bank. He has also published several papers in peer-refereed financial journals; contributed numerous articles and chapters to financial newspapers, magazines, and books; and regularly speaks at industry conferences. He is on the board of directors of CAIAA (Chartered Alternative Investment Analyst Association). Ineichen is also the author of the widely popular *Absolute Returns: The Risk and Opportunities of Hedge Fund Investing* (ISBN 0-471-25120-8).

Index